Does Grace Have a Ceiling?

Does Grace Have a Ceiling?

The Anatomy of the Will

KYLE JONES

RESOURCE *Publications* · Eugene, Oregon

DOES GRACE HAVE A CEILING?
The Anatomy of the Will

Copyright © 2026 Kyle Jones. All rights reserved. Except for brief quotations in critical publications or reviews, no part of this book may be reproduced in any manner without prior written permission from the publisher. Write: Permissions, Wipf and Stock Publishers, 199 W. 8th Ave., Suite 3, Eugene, OR 97401.

Resource Publications
An Imprint of Wipf and Stock Publishers
199 W. 8th Ave., Suite 3
Eugene, OR 97401

www.wipfandstock.com

PAPERBACK ISBN: 979-8-3852-5256-5
HARDCOVER ISBN: 979-8-3852-5257-2
EBOOK ISBN: 979-8-3852-5258-9

Contents

Foreword ix
Preface xi
Acknowledgments xvii
Introduction xxi

SECTION 1
Chapter 1: The Intentful Archer 3
Chapter 2: Shared Wills 5
Chapter 3: Praise of the A-Moral Hero 12
Chapter 4: A little closer to morals 19
Chapter 5: Stage and Setting 21
Chapter 6: The Four Wills 24
Chapter 7: Vocabulary 30
Chapter 8: Our Common Themes 32
Chapter 9: The Failure of Human Reason by Human Perspective 41
Chapter 10: Predetermined *Teleon* as we naturally see it 44
Chapter 11: Man Made Diatribes 48
Chapter 12: The Story that Tells it All 56
Chapter 13: *The First Noble Truth – The Predeterminism view* 64
Chapter 14: Professor J.R.R. Tolkien 70
Chapter 15: The Inability to Repent Leads to the Ultimate Gratitude 73
Chapter 16: A One-Way Street 77
Chapter 17: An Old/New Physics 80
Chapter 18: The Stacking or Sandwiching of Predestination and Prophecy 81
Chapter 19: *Second Noble Truth – Teleological View (the arrival of meaning)* 88
Chapter 20: Being Halted 101
Chapter 21: *The Third Noble Truth – The Apocalyptic View* 104

CONTENTS

Chapter 22: *The Fourth Noble Truth – The Prophetic View* 109
Chapter 23: *The Fifth Noble Truth – Universal Salvation* 128

SECTION 2

Chapter 24: Born In Memphis 135
Chapter 25: Suffering Has Meaning 139
Chapter 26: Leaving My Eden 142
Chapter 27: Jumping Forward 145
Chapter 28: Continued Pain 148
Chapter 29: My Parents" "Sketch" and "Color" 151
Chapter 30: Enters The Holy Ghost 154

SECTION 3

Chapter 31: Theology 159
Chapter 32: What Predestination Is and Not 161
Chapter 33: Determinism Is Not Predeterminism 166
Chapter 34: Terminologies 178
Chapter 35: The Rocks Would Cry Out 184
Chapter 36: The Intangible That Naturally Cries Out 187
Chapter 37: Return to the Reason of Universal Salvation (*apokatastasis*) 193
Chapter 38: Harder Sayings That Connect the Dots 206
Chapter 39: The Pagan's Prophet 212
Chapter 40: Children Walking and Learning in The Kingdom of God 223
Chapter 41: Paideia to Archer 226
Chapter 42: A Prelude to Satan 232
Chapter 43: Satan is an Element of Predestination 236
Chapter 44: A Hyper Focus Using Paideia/Twisting Texts on Hell 244
Chapter 45: What is Judgment Again? 248
Chapter 46: Sin and Hell Unto Repentance 258
Chapter 47: A "Kind" of Condemnation 264
Chapter 48: Are We a Third Party? 271
Chapter 49: Therefore, What is Hell? 275
Chapter 50: Objective to Abstract forms: Eternal, Eternity and Permanence 283
Chapter 51: Configurations Unto a Mytho-Theology 285

CONTENTS

Chapter 52: Messiah VS. Hero 287
Chapter 53: Eternity, Everlasting, Era, Limited Duration, Unending 292
Chapter 54: Do We Fear the Powerless 299
Chapter 55: Jesus and Beelzebub – Jesus as a "Type" of Beelzebub 305
Chapter 56: Jesus as Exorcist 310
Chapter 57: Importance of Plato's Vocabulary as the *Praeparatio Evengeli* 316
Chapter 58: Satan Is God's Cookie Cutter 323
Chapter 59: The Scapegoat and the Sacrifice 327
Chapter 60: *The Five Noble Truths Summed* 333
Chapter 61: Final Words: Synthesizing vs. Sandwiching 337
Chapter 62: *Teliko Sumperasma* 346

Postscript 349
Appendix 357
Bibliography 361

Foreword

FOR THE PAST EIGHT years, every Sunday afternoon in Nashville, I have had the privilege of sitting cross-legged on the floor across from Kyle Jones, ostensibly to learn the Tabla, but in truth to learn far more. What begins as a percussion lesson reliably unfolds into a conversation about philosophy, purpose, and the quiet ways in which meaning reveals itself. Week after week, I have come to know Kyle not only as a gifted musician and teacher, but as a thoughtful, grounded, deeply sincere human being whose intellectual curiosity is matched only by his spiritual humility.

This book is an extension of those conversations. In it, Kyle undertakes a bold and compelling theological synthesis—what he calls the "stacking" of five noble truths: Universal Salvation, Predeterminism, Teleology, Prophecy, and the Apocalyptic view. He weaves them into a coherent, orthodox framework that seeks to restore the unity, coherence, and narrative beauty of Scripture. His exploration of God's sovereignty, suffering as a form of divine calibration, and the tension between fear-based and hope-based belief systems is both challenging and deeply comforting.

What strikes me most is that Kyle writes with the same spirit with which he teaches: patient, searching, humble, and profoundly anchored in love. This work is not merely an argument; it is an invitation to see Scripture as a living, cohesive narrative, to understand suffering within a purposeful arc, and to embrace the possibility that grace extends further and deeper than we imagine.

I highly recommend both this book and the man behind it. Kyle has shaped my understanding of rhythm, but more importantly, he has shaped my understanding of meaning. I hope these pages offer you a fraction of what his friendship and guidance have offered me.

Dr. Pranav Mehta, President of H.C.A.

Preface

THIS WORK IS A sifter of sorts using what I call The 5 Noble Truths. Some people might wince when the word "truth" is used, however, I use the mother meaning of the word truth found couched in classical Greek, Hittite, Sanskrit, and the early reconstructed Proto-Indo-European (P.I.E.) language. I did this in order to elicit a time capsule of rich meaning supporting the word, truth, showing its linguistic gold as it tethers to our bank of current words. For truth was bigger than a relative transient meaning. It was interconnected with a series of other ideas that completed a broad matrix of meaning.

The meaning of truth, from its earliest P.I.E. inception, was: *dr- "tree", as in "root, stem, and branches". Compare "truth"/"daru"/"dr-" with "druid": (daru ["tree", "truth"] + eid ["wit", "vision", "witch", "videre", "video", "to see"])", i.e., "tree seers"/ "wise ones"/ "seers within the trees"/ "steadfast ones", etc. {Shipley, Shippey, Watkins}).

Such a term was not lightly thrown around for millennia. Just as a test, take the true meaning of true and apply it to anything you want to find out. Simple things like where you put your keys that you lost. You mentally track your steps back to the last time you had your keys and follow the sequence of your activities. Possibly asking others that were around you as witnesses to your day's journey to help as to when they last saw you with your keys. Finding your keys uses solid realities to find your real keys.

Circa 4,000 years after the Proto-Indo-Europeans gave us a zero-grade (linguistic inception) meaning for truth (*dr-/ daru) we read the following as an example of an a-moral sense for the word, truth: Pontius pilot asked Jesus (John 18:38) the question, "what is the truth ("ti 'estin 'alay'theia" ['alay'theia: objectve facts and not illusion])"? Jesus did not reply for Jesus is the cause of the truth: root, stem, and branches

PREFACE

of created objective reality. Furthermore, Jesus calls himself the Alpha and Omega [Revelation 1:8, 1:11, 21:6, 22:13]) qualifying Jesus as the objective "truth" living-breathing among us. Therefore, the gospels, being qualified by Jesus, do qualify what truth is. Note: the P.I.E. etymon, daru (dr-), and the Greek, 'alay'theia, are not the same words but hold the same meaning. The truth still exists within the words.

The ones that could see the truth in the deeper sense were those who traveled with Jesus and witnessed all that Jesus the Messiah would fulfill. This meant the disciples (Greek: mathetikon-"mathemeticians"; "accounters") took account of Jesus' words, deeds, fulfillments, universal truths, parables, etc. Therefore, how could there have been a correct reply from truth itself when Jesus is the truth standing before you? For Jesus is the beginning and end, the Alpha and Omega - which also fulfills the word, telos.

Another term that needs to be addressed in our world of illusory free agency is the aged idea of free will.

Free will as it should be known:

Probability within modern psychiatry aids us from subjective to objective data driven classification into a type of clarity. Such factoring gives an epidemiological approach which shows us that Axis I (mania) and Axis II (hypomania) Bipolar (as is listed in the DSM-TR-5), schizophrenia, etc., are what I call "states of free agency" in that (if untreated) they will exist freely from the neurotypical standard. I also state that a person who is diagnosed within the gamut of dysregulation is medically assigned to that free from neurotypical state of existence. Currently, a goal for such a person by the medical provider, and patient's surrounding community, is the aim for the neurotypical standard.

As we have advanced in the neurological sciences we are finding profound events that occur upon the will of the neurotypical and the dysregulated. Dr. Sam Harris, a neuro-scientist, offers a very brief but intense treatment concerning the study of our very being (ontology) in his book, "There is no Free Will". To further this, Dr. Harris, a professed atheist-naturalist, attributes natural causes upon the human will making the human being incapable of having free will. Dr. Harris attributes genetic, random quantum fluctuations, the micro-biome relation (i.e., the gut-brain axis), parasitic influences - making us act less fearful, etc. Dr. Harris proposes such "outside causes" acting upon us remain outside our control. Therefore, Dr. Harris concludes we have no free will.

So, if it is true that our human condition, whether neurotypical or socially aberrant due to dysregulation, is acted upon by preceding causes then what is free will from the current theological and scientific perspective? Where is the condemnation or merit to be found? Whether "sinner" or "saint", one will "act out" from their state or condition. If we can prove theologically and scientifically that neither rogue agency nor free agency is a force derived from the individual then who or what is left to be put to the merit or blame? If it is merit, then the only direction to look to is to look backwards for it was something else that was driving you to act. If blame, you would still need to look back and do the same. In either case, if natural-fated-causation is the current adequate argument for the outcome for anything, then we can most definitely eliminate accountability. That is, the elimination of the kind of accountability that holds judgment upon the object of receiving such merit or blame.

But what if there is an entire new/ old way to look at causation within a forgiveness paradigm? Again, holding to a temporary suspension of disbelief (if one is an atheist) one could imagine heaven with God eternally existing where there is no blame. Reasonably, this idea could become a wonderful reality enacted by us all in the primary-corporeal world if it wasn't for our free wills to sin against each other for that is what the world does. Therefore, free will is hypothetically not of God if defined as free agency and therefore a third party to choose God which is not biblically sound.

Sin: can sin be amoral in the telos meaning?

Linguistically, the word sin holds quite a different angle than what we might think of in the old European and Hittite world. The Proto Indo European gives us *snt-ya- and its root, *es-ont- mean: "a becoming to be"; "a truth", "a root-to stem-to branches" observation, etc. while the Hittite's word for truth ("ess") gives us a formula of confession as follows: "as it is being", "as it exists", "as it is existing", etc.

To sin is to show the truth via the etiology and ontology of the one who trespasses. This would, to its furthest extent, show the reasons, i.e., the "why", and/or the etiology for one's sin. Would we not understand the truth of their sin in this fashion? Would we hold judgment to those for whom we understood why their sin came to be – the cause of their being, the theological teleology of one's being?

Furthermore, to see the becoming of someone, knowing they are being caused to "become" by an outside agent, would we hold blame upon the cause or causal agent of the one coming to be? Therefore, how could we judge the one "becoming"? To conclude this thought: sin must be understood as being aligned with truth as truth is to be known.

To blame your fellow human for being a transgressor of the law is much like blaming a barking dog for its barking. It is in its nature to bark, therefore, a dog is not free from its state of being a dog. A dog could be said to be guilty of "doggery" in the same breath that a human can be said to act all too human. I am not shocked in either case, dog or human.

In the philosophical teleological view, it is the mere explanation of phenomena in terms of the purpose in which they serve rather than the cause by which they arise. This method annuls a theological/God causality opening in which a temporary suspension of disbelief for the non-believer cannot be employed. This faith in "anti-faith" adopted by certain atheists of all walks of life holds no more substance of a grounded argument than does a religious radical laden with faulty beliefs threatening to blow up a building in the name of their god does. This is an unfair approach, for all novice to seasoned scientists have been allowed their beliefs in their field to allow ideas of the "what ifs" and the "thens" and the "therefores", etc. Why fear to "act" in belief or disbelief if the thing that is being tried (Aristotle's "telos") does not yield results as you "wished"? Worse yet, one would be showing a poor ethic of practicing good science and/ or theology, due to the thing observed showing its "trueness"? Should I ask: why fear the things claimed to be spoken by God on earth if one is to use the scientific, linguistic, anthropological, and sociological approach to disprove God or prove his existence?

This work more than adequately shows the possibility of the conjunction of these sciences/ -ologies to prove a consistent God narrative.

It is here that I refer back to one of my favorite dialogues of Plato called "Cratylus".

Hermogenes' and Socrates' daimon (Greek: "spirit") employed by Plato for use in Plato's dialogue which shows that "sin" isn't necessarily "immoral". It does not, however, disprove that "sin" is not immoral when its context is within a critique requiring "sin" as the source of a fault. What I have found is the uncanny beautiful horror that it is never found to be objective.

Right, Good, Evil, Sin

[420.B/ Loeb classic; Cratylus] Socrates: "Doxsa (glory, rightful, worthy) is derived either from the pursuit (dioxsis) which the soul carries on as it pursues the knowledge of the nature of the thing, or from the shooting of the bow (toxson); the latter is more likely; at any rate "oiesis (belief)" supports this view, for it appears to mean the motion (oisis) of the soul towards the essential nature of every individual thing, just as intention (boule) denotes shooting (bole) and wish (boulesthai) as well as plan (bouleuesthai), denotes aiming at something. All these words seem to follow doxsa and to express the idea of shooting, just as ill-advisedness (aboulia), on the other hand, appears to be a failure to hit, as if a person did not shoot or hit that which he shot at or wished or planned or desired.

The Greek in the classical and New Testament holds sin as armateia (without portion): "a" = "not" + "meros" = "portion". It is here that we find Plato's "sin" - "aboulia" to match that of the Greek New Testament's harmateia and the Semitic (both secular and religious) "qat".

For, harmateia etymologically conveys loss, forfeiture, no part of, due to not hitting the target; missing the mark, etc. Sin, as I previously stated, in secular Semitic and religious sources, finds itself in the Old Testament Hebrew, giving us the root "CH-T-' (qat) indicating "a verb of motion" that is "in the missing of the correct point".

Such a verb of motion as "qat" can be denoted in Psalms 19:2: "he that hasteth with his feet goeth astray (ats berag'liym qot')." The rushing, speeding, hurrying, making haste, etc. is the root to "going astray" and is in one motion. Qat is very interesting, indeed for it seems to follow an idea of "fate" as known to the ancient Greeks, though fate's conclusion is quite different in that it leads to "fatality" whereas qat leads to a lesson learned unto life eternal. Qat, to the ancient Semitic mind, denoted a sphere of motion as an "outside agent" prior to human action acting upon the objective individual causing both the nature of evil and the fruit of evil!

To understand sin, Semitically speaking, we can apply etymological formula for truth in the "dr-/truth" sense, i.e., "root, stem, branches", making the root the "qat" as sin, the stem is the recipient of qat, and the sinful acts are the branches of qat. Not only this combined series of motions of truth coming from an outside agent, these motions also require a reconciliation as in "atonement" which is connected with the feminine form of the masculine qat. Therefore, the beginning of qat requires the end–much like Plato's "eternal shapes". The idiom, "nasa chatta'th" is the verb with the feminine object and always means "the carrying away of the sphere of guilt from the sinner by a third party who intercedes vicariously taking away the consequence of death (Ex. 10:17; I Sam. 15:25).

In all cases above we still haven't found objective direct blame upon the individual by which we should rank as either right or wrong. So, where is the judgment if the causal agency is outside the sphere of our first act driving the motions of sin upon the object unto reconciliation?

Through the sifting of my 5 Noble Truths (5NTs) I attempt to dispel unnecessary moralizations of words and ideas that can cause dissension within my target audience. Such a method, as you will see in this work, will allow morality to ring true as it should.

Acknowledgments

I DEDICATE THIS WORK to my oldest daughter, Alicia (32) and her husband, Everett. Alicia has been a residing spirit that will always rest deep in my soul. I promised her two things when she was a child: the first was to build a "Hagrid House" for her and the second was to write a book in dedication to her. I have somewhat done it here, though, I will always feel the need to correct and add more and more. Alicia is my pride and joy having surpassed me in all things. She is a practicing M.D. who has an evangelism all of her own in the healing arts with Jesus Christ.

I dedicate this work to my wife, Samantha. Samantha has been the answer to my prayers having given me 3 wonderful children: Ethan (20), Fiona (17), and Eden (10). Samantha, more than anyone, has challenged me on every level of science, religion, myths, politics, social issues, etc. to "see" a bigger picture.

Infinite gratitude to God for gracing me with the world's top scholars in their fields to help guide and shape my way of thinking. Dr. Robin Parry for quantifying biblical universal rectification with a tender spirit to boot. I thank a tough but endearing mentor, David Rohl, for synchronizing Proto-Sinaitic, Egyptian, and Sumerian cultures with a fresh new look at the biblical timeline as backed by Ancient Near Eastern (A.N.E.) comparative archaeology and scripture. I want to thank my most intense comic – scholar cum laude, Dr. Irving Finkel, for his unbounded knowledge of Babylonian cuneiform tablets, his studies and books on Mesopotamian ghost stories, the Mesopotamian flood, chess, and, finally, his hopes of getting into a rock band with me and David Rohl (seriously). Dr. Anna Meshke for her unparalleled brilliance shown in her doctoral works concerning Kartvelian languages and culture as pre-Sumerian. Her works: *Kartvelian Linguo-Culturology*, *Kartvelian-Sumerian-Egyptian Linguo-Culturology*, and *The Unwritten History of*

ACKNOWLEDGMENTS

the Meskhis shows the link between pre-Georgian, predynastic Egyptian, and Sumerian language and culture. She is truly a one-of-a-kind scholar and dear friend to me. Though I failed to communicate with Dr. Hamlet Martirosyan in his modern native Armenian tongue, his doctoral work called: "The Lion Character" was a great influence upon me. Dr. Martirosyan's comparative analyses of proto-Syunik (ancient Armenian) and Sumerian cultures helped me with ancient Ururtian/Ararat culture which supports the Noah/Utnapishtim/Atrahasis character's development. Dr. Verlyn Flieger, my dear, dear friend! My unbounded thanks goes out to Dr. Flieger. Anyone who knows J.R.R. Tolkien will know her endless endeavors in editing nearly every posthumous work that J.R.R. Tolkien did. She is regarded as a scholar of scholars in her Tolkienian field and furthered fantasy (fantastic) writings. She continues in her 90s to teach Icelandic language at "Politics and Prose" in the D.C. area (both online and in person). Dr. Gerald Schroeder, an M.I.T. graduate and professor with a double PhD. physics exposed me to what the Hebrew Torah has to offer in modern scientific findings. Such works of his are "Genesis and the Big Bang," "The Hidden Face of God," etc. Everyone mentioned above has called, "skyped (now – "Microsoft – teamed"?), emailed, "messengered," texted, etc. with me on their very important time to "give me an answer." I am truly indebted to these beautiful people. Furthermore, I have interviewed all of these wonderful people which can be accessed on my website, fomcm.com, in the "interviews" category. While I find it impossible to account for everyone who has taught me, I thank you and will put you in future "revised editions." I dedicate this work to Dr. David Lawrence offering his patience with me as I argued with him in college nearly every day concerning his Arminian views at the time. We became very close friends in college as I was just a student and Dr. Lawrence a professor. Many lunches after class at a famous authentic pizza parlor in Nashville ("Caesars" [to be distinguished from "Little Caesars"]) discussing predeterminism, Arminianism, predestination, and free will.

David had a "conversion" to Calvinism after many meetings, especially after a brief hiatus in my musical touring schedule. Coming back from my tour and a semester break we did two radio shows together. The first on "collective theological and secular thinking" and the second show called "The Finnish Mazzaroth." Such a treatment I was very fond of. It was a work I had been doing for some time prior that was my hidden door to the universal idea that is found in Romans 10:18: "Have they not all heard? Of course they have; "their voice has gone out into all the earth, their words to the ends of the world."

I also dedicate this work to my 2 dear friends in the music business. The first is to master guitarist, Phil Keaggy, for whom I have played drums and percussion with for over 27 years, having done many recordings and live performances together. Our mutual friend, Gene Ford, was the first to introduce me to Origen's views of apokatastasis (universal rectification) and hit me from a biblical eschatological-teleological perspective to universal salvation. I fought Gene hard with a hotchpotch of Greek linguistic-gymnastics and Calvinistic "hellologies." In the end, thanks to the consistency of Gene's presentation of apokatastasis and countless other God ordained events, reason took me over, wiping away my cold Calvinist views and replacing them with theological and emotional sanity. I still maintain that my 30-plus years of biblical Greek immersion is stronger than ever but blanketed with the warm doctrine of apokatastasis-universal sanctification which is my lode-star.

I dedicate this work to my students: Sam Glenn, Addison Macardle, Alec Bahmed, and Brandon Heinzelman, my son in law-Everett Bowles, and Matthew Joy who have helped me to continue this work in some aspect of time, funds, research, challenging me, reading this work with me (over and over), etc. I acknowledge the combined editorial efforts of Xavier Burval, the Wyrdhoard editorial staff, and much flawed attempts by me.

I dedicate again this work to Brandon Heinzelman in his indefatigable efforts on putting up my ministry's website: The Fullness of Meaning Christian Ministries.com. I consider this a joint ministry with Brandon for we both work together to get out challenging information for the believer and non-believer.

I dedicate this work to my mom and dad. My heart is with them though having passed on ca. 15 years ago they carry my spirit through this life. I still feel their love in Christ to me. Without them I can only say that I am being silly, for I know that God granted me them, my friends, influences, etc. in God's perfect plan.

Finally, I dedicate this work to the tender Christ that I know and love. I moan for that day that my love for him will have the substance that his love has for me.

ACKNOWLEDGMENTS

I encourage the reader to read the copious footnotes which strongly support the main body of this work. I regard the footnotes as "the other book within this work."

As a disclaimer, I'd like to say that no one that I have mentioned above necessarily holds to every facet of this work nor have they influenced me on every facet of this work. I do take a personal interest in presenting this treatment as an original work.

Introduction

THIS IS A VERY easy book to understand. It merely consists of the following ideas that you should be comfortable with in comprehending this work. Below, I give you 5 themes that repeat over and over again. I will repeat each theme from different vantage points all throughout the book ad nauseam but I will always return to our 5 simple themes. Let's get started and cover these 5 themes.[1]

1. First theme: there are only five points that I will attempt to make in this entire work. These five points (to be distinguished from these 5 themes) are what I call "The Five Noble Truths" or 5NTs. These 5NTs are: *the predeterministic view* (as it should be defined), *the teleological view*, *the apocalyptic view*, *the prophetic view*, and *the universal salvific view*. I qualify all of these 5NTs as being under the Sovereign Will of our Father, the Lord of Grace – Christ Jesus, and The Holy Spirit (*O Hagios Pneuma* [*O Hagios Parakletos*]).

2. Second theme: I "sandwich" or "stack" these developed 5NTs[2]. Here, we will see a multi-layered or dimensional view of God's hand. You will be able to conceptualize through scripture how God could work out of time, into time, and within time. The only limitations that the 5NTs hold are the innumerable aspects of God's being that we have yet to understand in eternity with him.

3. Third theme: I will show that these 5NTs support my argument that all events in your life are *full of meaning*, hence my ministry and website's name: fomcm.com (a.k.a. *The Fullness of Meaning Christian Ministries*).

---

1. Which are to be distinguished from the Five Noble Truths (5NTs).
2. we will anatomize each Noble Truth to exhaustion.

INTRODUCTION

4. Fourth theme: I will establish a kind of primer from the first chapter of Book I. You will be introduced to basic nomenclature of Greek archery and the archer's participation with the "Will[3]" to the bullseye in order to see the analogies of the Will of God in *relation to our will*. Such a rich language bank has loaned itself into the first century's Greek New Testament redactions and early Paideia[4]. This led me to make a lecture series called, "The Anatomy of the Will." I nearly chose this for the title of my work that I present to you, but in the end I decided going with the title, "Does Grace Have A Ceiling?."

5. Fifth theme: As the title of my book (just mentioned) should give you a big hint to this work, I repeat the theme of grace over and over again. For grace means "unearned favor." We get our word "charity" from its Greek origin, *Xaris*.[5] Either it is either the law or grace that abounds in salvation for all. Who gives grace but the gracious God of salvation, Jesus Christ.

Terms:

The Five Noble Truths (the 5NTs):

1. the predeterministic view (as it should be defined),
2. the teleological view,
3. the apocalyptic view,
4. the prophetic view,
5. and the universal-salvific view.

Other very important terms are:

A) *Stacking* (I interchange as "sandwiching"): to place one or more of the Five Noble Truths on top of each other

---

3. I use the capital letter, "W," to understand "God's Will" vs. "our will." The archer's "will" lines up with the "already made shot on the bullseye," or, the "Will" to the bullseye. We shall continue in the Greek words for *will* as in *boule* as is mostly shared in the Greek: "*thelos*" for "intention," "desire," "will," "wish," "compulsion," etc.

4. largely in part to Alexander the Great and his influential teacher, Aristotle: "Cyclopedia of Biblical, Theological, and Ecclesiastical Literature," (Strong and McClintock, *Cyclopedia of Biblical*, 1:138–40).

5. Strong's 5485

INTRODUCTION

B) *Layering*: to place one or more examples of just one of the 5NTs on top of itself

Below, I used layering (in contrast to stacking) since it was for only one of the 5NTs. I chose the prophetic view[6] to make an example for you of layering one of the 5NTs (Five Noble Truths[7]) which supports my methodological approach for unlocking Scripture.

Stacking and Layering used in conjunction

For our methodological approach, one can *only stack* the 5NTs. In contrast, one can only *layer* one of the 5NTs with various examples of itself (as seen below).

The importance of layering

The more *layering* you have of a single Noble Truth then:

(1) the more sustainability that one Noble Truth has against academic scrutiny

(2) the more informationally fortified our methodological approach can be

(3) the more confidence the Bible layperson will have to quote from the Bible as "the Authoritative Text."

As we unfurl this work, I believe that you will see that the Five Noble Truths, especially when stacked, rid us from the litany of contradictions found in the English and Latin *versions*[8].

---

6. one of the 5 "noble truths" that supports my thesis.

7. All of the Five Noble Truths that I present contain each other. I had toyed with the neologism "simplexity" (first used in 1924 by an unknown author) but found that the terms *"stacking"* or *"sandwiching"* fit better for expressing the self-referencing/self-containing attributes of the Five Noble Truths. Furthermore, I felt the term simplexity crossed over into the boundary of "synthesis" which is what I'm trying to pry English biblical versions from. These two terms will come to your full attention both now and nearing the end of this work once my Five Noble Truths are fully comprehended. My goal is that you will see that "stacking" or "sandwiching" (even if only using the prophetic view) offers a rich "sketch" of Jesus through 3 distinct prophecies.

8. what I might call, "the synthesized Bible versions".

INTRODUCTION

This particular example of the *prophetic view*[9] consists of only *layering* three prophets. One of the prophets is considered "pagan," which I refer to in the "a-moral" sense. The other two prophets are "messianic Jews" in the truest sense of that title. All three prophets share a portion of Jesus' character sketch[10].

As I see it, the two messianic prophets[11] that lived before Jesus the Messiah had a specific role. Unlike the Sybil of Cumae (Virgil 70 BC), the messianic prophets were to thread prophecy with the law using prophetic-poetics[12] as the suture.

> "The world was not created but only for the Messiah."
> – Sanhedrin 98 b

9. One of the Five Noble Truths. The other 4 are: the teleological view, pre-determinative view, apocalyptic view, and universal restorative view (i.e. *apokatastasis/apokatakaleo*).

10. It is claimed by the Oxford Doyen, Dr. Alfred Edersheim, that there are at least 456 prophecies from the Old Testament that were fulfilled in Christ Jesus alone. If this is true then the collage sketch of Christ's life would be more than ample evidence to claim Jesus as the Messiah: Book II: chapter 5, page 163:"Their (the ancient synagogue) number amounts to upwards of 456 (75 from the Pentateuch, 243 from the Prophets, and 138 from the Hagiographa), and their messianic application is supported by more than 558 references to the most ancient Rabbinic writings." Edersheim; "Life and Times of Jesus the Messiah."

11. There are, of course, so many prophetic visions that I did not pick. So many of these prophecies bear precision with calendrical accuracy: McClain's "Daniel's Prophecy of the 70 Weeks or *Shavua*," esp. graph on 68 and 69; Machen, "Virgin Birth Of Christ"; Hughes" "Star Of Bethlehem" —an astronomer's confirmation, 50 – 84; Molnar's "Star of Bethlehem" —the legacy of the Magi; Hoehner's "Chronological Aspects Of The Life Of Christ"; Ladd's "Blessed Hope"; Kyle Jones's audio Lectures on "The Fullness Of Meaning Christian Ministries (https://fomcm.com./christ-of-the-zodiac)" audio category, "The Vanderbilt Lectures," Lectures 5-10.

12. The Book of Revelation is a "Gospel culmination" of law, prophecy, allusion, allegory, *poetics*, etc. (Koester 2014); "Revelation," esp. pg. 73: "the glass sea" as the motif within the Canaanite sea god & its religion – "Yam" – "sea" which plays an important role in Ugaritic Epic poetry (Ford 1975). The possible sharing of symbolism might come into play without insult to the validity of Jewish to Christian symbolism. Such is the case as the Bronze Sea in Solomon's temple: 1 Kings 7:23–26. Dr. Albright, in his "Archaeology and the Religion of Israel," 148-50, shows the Brazen Sea as a cosmic significance. The word *yam* is similar to the Mesopotamian word "apsu" in meaning which refers to both the fresh water and/or ocean from which all life and all fertility were derived: and to a basin of holy water in the temple. The author of this part of Revelation, because of his interest in liturgy, may have been thinking not only of Solomon's temple but also of the significance of blue in the priestly vestments (Thavapalan 2019); The fresh blue ocean waters are relatable to the Sumerian word GIN, the Akkadian ZAGINNU, Hittite KU(wa)NNASH, Ugaritic "IQNU, Greek KUANEOS —which all relate to the color of Lapis Lazuli — as we see "the pavement" as Lapis Lazuli under God's feet in heaven – cf. Exodus 24:9–11.

INTRODUCTION

"All the prophets prophesied not but of the days of the Messiah."
– Sanhedrin 99[13]

Example of layering the prophetic view:

First Prophecy

King David was not just a warrior king but a prophetic voice/medium through which Jesus spoke ca.1,100 years before Jesus walked the earth. Let's take a look at this poetic prophecy in the book of Psalms.

Psalm 22:13-21

"They gaped upon me with their mouths, as a ravening and roaring lion. (14) I am poured out like water, and all my bones are out of joint; my heart is like wax; it is melted in the midst of my bowels. (15) My strength is dried up like a potsherd; and my tongue cleaveth to my jaws; and thou hast brought me into the dust of death. (16) For dogs have compassed me; the assembly of the wicked have enclosed me; they pierced my hands and my feet. (17) I may tell (Hebrew: "a-sap-per" – "I can count") all my bones; they look and stare upon me. (18) They part my garments among them, and cast lots upon my vesture. (19) But be not thou far from me, O LORD; O my strength haste thee to help me. (20) Deliver my soul from the sword; my darling from the power of the dog. (21) Save me from the lion's mouth; for thou hast heard me from the horns of the unicorns (Hebrew: "qeren"; sharp tooth/teeth within the jaws of a strong beast or horn(s) of a wild beast)."

---

13. Edersheim, *Life and Times of Jesus the Messiah*, 1.

INTRODUCTION

Second Prophecy

The second "prophet"[14] or "prophetess" was amongst the oracles of the Roman Sibyls of Cumae[15] in the early sixth century BC. She has been mentioned as the particular crone[16] of notoriety amidst a Greek colonial assembly near Naples, Italy. It was to her that most give credit to 9 initial oracles. There was a particular oracle amongst the remaining three (6 having been burnt by king Tarqin until his belief in her as a true "seer") that Virgil recounts in his work, *Georgics*.[17] This *heathen prophecy* (I use in the a-moral sense) shares with Deutero-Isaiah within a similar time frame in which the Jews had their three deportations into Babylon (ca. 586 BC). It seems that there were other Messianic allusions already in existence at this time but the Sibylline accuracy of the oracle that was loaned into Virgil's hope mentioned in his Georgics supported the prophetic foresight of Deutero Isaiah's prophecy in Isaiah 53:1-12. Such pagan and believing voices rang in exaltation a *harmony* which arrested my attention, intellect, and heart. With high precision from three very distinct personages, religions, and locations, one can see that Jesus the Messiah's life, crucifixion, and resurrection were on prophetic point as the Gospels exhibited their fulfillments.

Virgil, the pagan poet (ca. 70–60 BC).

> "Now is come the last age of Cumaean song; the great line of the centuries begins anew. Now the virgin returns, the reign of Saturn (Saturn meaning: renewal, dissolution, abundance, liberation) returns; now a new generation descends from heaven on high. Only do you, pure Lucina (the moon and her gestation period to birth), smile on the birth of the child under Whom

---

14. The root of Nabi (Ne'evi) is Naba, meaning, "to bubble forth" like a fountain; Strong's Concordance #1301 – NB "flourish, fruit, prophecy, seed inside"; NBB = "hollow" as a container to hold something; NBA = "prophecy [as inside a man not being known of the 5 senses]; N-BYA = "one who brings forth the inner fruit" —cf. to Strong's Concordance # 5029 and #5030 (Strongs 1980) and The Brown-Driver-Briggs Hebrew and English Lexicon", pages 611 and 612 – #5030 (Brown, Driver, Briggs 1906). The emphasis of this word and its variants starts with the earliest forms of pictographic Hebrew which phonemes were represented by pictures. Such evidenced inscriptions can be found at Wadi El-Hhol and Serabit El-Khadim in the Sinai Peninsula, dating back to around 2,000 BC. Cf. Marc-Alain Quaknin's "Mysteries of the Alphabet (Quaknin 1999)."

15. Virgil, *Eclogues*.

16. Crone: Anglo-French: *carogne* – "an insult;" French: *charogne* – "*a disagreeable woman*'.

17. Virgil, *Eclogues*.

the Iron Brood (Rome's use of iron smithing for weapons) shall at last cease and a golden race spring up throughout the world! Your own Apollo (Son of Zeus) now is King!" (cf. footnote [18])

Third Prophecy

Deutero Isaiah 53 (ca 538 BC)[19]

מִי הֶאֱמִין לִשְׁמֻעָתֵנוּ וּזְרוֹעַ יְהֹוָה עַל־מִי נִגְלָתָה:

"Who can believe what we have heard?
Upon whom has the arm of GOD been revealed?

וַיַּעַל כַּיּוֹנֵק לְפָנָיו וְכַשֹּׁרֶשׁ מֵאֶרֶץ צִיָּה לֹא־תֹאַר לוֹ וְלֹא הָדָר וְנִרְאֵהוּ וְלֹא־מַרְאֶה וְנֶחְמְדֵהוּ:

For He has grown, by God's favor, like a tree crown,
Like a tree trunk out of arid ground.
He had no form or beauty, that we should look at Him:
No charm, that we should find Him pleasing.

נִבְזֶה וַחֲדַל אִישִׁים אִישׁ מַכְאֹבוֹת וִידוּעַ חֹלִי וּכְמַסְתֵּר פָּנִים מִמֶּנּוּ נִבְזֶה וְלֹא חֲשַׁבְנֻהוּ:

He was despised, shunned by others,
A man of suffering, familiar with disease.
As one who hid His face from us,
He was despised, we held Him of no account.

אָכֵן חֳלָיֵנוּ הוּא נָשָׂא וּמַכְאֹבֵינוּ סְבָלָם וַאֲנַחְנוּ חֲשַׁבְנֻהוּ נָגוּעַ מֻכֵּה אֱלֹהִים וּמְעֻנֶּה:

Yet it was our sickness that He was bearing,
Our suffering that He endured.
We accounted Him plagued,
Smitten and afflicted by God;

---

18. Virgil. «Eclogue 4,» in *Eclogues*, 49. Also cf. Isodore, *Etymologiae* viii.8.5;" Servius, In Aeneida vi.72, 321; Lactantius, Divinae Institutiones i.6.10–11; Solinus, Collectanea rerum memorabilium ii.16, 17, 18

19. Still debated in certain circles, many scholars suggest a later date than what they would consider the "second prophet and evangelist known as "Deutero-Isaiah (*secundus propheta et evangelista Esaias*)." This beloved prophet, distinguished from the first Isaiah, was to be set in the Babylonian exile, ca. 538 BC. These "argued" dates still give us at least ca. 560 years before Jesus fulfilled Deutero-Isaiah's "Christ-Character" sketch. My argument stands that the proto-Isaiah was a different prophet than the second Isaiah and not a historical blunder of scripture but a validation of two different authoritative prophets who bore the same shem or "authoritative title-name." I conclude that two distinct prophets under one salvific God bearing the *shem* "Isaiah (Hebrew)": "*Yeshayahu*" → "Salvation of the Lord." A treasure trove for this topic can be found in Keil & Delitzsch's *Commentary on the Old Testament*, 7:38–42.

INTRODUCTION

וְהוּא מְחֹלָל מִפְּשָׁעֵנוּ מְדֻכָּא מֵעֲוֺנֹתֵינוּ מוּסַר שְׁלוֹמֵנוּ עָלָיו וּבַחֲבֻרָתוֹ נִרְפָּא־לָנוּ:

But He was wounded because of our sins,
Crushed because of our iniquities.
He bore the chastisement that made us whole,
And by His bruises we were healed.

כֻּלָּנוּ כַּצֹּאן תָּעִינוּ אִישׁ לְדַרְכּוֹ פָּנִינוּ וַיהוָה הִפְגִּיעַ בּוֹ אֵת עֲוֺן כֻּלָּנוּ:

We all went astray like sheep,
Each of us going our own way;
And GOD put upon Him
The guilt of all of us."

נִגַּשׂ וְהוּא נַעֲנֶה וְלֹא יִפְתַּח־פִּיו כַּשֶּׂה לַטֶּבַח יוּבָל וּכְרָחֵל לִפְנֵי גֹזְזֶיהָ נֶאֱלָמָה וְלֹא יִפְתַּח פִּיו:

He was maltreated, yet He was submissive,
He did not open His mouth;
Like a sheep being led to slaughter,
Like an ewe, dumb before those who shear her,
He did not open His mouth.

מֵעֹצֶר וּמִמִּשְׁפָּט לֻקָּח וְאֶת־דּוֹרוֹ מִי יְשׂוֹחֵחַ כִּי נִגְזַר מֵאֶרֶץ חַיִּים מִפֶּשַׁע עַמִּי נֶגַע לָמוֹ:

By oppressive judgment He was taken away,
Who could describe His abode?
For He was cut off from the land of the living
Through the sin of my people, who deserved the punishment.

וַיִּתֵּן אֶת־רְשָׁעִים קִבְרוֹ וְאֶת־עָשִׁיר בְּמֹתָיו עַל לֹא־חָמָס עָשָׂה וְלֹא מִרְמָה בְּפִיו:

And His grave was set among the wicked,
And with the rich, in His death—
Though He had done no injustice
And had spoken no falsehood.

וַיהוָה חָפֵץ דַּכְּאוֹ הֶחֱלִי אִם־תָּשִׂים אָשָׁם נַפְשׁוֹ יִרְאֶה זֶרַע יַאֲרִיךְ יָמִים וְחֵפֶץ יְהוָה בְּיָדוֹ יִצְלָח:

But GOD chose to crush Him,
That, if He made Himself an offering for guilt,
He might see offspring and have long life,
And that through Him GOD's purpose might prosper.

מֵעֲמַל נַפְשׁוֹ יִרְאֶה יִשְׂבָּע בְּדַעְתּוֹ יַצְדִּיק צַדִּיק עַבְדִּי לָרַבִּים וַעֲוֺנֹתָם הוּא יִסְבֹּל:

Out of his anguish He shall see it;
He shall enjoy it to the full through his devotion.
"My righteous servant makes the many righteous,
It is their punishment that He bears;

לָכֵן אֲחַלֶּק־לוֹ בָרַבִּים וְאֶת־עֲצוּמִים יְחַלֵּק שָׁלָל תַּחַת אֲשֶׁר הֶעֱרָה לַמָּוֶת נַפְשׁוֹ וְאֶת־פֹּשְׁעִים נִמְנָה וְהוּא חֵטְא־רַבִּים נָשָׂא וְלַפֹּשְׁעִים יַפְגִּיעַ: (פ)

xxviii

INTRODUCTION

> Assuredly, I will give Him the many as His portion,
> He shall receive the multitude as His spoil.
> For He exposed Himself to death
> And was numbered among the sinners,
> Whereas He bore the guilt of the many
> And made intercession for sinners."

Why did I list these three prophets?

God does not discriminate against his own voice, a.k.a., his own prophets.

I picked three distinct prophets (seen above) who were removed by time, and for one, their culture. I presented these distinct characters to show that God is not limited by who we think someone is, especially the pagan prophetess at Cumae. As we arrive at chapter 22 in this book concerning prophets, professing, prophesying, seeing, visions, etc., we will come to understand that there are many kinds of "prophecies" and many kinds of "prophets." Some are simply bold sayings of someone who sees sin to be repented of, whether it be their own sin or the sins of a select group. However, isn't it possible that God was behind these "simple bold sayings" all along?

As we shall see in this book nothing is outside the "fullness of meaning" which is orchestrated by God. Other prophecies are poetical visions ladened with ordained judgments holding both *warning and recompense*. Many times, higher prophecies of this nature call upon prophetic literary devices such as prophetic poetics that deal with events seen as *forms and shapes of time*, i.e., correlations of "*sin unto repentance*" as one shape containing many moving pictures. Through the medium of intentional anachronism, we can feel in the high prophetic style a sense of *euphony*- the musicality of poetical flow with all of its blissful sentiments.

Some of the prophets, such as King David and his son, Solomon, brought us a *euphoric musical style* (euphony) which was reality based, yet *above reality* at the same time. Such euphony can be experienced in the prophetic cantos of David's Psalms. David's poetical peaks are laden with a combination of supreme agony and supra-a-sexual dispositions which are found in David's words paralleling what Jesus spoke to his Father in Psalms 22:20: "Deliver my soul from the sword; my darling from the power of the dog."

INTRODUCTION

Poetics, without the need for calling them "prophetic (for they simply are prophetic)," can be found in David's son, Solomon. Let's read Solomon's Song of Songs 1:1

> "Let Him kiss me with His mouth's kisses! Truly, sweeter is your love than wine, Than the smell of your precious oil. Turaq oil is your name. Therefore the girls love You. Draw me after You, let us run! The King brought me to His chambers. We will exalt You and joy in You. We will savor your love above wine. Rightly do they love You."

Other[20] prophetic devices involve *irony* implying a distance between what is said in the corporeal world and what is meant in the metaphysical sense. Irony can be garnered within the context of the prophet's scenario, situation, and figuration of apocalyptic application. Many times, irony is wrapped within euphony, arresting the senses while introducing the sublime. I am in awe of such speech patterns for these were just a few of the prophetic mechanisms by which the prophets used. Through the prophets' prophetic pantomiming, heaven and earth met.

Prophecies that did not fail will always continue *unto* the eternal sense of total meaning because they are *from* the eternal being *in* his eternal abode. That is to say, prophecy thrusts itself back to where it came

---

20. A somewhat similar secular poetic style using intentional anachronism might be found in James Joyce's *Finnigan's Wake*. Though not Scriptural, James Joyce's modus operandi of writing *Finnigan's Wake* could be compared to John the Revelator writing in his Apocalypse. In my mid-twenties I dove into the dream space of Joyce's use of semiotics and dream-speak or "out of time speak" (Campbell 1995/Tindall, William York 1969). Professor William Tindal quotes James Joyce concerning Finnegans Wake: "is about anybody, anywhere, anytime.," or, as Joyce puts it (5981.1) "about every those personal place objects…where soevers (Tindall 1969 [pg. 3])." I bracketed supporting historical and geographical points to show Joyce's references (McHugh 1991). Such nonlinear sentences from the beginning of his book go as follows: "riverrun, past Eve and Adam's (i.e., beside the river Liffey by a tavern site of the same name and present day shopping center), from swerve of shore to bend of bay (Dublin Bay), brings us by a commodius (Roman Emperor) vicus (i.e., Vico road, Dalkey [cf. to Dalkey Island]/also, a "vicious circle'→ travelling around the island's course with reefs, funneling winds, strong currents, wind over tide conditions, etc.) of recirculation back to Howth Castle (The legendary Sir Tristram, i.e., Malory's Sir Tristram of Howth Castle), and Environs (Joyce 1976)" begins the Joyce tome central to Dublin, Ireland. Through Joyce's literary-poetic mechanisms one is allowed to experience several stories/events at the same "eternal" or 'a-tempo" "time." Joyce's mastery of languages and history were used to convey the history of man, his fall, Joyce's diatribe against Catholicism, aspects of the Irish funerary wake from its Druidic origins, etc. drawing many timeless points together into one book. To say you get a college education from *Finnegan's Wake* is far reaching but it offers a lifetime of analysis, if you so *choose*.

from, that is, the eternal. Therefore, what greater poetry is there than the eternal poetics of the Ne'evim or prophets[21]?!

The revered and feared prophet's office was to bring about the inevitable. For sure, they brought "judgment" as was *ordained* by yhvh. But "judgment" was only the schoolmaster's whip to guide the children of Israel not only into line but to make them recognize the whip was not a sustainable option, therefore, there must be a better way. The prophets presented something far past the whip for children of Israel. They presented a *hope* past the sting of the whip when the objective "keeping" of legalities of the children of Israel were found wanting. To say that one "kept the law" was a sham. The prophets declared a "hope" of grace above the condemnatory law that would show the law's "failure to acclimate" when compared to our growing relationship with God, becoming more like him in his image (Romans 8:29–31).

The law was at a crux when the messianic prophets came and more than that: when the Messiah came, the believing Jew (who lived among the prophets/Nevi'im) held that to reject the prophets would be to reject God's mouth, law, dabar, word, etc. The law indicated its own death when held in the face of a messianic hope which forgave sins condemnable by the law.

The Importance of the Law within Prophecy

The Prophets were using the law to traject hope, hence, a correlative failure for the law to continue to condemn. The prophets never dismissed the law/Torah.[22] The law, in a sense, was the rear sight aperture by which "the aim" was rooted though it had no "leading directive" or frontal sight. What was the law "aiming for"? The prophets were the ones who "aligned" these two sights.

As Jesus said in Matthew 5:17–18: "Think not that I am come to destroy the law, or the prophets. I am not come to destroy, but to fulfill. For verily I say unto you, Till heaven and earth pass, one jot or one tittle (of the law) shall in no wise pass from the law, till all be fulfilled." It is in his

---

21. Other mentionings of prophets, poetical literary devices, anachronism, allusion, allegory, etc. can be found in Koester, *Revelation*; Ford, *Revelation*; Pope, *Song of Songs*; McClintock and Strong, "Cyclopedia of Biblical, Theological, and Ecclesiastical Literature, volume VIII, Pe-Re.

22. Schurer 1890.

grace and his grace by the law that "all in all should be subjected to Christ and submitted back to the Father in Christ." (1 Corinthians 15:20–28)

Imagine a "place" or existence of eternal kindness, treating others as you would have them treat you. Is this not the eternal grace we all seek on earth? The law of the Jews, as used as a device within the poesis of the prophets, became allegorical. Not just the prophets but the epistles are filled with mentionings of the law in order to understand grace. Without the law, grace could not be fully understood. In Romans 6:6, Paul says: "Knowing this, that our old man is crucified with him, that the body of sin might be destroyed, that henceforth we should not serve sin. (7) For he that is dead is freed from sin". This will be one of many passages in scripture that will show that the old man, our old sinful being, who was naturally damned yet saved in Christ. Cf. to Ephesians 2:1–ff concerning our old damnable selves that were saved by grace, and not of ourselves or of the law that damned.

The Process from Law, to Prophet, to Jesus

One could call this section "*a necessary process*" or "*evolution of understanding*"[23] by which *objective* thinking (i.e. The Torah) moves forward into the abstract world of prophetic poetics.[24] Then, with a forward march, we move into the *objective* again but with a twist; the *objective* is also purely *eternal* in word and deed. Jesus is the "form" by which we observe eternity in motion in our limited time which creates the ultimate paradox. It was Jesus' messages that baffled even that of Plato's standard of the eternal form as the unalterable.[25] For he, Jesus, abides in the (1) *eternal form* of divine time (immovable/inalterable), (2) physical time or divisible time (day, night, hour, minute, sec.), and (3) psychological forms of time (past, present, future). All of Jesus' "abodes" would have baffled Plato's "eternal form" and "divisible" time in that Jesus, bearing eternity, participated within time's *moving pictures* (or "slices" or "divisions") that represent "portions" of eternity.

23. Barfield 1973.
24. Koester 2014/Ford 1975.
25. Plato *Timaeus* 38.

SECTION 1

Chapter One

The Intentful Archer

"Even if the Bible was approached as a work of fiction, the elicitation of truths brought out by its own intertextual and extratextual agreements would be enough to build a strong theological treatise.[1]" — Kyle Jones

This is a theological work using both Christian and non-Christian sources to create a rich nest of meaning in that we may promote a greater understanding of the Gospel of Jesus Christ.

The above icon represents "the intentful archer[2]." To me, and hopefully to you as you read through this work, it will represent the participation of both the "will[3]" of the archer (within the constraints of physics) and the "Will[4]" of God (outside the constraints of physics).

---

1. This quote was taken from one of my podcast interviews with the great Tolkien Scholar, Dr. Verlyn Flieger. I found it necessary to place my name after this quote in respect of whatever views Dr. Flieger holds. Our interview (one of 12) concerned the validity of Christ in the pagan world and the idea of "pagan saints" in Nordic literature. Verlyn and I continued to cover the idea of *true-ness* within the world of *pure fantasy* as a "reality." Our friendship has endured time's testing through ostensible differences in which we laughingly found ourselves on common ground.

2. Greek: the *"toxotayce"* = "archer" [toxsadzomai [(toxson)—aorist optative: "toxsassaito" *shoot with the bow*; [Greek: *tinos*: "at something"], author: Georg Autenrietth, *A Homeric Dictionary*, copyright 1876,1901, and 1904, new edition: 1958 by the University of Oklahoma Press, Norman, Publishing Division of the University.

3. Greek: *"protithaymi"* = *"pro"* = "pre" + "thought" = *"tithaymi"* (intent/place/set/purpose/[Hebrew equivalent: *machashabah* = "thought" or "plan'-cf. Jeremiah 29:11].

4. *Boule [Boulayn]* – Strong's Greek # 1012; Noun, Feminine; Counsel, purpose, will, plan. It is important to note with the word "boule" that it is more than "God's immutable plan of physical circumstances." Rather, boule always includes in its meaning the LORD's purpose in arranging all the physical scenes of history before creation

We will see in reading this work how these two shared wills, i.e., the archer's "will (i.e., our "will")" and God's "Will," work together synergistically as an "anatomy of actions and/or wills." We must take note here that these "wills" are not to be understood as equal wills in their respective functions. That is, God's Will and humanity's will only share in "definition" or, if you will, their definitive aspects, not actualities. Take note: God's name YHVH is a verbal construct, hence his office or name—> **God is a verb**[5].

Such wills become more easily understood as we begin to understand participation in God's verbal motion upon us. Participation involves cognizance and will. With or without a conscience towards God we are fully aware of our despair and depravity, if only for moments at a time. Over motions of time, when "a time" or "era" has completed its duration, we can bear witness to a result. Either the result resides in sin or repentance. In the end, depravity and desperation are not sustainable "options."

THE GLORIOUS WITNESS

We, as conscious believers, bear witness to our (1) incarceration unto redemption, (2) our purging unto purification, and (3) our shaping unto perfection only in God's grace. These 3 examples of "forward motion" make witness of the momentum with an intended directive in us. The world which sees this verb of motion acting upon and within us, in a sense, is reading the active WORD of God as scripture comes to life. We are the witnesses by which God is expressed.

DEFINING "GOOD" AND "WILL"

Mark 10:18— "There is none good but one, that is, God."

Philippians 2:13— "For it is God which worketh in you both to will and to work according to His good pleasure."

---

with ultimate intent and/or purpose. One can refer to Ephesians 1:11: "In Him we have obtained an inheritance having been predestined according to the purpose of Him Who works all things according to the *BOULE/Boulayn* (counsel) of His will (Greek: *thelaymatos*)."

5. Maimonides, *Guide for the Perplexed*.

Chapter Two

Shared Wills

As a Greek Christian, to know what good is one must know what "evil, will, free, bound to, sin, …etc." are. It is only when shared "intents" or "wills" of participant and God work together[1] in participation (cf. footnote: participant archer[2]) that one will see what "will" and "free" (i.e., the real "free will") mean—for this is the definition of good (*agathos*: profitable, beneficial[3]). The term "free" is a prepositional word meaning "free from" something but "bound to" something else[4].

Is it a "sin" to be free from the Will that makes the shot to the bullseye? Should I ask, is this a question of moralities, or, is it a question

---

1. Greek: [*sunmorphay*] = *sun* (with) + *morphe* (form to); Romans 8:28 – "And we know that for those who love God all things work together (*panta sunergei*) for good…." Romans 8:29: "For those whom He foreknew also He predestined to be conformed (*summorphous* – [*Strong's* #4832] jointly formed, (figuratively)) similar to "fashioned like unto") to the image of His Son…"

2. The *participant archer* is the believing Christian who acts upon God's logos with obedience and submission. This kind of humility is necessary in order to be a disciple (Greek: *mathetikos*-'mathematician") of Christ as the "Archer of Christ." These same *toxophilia* (Greek: love of archery/knowledge of archery) principles are not only applicable to the *literal – secular* archer but are the secular root by which the *Christian-Archer* acts. I say, "Christian Archer" without the usage of literal bows and arrows, but with that "*toxotayce* (Greek: the archer: *toxotayce*)" faith applied to the principles of literal archery. Such a *toxotayce* obeys the math in order to hit the bullseye. I shall fully qualify this in this work.

3. Kittel, *Theological Dictionary*.

4. Hindus hold a *Mahavakya* ("great saying") from the Chandogya Upanishad 6.8.7 of the *Sama Veda*, also with "*tat*" in 6.8. "*Tat Tvam Asi*" (in Sanskrit), meaning that "You are that" or "fundamental identity" of the Individual self—the ultimate reality (a.k.a., "*Braham*)." This vedantic belief holds that there is no dualistic reality and the "interconnectedness" of the individual soul is with the universal essence.

of technicalities? Likewise, are we to be praised (Greek: "*doxa*": glory, worth, praise, valued) for our moral ethics if we are possessed of an Eudaemonia (a good spirit/a good mind)[5]? That is, if we are in the Will that makes the bullseye are we to be praised for "making the shot"?

We will see the basis behind "good (Greek: "*agathos*")" and "sin" from its technical beginnings prior to what we would claim as "moral" or "moral-ethical" later on.

Such examples of good and sinful "a-moralities" goes as follows:

TECHNICAL A-MORAL "GOOD:"

Jane, a local archery lover (*toxophilay*) and Athenian, was a profound student of archery. When she competed, she applied art, math, athleticism, form, breath, calm, etc. "in order" to hit the bullseye. Therefore, she followed the math and hit the "*boulesthai*" or "sticking point [-*sthai*]" of the *boule* (the ballistics, bullet, directive path, intention, will, desire).

A GLOSSARY OF TERMS SUPPORTING THE ANATOMY OF THE WILL FROM THE HEBREW PERSPECTIVE.

A complement to the Greek *toxiphilus*/lover of archery.

The Hebrew Arrow

I mostly dove into the biblical and classical Greek to find the materials that supported my proposed theory on "the archer of intent" and "his/her" linguistic anatomy. Only later in my search for truths did I find my archery maxim to be substantiated in the Tanach (Hebrew Old Testament).

I found it necessary to place this short treatment of the Hebrew's notions of the archer's "shot to the directive" in order to prime you for reading this book. I will cover the Hebrew significance of the arrow and

---

5. cf. Aristotle's *Nicomachean Ethics* (Aristotle, "N.E. II.2): *Eudaimon* = "eu" = good + "*daimon*" =spirit/deity. Cf. Joseph Shipley's "*dei*" or "*dai*" = god, deity, demon [good or bad], "divider [as in "time segments (cf. "*Chronos*" —the *kakos demon*–i.e., the "divider of time"). Also, refer to my audio lecture, "Tempo Is Tempter"; on my website: fomcm.com.

its shot within the Hebrew roots Y-R-H, D-A-T, and T-R-H (Torah), M-R-H, and Y-D-A. I will show their interplay and significance in biblical wisdom literature in order to suture archery and archery's metaphors to the concept of *intentional guidance* towards divine understanding.

Words that complement the aimed arrow of wisdom: Y-R-H, D-A-T, T-R-H (Torah), M-R-H, Y-D-A in biblical Hebrew:

Such an exemplary case is to be found in the Hebrew root Y-R-H (יָרָה, pronounced yah-RAH), meaning "to shoot" or "to teach," embodying an imagery of an arrow aimed at a target—whether it be a physical bullseye or the path of divine wisdom offering solitude for the body and mind.

Similarly, D-A-T (דַּעַת, pronounced dah-AHT), comes from the root Y-D-ʽA (יָדַע), signifies a deep and intimate and relational knowing of God's Will, not just an intellectual awareness God.

At the heart of these concepts lies T-R-H, or Torah (תּוֹרָה, pronounced toh-RAH), which is a feminine noun derived from Y-R-H. Torah encapsulates "divine instruction", "guidance", and "law".

Together, these terms (Y-R-H, D-A-T, and T-R-H) weave a theme of purposeful direction and covenantal understanding akin to an archer's disciplined aim.

Below are some scriptural references to these *directional* words:

[BB] 1) Y-R-H – The Arrow of Teaching

The Hebrew root Y-R-H (יָרָה) is a multifaceted term, often translated as "law" but carrying a broader sense of teaching, instruction, or guidance. Its literal meaning, "to shoot (as in shooting an arrow)" and is imbued with a sense of direction and intentionality. In the Hebrew Bible, Y-R-H can refer to the entire Pentateuch, a specific rule, or wise counsel, as seen in its varied applications. For instance, in Genesis 46:28, Y-R-H is used in the context of "showing the way," where Jacob directs Judah to Joseph, employing the root to mean "to point or direct" (le-ho-w-rot, from Strong's H3384: yarah, "to point, direct, cast"). This directional quality aligns with the metaphor of an arrow, guiding one along a path.

Similarly, Torah (תּוֹרָה) is derived from Y-R-H. T-R-H is not merely a set of rules but divine instruction. T-R-H is as a lamp guiding one's steps "straight and true like a well-aimed shot" (Proverbs 6:13). Grammatically, Y-R-H in verbal forms like the past narrative vayyareh (וַיָּרֶה, "and he taught"), present action such as horeh (הוֹרֶה, "he teaches"), etc. Another example might be found in the imperfect hiphil yar'eh (יַרְאֶה) –"he will cause to teach/ shoot". To me, it is amazing that the abstract sense of the ancient Hebrew conveyed archery shooting with teaching. In Proverbs 4:4, a father says, "I was taught (horeni, הוֹרֵנִי, from Y-R-H) by my father," emphasizing guidance toward wisdom. The root's archery imagery underscores its role as an intentional act of aiming someone toward God's Will.

2) D-A-T – The Intimacy of Knowing

The noun D-A-T (דַּעַת, pronounced dah-AHT), from the root Y-D-'A, signifies a knowledge that transcends intellectual understanding. It implies experiential, relational, or intimate insight. In Genesis 4:1, when Adam "knew (yada, יָדַע)" Eve, the term Y-D-'A denotes an *intimate connection*, not mere awareness. This depth makes D-A-T central to biblical thought, where *knowing* God or his ways is personal and covenantal. In wisdom literature, D-A-T is a prized outcome of following divine guidance. Proverbs 1:7 pairs D-A-T with yirah (יִרְאָה, "fear" or reverence) stating, "The fear of the Lord is the beginning of D-A-T (דַּעַת)," where yirah—a feminine form related to Y-R-H—implies a *reverent focus* that leads to practical, intelligible living. This "fear" is not terror but an awe-filled acknowledgment of God's sovereignty (ribonoto shel Elohim), guiding one to "know (yada)" and obey him. Proverbs 9:10 reinforces this: "The fear of the Lord is the beginning of wisdom, and D-A-T of the Holy One (D-A-T qedoshim, דַּעַת קְדֹשִׁים) is understanding". This highlights the *relational* grasp of God's nature. D-A-T also appears in legal and practical contexts. In Exodus 35:31, artisans are "filled with D-A-T" for skillful work, indicating expertise or know-how. The root Y-D-'A produces derivatives like yodea (יוֹדֵעַ, "one who knows") or moda'a (מוֹדָע, "acquaintance"). In the causative stem, hodi'a (הוֹדִיעַ, "to make known") appears in Psalms 98:2, meaning to inform or reveal. Grammatically, D-A-T is feminine, often paired with prepositions like l' (לְ, "to/for") in phrases like l'da'at (לְדַעַת, "to know" or "for knowledge"), as in Proverbs 2:10, where "D-A-T is pleasant to your soul (l'nafshekha, לְנַפְשְׁךָ)," showing internalized understanding.

3) T-R-H (Torah) – The Path of Divine Instruction

Torah (תּוֹרָה, pronounced toh-RAH), derived from Y-R-H, is more than law; it is divine guidance, an arrow pointing the way. In Exodus 24:12,

God gives Moses the Torah and commandments, encapsulating divine instruction. In Proverbs 3:1, a teacher urges, "My son, do not forget my Torah (torati, תּוֹרָתִי), but let your heart keep my commandments (mitzvot, מִצְוֹת)," where Torah extends beyond the Pentateuch to parental or wise teaching rooted in Y-R-H's directional sense. Proverbs 13:14 calls the Torah of the wise "a fountain of life," guiding like an arrow to a well-lived life.

Grammatically, Torah is a feminine noun, often paired with verbs like SH-M-R (שָׁמַר, "to keep") or L-M-D (לָמַד, "to learn"), as in "keep the Torah" (shamor et ha-torah, שְׁמוֹר אֶת הַתּוֹרָה). It frequently takes possessive suffixes like toratkha (תּוֹרָתְךָ, "your law") or the definite article ha-torah (הַתּוֹרָה). In Psalm 119, Torah appears 25 times, as in verse 18: "Open my eyes that I may see wonders from your Torah," emphasizing its role as a source of divine insight.

The Interplay of Y-R-H, D-A-T, and T-R-H:

The roots Y-R-H, D-A-T, and Torah converge in wisdom literature, creating a tapestry of guidance and understanding. Proverbs is a goldmine for these concepts. Proverbs 1:2 states, "To know (ladat, לָדַעַת) wisdom and instruction (musar, מוּסָר)," linking Y-D-ʻA to the goal of D-A-T. In Proverbs 2:1-5, accepting Torah and commandments leads to "D-A-T elohim (דַּעַת אֱלֹהִים, knowledge of God)," where Torah (from Y-R-H) is the aimed path and D-A-T is the bullseye of divine understanding. Proverbs 4:2-6 ties them further: "I give you good instruction (leqach, לֶקַח); do not forsake my Torah," implying that Torah leads to D-A-T, the understanding gained by following guidance.

Psalm 119 reinforces this connection. Verse 66 prays, "Teach me (lammad, לַמֵּד) good judgment and D-A-T, for I believe in your commandments," where D-A-T is the outcome of following Torah. Verse 104 adds, "Through your precepts (piqqudekha, פִּקּוּדֶיךָ, a Torah synonym), I gain understanding (etbonan, אֶתְבּוֹנָן, related to D-A-T)," and verse 125 uses Y-D-ʻA: "I know (yadati, יָדַעְתִּי) your judgments." Isaiah 28:9-10 further illustrates this interplay: "To whom will He teach (yoreh, יָרָה) D-A-T?" uses Y-R-H in the hiphil stem (causative), showing teaching produces knowing, layered like "precept upon precept," reminiscent of Torah's guidance.

In Jeremiah 3:15, God promises shepherds who will feed with D-A-T and insight, implying they teach (Y-R-H) Torah. Job 6:24 uses Y-R-H in the hiphil form (horeh, הוֹרֵנִי, "teach me"), and Ecclesiastes 7:12 uses D-A-T with suffixes like da'ati (דַּעְתִּי, "my knowledge"). The metaphor crystallizes: Torah is the arrow, Y-R-H the act of shooting, and D-A-T the bullseye of understanding.

Other Hebrew terms concerning instruction

M-S-R (Musar) – The Discipline of Instruction. The term musar (מוּסָר, pronounced moo-SAR), meaning "instruction" or "discipline," complements Y-R-H and D-A-T. In Proverbs 8:10-12, Wisdom declares, "Take my musar instead of silver, and D-A-T rather than prized gold". Therefore, it is D-A-T that is the prize of heeding to musar's guidance. In Proverbs 1:7, musar is paired with D-A-T: "Fools despise wisdom and musar," contrasting with those who pursue D-A-T through reverence. Musar aligns with Torah's directional quality, guiding one toward a life well-lived.

Hebrew Grammar and Morphology – Steering the Arrow

Hebrew words are dynamic, shaped by prefixes, suffixes, and infixes that steer meaning like an archer adjusts aim. The root Y-R-H (יָרָה) flexes with prefixes like le- ("to"), as in le-yareh (directing the shot), or hi- (intensifying), as in hi-yareh (strong guidance). Te-yareh points to specific teaching with purpose, reflecting Y-R-H's intentional trajectory. Similarly, D-A-T pairs with prepositions like b' (בְּ, "with"), as in b'da'at (בְּדַעַת, "with knowledge") in Proverbs 24:4, or l' in l'da'at. Torah takes suffixes like torati (תּוֹרָתִי, "my teaching") or toratkha (תּוֹרָתְךָ, "your law"), personalizing guidance.

Prefixes like b- ("in, with") turn bayit (בַּיִת, "house") into babayit (בַּבַּיִת, "in the house"), and l- ("to, for") shifts shomer (שׁוֹמֵר, "guard") to lashomer (לַשּׁוֹמֵר, "to the guard"). M- ("from") yields mitoch (מִתּוֹךְ, "from within"), and k- ("like") makes kyad (כְּיָד, "like a hand"). Suffixes include -a for feminine forms (shomera, שׁוֹמְרָה, "she guards"), -im for plural (batim, בָּתִּים, "houses"), and -v for "and" (v'hu, וְהוּא, "and he"). Infixes, like the hitpa'el pattern with -ta-, create reflexive forms, as in hiktatav (הִכְתַּתֵב, "self-writing") from katav (כָּתַב, "to write").

Roots like shamar (שָׁמַר, "to guard"), katav (כָּתַב, "to write"), and yalak (יָלַךְ, "to walk") illustrate this. For example, b'shmeret (בְּשִׁמְרֶת, "in custody") in Numbers 18:8 or yiktov (יִכְתֹּב, "he will write") in Joshua 24:27 show how prefixes and vowel shifts reorient meaning. Every letter in Hebrew pulls the reader somewhere, guiding like an arrow.

Cultural and Linguistic Archery Connections

The archery metaphor extends to cultural terms. The Hebrew and Syriac name for Sagittarius, Kesith (קֶשֶׁת), means "the Archer," while the Arabic Al Kans means "The Arrow," and the Coptic Pimaere signifies "the graciousness/beauty of the coming forth." These terms echo Y-R-H's imagery of aiming with purpose. The Talmud (T-L-M-D, תָּלַמַד) further aligns with Y-R-H, emphasizing teaching as pointing truth directly at the learner, not just imparting facts. It is an interesting word that the Hebrew holds for a 'misdirected shooter': Kesil, meaning a "far darter without intent", "shooting amiss", and the euphemistic notion of "spreading your seed without thought". This Hebrew word is the equivalent to the "aboulia" in Greek. Aboulia meaning "ill-advised", "fail", "missing the instruction", ignorant to the math that takes one to the shot's bullseye.

Conclusion within the Hebrew Arrow

Hitting the Bullseye of Divine Wisdom

In biblical Hebrew, Y-R-H, D-A-T, and Torah form a constellation of meaning, each reinforcing the others. Y-R-H is the act of shooting the arrow—teaching with intention, Torah is the arrow itself – the divine guidance pointing the way, and D-A-T is the bullseye, the deep, covenantal knowing that results from following the path, the prize. As Proverbs 2:5 (yira[t] and da'at) and Psalm 119:66 (da'at) illustrate, accepting Torah's guidance leads to D-A-T elohim, the intimate knowledge of God. Like an archer aiming at a target.

These concepts direct the heart toward wisdom, aligning human life with divine purpose. Within this interplay of these mentioned directive verbs, the Hebrew sings, guiding us to live rightly through reverence, instruction, and understanding.

Chapter Three

A culture's praise of the a-moral hero is the indicator of anti-Christ.

GOD'S GOODNESS IN THE FACE OF THE TRENDING "ANTI-HERO."

Relativism is the fruit of chaos.

It is interesting that these technical terms in ancient Greece did not necessarily hold the moral weight that we might think of today. Much of ancient Greek society was based around the Epic (praised through song/poetry/etc.) One, i.e., "the one of glory" or "hero," i.e., "the one for whom all speak well of," the "*doxa* (PIE. – "dek" = "the one of worth"; "to have an opinion as opposed to knowledge[1]" due to their cultural worth[2])" – "the one of splendor," etc.

Within such an epic based society, as in the ancient Greeks of Homer's day (and epic successors following the days of Homer), came a correlative shame to guilt culture–i.e., "those" who were not epic, without opinion, worth, weight of value, glory, etc[3]. One would think without accountability the attributes of "shame" and "guilt" wouldn't be par for the course. But the larger reason shows us that this is not the case. Even if there was "success" for the Epic one/hero, the value of self-worth was nil due to the rule of fate, not worth. Just as if one is genetically disposed to be a runner or discus thrower.

1. Plato *Timaeus*.
2. Shipley 1984/Kittel 1985.
3. Dodds 1951, 28–63.

SHARED WILLS

The participants of shame to guilt had "no will" to associate their worth since whatever one did wasn't them but their "luck" or "allotment," hence the apportionment of the fates.

It is fascinating that the misunderstanding of the lack of self will within fate gave rise to shame and guilt. For if the "will" was one's "identity" of acting upon valuation things and that which they valued, yet, the "will" was "fated" or "allotted," as in Macbeth. It is in the identity of "shared wills" with a gracious God of good intention (contra. to a fate of debt and repayment) that we see ourselves as exemplars of God, will, Will, goodness, correct value, correct worth, etc. This runs into the face of the Moirai, Parcae, Norns, Graces, etc. —the Fates.

The fascinating part to "success," "failure," "shame," "guilt," etc. was more to do with the attribution of a "participating daemon." That is, from the time of Homer, *moira* or portion was perceived as a kind of luck, or "apportionment," having been built into the participant rather than an extraneous accident (such as a concerted effort to alter someone or something). Rather, natural beauty, good genetics, etc. were not earned, they were "deemed" by the fates. Even in the days of Herodotus kings and generals succeeded or failed not as an extraneous accident/concerted effort nor "consequence of character" but "what had to be" – i.e., fate. This archaic belief took personal "free will," "personal morals," or "personal success" out the window, attributing all things to the *moirai* ("those who apportion" or "fate"). This lightly developed topic might now help to continue our theme for a-morality.

An a-moral hero/anti-hero that is lauded today is no new thing. It is an indication that our current culture has made "events" a kind of "fate." This, to me, is the revelatory female daemon – or "divine goddess" that the pagan poet, Robert Graves in his *White Goddess*[4] raved about. Graves lauded her while John, the Revelator, expressed her as vileness in its utter form (Revelation 17:1–18). Quite frankly, both the laudation of this "goddess" and reprimand of the same as "The Whore of Babylon" by John, the revelator, gives enough weight to make "her" a substantial entity. In both the high poetics of Robert Graves and John's fully inspired prophetics have "done me in," per se. That is to say, I am convinced that "she" is real in a bigger sense than just the natural.

---

4. Graves 1948.

THE SOCIAL CLIMATE OF FATE CULTURE AND THE ANTI-HERO

1 Timothy 6:10 "The love of money is the root of all evil."

Doxa = praised = price = commerce = prized = worth = value = merchandise = trafficking of merchandise.

First fictive example of the "praised/valued one:"

There was a local "hero"[5] who often beat his servants often but won wrestling matches for the betting fans. Since the betting fans won lots of money based on the hero's consistent victories the hero is to be praised (*doxa*). That is, his "opinion" has "worth" ←-(hence, this fictive example elicits the definition of *doxa*). Though he wasn't a scholar, he had a "platform" to speak his mind and set trends. Shoes, shirts, shorts, etc. bore his name, people coming in droves to purchase merchandise "by association" of the anti-hero.

This kind of secular hero/anti-hero can be found in many of our modern sports heroes (including the heroes of antiquity). The substantive "good" is not necessarily defined as "moral" here, rather, "successful." So, in this case of "good," we see how this word takes on an "a-moral" meaning in the sense of utilized vs. moral.

Second fictive example of the "praised/valued one":

"Joe is a prized running back who benefits the commerce of the city— so, we don't look into his personal life nor is it any of our business." This second modern example (as was the first) of "the one of praise" or "the one of value," for now is found in doxology[6] which all relates to "value," "praiseworthiness," "worthiness," "praise,[7]" and/or "words or hymns of praise." The question is "to whom" is the *toxotayce*/anti-hero found worthy?

---

5. *i.e., epos* "a song/hymn of praise" --especially to a brave hero, an "epic one."

6. Doxology: "hymn of praise to God." From *dokein* – in Proto-Indo-European as from its root, "dek-": "to take, to accept, to receive, etc. (ambiguous: possibly as "in the 10 fingers, i.e., the hand"). More leanings are to the Sanskrit "*dasasyati*" – shows honor, is gracious, *dacati*= "makes offerings," "bestows," etc.

7. praise: Proto-Indo-European: pret-yo ["per "] "to sell," "to traffic in," Latin: *preciare* = "price," "worth," "reward," "prize," "value," "worth"; Old French: *preisier*: "to value," "to prize."

The anti-hero holds an "amoral" status in word and deed[8] (Herakles, the anti-hero "guest") but maintains the delusional freedom to act *relatively* immorally or morally in relation to the people's stage and setting who deem the anti-hero "worthy." The people are the "prop" and the anti-hero is their "icon." The common phrase, "it is what it is" is the "*logos*" of the *daemon apportioning goddess*[9] who "grants" the Hero's fame-status until his/her "fatality" (See *Macbeth*). That is, they are their own law, their own reference point, their own "goodness" to their fated end, in the blanket of "fate which doth rule."

For me, this comfortable "set up" of a journey unto demise already indicates a "freedom from" something "other than" what they knew they needed. It is a "will-full" flesh thing. "It is what it is" carries another sibling thought in our modern daemon-culture coined in the phrase: "you do you." Again, if I were a cannibal who lived next door to the person who told me that I might most graciously act.

We can say without a doubt that "she" is being indicated as the "spirit of" our postmodern culture of relativism. To elicit her fallacy, one might find "her" spirit-logos (logeia) generating Adolph Hitler to live out "you do you." If there is no good or bad in the relative sense of God, then, relativity will cannibalize us all as "she" is the queen of relativism.

Within an "a-moral" culture what can people possibly hate?

People hated (Greek: *miseo*: "dismissed," "rejected [*re*- "back" + *'iactere* -'throw'], "despised," [*de* – "down" + *spek* – "to observe" = "to look down on with hubris") Jesus because their deeds were evil (Greek: *poneros* – hurtful, painful. laborious, pain ridden, grievous). John 3:19: "This is now the judgment (*krisis*: "crime") (Greek: *krisis/krima*/crime) that the Light has come into the world and men loved darkness rather than the light for their deeds (*erga*) were evil (*ponera*)." "Evil" might be looked at as the spirit which engenders "hubris" as in "above-ness." As applicable to *aboulia* (lit. "without" + "will" ["without skill"]) or "evil," as we have mentioned in prior chapters, it follows that the property "evil" cannot, by itself, "align" or "abide" with the boule[10] of God: Psalm 5:4 "For You are

---

8. Watkins, *American Heritage Dictionary*.

9. Jones, "Theodicies." The doctrines of the feminine "logeia" – i.e., receiving allotments vs not inseminating; cf. both of my lectures on logeia.

10. "ballistics," "will," "volley," "toss," or "determinate council."

not a God who takes pleasure in wickedness; No evil can dwell with You." This does not discount the "usage" of evil men and actions that bring about a beneficial outcome (Acts 2:23 "This Jesus, delivered up according to the determinate (*horismene*/"ordained") plan and foreknowledge of God, you crucified and killed by[11] ("by" is not in the Greek) the hands of lawless (*animon*: "animosity") men."

Hostility to the laws of God, disrespect of humanity, and disrespect to the innocence of Jesus were defined as evil because Jesus is the light of men and men love to walk in shadows.[12] Therefore, whatever vacillating "reason'[13] humankind is residing in for the trending day, the disregard for Jesus is the very definition of evil, hence, the idea of being "apportioned" by the goddess of dispensing, the *moirai* (cf. my *logeia* [feminine "receiving" vs. masculine "giving"] lecture on my site fomcm.com). If we are not proclaiming im, we are "hating" him, and not only him but all that he has preordained and predestined. Even in secular understanding, we know we are all guilty because all of us know the standard or golden rule by which we should treat ourselves, therefore, we all know how to treat others. We even know humility as pagans or prior pagans.

In Matthew 7:12 and Romans 2:15 we are universally instructed that not only is there a "nature" to be understood on how to treat others as ourselves, but, the actual law of God is written on all of our hearts convicting us all. Paul continues to tell us in Romans 2:15 that the natural man's conscience also bears witness, and his thoughts sometimes accuse him and at other times, it even defends him.

There is a "waffling" that never ceases in one's own nature for the nature of man is itself in conflict. Even secular mental health therapists are called upon to psychologically "excise" or "cut out" that part which causes the natural man's "course" of actions to waiver. It is in this therapeutic endeavor that we must, as secularists or believers, recognize the conundrum of being human and what we unnaturally need in our naturally destructive path to be remedied.

---

11. *"dia"* = *"through the hands of wicked men."* the hands of lawless men.

12. Shippey, *Shadow Walkers*: John 3:20 "For every one that doeth evil hateth the light, neither cometh to the light, lest his deeds should be reproved (John 8:12 [Jesus speaking to the Pharisees]) "I am the Light of the world. Whoever follows Me will have a life filled with light and will never live in the dark."

13. or "ration"/"ratio"/"apportion"/"moros [moirai/merimnao]."

No one is guiltless

Romans 2:12: "For as many who are without the law have sinned and those for whom have sinned by the law they shall be judged (cf. Greek: Krima/krithaysontai – "incriminated," "crime")." Where do "all" of us go then? Fortunately, Paul is using a rhetorical approach here to grace in his "Romans Road" message.

Matthew 7:12: "So in everything, do to others what you would have them do to you, for this sums up the Law and the Prophets (Jesus [no copyright date found])." Well, Jesus gave us the answer right here! So, how do we fulfill this? Have you made it through a morning with your kids, spouse, family members holding to this golden rule? I haven't.

How do I fulfill the law and the prophets, i.e., how do I do good and not evil? How I "do good" is to understand how I am known in God in the eternal sense. There is not a waffling cultural reference when defining good in the eternal sense. Eternity is a stative or unchanging form, as Plato said.

God, the unalterable eternal "being verb"

Psalms 119:89: "Your word, LORD, is eternal; it stands (Hebrew: *natsab* – "station; to station; set") firm in the heavens." Psalms 119:111–12: "Your statutes are my heritage forever; they are the joy of my heart…." Other Hebrew words found in conjunction with Plato's eternal-unalterable form can be found here in Psalms 119:89, 111–12: establish (*kownanta*), endures (*emunateka*), abides (*wat-ta'-a'mod*), continue (*amedu*), forever (*olam*) ← all in the eternal sense.

God and true "good" share an attribute: they both share the attribute of eternity, or that which is "eternal." Eternity is a property of God. "True goodness" is a property of God. God's expressed abode is stative in that it never wavers and this is "good" for all of us. Therefore, true "goodness," if it exists with God, never wavers —unlike our natures—, which constantly fluctuates. Hence, we can never be truly good in this life.

THE MOTIONS OF TRUE GOODNESS

Continuing the idea of good and bad we shall see the evolution of humankind's ideas of morals (that is, humankind's ideas of good and bad) press forward into a reasonable theology if we are to hold that God is sovereign and all things are predetermined unto an *apocastatic* point. Plato said, "time thrusts itself unto eternity." I concur with Plato's thought and add that all particulars (all instances) consumed within the moving pictures of time will conform to its eternity, its unalterable state, i.e. a divine place with the eternally divine. It is in this reason of Plato that we can see God's universalistic hope of humanity bleed through. Whether of good or bad categories, all things are being "thrust" towards God by his own Will and into their "eternal forms."

1 Corinthians 13:12: "For now (*arti*- "in the immediacy of time"; "at this moment") we see through a glass darkly (*ainigmati*- "in riddles"), but then, however, face to face. Now I know in part (*meros*- "portion"); but then shall I know, even as also I am known (by God)."

Chapter Four

A Little Closer to Morals

STEPPING INTO THE ANATOMY OF GOOD AND EVIL

Ethos[1] means the "genius of a person or people within their "habits, manners, morals."[2] Morals[3] are close to the "morale," "mood," or "mores" of the group. That is, how the individual or the group "handles[4]" the day's situation. Ethics, customs, manners (Latin: manus), character, etc. can all be seen to work in a "synagogue[5]" of characteristics "towards a goal." How one "handles" the matter exposes their ethics and/or character. All of the elements of "character" work unto a goal, ending point, teleology, the bullseye, destiny[6]. So, we can see that morale, mood, mores, ethics, and character are tested within a group or unit and not a vacuum.

    1. Aristotle's *Rhetoric* ll xii-xiv; ethos is also known as "the spirit of a time;" Proto-Indo-European: root: s(w)e- 3rd person pronoun and reflexive ["self," "to one's own']; "manners," "habitual character and disposition;" "moral character."

    2. Sanskrit: "Yuj" = "to join," "to yoke," "to unite": join (gn/"genius"); the culture together: P.I.E. "sue-" = "personal relations within a group or unit"; Hittite: "yugan," Greek: "zygon," Latin: "iungere," Welsh: "iou."

    3. Shipley, "Origins of English Words," 257.

    4. Latin: "manus'—as in "manual," "manipulate".

    5. Greek: "syn" - "together; a bringing together" + "agein" = "put into motion," move, etc. From the Proto-Indo-European root ag- "to drive, draw out or forth, move."

    6. "*Character is destiny*" – Heraclitus; 1000 BC. Heraclitus neither meant this as a predetermined path of "character" nor an "interchange" of meaning such as "character = destiny." Rather, he meant that you have the "free will" to act in a way that brings about a destiny of your will. I do not agree with this. This view dismisses the many who never "chose," rather, his view includes the idea of those who could choose worldly success based on unforeseen external impositions such as oncoming diseases, mental

But from here I must digress for we are still just looking at the working parts of the machine and not the driver.

First, as I have stated, the ordained or destined path which carries the participant unto their end is the state of character (cf. footnote 18 again) that blankets the participant unto a desired effect.

Secondly, the analogue of the believing Christian, the toxotayce (Greek: archer), is the participant of God's verbal motion. Such a participant can also be called an observable actor or martyr/witness who carries the destined shot to the bullseye. It is the "observable actor" who indicates the invisible motions of God the verb upon him/her.

Thirdly, this pagan's idea of a "blanket destiny" that carries, drives, overwhelms, inwhelms, baptizes, rushes upon, convicts, etc. the observable actor all the way through the play until their end ("teleon") is revealed in a "relational" sense.

Fourthly, the "character is destiny" phrase by Heraclitus is not one of fluctuations by which the flesh acts for no one — (being that of the fleshly desires) — could hold their own character intact. This includes both good and evil in the sense of "a-moralities" and later "moralities" as we have come to understand them.

How do we participate if God has sovereignly predetermined and predestined all things?

---

illnesses, deaths, war ending the dreams of many, brutalities brought on by inner societal disputes which led to physical violence, etc. This is delusional for free will is delusional in this se se. I do, however, see "character is destiny" as both *eternally stative* (a fixed intent prior to time in the mind of God) as well as a "condition" set upon the participant. Such "condition" being fixed with the eternally stative is, in the here and now, unfurled or reeled out, as the "journey" or "path" within time. Such a formula, "character is destiny," though not Heraclitus's intended formula, fits the bill for a pre-ordained road that led to the participant's destiny. Such a pre-ordained road, parth, or journey filters out the necessary flesh of the participant while building the character of the participant *unto* a "perfection" or *teleon*. One way to look at this "destiny" and your "character" is recognizing who you are right now, looking back at the most painful periods of your life that you would never have "chosen" to have endured yet realizing those past sufferings are part of the process that brought you to who you are, i.e., your "destiny" and "character." Conferring to Ephesians 1:11 again, we have the following: "In Him, we have obtained an inheritance having been *predestined* according to the *purpose* of Him Who works all things according to the Boule (Greek: *Boulayn* counsel-intention, will, purpose) of His will (Greek: *thelaymatos* – desire, wish, want)."

Chapter Five

Stage and Setting

(A Necessary Process to Elicit Meaning)

The "enactment" of God's stage and setting is the unfurling of our lives. Somewhat like a Shakespearean play, our life's dramas convey the "moral of the story." For, if we find at the end of this unfurling that we are "saved by grace" and saved from our hostile directions towards God and each other, then how could having character unto goodness be an independent act of personal will alone? Prepositions such as saved by grace and saved from our hostility towards God are without or outside of our "wills."

Free Will Without a "Tethering Line" is a Nonce Idea

Some Christians use the term "free will" to promote an erroneous idea that you are an independent agent to either "reject" or "accept" God (or anything for that matter). Nothing is independent, nothing operates in a vacuum. One can say, "look, there's a stick over there! I'm going to pick it up because I choose to ." Is this an independent "free will" action, rogue agency, illusion, delusion, or participation in the figuration of God's mathematical design by which it was fashioned before time and space began? I say both. For we operate in time as an image of eternity in the sense that we have already been as Solomon said. We operate in sequences using a language somewhat "meta" of eternal inalterability.

Many philosophers, scientists, and theological scholars profess that all things are in motion[1] and are based on external forces. I agree with this. Therefore, things that you have ostensibly (seemed to have) chosen[2], reject, or accept in the observable sense, are "enigmas" or "riddles (Greek: *ainigmati*/enigmas)" which are mentioned in 1 Corinthians 13:12. We find the word that was "translated" as "darkly" in many Bible versions was actually the word *ainigmati* (enigma) as in a "riddle" to be "reasoned" or "analyzed"[3].

QUANTUM PHYSICS, OWEN BARFIELD, AND SOLOMON

Modern astrophysicists who implemented string theory found how our universe was "brought forth" or "became." Many quantum physicists are speaking as though the Bible from beginning to end was on the tip of their tongues.

For sure, quantum physics can also agree with the writer of Ecclesiastes (1:9 and 3:15 [ca. 1,000 BC]). My interpretive paraphrase of both very similar passages might go as follows: "all events in the past require all events in the future and events that will happen will happen again, therefore, all events happening now have already happened in the past, and all things in time require each other, therefore, there is no new thing under the sun." This sounds very much like our latest findings in modern physics' "string theory." Please read Ecclesiastes 1:9/3:15.

I would qualify this paraphrase with Dr. Owen Barfield's terse but powerful word, "figuration." That is, we "act"[4] as we are seeing the configuration of the stage and setting which has beset us. It is within this

---

1. gestalt: Greek: *synogogay* (together [*syn*] + move [*ag*] + drive/lead) – i.e., *synagogue* in the truest sense.

2. Charles Harrington Elster: "choice" is a substitution word for "replacing one thing for another."

3. Proto-Indo-European: "*re-dh-*," from its P.I.E. root: *re- "to reason, count." It is interesting that the verb "*riddle*" means "sift, pass (as in, "through a riddle"), "coarse sieve," I find that the function "to riddle" something is applicable to the Satan figure as "a Riddler." The P.I.E. cognate, *krei-* means "to sieve," thus "discriminate," distinguish, etc. We later find our meaning for "judgment, crime, *crimen, cerne*, discern, Latin: *cribrum*, separate, (Old Irish) "*criathar*, (Old Welsh) *cruitr* – "sieve," (*Middle Irish*) *crich*: "border, boundary"!

4. Philippians 2:13 "For it is God Who works (*energon*) in you, both to will (*thelon*) and to work (*energein*) for His good pleasure."

"figuration" that we are known. Stage and setting are "set" to bring forth meaning, i.e., our meaning in relation to the meaning by which the author designed. We know who the characters are in a Shakespearean play by how they play their roles. Similarly, as we act in "character," both in the immediacy of objective reasoning and in line with the story's narrative throughout, we ostensibly "choose" to act which expresses our "being" or "personage" in so much as we think that we are conscious to do so. Yet, it is in our essence to "choose" God or "reject" him for the moment. That is, it is the stage and setting that we freely act both as his children and antagonists.

Though we have all "participated" in the shape and form of damnation and have felt many times over its eternal furies we are dragged back to rest in his kingdom from such eternal fires unto an everlasting hell being "motioned" into the arms of our creator. There is no one who is noble, no one good enough, all seek by their nature their own (Romans 3:9-21; Psalm 14: 1-7).

We have all naturally crossed the boundary line into such damnable shapes where the "daemons[5] (gods/drivers of the mind[6])" of lust, greed, pride, adultery, anger, covetousness, etc. reign and ravage us. In these damnable shapes we found ourselves "free from" the settled mind and soul of being in the shape/form/of God's children. Simply put, much like the design of heroin addiction, the "shape" or "form" of such a thing, when participated with as in its motion-direction, it has its determined end, or "eschaton," which is death. It is already done and there is nothing new under the sun! Let's look at our next chapter to see what "will" we actually do have. It is very promising.

---

5. dae/de-/d" = god/demon + mne = mind (Shipley 1984).
6. Dodds 1951.

Chapter Six

Examples of Five "Wills"

We can find throughout the Greek New Testament a glossary of words conveying intent, wish, desire, passionately affected, volition, will, etc. Here are only a few examples, distinct from one another, that have been "translated" as "will" in the New Testament. In other words, the English "translations" or "versions" can sometimes shortchange us from the "varieties" of "wills'—such varieties of will which all work together in the collective anatomy of will between our "will" and God's "Will."

1. *protithemi* ("pre + place").
2. *ballein/boule* = "wel" (Proto-Indo-European: "to wish, will;" Sanskrit: *vrnoti* – "chooses, prefers"/*varyah* – "to be chosen"; Greek *elpis* – "hope," desire, wish; Gothic: *wiljan* – "to will, wish, desire," "volition").
3. *thelos* – "desire, pleased with, to take delight in (i.e., take delight in doing)."
4. *thumos* – "great heat, desire, burning, rage, war, outburst."
5. *orge* – "rage, raging, urge" (literally where we get the word "orgasm"), bursting forth.

God's five wills fill in the aporias of the irresolvable wills concerning "free will" vs. "predeterministic ideas." Such resolve of "acting," "doing," "coming," "going," etc. might be in the analogy of a Shakespearean play called *As You Like It*. This particular metaphorical quote was from Jaques in Act II, Scene VII: "All the world's a stage, and all the men and women merely players." Simply put, we are all actors in a grand play, each playing their assigned roles.

Though I do not use Shakespeare on the scriptural level, I do find the careful handling of his poetic words of power to write to themselves. There is a mode of elevated trueness exhibited in the Shakespearean form. Mimesis might be the best approach for reading Shakespeare, for it puts you in his mental nest of meaning, elevating the mind from the mundane. Maybe this is why I am so fond of J.R.R. Tolkien as well as Shakespeare.

What greater author is there but our Lord? Aren't we to mimic Jesus' words and actions? If we are written into the Book of Life, should we attempt to jump off the pages and separate ourselves from the fabric of his master story? Would we truly want to "be free" from his Book of Life by demanding our autonomy?

Our five wills and God's five wills (as read in the beginning of this chapter) are seen as "equal" in the definitive sense but not in the relational sense. Both God's Will and our will become cooperative as we come into his likeness. Our wills become co-operative—even when our sin is on its occasion, it is still not outside the author's pen. These five cooperative wills of man and God "act" in their participatory functions. That is, these wills join together, though separate in function, making a "unified sense."

"COMING TO BE" INTO THE ETERNAL FORM

sunmorphe (Greek: *sun/syn* – "together," "join" + *morphe* – "shape," "form").

Romans 8:29: "For those whom He foreknew He also predestined to be conformed (*sunmorphe*) to the image of His Son... ."

'*ehyeh 'asher 'ehyeh* = I will become what I choose to become (Exodus 3:14).

God is saying: *I choose to be Who I will be before I come to be.* Another way to understand this might be: God is before any event in time with full sovereign power to will what form/shape/extension he will take on in time as he will be "becoming." This simply transcends any logic applicable to a measurable reference.

We were predestined to "become" into the "likeness" of Jesus, as Romans 8:28–31 tells us. We are his body "coming to be" in his image.

We are being affected and filled up by our Lord as we exist here and now. he is the prime cause (i.e., the *Qal imperfect* first-person form of the verb *hayah* = "I will be" = YHVH–God [cf. *ehyeh asher ehyeh* = "I Am that I Am" = YHVH]) that precedes us to act, breathe, think, be, etc. His Will acts upon us and fills us up with "resolve" as we share (participate) in the likeness of his Will—hence, his son—as he is "coming to be" in us into the perfect eternal form.

Now that our wills are becoming subsumed in his Will, we are being given abundant saving grace and its correlative humility to overcome the trending dissimulation of fashion and bling, the lashings of "group speak," exclusion of those that aren't accepted by the "in crowd," the social cannibalism of the cliques or gangs who would show their "power" over the weak, etc.

JESUS = THE TENDER PLANT, THE *TSEMACH*, THAT IS "COMING TO BE" IN US

The only good example that we could live by is Jesus in this fallen world. Jesus' patterning of word and deed followed his Father's Will. Jesus followed his Father's plumb line (Zechariah 4:10) while trodding through the trenches of this world's vain glories. Meanwhile, the god of this chronological age gnawed at his feet.

Jesus' relationship to us is also rhetorical in that he is without cessation teaching us of our constant inability to "choose" him by our naturally condemnable state. Yet, the *ehyeh-asher-ehyeh*-God is "coming to be" in us—as planned for us, through (*dia*) us, and by (*dia*) his effort/work/ Will, not ours. As we read in Philippians 2:13: "For it is God working (*energon*) in you to both will (*thelein*) and work (*energein*) according to His good pleasure (*eudokias*)." This is the same God who "works (*energon*)" through (*dia*) us as he works through (*dia*) evil (*animos*) men to bring about his Will (as we just covered in Acts 2:23).

In his grace, he leaves us with the "sense" that we are participating with him in our shared wills. This is our character identity, our name of authority. This sense is not as though God is simply appeasing his pet by throwing us a bone, but in a broader sense—in the apocalyptic view (fully revealed view)—we feel that we are a part of a bigger plan than what we just see in the objective case. We are bigger than the limited and damnable "will of the flesh"

EXAMPLES OF FIVE "WILLS"

As we are drawn closer to him, our wills become more identifiable as his Will. We become lost, as all lovers are, in one another. Lovers say, "You have never really lived until you have met her/him." Is this not the bliss we have in Christ as we "lose" ourselves in our marriage with him? I think so, no matter how depressed we can get in this world. For sure, this depression is necessary to see the contrasting "kingdoms" of the world and of heaven.

DOES GOD PREORDAIN SIN?

Necessary Rhetorical Sin

At the fullness of our lives (the completion; the *teleon*), we should be able, with humility, to say, "I didn't do the things that I would have done, and the things that I did do were shameful, but by God's grace I have been absolved of this damnable flesh and freed from this damnable flesh, only because of you, God. Thank you, God, for loving the unlovable" (cf. Romans 7:18–25). This is the participation of our sin that reflects the necessity of salvation in Christ alone.

What we fail to see in the flesh (as believers, by and large) is the Will of God, which has ordained our sins unto salvation—in contrast to understanding that he has predetermined us as his elect unto salvation before we sinned. Therefore, God's *ordination* is to be distinguished from God's *predestination*. In other words, God ordained a sequence of events (i.e., having to do with things in this world's time) within the muck and mire of this world that would lead unto salvation—i.e., a place *beyond* time's grasp.

God is sovereign on all accounts:

1. He had a deeply known relationship with us before the world began.
2. He "pre-timed/pre-spaced" us in his love as his own.
3. He also taught us what is worthy by distancing us from him in our natural-heretical flesh.

In his distancing himself from us, we gain the respect of what God-Father did to save us. This display of sacrifice from the Father—let alone the Son—is more than anyone could bear to do. It would take a God with a plan to commit these acts to fruition.

Might I say that Jesus' worth has always been, but for us, the limited observers, we "see" the value in Christ by his actions? In the fullness of time, we will be ready to value him more than we did in our youth and its young lusts. He commands our saved spirit into obedience through our ordained condemned sin in order to make the refined shot to God's intention—no matter what we believe for the time. In this justifiable theological approach, ordination and predetermining do not conflict nor breed the heresy of dualism. In short, God's ordination of evil (i.e., destruction/sin, etc.) is a sequenced thing in time which leads us unto salvation while condemning our sinful natures.

We—not God—are naturally out of control, watching the movie of our salvation as it runs its full gamut. We are constantly seeing the will of the flesh and the Will of God work in a unified field. In our Christian youth, we longed for both the will of the flesh and God in the same breath. Our opinions about God's Will to make the shot to his objective bullseye (himself) can be very discordant to our perceptions, for it is the flesh that is the schoolmaster teaching us to "hit the miss."

It is our opinions that naturally got us in the weeds to begin with. Yet, being "in the weeds" does not imply "free will," as we say in modern Christendom. "Being in the weeds" is a natural concluding factor due to the state that we are in—i.e., fallenness. Therefore, we could only "choose" to be in the weeds. We are not free to "choose" another by our state or condition.

A NEW CONDITIONING

Our shared wills (i.e., God's and man's wills) are a sign of eternity's "expression" on earth. These shared wills are the "correlation" of wills unto salvation by, for, of, in, and with Jesus Christ in his love. How wonderful it is to share in time with an eternal living God living through us—all in "divine time."

Participating in time and eternity is a human's paradox, rectified in sovereignty, not human understanding. For God freely and openly operates in the eternal heavenly abode without the possibility of paradox. A freeing thought might occur to know that you are limited to God's infinite possibilities on earth and in heaven. We have been given "possibilities," as we might call them, within his limitations that he has prescribed to us. Even if God "limits" (Greek: *ordains – tasso*) us to act in a certain way in this life, the limitations are "settings" by which we are being calibrated unto eternal possibilities.

This is a much greater reckoning than being limited to the flesh, or physics, which is preordained to natural death (versus predestined unto salvation). Therefore, God preordains sin, failure, collapse, etc., but predestines our salvation and relationship with him. Our confidence lies in Romans 8:29—that we are already in a condition of being saved, but our process is a predetermined journey into the likeness of his Son through ordained suffering.

We also know that Jesus suffered unto death while he was being conformed to the *eikon*, or image of God in his fullness. Are we also to be "conformed" in the like manner? I think so, as Romans 8:28–31 tells us.

Chapter Seven

Vocabulary

Seen below are several very important New Testament Greek words to know. The following biblical Greek words explain "real life" scenarios as used to reconstruct biblical history. The integrity of the building of scripture is reliant on knowing these words in their historical setting. Many times, this is not what I have found in popular English Bible versions.

I also have dispersed these common biblical Greek terms throughout this work to show how they explain our modern experiences that we all share yet might not have the exact word or words for such experiences.

I do hope that you, the gentle reader, will grasp their potency in answering real life scenarios that are in accord with the original biblical text and your current life. Please take time to learn each of these Greek definitions placed directly below and how they are understood in the following few paragraphs. May you see this book as a kind of "self-referencing" work with many external sources to support itself. This book is not a "complete answer," of course, but if you get inside it, much like a multi-dimensional hologram, I think you will "see" new things that might be helpful to you in your relationship and journey with God.

NEW TESTAMENT GREEK WORDS TO KNOW

1. *Krino/Krima* (crime, judgment/categorize/separate/judicially prove (sounds like kree-know)).
2. *Pro-horidzo* (predestination (pro-ho'reed-zo), pre/be-fore + the horizon of time/space).

VOCABULARY

3. *Apocatastasis* (renewal of all things/born again (sounds like uh-pah-kuh-tuh-stah-siss)).

4. *Teleon* (the meaningful summation point of all things (te-lee-on)).

5. *Apocalypto* (the revelation of all things as they were once hidden (ah-paw-kah-lup-toe)).

6. *Prophetayce* (confirmation of God's Sovereignty through the revealed "Glimpse" via His prophets (prah-fuh-tayce)).

7. *Eis* (unto → a directional advancement of "going into" or "at" something).

8. *Xaris* (Grace/unearned favor/unmerited favor (sounds like Kareece with a trill on the "r")).

9. *marturos* (martyr, a "witness," "one who dies for the sake of something [Sanskrit: *"smarati"* "to remember"/Proto Indo-European: **(s)mrtu-*/Latin: *memor* – "mindful").

How does what I have said so far apply to your life?

Chapter Eight

Our Common Themes

WE ARE BORN CRYING as we leave the comfort of our nascent-conscience that has no pain or suffering, only the nurture of the mother's womb. As we get a little older, we are placed into "orders" or "categories" that we must unnaturally "fit" into such as pre-kindergarten, kindergarten, and then onto grade school.

Each grade requires more "death to self" in the sense that we are leaving our first nurtured state reference point – i.e., our first "ontic referent" – which will always be imprinted onto us. Some of us adapt to change better than others. We are all in a sense "called" to adapt as we are separated further and further from the matrix[1] of our mother (whether physical, spiritual, or both).

Then puberty hits with all of the hormones playing havoc upon our body's chemistry which some thought were just getting the hang of it ("growing up"). Then relationships kick in. Many of these relationships are immature and unstable. This, of course, is to be expected. Many hearts broken, questioned inadequacies taking place, possible jealousy, competition, etc. Then, we enter high school, college, jobs, serious long-term relationships, having kids of our own, death of our parents, death of our loved ones, and then our deaths.

For me, I have missed and hurt over all of these formed bonds that were torn away. I sit here writing about past relationships and parents all the while continuing in my "processing" journey, hopefully, within the reason that God has given me. So much pain.

---

1. *matrice* (Old French) – "uterus, womb" —> from the Latin: *matrix*: "pregnant animal; source of origin."

I looked at another approach to "handling" our suffering. I call this "approach" "holding position." Maybe you are "holding position" in order to tell yourself that you are going to "overcome" all of your pains, losses, injuries, etc. The problem with "holding one's own" or "holding position" is that this approach to pain and suffering has no substance[2]. Therefore, technically, "holding one's own" is meaningless. One can "hold position" until the next event comes to erase or dull the memories and feelings of the past hurts and heart aches through sheer physical "will" but this just covers up past issues that will reoccur. Furthermore, this physical "will" is the very kind of will that separates us further from God. The attempt to be "tough" and to "hold one's own" is a very different stance than believing that all things have fullness of meaning. But to hold the view that all things have meaning, purpose, direction, significance, etc. is a conditioned view. This view only occurs when we are ready[3] to throw away our trust in human will power.

THE DIFFERENCE BETWEEN PREORDINATION AND PREDESTINATION (FROM THE GREEK)

If God is sovereign in everything, does he also "do" and/or "create" evil?

A study of boundary lines

"Pre-Horizoned"/"Predestination"/Greek: *Prohorismenos* [key root: pro + *horos*]

is not

"Determined/Determinism"/Greek: *Horosmenei* [key root: *horos*].

Have you ever heard anyone say, "only good things come from God?" What if all of our experiences of pain and suffering in this lifetime were a determinate plan unto eternal meaning and joy? What if there was a grand intent by which we were ordained to suffer unto salvation from beginning to end – within the boundaries of time's juridical frontier?

---

2. *substance* = "sub" + "stance" = *hupo* (under/sub/rooted) + *stasis* (standing) = (Greek) *hupostasis*.

3. at the point by which meaningfulness has culminated to the "here and now" and one is at their *"kairos"* – "at hand" time to deal with things healthily.

What if I told you that predeterminism and determinism worked hand in hand but were two very different things?

Pro-tasso

The word "determine," from Latin, means something that is "*de*" – "off" + "*terminus*" – "limit," "end." It also means "to render judgment"; "to find the solution of a problem." Finally, Proto-Indo-European gives us "*termen*" as a "peg, post, boundary marker, etc.." It is in the deeper study of this "terminal" as "peg" where we get "*paginus*" or "*pagan*" from. That is, "those demarcated from the cultivated village by a series of pegs."

The "hand of blame" or "dark hand" is that which "handles or manipulates" while remaining obedient to God's sovereign determinism. Though seen as "lawless," or better yet, "antagonistic," we see the "dark hand" in the Book of Job as the Satan figure. This "satan figure" roved *to and fro* (literally meaning "Satan" in Hebrew: *Mi-SHUT* [*Shat- (an)* -as is animated into a being) seeking "*on* [Hebrew: "*ba*"]" the earth, and "from walking up and down "*on* ["*ba*"]it." As the *miSHUT* (the Satan figure) "roved, seeked, walked to and fro" as did the lawless men who put Jesus to the cross having their hands worked unto God's fulfillments as they "acted" solely by God's ordination. Let's look at the boundaries where they contain such workable evil.

Note: Please refer to the diagram of Greek/English prepositions in chapter 10.

Judgments within boundaries

Determinism refers to judgments which have been rendered. It means to settle, decide upon, state definitively, fix the bounds of, limit in time or extent, give direction or tendency to, mark the end or boundary, and find as the solution of a problem (i.e. the "terminus" of the problem). Terminus qualifies the argument for "determinism" within the boundaries of space and time, i.e., a "place" which is not of limitlessness.

Scripturally speaking, these "judged events" happened from the *horos*/boundary of creation. We find time's first moment at the "horizon" as "entering" or the Greek's preposition, "*eis*." The Greek philosopher, Plato, rendered "*horidzo, horus*, horizon, hour as *physical divisions of time* which were only shadows of immovability, a.k.a. the inalterability of eternity. Hence, we are moving pictures in "time" or "divisions" representing a full shape (eternity).

To note: in Greek myth, the anthropomorphized god of time was named Chronos. Chronos, as the god of time, was the "eater of all things" since "time." Chronos would consume all until his end or terminus.

The beauty of Greek (and Hebrew) names are found in their function and it is here that we see Chronos's boundary line offering no other place to go. His function is to consume, divide, cut asunder, section (as we shall see later in this work in *"timon"* or *"de'-mne"* – as the *demon*, "time"). Arguably, the Shemitic mind, especially that of the Hebrew mind, seems to be more *dynamic* being that God is the verb who is acting upon all things or who is the action of all things while the Greek mind is more "measurable." I might paraphrase the great Scandinavian theologian, Dr. Thorlief Boman, as follows: An ancient Hebrew would define a pencil as in the attribute of writing or marking while the Greek would define the pencil by its physical dimensions. Nonetheless, Dr. E.R.R. Dodds gives us plenty of examples of "abstract" notions in his "Those Irrational Greeks[4]" as does Plato in "things" in motion that "cause" the next event[5]. With that said, we can look at Chronos as an agreeable mythical god-figure of the age by which Paul refers to. The "god of this age, era, aeon, time," as the biblical Satan or Greek mythological Chronos abides now, lives in his court as the prince of the power of the air. That is, the *god (theon) of this age* (aeon, era, time) as we find in 2 Corinthians 4:4 and also in Ephesians 2:2. In these passages we have mention of the ruler (archon) of this age (aiona/eon/aeon) as can be applied to the Satan/Antichrist/Chronos, as the god (theon) and ruler (archon) of this era as he fulfills the role of the Biblical Satan and the mythological "horned one." I might add that history gives us Nimrod as the "god" of his age wearing horns (Hebrew: "qeren"/Greek: "kerata") of a bull on his head to show dominance[6].

In Greek myth, Chronos's wife, Ananke, was the goddess of objectivism and lust. She also carries with her toil, anguish, and anxiousness as Plato tells us in his dialogues of Cratylus: "Ananke is likened to that of traversing a stream/going against the current." Chronos is seen as the "horned one" from which we get the word, "corona" which is also another cognate from its guttural (h, x, k, ch) + rotex (l, ll, y, r) configuration to

---

4. Dodds 1951.
5. Plato 1926, "Cratylus".
6. Reverend Alexander Hislop did a wonderful treatment on the history of deified leaders wearing horns/crowns in his,"Two Babylons."

that of Chronos. Chronos finds himself in the crown for most crowns consist of a corona/and the horns attached to it, thus symbolically expressing "power" to alter the times and land appropriation.

In contrast to the existence within the boundaries of Chronos's circle, *prohoridzo* or predestination is an existence outside the boundaries of time, being bound to God within his eternal intimacy. All things existing outside the boundary of time are in the pre-boundary (pro-horidzo). Therefore, *prohoridzo* is a state (stative condition) that does not "sequence." Rather, this condition is not in time. For pro-horizon/predestination/pro-horidzo is eternal in the everlasting without end sense. Therefore, "drama," "trauma," or "unfurling" cannot and does not occur in the physical-chronological sense.

A few years back I did an audio lecture called "Trauma, Drama, and Thing."[7] It was a look into time as it unfurls as a "thing (an eternally stative form/thing)" of trauma. Truly, trauma occurs in the unfurling of time and as an "idea" in the stative shape or form of "that which was/is/will be" unfurled.

The Distinction

We need to categorize determinism (*horidzo*/Horai[8]) from predestination (*prohoridzo*). Determinism, as in "ordained," usually refers to a "timed" sense by which events will occur around. Cold determinism, as held as an ideological belief, holds that many events will lead up to the "determined" event–but by what driving force is begged to be answered. Hence, its meaning is "to enclose, bound, set limits to (Latin: *de* – "off" + *terminus* – ending point, boundary)," etc.

We read in Acts 2:23: "By the determinate (*horosmenei*) will (*boule*) and foreknowledge (*prognosei*) of God, He (Jesus) was delivered up (*ekdoton*) and crucified by (Greek: "dia" – "through" [not "by"-as many "translations" horribly read]) lawless (*anomon*) hands which you put unto death (*aneilate*)." Therefore, God used lawless men to "work through (*dia*)" to do his determinate plan. This is answerable to "evil" not abiding with, of, in, etc. God.

---

7. Jones, "Trauma, Drama, and Thing."
8. Horai: the Greek goddess of processional seasons, natural order, and time. The Horai were young beautiful maidens also known for keeping order and justice

In another passage (Revelation 13:8) concerning ordained crucifixion. We find Jesus as "The Lamb having been slain from the founding of the world." When we look at "slain" in the Greek, *esphagamenou* [es-fah-gah-meh-noo]) we find that it is in the perfect tense, i.e., it already happened to completion. We read that this "slaying" was from (*apo* – off/of) the founding (*katabolis* – depositing, sowing, act of conception) of the world." In both instances, it was from, at, or in, the beginning of this world's foundation – i.e., where "fallenness" begins and reigns. God is Holy, always resolving with Holiness, but he ordains through (*dia*) evil (within Chronos's reign) his ultimate plan which is to purify and reconcile all[9] things back to himself (Col. 1: 20).

Again, "time" is involved in "ordination" or Horidzo/Horai/Hora. While predestination's root is found in "pre" + "time/hour/boundary" existence. Furthermore, *prohoridzo* (pre-horizon/pre-time) was in a relational or marital sense before "time" or "around, beyond" time. Though "determinism" as used in the "Determinate Counsel" absolutely implies a "sovereign" aspect of God. But this "determinate" Lord is "relational" as a husband to us found in Hosea 2:16 (ca. 720 BC). God defines himself as a "contrasting Lord" to Ba'al (master of time/land). In Hosea he calls himself by his title to us as "*ISHI*," a.k.a. "Husband," vs. "Ba'al" which means an "owner" of chattel (including the wife).

This is why I say the potency of God's sovereignty lies in his kindness as our husband who has taken us from the world (*kosmokriton*) and into his arms. We are "free from" the peril of time and eternally into his bosom.

Throughout this work you will see me repeat the word "unto" quite a bit. The reason is that "all things" are working together unto our reunion with God. This idea/reality also means going "out" of time. All determined destructive things that occur to our damnable flesh do their work unto our return with God. It is in God's determined orderly arrangement that we will fall into the order (sequence of Chronos[10]) that leads to God. In this "fateful" world, God's "Will" is that we will dwell with him beyond the boundaries of time. As pastors, bible scholars, bible teachers, etc. we should not dare obfuscate terms such as "predetermined, ordained, determinism/determined, fatalism, and fate as synonyms.

---

9 panta: "every, all, the whole, everything whatsoever [Strongs 3956]

10. This is a crucial point to understand. God ordains us to be "sifted" through time *unto* salvation.

DEFINING WHAT SOMETHING IS WILL DELINEATE WHAT IT IS NOT (SEMIOTICS, LIMITATIONS OF MEANING)

Pro-horidzo

What exactly does "predestination" mean? Pretty much what you might guess. It means that something was set *(tithemi/taxis)* by idea and intent to happen before it happened. In a little more extended way of saying it: it means a "pre-set-boundary" by which potential events that have not instantiated/happened, as of yet, will happen in time as time unfurls its dramatic stage. We can look at it like this: before the "potential event" met the boundary of time, the potential event(s) had not been unfurled into the fabric of time and space. When the "potential event(s)" penetrated the bounded time or "horizon of time (the *horos*[11])," they unfurled into bounded time ("horos"/"mountain"/"place of boundary of man from the gods") and became[12] "instantiated/actualized/actuated/"[13].

Oros/Origins

To thicken the views of the Greek "mountain (*oros*)" as "time, no time, boundary marker, etc." we might give another angle on this same biblical-theological principle. Jesus tells us in Mark 11:23: "For verily I say unto you, that whosoever shall say unto "this mountain ("*toutoi -orei* [root–*oros*]" — demonstrative pronoun — "this mountain/boundary [of self]),"

---

11. Both *oros* [*horos*] in Greek and its Hebrew equivalent – *gebhal* – mean "mountain" as in a "boundary line" between the gods and men. *Oros* and *gebhal* are where the arch of heaven and earth touch. Both terms establish the "boundary line" idea of ocean and land, fence and field, village and heath, dark and light, etc. In our English word, "hour," we see *oros* as the etymon for "hour." "Hour" or *oros* is a "dividing" line of time. Such examples of horos are found as a minute, hour, day, week, month, year, etc. —in which all "divisions" of time are considered invisible dividing lines.

12. *egaygermai* – "to excite, arouse, awaken [cf. Matthew 2:13]."

13. Ephesians chapter 1 not only explains our predestined relationship with God before the world began but the "reconciliation" of ALL things back to the Father in Christ after the world goes away and back to the Father in our "born again (anothen)" state. This also flies in the face of Plato's non-belief of "instances" or "instantiations." Such philosophers as Parmenides and Zeno touched on the ideas of fabric of time and space. Immanuel Kant also considered our minds to be the "shaper" of space and time." Recent discoveries with physicists such as Brian Cox's show a complex network of information within black holes as being held like "bits" as they are collected and re-emerged into other Big Bangs.

"be thou removed, and be thou cast into the sea; and shall not doubt in his heart, but shall believe that those things which he saith shall come to pass; he shall have whatsoever he saith. (24) Therefore I say unto you, what things soever ye desire (*aiteisthe*: "ask, entreat), when ye pray, believe that ye receive them, and ye shall have them." Jesus is not preaching health and wealth. On the contrary, he is giving you the empowerment of heaven to "remove" your "mountain of pride" and send it to the abyss/sea/unseen place/hell. This prayer is in contrast to the acquisition of stuff and things. He is empowering you with a clear mind that if you pray, even within this boundary of self/sin, you can remove it, and have the desires (shared with God's desire) of your heart, which will be one and the same as God, not stuff and things of objectivity.

Secondly, such an idea as the Logos's "coming into being" or "becoming" within the flesh[14] is the human paradox. This relationship of intent: idea: coming into, becoming, etc. was already established out of time, or before time, as "idea, purpose, will." This is the definition of predestination prior to creation. That is, creation was intentful, purposeful, meaningful, etc. We shall see that this covers the meaning of one of the 5NTs, i.e., the teleological view.

This makes a separate theological idea of WORD or Logos that we have in John 1:1–51. John explains the principle of "potential" to "actualization" in that the Logos became flesh (actualized) and dwelt among us[15]. John tells us that this same Logos "actualized" and that all things came into being (*egeneto*: "came into being" [King James: "made"]) including himself by himself as "actor," as triunitively shared with the Father and Holy Spirit. The Logos "actualized" himself into flesh and existed among us in the flesh. The Logos entered the flesh of Jesus as an "eternal form in moving pictures." Separated only by time, Jesus acted solely upon the eternal form of holiness of his Father's Will, being full of meaning in every chronological step.

The anarthrous "beginning" means that there is *no specified time*, only a concept to be apprehended of eternity unmodified by linear time. John continues to say the logos was "*pros ton Theon* (i.e., pros: "towards/facing/*with*" ton: "the," *Theon* "God")." John equates the Logos as facing, or "pros," with God. *Pros*, or "facing" does not mean "equal" or "same." For, the WORD is a part or "office" of the trinity. Therefore, the Logos,

---

14. Greek: *sarx*: flesh. That is, the eternal form (The *Logos*) crossing through the *oros* into time

15. *Immanuel* – Hebrew: "*God is Among us*": Isaiah 7:14; Matthew 1:23

Father, and Holy Spirit comprise the compound plural masculine "*Elohiym.*" There can be an argument here that the angels are a part of the "*Elohiym.*" But, as the Trinity is concerned within the "Elohiym" (better yet, the *eyeh – asher – eyeh* YHVH) there is none like "Him" or the Trinity expressed through ONE (Jesus) as one God. John tells us that not only did all things come into being (*egeneto*) through him (the *Logos*) but that nothing came into being without him.

So, we could reason from scripture that the Word (Jesus Christ/Logos) acted outside time and space and then entered into (Greek: "*eis*"- "went from outside to inside") time/space and intent preceded the act. Jesus brought all things into being while the Father acted before time (Greek: *pro-horidzo*: "before the boundary/time) and space with intent and purposefulness agreeable with the Holy Spirit. He Willed, through his Son's actions, a bringing into being through the formless black matter (*tohu va bohu mayim*) as mentioned in Genesis 1:2:[16] into form (Greek: *taxis* – "order"). Such an act of materialization acted in agreement with the laws governing time. Before this actualization nothing was actualized (only potential in the intent of God-Father).

This is an explanation of creation from combining Genesis 1:2 with John 1:51. That is, before creation there was "action." Before action there was intent/reason/thought. This is a way to explain *pro-horidzo*, "pre-time," "pre-event," "pre-boundary line."

Why do we not want to believe in predestination when so clearly it is laid out in the acts of creation? We certainly do not have a problem, as believers, with God creating mass, time, light, heaven, earth, etc. Some argue that the problem of predeterminism is that our "free will" is taken away. Yet, as believers, we must read Romans 8:28-31 that God predestined our salvation, knew and loved us before the foundation of the world, and predetermined us to be conformed (Greek: *sun* ["with"] + *morphe* ["shaped, conformed"]) to the image (icon/*eikonos*) of Christ. These were all acts before creation. Predestination is not master puppetry. Rather, "before time (*pre-horos*)" is a place of unbridled freedom in a form of eternal marriage with our Lord. Predestination is marital.

---

16. Hebrew: *Tohu va Bohu* – "formlessness and void"/*Mayim* [black substance; urine, waste] – "chaos"]

Chapter Nine

The Failure of Human Reason by Human Perspective

Predestination has become a theological buzz word in certain circles making some people fearfully not wanting to fully approach it, let alone dissect it. I understand this completely. It's a kind of fear that this "unknown" might become the very thing that unravels your fabric of understanding or belief system. It can make a minister fearful to be associated with ideas of "predestination" in that some may associate the minister with Calvinism, automatism, puppets on a string, etc.----all of which I have purposefully been addressing and ridding from what true predestination actually is.

I remember all throughout my college years there were around the clock arguments concerning "free will" vs "predestination." This can be healthy, except I hardly ever heard the proper definitions of both of them in an "agreement context" or "synergy." Free will and predeterminism (as defined by undergraduates) always seemed to be bantered within a "versus" context. This led me to start thinking "out of the box of time (linear time)" as I got older. I began to think of justifiable reasons for having both predestination and a "kind of" free will to work together as a unified supporting mechanism within a larger scope, with bigger dimensionality, i.e., a "marriage" of two ostensibly competing ideas. It was never enough to just look at this clean running hybrid idea consisting of definitive free will and definitive predeterminism unless they were joined as a marriage within the context of endless love/marital love (Greek: *gamos* – "married, joined, union") of God and us. "Marriage" or *gamos* was the glue that bonded the entire equation.

Eternal/endless love can be seen in scripture as a conjunction of his predeterminate counsel and our participation as he works through us unto the consummation of our marriage. This Will does cause all things to act for good unto a meaningful end, i.e., the marriage consummation, the *teleon*, God's bullseye.

Aren't we good enough to choose good things?

OUR NATURAL WILLS ARE HOSTILE TO GOD

Before the world was created into physical-time I was known and loved by him more than anyone in this world could love me. God loves me because he made me his child in all of my ordained[1] sins and I shared glories with him as an eternal innocent. Yes, that's right, my sin was ordained. I am an ordained chronic sinner, that is, a child of nature, naturally hostile to God (cf. Ephesians 2:1-18). Interestingly, my hostility towards authority, especially God, was always when I wanted "my way"- "my will" – "my choosing" as in the "natural man's desire." The unnatural/supernatural condescension of the Son to save me was and is still beyond my sinful human understanding. Without force, will, or choice of my own, I have naturally sinned against God unto death. Without force, will, or choice of my own I (identified only in his working through me) have "chosen" God unto life. Philippians 2:13: "For it is God who wills and does all things in us according to the good pleasure of his Will." I could only receive his call at the appointed time (*kairos*: "at the hand" [*kairon*]) by which God had set. I could only act upon his command to believe in him at his appointed time and through his works (Greek: *ergon* – work, energy, generative power) through (*dia*) me.

Therefore, I see him as the only one who could save me from the wages of sin (death, Romans 6:23) and bring me towards him. Such an act of God proves him alone to be worthy above all things. And, for this reason, the act — the story — the narrative of my sin and my journey unto God has fullness — it has the fullness of meaning. This meaning

---

1. Through the evolution of this work, we will find that "natural" humankind is "ordained" to damnation. Predestination has to do with a marital existence with God. "Knowing," "loving," "intimately existing with" is "before the fallen world." Pre, pro, be-fore, etc. are prefixes to show us "the state of being before our fallenness in this "hour," "boundary of time and space," this aeon, age, era, etc. of "purging." Therefore, "ordained sins" is a must within the theological confines of expressing the "nature of the world" or "nous monde."

resides in God's sovereign grace. My rebirth is the second birth being "born out of" the flesh and into his spirit by his sovereign Will, not mine. For my first fleshly birth was ordained to condemnation before it had a "choice" to only sin by the litany of our sin nature (Galatians 5: 18 – 22). See this passage if you think you're above this condemnation of fleshly/natural "works."

All of my pains that I have had, am having, and will have, are shaping me into the person that I have no control of becoming. Yet, I see that all of these pains have "calibrated" me overtime unto the likeness of Christ. Haven't you ever looked back at your life and said to yourself: "had I not gone through such hardships I would never have been the person I am"? You would never choose such hardships but you are now thankful that you went through them.

More and more I[2] acquire trust in his predeterminate Will. More and more I have less trust in my natural flesh which "chooses" sin. I am starting to understand that I am being purified in this harsh reality called life. More and more I see myself becoming a child of God. I see my "becoming" as a forward movement steadily marching unto the day that I will see him again. I will be fully restored as a child again. This is the "renewing/refreshing (apocatastasis)" that Acts 3:20, 1 Corinthians 15:28, and Colossians 1:14–20 speak of in that all things are made for, of, by, through, in Jesus in love – both visible and invisible existences and will be restored back to their original state of "beginnings." We shall all come to the "renewal process" that Jesus demands. Jesus says in Matthew 18:3: "you must be turned (*straphatay* – "take a divergent course; an "about-face [Strongs 4762]") as a little child (Greek: *paedion* – one who submits and obeys with innocence)[3] in order to enter the Kingdom of Heaven." As to what Jesus means will be unfurled in this book.

---

2. "I" as in my intangible spirit "coming to be" with the God called eyeh asher eyeh ("I Choose to Be Whom I Will Become") or YHVH.

3. Jaeger 1961.

Chapter Ten

Preordained *teleon* as We Naturally See It

All of us have interests that require us to already "believe" before we "know" what we want to do. Whether a physicist, evolutionary biologist, archaeologist, etc., we all exercise a "belief" in a *potential* profession. The journey that got you onto the road to make that next "decision" to become an archaeologist was a journey of many adventures of the mind and body. "The journey," or "path," *unto* anything always has both *eschaton* and *teleon*.

Another way to look at that is to conceptualize a path unto the bullseye for an archer. One could analogize this as a train on a one-way track (i.e. the path, direction, will). With these analogies one can see the "journey" or "path" of a drug addict (if continued) is destruction (*eschatos*), i.e., it is a predetermined path that naturally takes you to "conclude" your next step. Many heroin addicts have said that heroin is its own predetermined path and its ending (*eschatos*) is destruction. Take the path of the embodiment of heroin and it concludes you with its own fate/fatality (eschatos). Theologically and philosophically speaking, teleology is an embodiment of the finality of meaning unto a glorious summit. *Eschatos* demarks the final period of destruction of the thing. In contrast, it is *teleon* (though it occurs during the final eschaton) that gives us the meaning of "completeness," or "fullness of meaning."

Aristotle referred to the relation of the acorn and the oak: "The Oak tree is the *teleon* of the acorn." Aristotle said, the "*teleon* answers to the "whys" of something that exists or changes under the laws of *phusis* (nature). Aristotle concludes this thought with *teleon* as the definition of "meaning" or "explanation"[1].

PREORDAINED TELEON AS I UNNATURALLY REALIZE IT

It is hard at times to separate *teleon* from predeterminism except that the *teleon* is the explanation (the why) of all that has and will happen. The *teleon* will refer to God's intent only when it has completed in its unfurling ([P.I.E. – *dran*], drama, trauma). We will see all things as to their "why (*teleon*)" when time comes to its fullness of meaning. All "things" that have been seen, touched, felt, heard, etc. will be seen for their Reason in full at the final explanation (*teleon*). Therefore, I say: everything is *meaning-ful* (full of meaning) in his predeterminate Will unto its destination point or summit (*teleon/teleos*) prior to time as his "potential." To me, to ask in the English connotation "what is God's "potential?" mocks what He IS. So, I use "potential" in the truest sense of power, Lord, force, might (cf. P.I.E. *poti* – "Lord, mighty").

If you have been paying careful attention to reading this work you can already see how "teleology (the study of the "whys" unto the fullness of meaning)" and God's predeterminism are intertwined. Predeterminism is the prima causa, the intent, the act by which the Father establishes meaning and then expresses himself through his creator-Son to "act" out creation by which teleology is fully explained when time is fulfilled, i.e., the *atia* – "the why-ness." This is the "*arche*" of predeterminism unto the eschatological end and the summation of God's "teleological" intent of the act of creation. This *arche* does indeed mean "author," "arch," "beginning," —finding its cognate in "*atia*" – "the cause, the accused.." .i.e., "to the one/thing who did." This is where we get the word etiology – "study of the cause(s)." God's *atia/teleos* ("directive to the fullness of meaning")

---

1. For "*cause;*" "*why;*" "*teleon*" – > cf. Aristotle's *Physics* ll.3; *Metaphysics* V.2. Aristotle held that there are 4 *causes* (Greek: *aitia* – "cause"/"author"/"*arche*-archon" [accused/"*ac*" = "to'- + "-cused" = "cause']) upon something in nature. The first is the material cause. The second is the formal cause. The third is the efficient cause. The fourth is the final cause. Such an example is illustrated in a dining table: wood is the material cause, the structure is the formal cause, carpentry is the efficient cause and dining is the final cause for the teleos of the dining table. Therefore, a "configuration" of these 4 causes would be necessary to explain "a thing." This is very similar to the Five Noble Truths in *explaining/concluding* (teleos) a meaningful systematic theology.

and *diatasso* ("to set in arranged order") work together (*sunergo*) in order to explain the meaning to the question of "why?".

At the state or condition of being with God again I will be shown how all things synergistically worked together for his and our good outcome that God had predestined and preordained before the world began (Isaiah 46:10, Ecclesiastes 1:9, 3:15). Even during my "coming to be" in this life I have already been given "glimpses" of his master plan based on sola scriptura in my sufferings and not in some special vision into the future or extrinsic philosophical ideology.

Ephesians 1: 10, 11, 22, 23, and 2:5: (1:10) "That in the dispensation of the fulness of times HE might gather together in one all things in Christ, both which are in heaven, and which are on earth; even in Him. (11) In Whom also we have obtained an inheritance, being predestined according to the purpose of Him Who worketh all things after the counsel of His own Will, (22) And hath put all things under His feet, and gave Him to be the head over all things to the church, (23) which is His body, the fullness of Him that filleth all in all." 2:5 – "Even when we were dead in sins, hath (He) quickened us together with Christ, (by grace ye are saved)."

> Romans 3:23 "For all have sinned and fallen short of the glory of God."

If we are to be loved when we (a) in times past not aware of true love or (b) antagonistic towards God and his children then how can we be judged as being unloving or even hostile towards God when all things are ordained to the fullness of meaning? Since all of us existed in the state of animosity towards God (and sheer ignorance of true grace) how much more thankful should we be now since we know what true love and grace is? Did not our parents or someone who parented us love us enough that we are standing here? These are very simple scenarios and questions that should evoke profound theological questions and hopefully promote the correct answers.

You have already come quite a way with me on this journey. By now you should know that you can't be a lazy reader to read this book, but if you are hungry to have your questions about life answered I believe that this book has much to offer. Take patience with this book and wait until the end of reading it before you form your conclusions. The book answers to itself and needs its entirety read before put to scrutiny.

I give you a diagram of frequently used prepositions in the New Testament. Keep these prepositions in mind as we begin to understand how we are "acted upon" and "do act" within the accord of God's verbs of motion.

The prepositions in this diagram (Harris 2012) can be easily looked up in your Strong's concordance. Terms in relation to God acting "upon," "to," "on," "within," "going into," "around," "by," "fore/pre," "unto," "at," "above," "para/beside," "downwards," "under," etc. can be seen multi-dimensionally. This chart refers to how God acts within time upon us. All prepositions "precede" and then go at, to, into, upon, etc. the "box of time and space" where we are placed for now.

PREPOSITIONS

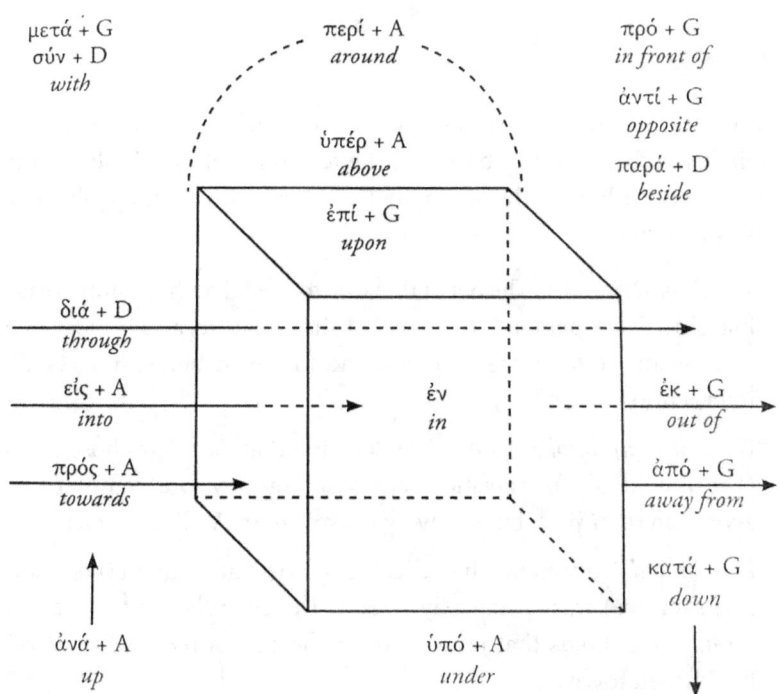

Diagram of the Spatial Meanings of the Seventeen New Testament "Proper" Prepositions

Chapter Eleven

Man Made Diatribes

I present the two main arteries of modern Christendom by which the Western churches are founded. I do not make an argument as of yet to the obvious contradictions found within both systems.

CALVINISM

Calvinism is a branch of Protestant (i.e., "that which protests the Roman Catholic Church") theology based on the teachings of John Calvin. It is often summarized using the acronym TULIP, which represents five key points of doctrine:

1. *T – Total Depravity*: The belief that due to the fall of humanity (original sin), every person is born with a sinful nature, and is incapable of choosing to follow God or respond to the gospel without God's intervention.

2. *U – Unconditional Election:* The doctrine that God has chosen *certain* individuals for salvation, not based on any foreseen merit or action on their part, but solely by his sovereign Will and grace.

3. *L – Limited Atonement:* The belief that Christ's atonement (his death and sacrifice) was specifically intended to *save the elect, not all of humanity.* It holds that Jesus died for the sins of *those* whom God has chosen to save.

4. *I – Irresistible Grace:* The teaching that when God calls someone to salvation, his grace cannot be resisted. The Holy Spirit works in the hearts of the elect to bring them to faith in Christ, and this calling cannot be thwarted.

5. *P – Perseverance of the Saints:* The belief that *those* who are truly chosen by God and saved will persevere in faith to the end. Once saved, a person cannot lose their salvation, as God will preserve them in their faith.

These doctrines are central to traditional reformed theology and are often associated with Calvinist thought.

ARMINIANISM

Unlike *Calvinism*, which has the well-known acronym TULIP, Arminianism doesn't have a single, widely accepted acronym that encapsulates its key points in the same way. However, some people informally use the acronym FACTS to represent the five points of Arminianism:

1. *F- Free Will:* The belief that humans possess genuine *free will* to choose or reject God. While humanity is affected by sin, they are not spiritually incapable. People have the ability to respond to God's grace and the gospel message freely.
   - *Key idea:* People have the ability to accept or reject God's offer of salvation.

2. *A- Atonement (Unlimited):* The belief that Christ's atonement is *unlimited*, meaning Jesus died for the sins of all people, not just a select few. His death is sufficient for everyone, but it only becomes effective for those who choose to believe in Christ.
   - *Key idea:* Jesus's death was for all people, and anyone can be saved if they choose to accept the gospel.

3. *C- Conditional Election:* The belief that *election* (God's choice to save) is *conditional* upon God's foreknowledge of who will freely choose to respond to his grace. God elects individuals based on his knowledge of their future faith, rather than any merit or action on their part.
   - *Key idea:* God's election is based on his foreknowledge of who will choose to believe. Therefore, God's decision is contingent upon your actions.

4. **T – Total Depravity (Weakness, Not Inability)** *Definition:* The belief that humanity is *totally depraved*, meaning that sin affects every part of human nature. However, this depravity does not result in total inability. Humans retain the capacity to respond to God's grace through the enabling work of the Holy Spirit.

    - *Key idea:* Humanity's will is weakened by sin, but people are still able to respond to God's offer of salvation.

5. **S – Security (Possibility of Apostasy):** The belief that while a person is truly saved, it is possible for them to *fall away* from grace. A believer can lose their salvation if they choose to reject or renounce their faith. This contrasts with the belief in *eternal security* found in some other theological systems (such as Calvinism), which holds that once saved, a person cannot lose their salvation. *Key idea:* A believer can forfeit their salvation through persistent unbelief or apostasy.

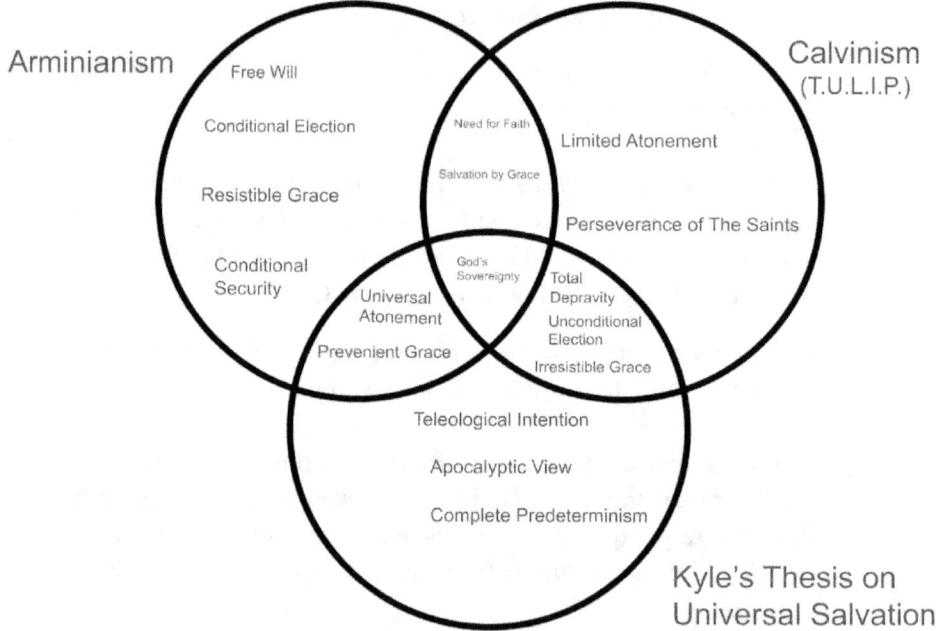

TWO DOMINANT BELIEFS

I have displayed a Venn diagram[1] showing 2 dominant systems of orthodox views. The third system, mine, shows how *Christic*[2] *predeterministic universalism* adds up between these two dominant and trending views. Minus my view for now, we can see these two medieval orthodoxies still remain fairly unchanged over the past 500 years for better or worse. Currently, most orthodoxies fall into the camp of either the Arminian[3] or Calvinistic view[4]. Simply put, these two medieval theological views are tethered in some way to many of the prevailing doctrines found in the contemporary High and Low Churches.

Such High Churches can be denominationally recognized as Anglican, Episcopalian, Methodist/Wesleyan, Lutheran, Roman Catholic, Tractarian, etc. The Low churches that didn't exist until after the Reformation can be recognized as follows: Baptist, Pentecostal, Quaker, Amish, Southern Baptist, Church of Christ, Anabaptist/Mennonite, etc.

CALVINISM AND ARMINIANISM

My focus in this preface displays the Arminian and Calvinistic traditional positions. These two oppositional systems shared qualities within their particular doctrines that freed Europe from a theocratic state, i.e., The Medieval Roman Catholic Church. Both Anglican-Arminian, Calvinistic/Lutheran and Roman Catholic institutions were forces to be reckoned

---

1. Thanks to Addison McArdle for making the above Venn diagram for this book. Addison, a student and friend, has consistently asked me theological questions concerning what she had read in my book's formative months. Adding to the book's editing, Addison has brought critical information to the table in order for this to be a better treatment for the reader.

2. I use the term "Christic" to convey "Christ" vs. "Christian" or "Christianity" as a conglomerate. The term, Christic, should be taken as pre-orthodoxy, i.e., *pre-high church*.

3. The Arminian acronym, *D.A.I.S.Y.* represents the 5 points of Arminianism.

D.A.I.S.Y. stands for D-diminished depravity, A-abrogated (repealed, canceled, or abolished) election, I – impersonal atonement, S-sedentary grace (God calls everyone but many freely reject it), and Y – yieldable justification (the saved can fall from grace and lose their salvation).

The Calvinistic acronym, *T.U.L.I.P.* represents the 5 points of Calvinism.

T.U.L.I.P. stands for T-total depravity, U-unconditional election, L-limited atonement, I-irresistible grace, and P-perseverance of the saints.

4. cf to "The Story of Christianity" volumes 1 and 2 by Justo L. Gonzalez for a fuller treatment.

with in their day. "Taking sides" with one or the other had its benefits and downfalls (including saving or losing your life) depending upon how politically savvy you were.

The Story of Christianity (Gonzalez 1985) and *Bible and Sword* (Tuchman 1978) are good reads for understanding the power by which the Medieval Churches had (including the Roman Catholic Church) no matter which orthodox they were. I will expedite as best as I can these two main orthodox views to establish a higher theological ground.

MY EXPERIENCES WITH BOTH SIDES

I have come out of both Arminian and Calvinistic churches with an open profession that they are not theologically sound. The term "recovery" is not an overstatement once you find out how devastatingly wrong the mainstream views are in most trending American "orthodox" churches, whether Arminian or Calvinist[5].

It took over 3 decades for me to overcome these religious traditions that we are steeped in. In my overcoming process having gained many companions along the way who recognized the same inconsistencies within their church experiences. No matter what church it was, there were always the same *core problems* consistent within these "orthodox" errors.

---

5. Amyraldism hits close by taking out "Limited Atonement" in T.U.L.I.P. and replacing Limited Atonement with another "U" for "Unlimited Atonement" making for a kind of "Universal Salvation" within the structure of Calvinistic theology. Sounds promising but problems arise with the hotch potch of Amyraldism now mixed as a compromised "new" 5 point Calvinism which still held to Calvin's views on execution of criminals which flies in the face of "kolosin" – i.e., *grace-reformation penal system*/"condemned to salvation." Amyraldism fell short of its self-proclaimed Unlimited Atonement by still being Calvinistic-Centrist which inherently opposed the forgiveness that we all must have to continue as a society unto heaven (Romans 14:1–23).

All such views of Amyraldism are just the start of contradictions that "God *knew* that not all would respond in faith to Christ's atonement (due to man's total depravity), He elected some to whom He would impart saving faith." This is a contradiction of the *unlimited atonement* that Amyraldism held (i.e., the works that damn/or save). It also gives less sovereignty to God (via doctrine) by having God simply "know" that "not all" would respond.

MY PROPOSED ANSWERS

The five core premises (or, "the five noble truths")

As seen in the Venn diagram, I present Five Noble Truths or "core premises" that will appropriate clear contextual reading of scripture[6]. These Noble Truths or 5 core premises[7] are: predestination, teleology, the apocalyptic[8] view, prophecy, and Christian universal salvation[9].

Amongst the Five Noble Truths, *biblical predestination* connects the other 4 core premises. My belief is that these 5 core premises hold the key to unlocking the Bible's inner consistency for us to experience. Through this "sandwiching" or "stacking" of premises, one can witness how God speaks to us through time within his eternal essence.

Oppositions will come

Predestination as a religious and social buzz word

Just to mention the word "*predestination*" can awaken many religious associations that come to mind, good and bad. I will attempt to address what biblical predestination *is* and what it is *not*.

What Biblical Predestination is not:

1. Biblical predestination is *not* exclusive.
2. Biblical predestination is *not* to be understood as a "*counter*" doctrine to Arminian "free will" – (i.e., Biblical predestination is not a "counter" argument to Arminianism).
3. Biblical predestination is *not* altered by human volition (or, B.P. *cannot* be altered by human volition).

---

6. I say this because I hold that without looking through the "lens" of these "Five Noble Truths" it will be hard to read the Bible as a coherent text

7. some might look at these like "beads" that are threaded through.

8. *apo* – "off with"/to take off + *kalupto* – "cover." I used the word apocalypse not just for end times or *eschatos* but for "revealing the meaning of everything" which justifies the Greek usage of the word.

9. i.e., the consistency of Christian universal soteriology as opposed to pantheistic universalism

What Biblical Predestination is:

1. Biblical predestination *is* the agent of limitless salvation to all.
2. Biblical predestination *is* unquantifiable in mercy and without comparison.
3. Biblical predestination *is* about God planning His salvation for all before the world began–which is incomprehensible to the human mind.
4. Biblical predestination defines what "marriage" really means.

When we speak of free will we speak of free will "unto," "by," "from," "into," "out of" where to what, what to where, where to where, or what to what? That is, what are you intending to "choose" in order to be bound to and what are you intending to be free from? You're always "with" something if "away" from something. What do you "will" this status be? This "free will" to act is to be "free from" something and "near" another. This "free will" is "prepositional." But how about if God wants you here or there for a reason. How about if God pre-planned you to be bound at some point in time to be at a specific place in order to make you become more mature. Your child nature would "will" every time to be in a place that feels good but this may not be what God wants for you. We think we are making sense to ourselves with our plans but it is either your "free will" or God's free Will that makes the plans for everything and everyone. We're infinitely "free" from sin if we are bound to God's Will. But this takes a long time, a long journey, it is a long road. To mature means, in a sense, to be "martyred" to one's desires. Maturity puts you in a state or condition of mind that oftentimes doesn't allow you to have it your way for the betterment of all that is around you. In this sense, you are martyred to your desires and have become a "witness (*marturos*/martyr)" of authority as a parent, guardian, etc. This, for sure, doesn't happen all at once to the freshman at college, though they might have a sterling G.P.A., looks, talents beyond measure, and no handicaps, etc. It takes a long journey to humble a person unto God and "away" from their flesh and this humbling is not chosen by the martyr. That is: it is not a natural choice. It is God's supernatural decision upon us to make us "choose" him. Moreover, it is God willing in us to do God's good pleasure – Philippians 2:13.

We are naturally free from God while we act in our sin "freely." Yet, we want to be saved "from" sin's wages. We can't will our salvation any more than one can will oneself to stop sinning. So, free will, want, desire, sin, intent, etc. all need to be categorized carefully to see how this rebus of ideas acts within a component of free will "unto" its end.

Predetermined "unto" what end? God predetermining you unto salvation? Unto hell? If there is a "judgment," what is it? Is the judgment from God "unto" us intently salvific? or damnable? Or is judgment already set on all of us? Could all of us be doomed and saved? Again, what does "judgment" mean? What does "doom" mean?

Chapter Twelve

The Story Tells It All

DAMNATION DOES NOT HAVE TO MEAN "UNTO ETERNAL BURNING HELL"

Misreadings of John 3:1–19

JOHN 3:1– FF "THERE was a man of the Pharisees, named Nicodemus[1], a ruler of the Jews: The same came to Jesus by night (for Nicodemus did not want to be seen by the Pharisees with Jesus) and said unto him, Rabbi, we know that thou art a teacher come from God: for no man can do these miracles that thou doest, except God be with him. Jesus answered and said unto him, 'Verily, verily, I say unto thee, Except a man be born again[2], he cannot see *the kingdom of God*' Nicodemus saith unto

---

1. His Hebrew name is Naqdimon. Naqdimon (Nicodemus) is spoken of in the Talmud as one of the richest and most distinguished citizens of Jerusalem (cf. Taan. 20 a; Kethub. 66 b: Gitt. 56 a; Ab. de R. Nath. 66 b: 6 comp. Ber. R. 42, Midrash on Ecclesiastes vii.12 and on Lamentations 1:5. But this name was only given to him on account of a miracle which happened at his request, his real name being Bunai, the son of Gorion. Bunai's mentionings in Talmudic references usually concern how Bunai and his daughter, after immense wealth, came to most abject poverty. There can scarcely be any doubt that this somewhat legendary Naqdimon was actually one of the disciples of Christ. For Naqdimon is mentioned in the Talmud among the disciples of Jesus, reasonably, and more substantial for the story's sake, the well to do Nicodemus would have indeed lost everything to have become one of the followers of "the way" or the "*Chrestoi*."

2. Greek: *anothen* "anew, from its origins, from its beginnings," –i.e. *anothen* is a cognate to *apokatastasis* meaning "restored to its original state." What Jesus said here is what he will do in 1 Corinthians 15:28 (brought back all things to their original state of newness in Jesus and returned to the Father as "restored"). Cf. John 3:4–7: "How can a man be born when he is old? He cannot enter his mother's womb a second time and

him, 'How can a man be born when he is old? Can he enter the second time into his mother's womb, and be born?' Jesus answered, 'Verily, verily, I say unto thee, Except a man be *born of water and of the Spirit*[3], he cannot enter into the kingdom of God. That which is born of the flesh is flesh; and that which is born of the Spirit is spirit. Marvel not that I said unto thee, *Ye must be born again.* The wind bloweth where it listeth, and thou hearest the sound thereof, but canst not tell whence it cometh, and whither it goeth: so is every one that is born of the Spirit.' Nicodemus answered and said unto him, 'How can these things be?' Jesus answered and said unto him, 'Art thou a master of Israel, and *knowest not* these things? Verily, verily, I say unto thee, *We speak that we do know, and testify that we have seen; and ye receive not our witness.* If I have told you earthly things, and ye believe not, how shall ye believe, if I tell you of heavenly things? And no man hath ascended up to heaven, but he that came down from heaven, even the Son of man which is in heaven. And as Moses lifted up the serpent in the wilderness (i.e., the prophetic-pantomiming of salvation to come), even so must the Son of man be lifted up (the reality of our salvation): That whosoever believeth in him should not perish, but have eternal life.'" (Emphasis mine.)

For God so loved[4]

"For God so loved the world, that he gave his only begotten Son, that whosoever believeth in Him should not perish, but have everlasting life.

---

be born, can he?"

3. John 3:1: "*gennaythay* (born) *exs* (of) *hudatos* (water) *kai* (and) *pneumatos* (spirit)." I have always wondered if Jesus had referred to a popular philosophy proposed by Thales and/or stated the facts by which his creation works. Scientifically, Jesus was of course right but I love the idea that Jesus would relate to the early followers and nonbelievers as to what was understood to be right "philosophically/scientifically." Thales stated that water is the fundamental substance from which everything is derived (*gene-*) or generated. This would agree with Jesus' "*gennaythay*" of water and spirit. Thales's philosophical idea was considered the "arche" or "first principle" and established the groundwork for future scientific inquiry. Ironically, Thales's proposal of the "arche" was postulated roughly the same time (ca. 586 BC) that Judah was taken in 3 deportations into Babylon. I propose that this is a divinely appointed demarcation of YHVH's (and/or the Greek's abandonment of other gods) separation from humankind to science as one of the replacement "belief" systems that humankind desired in their natural declination from God and humankind's relationship. Today, we know that all living organisms are made up of water and humans are composed of 90% water. Interestingly, Thales, the "first philosopher," marked the first shift from the mythological to the scientific.

4. Romans 5:6-10 "*For when we were yet without strength, in due time Christ died*

For God sent not his Son into the world to condemn the world; but that the world through Him might be saved[5]. He that believeth on Him is not condemned (*krino* – "incriminated" (*Krino* = *Krima* = "Crime"): but he that believeth not is condemned (*Krino/kekritai* ("has been *Krima/* judged/incriminated) from where we get the word "crime" or "incriminated") already, because he hath not believed in the name of the only begotten Son of God[6]. And this is the condemnation (*krisis* – decision, judgment – as in a civil case/judicial case), that light has come into the world, and men loved darkness rather than light, because their deeds were evil. For every one that doeth evil hateth the light, neither cometh to the light, lest his deeds should be reproved[7]. But he that doeth truth cometh to the light, that his deeds may be made manifest, that they are wrought in God." Colossians 1:21 "And you, who once were alienated and hostile in mind, doing evil deeds (22) He has now reconciled in His body of flesh by His death, in order to present you holy and blameless and above reproach before him."

There is an overuse of what I call singularity-passages[8] which are used to argue for "judgment unto damnation unto hell. John 3:16-19 is used by some as a "singularity-passage" to attempt to make our salvation

---

for the ungodly (us). For scarcely for a righteous man will one die: yet peradventure for a good man some would even dare to die. But God commendeth his love toward us, in that, while we were yet sinners Christ died for us. Much more than, being now justified by his blood, we shall be saved from wrath through him. For if, when we were enemies (i.e. by our natures, God's enemies), we were reconciled to God by the death of his, much more, being reconciled, we shall be saved by his life. So, we were already reconciled while being his enemy for God knew and ordained when and where we would arrive at his feet."

5. 1 Corinthians 15:28; Colossians 1:14–22 (both passages contain "All things reconciled").

6. That is, we were "condemned [*krino*: "crime; incriminated] already" when we, once upon a time, were hostile to God (Ephesians 2:22).

7. This is the state of the natural man that MUST BE "*anothen*," "renewed," or, "born again" – which we see Jesus telling Nicodemus about since he could not see for he was blinded by the law. This is also mentioned by Christ in Matthew 19: 25, 26, i.e., no "free willing soul" can save his own self for it is impossible. Later, we see a "continuance" of Nicodemus' "salvation" upon him unto a tender, reverent, and believing heart. Salvation is shown to be a "work over time" upon a human's physical nature, not a "one-time-choosing" out of a vacuum.

8. Singularity-passages, refer to the scriptural favoritism of an individual's preferential selection of "out of context" passages by which one "picks" out of the New Testament (usually using the English) providing a "narrative" that one would like to argue. I believe, as this book will show, that we must look at the scripture as a "sandwiching" of passages that complete each other.

contingent upon a "choice to believe" or "choice not believe'[9]. We might call this "iso-glossing" or "foul-ball-theology." Many believe this verse to mean that if one doesn't believe right now, they are "damned." In a moment I will address the "coming to be[10]" in Christ vs. the immediate humanistic judgment.

I will also show that the "apocalyptic view (the full view)" is the view of multiple verses seen as one "sandwiched" idea giving clarity to the passages in question. Such an apocalyptic view disbands the singularity-passage approach (a.k.a. "iso-glossing") for a more interwoven view of scripture. Here is an example of a more careful reading of the journey of salvation (*sodzo*) and how it "acts overtime" upon the one who is "salted" or "saved" as we will read concerning Nicodemus's salvation process.

The "coming to be" of Nicodemus

Prior to John 3:16-19, Nicodemus, a Pharisee who was considered a *ruler of the Jews* (John 3:1; 3:10), came to Jesus by night asking Jesus various questions concerning Jesus' standing with God and salvation. Jesus tells Nicodemus "you must be born *again* (Greek: *anothen* – "from above")." Nicodemus was perplexed. At this juncture of scripture Jesus tells Nicodemus that he does not receive (nor know) the "witness" of those that have experienced God/Jesus. But Jesus only addressed the "single frame" of time, which in and of itself is an incomplete picture.

Nicodemus's salvation

In John 7:50-51 we have the account of Nicodemus standing up (no longer hiding in the dark of night) for Jesus's testimony and life. Nicodemus confronted the hypocrisy of the Pharisees by standing against both the officers and sanhedrin questioning them: *"Does our law judge any man, before it hears him, and knows what he does?."*

---

9. As though "belief is self-generated and "working" outside of the Will of God's intention.

10. "Coming to be unto the universal" and "theory of forms" is so beautifully explained by Plato in his *Republic*.

The teleon-salvation of the Scriptural Nicodemus

In John 19: 39 – ff: "And there came Nicodemus, who at the first came to Jesus by night, and brought a mixture of myrrh and aloes, about a hundred-pound weight. (40) Then took the body of Jesus, and wound it in linen clothes with the spices, as the manner of the Jews is to bury. (41) Now in the place where He was crucified there was a garden; and in the garden a new sepulchre, wherein was never man yet laid. (42) There they laid Jesus therefore because of the Jews' preparation day; for the sepulchre was nigh at hand."

Nicodemus was openly[11] there, supporting the cause of respect for Jesus' body. Though Nicodemus had not seen the resurrected Christ, he still held to Christ because of his words and deeds. Nicodemus's journey from a legalist Pharisee/"master of Israel"/member of the Sanhedran to the care of Jesus' crucified body is a statement in itself. It is a statement of continuance and belief[12], and in my opinion, indicating the process of salvation. Nicodemus was mentioned throughout the book of John until the last concern with the care for the body of the crucified Christ. Nicodemus's account in the book of John is enough to show me that Nicodemus never believed that Jesus was a fraud. Contrarily, Nicodemus, being such a staunch upholder of the Jewish law, would have reveled in Jesus' death had Nicodemus thought Jesus to be a fraud, blasphemer, demoniac, etc. Rather, Nicodemus was accompanied by Joseph of Arimathea who reverently placed Jesus' body in the sepulchre. These were the only two that were there with Jesus' body.

One might think (*krino*/judge) that Nicodemus was eternally categorized (*krino*/judged) by Jesus as "one who did not have salvation" due to the Scriptural passage in John 3:11–36. Jesus told Nicodemus in John 3:11 that Nicodemus did not receive the witness of Jesus nor his followers. But the "narrative" goes on. Jesus had only "judged" the state or condition of Nicodemus by the spirit of doubt for which he held for that instance of time. As we are "judged" guilty for the immediacy of our sins

---

11. Remember that Nicodemus was initially "concealed by night" for fear of other's opinions, esp. that of his fellow Pharisees. Conceal = "con" = with + "ceal" = p.i.e. = KEL IV = "hell" = "darkness."

12. Philippians 1:6 "God began a good work in you and He will *continue it until it is finished* when Jesus Christ comes again." This is "salvation" as God's "arrow" and his "shot" to the bullseye. This verse is one of many which I make the analogy in my lectures called "The Anatomy of the Will."

in the world of time – its moving pictures, we are conclusively universally forgiven by an eternal God with eternal grace and unwavering love.

What does all of this say concerning a Jew who was a leading Pharisee of the Sanhedrin? Jesus didn't condemn Nicodemus as a person. Jesus condemned (for that moment in time) the lack of Nicodemus's belief due to the law and more importantly, *"regeneration."* Jesus condemned the pharisaical notion that "keeping the law" was being moral. Finally, the momentary condemnation (Krino/criticism/critique) of Jesus against Nicodemus was against the condition, or lack of condition, of the mindset for "being born again." Only for that moment in John 3:11 – ff do we read that Nicodemus did not understand *"regeneration"/"born again* (Greek: *"anothen," "again," "from above," "from the beginning," "from the first," "anew," etc.)."*

Recap:

The initial presentation of Nicodemus's condition was *darkness*. I believe he needed darkness to "see" what he didn't have. The law was hell. Nicodemus was in hell. Jesus told Nicodemus that he was *separate from* Jesus and his followers. The words of Christ must have purged *through* Nicodemus' heart *unto* the end of Jesus' physical life, and in my belief, Nicodemus's salvation. Only Nicodemus and Joseph of Arimathea stayed with the dead body of Jesus in open daylight to properly entomb Jesus. This act alone would have, at the least, destroyed Nicodemus' position as head Pharisee. My conclusion here is that there was a "kind" of hell that purified Nicodemus *unto* conviction to openly confess his following of Christ.

Therefore, Jesus being the WORD, scans and scrutinizes that which he sees. It was in that moment in time where the condition of not believing in "regeneration" was the failure for meeting the "criterion (*kritein/ krino/krima*/judgment)." Nicodemus was simply wrong and simply judged wrong by Jesus, not condemned to hell, which doesn't fit the context of the story, even in the English versions. It is interesting that one of the 5NTs that I am proposing, i.e., universal reconciliation/regeneration, is at the heart of Jesus' point to be made with Nicodemus and the reason for Jesusjustified scrutiny. For Jesus was saying to Nicodemus: if you are not regenerated by an external God you can't live unto salvation, you must be "regenerated." It was here that Jesus made His critique against Nicodemus, (paraphrased) you don't have, as of yet, the engine that drives you unto salvation for it is God's regenerative power through grace and not your "goodness" that saves you or men. Nicodemus was only at the first stage of his processes to understand this.

RESPECTING THE LAW, RESPECTING THE LAWS OF OTHERS, RESPECTING SOCIETY, RESPECTING THE JUDGMENT OF GOD

Romans 13:1 – 14 makes it clear that every ordinance (*diatagay*), rulers (*arxontayce*) who establish municipal rule are themselves established by God for order, including the rules set by the Sanhedrin of Christ's day, the Nords, Roman, Greek, Babylonian, Codex Hammurabi, etc. For both rulers and laws were ordained by God as His expression (*nomos*). We, the believers in Christ, are to adhere to such municipalities under the different categories of government for there is no power (*exousia*) but that of God. In Romans 13:5 we are told that we must be subject in the societal holding pattern by which we too are subject unto the wrath (*orgay* – "rage") of God if we break such ordinances (*tagmenai, diatage, upo + tassestho, tatagmenai* (cf.antonyms: *anti-tasso'menos, anthestayken (anti + tas* [place])). We receive wrath (*orge*) from God when we don't (when our natural wills "act" on their nature) follow the laws set in place by God for the laws of the land. Not only "wrath" which is the "sting" of God through the secular law but the *krima* (damnation) of God mentioned in Romans 13:2 which is most emphatically used as a judicial case. The "whosoever" in Romans 13:2 refers not only to heathens, pagans, non-believers, etc. but the believers. As we shall see the believer receiving this same "damnation" alongside the non-believer. All to say: this "damnation" is not a "damnation *unto* hellfire everlasting."

Secondly, Romans 13:5 tells us that if we break laws appointed unto the heathen, pagan, secular or other, we lose our "good conscience (*suneidaysin*: "to know" + "together" – "to see as one")" toward God. So, if we breach such laws ordained (*taxis/tasso*) by God for good order (*taxis, tasso*), though they are for human behaviours, we cause rage[13] against us by Jesus and loss of a "joined" spirit, body, and mind (i.e., *suneidaysin*).

---

13. "*orge*" is a cognate to "orgasm." It conveys the sense of "blowing out," "forcefully acting out" or "going out with force." This seems to hold the office of Jesus who has the shared *emotional immediacy* with us. Unlike the Father who cannot look at us unless it is through Christ, the aspect of Christ is most plausible from the "humanistic

In the first and second centuries, *krino* was akin to the Latin *Damnus* when employing "discretion, judgement in the sense of categorizing and properly putting things in their place." The *krino* or damnation, as it should be known, puts the "non-Christian," for the time, into a state of confusion about the "ethics" of Christians.

Such a confusion about the Christian is very well understandable to me having friends with Arabs, Hindus, and Israelites alike. The innate legalists do live to the law (as Paul describes the one holding dietary laws – more than likely, our Jewish brother seen in Romans 14), many of them from birth all the way into the inherent legalistic behaviors of the culture promulgating such beliefs. Therefore, the legalist non-Christian accounts for the actions of their Christian brother. This does not make them, however, above the law or able to fulfill the law (though argued within their own indigenous theologies such as the Quran or Tanakh). This Christian, who by disregarding the law mentioned in Romans 14, caused a stumbling block/offense to the legalist brother.

---

compassion/humanistic expression" that I see fit. Although, an argument can be made that the *Parakletos-Holy Spirit* holds the title of *"carrier of our soul's journey"* and *"Convictor of our hearts"* Who, in my thoughts, is very capable of being the one who would "act out (orge-forcefully act out)" with piercing our hearts to repent which seems to fulfill both "wrath" and "conscience" mentioned in Romans 13:5.

Chapter Thirteen

The First Noble Truth: The Predeterminism[1] View

PREDETERMINISM IS NOT CALVINISM

THE DEFINITION OF PREDETERMINISM means that all events, including human interactions, thoughts, dreams, loves, hates, invisible and visible existences are pre-planned in advance. Predestination/predeterminism holds many distinctions from fatalism[2] which I will address later. In

---

1. *Strong's Concordance* # 4309: Predestine(-ed): Greek: *pro* = before + *horidzo* = the horizon, hour, time, event (establish limitation, boundaries beforehand).

2. "Fate, Fatua, Faye, Fairie, Fatale," Fates, Fatal, owing, etc. are all words bound in the term for fatalism. We really get our substantial meaning of "fatalism" or "fate" from the Norse "Fates" or "Nornir." Another cognate of Fate would be the Nordic "wyrd." Wyrd means "what is done; a deed; an action; speech; fore-wyrd, prologue, foreword; become; happen – be -; fate; on-ward; wierd (personified); *wierdan* – injure, destroy. Modern usages still continue this word to mean "to turn into" – "Wo *worth* the day." The Indo-European *HucVertere* – to turn (root: wyrd) – holds the idea "to turn," hence, "turn into" or "become." The Latin cognates are *vertere* "to turn" and "versus," "furrow," or a "line of verse" where the ox or pen turns back. The weird sisters of Shakespeare's Macbeth, for sure, take on the Icelandic Norn sisters (seen in my green ink sketch – illustration #1) are the "fatal" or the "destiny-wielding/wyrding/knowing/finalizing ones." *Urd* (*Wyrd* – Spell Cast/Cause), *Verandi* (Is being, happening (more importantly, "*Veranda*" – Anglo-Indian borrowed into Portuguese as "veranda" meaning, "a bar, railing, barrier, etc. "to hold in line, form, keep steady along the barrier, hold in"), and *Skuld* (*Should,* Could, Ought, Owe – *Shall*).

The UER "*swayed (as in "persuasion")*" the day….i.e., the wyrd/word/wield "turned the day into a sorrow" > UER = WORD in its most primitive form – i.e. ("zero grade Proto-Indo-European root;" Sanskrit: "vratam:" "Vow"; Greek: "eirein" – irony: a metal *brought forth (wielded/yielded)* by melting out the weaker ones, hence, the strong WORD, the HOLY WORD – iron- (Greek: *heiron*: holy – "irony" – comical: "*hilasteriou*" – the Holy Seat where the WORD of God is pronounced)--'to *excite* the god/God." In its

order to hold to predestination, theologically speaking, one would need to hold that an intention is set forth – for nothing can "plan" out an ordered cosmos with rules that hold in the physical sense[3] unless it is laid out in the mind of a God before it is executed[4]. If "reason (in the divine sense)" precedes predeterminism, as "ideas having consequences," then the being which intended the predestined acts did indeed precede the physical acts. There's enough scientific data that is up to date showing us that creation was much more than cold chance[5] or fate[6] (please see "chance" and "fate" in the footnotes).

MY MAJOR "BEEF":

Having heard many Christian elders of the churches that I have attended say[7] to me: "God is all knowing but doesn't "predetermine" things."

I simply quote the scripture here to begin with: "For those whom He (God) foreknew (*proegno* [pre-knew]) He *also* did predestinate (*proohrisen* [pre-horizon/time/*horos*/arched/i.e. "before time"]) to be conformed (*sun* + *morphe* = together likened) to the image of His Son..."

I say that "all knowing" is not enough to establish sovereignty. This kind of belief erroneously omits predestination out of scripture — especially that of Romans 8:28-31 and Ephesians 1: 4 – 11. To add:

---

usage, the UER is the "sway"/is the "wyrd." Greek: *orgay* – "rage," "orgasm," "excite out."

3. Please go to my audio lecture, Jones, "Two Creations." I explain that in Genesis chapter one (the first half) explains that God created the universe unto completion from beginning to end in his mind and then, in the second half of Genesis we read that his imagination was unfurled into the physical governed in time. This lecture was inspired by my talks with astrophysicist Dr. Gerald Schroeder.

4. Ideas have consequences

5. chance: (P.I.E. – *kad I*) "to befall," "to fall to the lot," "to befall," "cascade," "casual," "cadaver," "cadence," "to fall to," etc. The point to "chance" is that it is not what we would call a "random" event, rather, an "allotting" event.

6. fate (p.i.e. bha I) Latin: *fari* – "to speak"; Greek: *phone*; ...blame; "fay" – Fairy – fatal, Fata, etc. as in the fates that establish the fortune and fatality of the one they cast their "spiel" or "spell" on. This again, is not a random sentiment, rather, an ordered speech or spiel unto death. i.e., a path unto death governed by the word/weird/wyrd sisters.

7. This is where prophecy, teleology, and foreknowledge became such important factors in my thesis. To have these factors as the normally agreed upon categories in nearly every denomination my questions led to predeterminism as the logical outcome. I saw my thesis instantaneously as a young man but I could not quantify it due to the pressures of the authorities in the church which made me question my mind, my reason, and even my sanity at times.

"foreknowing" only "knows" what already *is*. The *is* or is-ness/*ontos* of "all things" is preceded by the intender who "predestined" what is to be known.

This conscious omission to say that God is "all knowing" without having the responsibility of all things becomes an inconclusive argument as to *why all things happened* (destructive and constructive [Isaiah 45: 7- ff]). Biblically-irrationally, the phrase "God is *all-knowing (implying "only foreknowing" and not predetermining)*" is an easy way to avoid the *entanglements* of the ever-so-involved argument over "free will" if one is in a peer pressured Bible forum. That is, if factored into the "orthodox" model" that God predetermined everything then there can't be free will." Ministers who are trying to "keep the peace" by non-committal and non-sense verbiage and doublespeak implement the kind of equivocation/ambiguities/mish-mash that I refer to in this book. I also call them lies. Lies keep the masses placated and depressed all at the same time. There is no logical resolve by omitting scriptural passages, filling the omissions in with "replacement theologies," and calling it "orthodox." I lived in confusion for decades due to this omission so how can I just let it go? There are others out there who actually want truth without ambiguities.

"All knowing" does not negate sovereign predeterminism, rather, it should work with it. Sadly, many "authorities" in the church "give" a modifier to God of "foreknowing" but not predetermining. As to how they assume their own authority to parse out the word predestinate in Romans 8:29-31 is beyond me: ("*hoti houos pro'egno* ("foreknowledge") *kai* (and) *pro'orisen* (predestined) *summorphous tayce eikonos au'tou tou uiou...* etc.")! "For God both foreknew and predestined us unto salvation."

"All knowing" does not in any way imply God's sovereign control when used alone to "modify God" as just "all knowing." Omission of the word "predestined" is what many orthodoxies cull for their religious interests doing damage to the coherency of biblical doctrine. To me, this abandonment of critical textual exegesis (to study the text from a cultural and linguistic point of view) falls within the same reasoning as recklessly justifying your lifestyle by not obeying municipal and federal laws (i.e., The kingdom of heaven and it's walk or "guidelines" on how to "handle one's self" within the heavenly court).

To describe God as having foreknowledge only does not convey a sovereign God and lacks the description for a God with the "fullness of intention." This deity, the one who intends all things, is the same deity that is mentioned in the Bible titled as: the I AM, YHVH, The Father,

THE FIRST NOBLE TRUTH

Eloah, etc. If limited to only "all knowing" then we have a *kind of deity* that *does not* represent the YHVH of the Bible.

If YHVH is expressed as having predetermined all things invisible and visible including all of our thoughts, dreams, loves, heartbreaks, feelings of anger, sadness, tragedy, sickness, etc. then we have the kind of deity that is represented in the scripture. Here's a look at these qualifications met in scripture for a predetermining sovereign God[8]:

> Isaiah 46:10: "declaring the end[9] from the beginning and from ancient times things not yet done, saying, 'My counsel shall stand, and I will accomplish all my purpose.'"
>
> Isaiah 48:5: "I have even from the beginning declared it to you; before it came to pass I shewed it to you: lest you should say, 'My idol did them, and my graven image, and my molten image, has commanded them.'"
>
> Romans 8:28 "We know now that all things work together for good for God to those who are called according to His purpose (29) For whom He did foreknow He also predestined to be conformed to the image[10] of the Son of Him."
>
> Ephesians 1:4, 5: "For He chose us in Him before the creation of the world to be holy and blameless in His sight in love. (5) He predestined us for adoption to sonship through Jesus Christ, in accordance with His pleasure and Will."
>
> Ephesians 1:11: "In whom also we have obtained an inheritance, being predestined according to the purpose of Him who works all things after the counsel of his own will."
>
> Colossians 1:16: "For in Him all (everything) things were created[11]; things in heaven and on earth, visible and invisible, whether thrones or powers or rulers or authorities; all things have been created through Him and for Him."
>
> Romans 13:1 "Let every soul be subject to the governing authorities. For there is no authority except from God, and the authorities that exist are appointed by God."

---

8. for an in-depth account of Sovereignty passages I encourage you to read Arthur Pink's "The Sovereignty of God."

9. beginning to the "telos."

10. *summorphous tayc eikonos* – "conformed to the image."

11. *ektisthay* – Strong's concordance # 2936 (root: *ktidzo* – "create what was not there before"/*ex-nihilo* to *nihilo* fit. To "found" or make a foundation from nothing.

Ecclesiastes 1:9: "What has been is what will be done, and there is nothing new under the sun (10) Is there a thing of which it is said, "see, this is new?" It has been already in the ages before us." (first and second law of thermodynamics).

Ecclesiastes 3:15: "That which is, already has been, that which is to be, already has been, and God seeks that which has been driven away."

Isaiah 45:25: "I form the light, and create darkness: I make peace and create evil[12]" (if evil and destruction exist—it is here either by randomness, i.e., an evil "counterpart" which lends to "dualism" as a belief system or God is totally sovereign).

Revelation 13:8 (the second ½ of the verse): "...The Lamb Who was slain from the creation of the world" —surely, this implies the series of actions from the beginning of time up to the Christ point[13] by which the fullness of Christ's mission was completed on earth.

James 4:13[14] "Come now you who say: 'Today or tomorrow we will go into such a city and will spend a year there and will trade and will make a profit.' For you know not what is on the next day nor know what is your life. For your life is but a vapor that appears for a short while and then vanishes. What you should say is: 'If the Lord should Will us to live and do this or that it will be God's Will – not your own.' But all such statements are bragging in arrogance of what you think you will do. All such boasting is evil."

Jeremiah 31: 18 "...turn me and then I shall be turned for Thou art the Lord my God."

Simply summed from these passages I believe that we could conclude that the scripture expresses that all things that exist, whether in thought, deed, action of the past, present or future were already pre-determinately created in the mind and act of God through his divine intention. Therefore, there is nothing we could acclaim to have done, chosen, acted upon, achieved, etc. that wasn't a part of God's willful intent before

---

12. Strong's concordance number: 7451 – Hebrew: "ra" = "calamity"; "breaking down"; "disease"; "famine"; "devastation": "malignancies," etc.

13. What I mean is the point on the line of time that demarks the "leading up to" from the past's signals and indicators (or "portents"). Cf. *Kairos* time – or "at hand."

14. please choose your favorite English passage for your own comfort for I have "interpreted" from the Greek to make this passage smoother to my own Greek ears.

the world was created. As I see it, we are dead nouns acted upon by the verb that acts—i.e. God.

Chapter Fourteen

Professor J.R.R. Tolkien

A BENEFICIAL DESTRUCTION/EUCATASTROPHE/ PREDETERMINISM'S INTENDER

Just having treated predeterminism, you might wonder why I'm taking up space to interject J.R.R. Tolkien in this work. Let me start by saying that his lectures and writings were that of a pure aesthetician, much like that of Joyce. The gifts that both writers had tells me they understood transcendence. Tolkien was the Christian Joyce to me who carried over theological themes of pure art and congruent orthodoxies bearing "inner consistencies" that only true art and theology can carry over from the sublime to needful humanity. Tolkien seemed to "*tell the tale*" with a cryptic theology, teleological aim, hope, trial by fire *unto* salvation (whether heavenly or social), and a journey with deep dimensions. Tolkien nearly makes the reader beg to be pulled out of their comfort zone. Finally, I offer you a "coming to be" statement totally inspired by Tolkien and scripture: we must be shattered before we can "see," hence, a "eucatastrophe."

> "The birth of Christ is the eucatastrophe ("well/beneficial destruction") of Man's history. The Resurrection is the eucatastrophe of the story of the Incarnation. This story (The Story of Christ) begins and ends in joy. It has the "inner consistency of reality. There is no tale ever told that men would rather find true, and none which so many skeptical men have accepted as true on its own merits. For the Art of it has the supremely

convincing tone of Primary Art, that is, of Creation. To reject it leads either to sadness or to wrath."

– J.R.R. Tolkien from his Oxford Lecture Series, "The Monsters and the Critics"; pg. 156, published by HarperCollins Publishers, 2006.

A KIND OF FAITH

Ode to Professor J.R.R. Tolkien

Maybe up to this date and time you haven't been challenged with predestination as a theological reality. Or, maybe you have held that predestination is *an unreality*. Speaking of "realities" and "unrealities," Professor J.R.R. Tolkien states in his lectures at Oxford called, "The Monsters and the Critics"[1] (Tolkien 1983): "in order to "see" rightness and trueness in a true, wholesome, and good fantasy writing one must temporarily suspend all disbelief that this fantasy piece is not real, false, fake, a lie, make-believe, non-truth, etc." Professor Tolkien continues to say that "All objects and subjects in a true fantasy writing are "signals" to direct the participant to meaning or ultimate truths that can be learned in our physical world – i.e., the "primary world."" These "truths" are not only relegated to our world but in the fantasy work – i.e., the secondary world. One must get into this secondary world of fantasy and live in it, breathe its air, feel its space, learn its language, acquire the "-isnesses" of the characters, surroundings, the nature of its sphere and the rules of the morphology of its growth patterns. "Realities" are both in the fantastic and physical world. Realities and truths do not have to exist only in the "reality" of the physical world but also can exist in the secondary world or "un-reality" of the physical-primary world.

Likened to Tolkien's concept about truths found in the world of fantasy, I address newcomers to apply a temporary suspension of disbelief concerning predestination and universal salvation.

If you are "willing" with this fantastic new faith (i.e., temporary suspension of disbelief) I would ask of you to believe just for a while (maybe through the rest of this book) temporarily suspend your disbelief that a sole predeterminer exists. I ask of you to hold that this predeterminer is

---

1. I'll paraphrase from Tolkien's treatment from pages 132 to 145; "The Monsters and the Critics and other essays; HarperCollins Publishers; published 2006.

defined as the prime cause for every action and the holder of everyone's salvation. I would ask of you to temporarily suspend your disbelief that it is he who established meaning itself and the endless paths of reasons by which we follow to get to his ultimate meaning, he is not a maze. I ask of you to believe that God is the author of our actions, generator-creator of our faith, the author of all destruction unto the restoration of all things whether it be in heaven or earth, especially all of us, *unto* salvation. Whether fantasy, fiction, "reality," or the divine, "truth" will bear its properties of "inner consistencies of realities" within the context that you both abide in and test.

Chapter Fifteen

The Inability to Repent Leads to the Ultimate Gratitude

Seen below are the beautiful words of the prophet Jeremiah concerning his lament over his inability to change, to repent, to turn to God, etc. we also find the joy by which God repents us:

> Jeremiah 31:18, 19: "(18) I have surely heard Ephraim [North Israel – taken away in 722 BC] bemoaning himself in this way: "You [God] have chastised me, and I was chastised, as a dumb bull unaccustomed to the yoke [bridle] yet saying to God: "turn me and then I shall be turned, for you are the LORD my GOD. (19) Surely after that [i.e., after that entreaty…then…] (1) I was turned, [then] (2) I repented; and after that [then] (2) I was instructed, (4) I smote upon my thigh; (5) I was [then and only then] ashamed, yes, I was even confounded, because I bear the reproach of my youth."

This takes me to the old adage: "we don't surrender, God surrenders us."

So, it is the redeemed person (who has been "repented" by God) that does the Will of God. They are "free from" what they "repented of." If Jeremiah is telling us the process unto repentance, then only God can do or superimpose repentance upon us.

Many sections of scripture seem to promote "an autonomy" to choose or reject God from an outside force[1] that one wields. That is, while we were dead in our sins we couldn't make a living decision nor

---

1. This leads to the irrationality of a "force" which is both outside God and fallen man. For if man is fallen and dead in his trespasses how can he generate a "living decision'—a beneficial decision? If outside of God, what "other goodness" is there than God to "choose God?"

a dying one. Our sinful flesh shows us to be without recourse to save ourselves. Our flesh, by its own nature, could not "choose" God by its own volition[2] anything other than death. Our fleshly nature has only one "will." This *"fleshly will"*[3] naturally patterns itself to death and hell. It is not free. It is bound. This fleshly will is not of ourselves either. Speaking to us old sinners: It is God who *"patterned" us unto salvation* using our *damnable natures* to calibrate us into new creatures for there is no good in us by our natures[4] alone. For how else could our salvation from death and hell have been? Here, looking back, we can actually see the immortal beauty of knowing what it took to save us.

Paraphrasing of an old minister I heard long ago:

> "Our very being stammered at his sovereign command. We were in his presence. Why would grace be given to us? Yet, grace was the only way to be saved from this sinful condition. Here he is, grace itself."

Yet, even now, we assume that we can make the efforts to "get saved" or have "acted upon" some pluperfect (i.e., perfected sometime in the past) decision to have "gotten saved" on any past effort of our own. We don't even use the meaning for the word "saved" in the correct sense. *Sodzo*, in the Greek, means to be *"preserved" as meat packed in salt from point A to B*. To be saved is to be salted and *carried through "unto"* your

---

2. Romans 7:15-18: "For that which I do I allow not: for what I would, that do I not; but what I hate, that do I. If then I do that which I would not, I consent unto the law that it is good. Now then it is no more I that do it, but sin that dwelleth in me. For I know that in me (that is, in my flesh) dwelleth no good thing: for to will is present with me: but how to perform that which is good I find not."

3. Galatians 5:19-21 NKJV "Now the works of the flesh are evident, which are: adultery, fornication, uncleanness, lewdness, idolatry, wrath, selfish ambitions, dissensions, heresies, envy, murders, drunkenness, revelries, and the like; of which I tell you beforehand, just as I also told you in time past, that those who practice such things will not inherit the kingdom of God." It is very important for me to qualify the phrase "kingdom of God" here because we will ALL miss out on the kingdom of God if Galatians 5:19-21 is referring to heaven at God's throne after time is no more. Romans 14:17: "For the kingdom of God is not a matter of eating and drinking but of righteousness and peace and joy in the Holy Spirit." I propose that we (in our spirits and new heavenly bodies) from eternal damnation. That only the works of our flesh are not only to enter this kingdom of God but that the works of our flesh go to eternal flame. We, known as subsumed in Christ (1 Corinthians 15:28), are all saved from ourselves in this world-*kosmokriton* (the world order).

4. Romans 3:10 "As it is written (also found in Psalms 14:1), There is none righteous, no, not one."

MEANINGFUL and INTENDED destination. This takes a doer of the salting. The agency of salt – the saviour, the destiny maker – the Father.

We still think there is some effort of the act of our "will" to "choose" a living holy God. We, as being dead in our sins, assume we can make a living decision. We think we can "choose" our heavenly parent before we were born, let alone our earthly parent as an earthly child for the analogy.

He signaled himself as a prophet concerning the ending of the temple at Jerusalem in 70 A.D and he spoke of himself concerning the son of man at the [5]teleos of his earthly ministry, himself as the temple that would resurrect in 3 days, and his second coming at the end of this aeon/age/era. Therefore, the finality in these "series" of events would end at the culmination of our existence: that we should see his physical presence again at the end of the world as we know it[6].

The fullness of meaning[7] was that the Father would send his Son to die for us and in this act he should resurrect us. This is the epicenter for the entirety of scripture. All past and future events rested upon this central moment on the timeline of creation. If this fullness of meaning is a reality, then no earthly transaction could compare.

Most recorded Christian martyrdoms took place after the resurrection of Christ. The eye witnesses of Christ's crucifixion evoked most of these witnesses to become the early martyrs of the foundational Church no later than the mid first to second century (ca. AD 35 to the AD 100s). There must have been something of substance worth dying for at this poignant time.

By the witnessed teachings, prophecy, deeds, and parables of Jesus in this life unto his death which evoked the precious martyrs to act must have shown the world that the promise of Jesus' resurrection was true. These first century events still affect us more greatly than any other event in recorded history.

Recap:

Jesus said he would resurrect in 3 days and now that it was proof to the unbelieving and faint of heart that there was something worthy to believe in and act upon. If the promise of Jesus' death and resurrection had not

---

5. *telos* – "telegraph" – "to the end of the toss, throw, trajectory."
6. especially Matthew 24:29–30.
7. *plerotayta* [plero–"full"] *noaymatos* [*ennoia/gnoia* "know'- "knowing" -].

come to pass then no one would have followed his doctrine unto their deaths. All would have gone back to their own lives with disbelief. But the power of Jesus' testimony in word and deed secured the contract by which all of humanity has hope.

Chapter Sixteen

A One-Way Street

GOD'S KINGDOM IS COMING to its *teleon* (meaningful end). We are headed to a place to be summed up in the fullness of God's intent/the fullness of meaning. This should be an exciting thing for us to believe.

Since biblical prophecy requires an "ending point," i.e., a "*teleon*," to the narrative of the Book of Revelation from the Old Testament, then, the Book of Revelation (both in written form and reality) requires the entire narrative of scripture (from its beginnings all the way to its end) to be in an exacting manner. This means that not one thing could be out of place in real time, that is, scripture must "meet" reality to accomplish prophecy[1].

Much like an author who has an intention behind his or her writing to take you on a journey to a destination (*teleon*: the fulness of meaning/meaningful journey). There were ideas first, then, the ideas were "reeled out" in a kind of "time" – i.e., sequenced onto print.[2] These initial *at-empo* ((ah-tim-po) "without time") ideas eventually entered into time

---

1. I look at prophecy as an "undissected reality" within our time. If prophecy requires the agreement of God to prophet, then the events leading up to the teleon and eschaton are required to be stitched from eternity into time. Moreover, I think prophecy is just a *glimpse* of the conjoining of eternity and time. In the systematic approach that I am offering, I simply present to you that all things visible, invisible, eternal, heavenly, earthly are stitched together for the fullness of meaning.

2. "print" as I see is a visual that is used to deduce information over a period of space (distance of the pages) and time, in the sense of how long it takes to grasp or apprehend the concepts which lead to the grand "idea."

by the author.[3] It is within this complete[4] "sequencing" or "reeling out" of ideas that we can now call the "narration." It is the author who must "authorize" the ideas in their head ("intent[5] of ideas") before the ideas become unfurled into time and space as linear words, i.e., words that are sequenced into time one word at a time in succession. Only the author can "authorize" the beginning to the end[6] of any narrative.

The narrative's road map is also another reflection of the author. There are many roads that the author could take for their own enjoyment. But what mirrors the quality of the author is the care for the "gentle reader" whose edification is of the utmost importance.

In the biblical sense, it is the author[7] (God the Father) that has laid out his eternity into a "narrative" by which we can be instructed/edified. Furthermore, it is the biblical author who mirrors himself through his word and gives us his eternal glimpse through his narrative (i.e., the Bible). God's (the author) eternal plan (and how creation is expressed) can be viewed in scripture as interwoven realities. If one only reads the prophets concerning the coming of our Lord and Saviour one would know that heaven and earth meet at the prophet and through the prophet's words. Prophetic acts also support the predeterminate Noble Truth —in that, prophetic acts are sewn into all of reality,[8] both physical and metaphysical.

---

3. I say *atempo* ideas because I'm attempting to convey the theology that conveys the eternal in the mind of God. Time is not needed there, nor does it exist (at least how we would understand). When this *atempo* narrative unfurls into time we should know, by this consistent theological approach, that there was no prior time to corrupt the story or narrative.

4. Greek: *pleon*/full.

5. or "will" seen in two words that are both similar in the Greek language: *thumea* (passionate drive; intent; overriding will; desire; aim) and *boule* (the volition; directed shot; aim).

6. literally everything that is evil, bad, happy, sad, good, malicious, etc. is a part of the narrative which will bring about the "Fullness of Meaning" (hence, my website and ministry's name: "Fullness of Meaning Christian Ministries) or the *pleon* (fullness) of the narrative.

7. Author = Greek: *sungrapheas* – i.e., "with/together" + "writing." We see that "authority (*exousia* – The existence [as in Romans 13:1–33 – there is no other higher existence/exousia than God] and "authorities [*archayce* – *archon* – leader]," if they "exist" are "existing" only due to the author (God).

8. this would include all joy, murders, rape, incest, genocide, success in business, etc. that "act out" within the drama by which space & time ("the fabric of creation") consists. That is, you can't just "pick out" an event in 1971, jump to 2026, and discuss how these two "time zones" are not entirely entangled. This is from a quantum physics

A ONE-WAY STREET

But it is here that intent, for me, is summed up in the biblical doctrines of predestination. For all that we receive, good or bad (as called by humankind), is for the narrative of meaning. Therefore, God's narrative is both word (written and read – i.e., The Bible) and the deeds (all events that we experience –confirming God's word/narrative) – are all combined as "written by/of/for/with (*sungraphe*) God.

---

approach without the discussion of God. The Bible has already taught us about "quantum entanglement" if we only read Ecclesiastes (though, throughout all of scripture do we see this). We have already been taught by the writer of Ecclesiastes (probably Solomon) and Paul in Romans 8:29–31; Romans 9:1–33; Romans 13:1–14 that every existent energy that is requires each other to complete "history" as God has written it before the foundation of the world.

Chapter Seventeen

Old/New "Physics"

Scientifically, we might call this the conservation of information which existed before time and space. Such a conservation of information would fit the theological narrative of predeterminism in God's intentful mind prior to time.

Scientifically/theologically, such conservation of information, being "relayed" in time and space fabric, could all be accounted for in entropy – or near infinitesimal compression inside a black hole – and then, over the aeons, science and scripture say this "information" or "knowingness of us" could be "born again" – i.e., born from a renewed (born again/anothen) sense. A "new big bang" would potentially match that of a biblical new heaven and new earth with the resurrection of us all to boot.

Astrophysicist Dr. Brian Cox explained this (without regard to this very theological idea) in terms of quantum entanglement and conservation of information. Dr. Cox is not a believer, nor does that matter for this purpose. He has brought (with his colleagues) a mathematical maxim by which physics is not broken down but rather altered into a different and unique way by which no time (or timelessness) is serving a great purpose for explaining new birth (anothen). A way that could very well run parallel to scripture as I am presenting.

This leads us back to narrative and deeds being predetermined before they happen as sequenced into time and space for our "relative" understanding of God. God has cared for us in giving us a coherent narrative by which we can learn his eternal nature.

Chapter Eighteen

The Stacking and Sandwiching of Predestination and Prophecy

As we enter (*EIS* – come at, go into) Daniel's 70th week,[1] ideas such as predestination, or predeterminism, have become "hush words" for many orthodoxies. This wasn't always so in the early Church (Ante-Nicene, ca. AD 33– 350). When predestination is addressed today, many ministers will at best say, "well, God knows all but you still have free will." It's nearly hilarious that these two concepts: (1) "the will's freedom in God"— i.e., 'free will" and (2) "predestination'—i.e., "pre-establishing before time

---

1. The *last 7 years* (Shavua) concerning our *teleos* and *eschatos* can be found in Daniel chapters 8 through 9 (esp. Daniel 9: 25 - 27 which was Nehemiah's commandment to go rebuild Jerusalem, backed by Cyrus's decree in 535 BC (almost a hundred years prior to Nehemiah), until Messiah the Prince.

The next "distance" of time will be what some call the gap between Messiah and "last *Shavua*" (a.k.a. beginning to end of Revelation) which concerns the payment of the engrafted and shared "responsibility of the Christian's "yoke" with Israel. Therefore, both Christian and Jew share the last accounting of pagan Asherah worship for 70 years. Israel and Judah paid dearly for that either in never returning as ancient Israel or the Babylonian captivity of Judah. Either way, from the "going forth to restore and rebuild Jerusalem until the Messiah the Prince was 69 Shavua (483 years [7 *shavua* + threescore and 2 *shavua* (or: 49 years + 60 x 7 + 2 x 7 = 483 years)]). Concerning the Christian, the last seven years (one Shavua) was signaled by Israel coming back as a nation in 1948. At the end of this generation (ca. 80 years), starting at 1948, Psalms 90: 10 makes it clear that 80 years is a full duration of a "generation" – full of strength, labor, and sorrow.

And it is here that we have our last few "signals" before the exposing of antiChrist and Christ's return: 2 Thessalonians 2:3 "Let no man deceive you by any means: for that day shall not come, except there come a falling away (Greek: *apo* = "off" + *stasis* = standing/stance/"rooted-ness") first, and that man of sin be revealed, the "son of perdition." So, it is a "ceasing" in time when prophecy is fulfilled that we should have understanding.

and space (i.e., *pro-horidz* – pre-horizon) are not fluid ideas working in conjunction with each other. Still, the "freedom to will in God (true free will)" and predestination should not be viewed as against the "foreknowledge" of God or a replacement theology of predestination. Romans 8:29 "For whom He did foreknow He also did predestinate."

Remember, predestination is the "pre-setting of events before the event horizon begins. That is, before the fabric of time and space were spread out, the unfurling of all events were in the mind of God. "Creation," in a sense, is a relative term for us, as "creation" is the physical unfurling of God's mental "creation." Foreknowledge is a correlative attribute of predestination (i.e. the Father having predestined all of creation) but it is not to replace or be interchangeable with predestination. What a godly ability foreknowledge is though! Foreknowledge is a characteristic that only God has. A gift of "foreknowledge" can be seen as time segments into the future – or glimpses – that God shared with the prophets.

We should now have learned that these 3 very distinct attributes (free will, predestination, and foreknowledge) work together but not be muddled as *combatant theologies*. As in sandwiching the Five Noble Truths, one can "sandwich" these attributes as easily if one only takes the time to study what "free will," "predestination," and "foreknowledge" means.

The conflicts of these theological concepts are not to be found in scripture but in the ministers or "biblical authorities" who claim to master holy writ from an orthodox perspective using the English rather than the authoritative Greek and Hebrew text.

I can reflect on how many times I have sat through "low church" sermons listening to "The Romans Road"[2] where nearly 100% of the time the ministers bypass Romans 8:28-31[3]. At best, the ministers don't even bother to read Romans 8:28–31 but "commentate" as follows:

---

2. The "road" from a destitute sinner without a chance of salvation *unto* salvation by grace. This is relief from our state of being. Yet, many ministers crop this grace point out.

3. Romans 8:28-31 "And we know that all things work together for good for them that love God, to them who are called according to His purpose. (29) For whom He did *foreknow*, He *also* did *predestinate* to be conformed to the image of His Son, that He might be the firstborn among many brethren. (30) Moreover whom He called, them He also justified: and whom He justified, them He also glorified. (31) *What shall we then say to these things? If God be for us, who can be against us?*" Ephesians 1:4 – "According as He hath chosen us in Him before the foundation of the world, that we should be holy and without blame before Him in love." ←- how is this possible unless we are fully restored? (5) "Having predestined us unto the adoption of the children by Jesus

"God foreknows who will be saved in the future and therefore predetermines their salvation because he (God) sees who will choose him." Ugh! What a conundrum of ideas and violation of scriptural coherency!

On the other end of the spectrum Calvinism sets forward a horrible idea of predeterminism that eliminates most people to hell without an answerable "why (teleon)" from God's reason. 5 point Calvinism is centered around the fear of not being the elect and establishes a type of hubris that leads one to believe that they are the elect, or select, over others for some unanswerable reason[4] that I can't theologically compute.

The Calvinist would resort to their blanket statement: "it's God's Will." The Armenian says, "it's a mystery." The "It" in both cases has to do with the intent of God and his plan, purpose, aim, trajectory, etc. The Calvinist says "who gets damned and who gets saved is God's decision" – yet, most "good Calvinists" speak as "the elect" and not the 99% damned in this world.

This Calvinistic "elected view" gives no hope to those (The Arminians and the rest of the world) who are taught that they should have the free will to choose God under "grace" since the flesh chooses sin naturally. "Grace" is now ill-defined because "grace (*xaris* – "charity" – "unearned favor") has been aligned with free human will or natural rogue agency and what it decides to act upon (versus God's plan).

Let me quote the conundrum of Paul that counters both views by reading Romans 7: 15-20 for it is a Biblical passage instructing us as to how inadequate we are to "choose" God.

Romans 7:15–20

> 15) For that which I do I allow not: for what I would, that do I not; but what I hate, that do I.
>
> 16) If then I do that which I would not, I consent unto the law that it is good.
>
> 17) Now then it is no more I that do it, but sin that dwelleth in me.
>
> 18) For I know that in me (that is, in my flesh,) dwelleth no good thing: for to will is present with me; but how to perform that which is good I find not.

---

to Himself, according to the good pleasure of His will. . . . (11) In Whom also we have obtained an inheritance, being predestinated according to the purpose of Him Who worketh all things after the counsel of His own will."

4. all of which this book answers to God's predeterminate *intent/"why"/reason* unto salvation.

19) For the good that I would I do not: but the evil which I would not, that I do.

20) Now if I do that which I would not, it is no more I that do it, but sin that dwelleth in me.

Paul, the writer of the majority of the New Testament, admits that he is in his sin as a minister and apostle of God. Paul speaks of the sin that he would not want to do but cannot stop doing it. He states that he is in a condition that needs help. Later, in Romans, Paul explains the external help by which God had performed and was still performing over time. This "coming to be" in Paul's life used Paul's sins as a witness to his continued transformation unto[5] righteousness and ultimately, his martyrdom. This is true sovereignty! This is applicable to us all. Paul makes it very clear that human free will chooses only death while God Wills death to self (human free will) through his pre-ordained process upon us.

Therefore, in response to both opposing views, I see that a dysfunctional "counter doctrine" has been developed in "free will" as taught in the churches (and secular society). "Free will," falsely defined (as I will address later), says that you can "choose" to accept God or to "reject" God. This view denies God's sovereignty over "all things." Somehow, the doctrines of man have led us to think that the flesh "needs space"[6] to move around with God via "free agency." This illogic supports the Calvinistic view of God's sovereign plan for the moment within these two counter theological sides. Yet, the Calvinist must still deal with the "momentary," "the now," "the field of time and decisions," etc. How does a Calvinist answer to the remaining micro-seconds of their lives "making decisions?" One of the best treatments I have read on such a matter is Dr. Sam Harris's "There is no free will." Dr. Harris explains the microorganisms that "act" prior to our "choice" which make our "choices." These microorganisms themselves are responding to yet an earlier impulse and so on and so on. Dr. Ben Carson, a pediatric neuro-surgeon explained something of the sort concerning how our brains are "made" to receive information. Truly, the deeper one goes, the more we see that we are preceded by a prior act upon ourselves. This kind of "pre-act" horrifies the Calvinistic who is still attempting by time bound language to "justify" their relation in the here and now to exhaustion. I have yet to meet a Calvinist who strips literally every aspect of thought and identity of

5. implying intent, trajectory, and teleological outcome.
6. as I call it, "*the illusory third agency.*"

PREDESTINATION AND PROPHECY

themselves away from the "overriding" identity by which their persona is subsumed in the infinite will of the sovereign creator. This takes all hubris away and actually gives us all the hope in knowing that our earthly identities must go. They must be destroyed and we will be assumed under a new name in Christ's new name.

We can assume hope if this is the case because Romans 3:10–12 says: "As it is written– "There is none righteous, no, not one: There is none that understand, there is none that seek after God. They have all gone out of the way, they are together become unprofitable; there is none that does good, no, not one."

Romans 3:23–24 continues this thought unto the great *teleos* or end of time (*ouketi kronos*): "For all have sinned, and come short of the glory of God; being justified freely by his Grace (not your choice) through the redemption that is in Christ Jesus."

Concluding with Romans 5:18: "Therefore as by the offense of one [Adam] did judgment [*katakrima* – *krinos*: the judgment mis-used in Revelation as judgment unto hell] come upon all men to condemnation; even so . . . by the righteousness of one [Jesus] came the free gift upon all men unto justification (*dikaiosin* = "to set straight;" "make right;" "rectify") of life."

Clearly, this is the perfect synthesis of God's narrative from beginning to end. Our problems always begin, not at reading the verse, but, when our thinking begins to bring in our connotative ideas such as "free," "will," "agency," "time," "grace," "sovereignty," "pre-time," "intent," "volition prior to time/space," "completion of beginning to end before time and space unfurl," etc. It is here where I believe you need all five noble values that I am presenting here to justify such verses when you fall back to the flesh's reasoning.

So, according to scripture, an unregenerate human of their nature cannot choose a supernatural God. An unregenerate person cannot see their failures to need a God. They cannot see their beginning or end.[7] Only in the "coming to be" or "process to" God can one "choose" God.[8] But this "act" of "choosing" is in fact God himself willing in us unto this righteousness, as stated in Philippians 2:13: "For it is God who works (*energon* = generates action) to both will and to work for His good pleasure."

---

7. i.e., they lack the "apocalyptic view" – one of the Five Noble Truths

8. i.e., Philippians 2:13 – "For it is God who works (*energon*) in you, both to will (*thelein* – "intention," "will," "design," "wish," "am willing," "delight," "purpose") and to work for His good pleasure— *eudokias* (*eu* = "good" + *dokeo* = "thinking, reasoning").

I see predeterminism as the prime act of intention by which God, the intender, predestines all things into perfect order and leads all things to a conclusive fullness of meaning. This act both damns our sinful flesh and saves our souls all while he is showing us the mathematics of his calibrating us over time. That is, God shows us our journey unto salvation (by which we did not choose in due time of our own "free agency/will'!).

Therefore, predestination should be defined by its own terms and not by an assumption. Again, learn the words: predestine/predeterminism are the Greek New Testament words: *pro* = "pre" + *horidzo* = "horizon"/"border"/"arch"/demarcation of beginnings. Thus, to predestine is to "set" or "determine" events before they happen. To establish the completion before the start. Who can do this? Only one can.

God predetermines all things, including our wills, for his good pleasure (intent – thelos). Romans 9:19 "Therefore He has mercy on whom he will have mercy and hardens whom he will harden. Who can tell God that He is wrong here?! For who has resisted his will?"

Is this not a prelude to Ephesians 2:22? "For we[9] hath He quickened who were once dead in our trespasses and sins –being in times past those who walked according to the course of this world, according to the prince of the power of the air" .... who worked within the children of immovability."[10] Yet, Ephesians 2 continues to say that God "generated" our spiritually dead souls out of that state of death and into the shared resurrection of Christ.

But it is the rhetoric of Romans 9:19 that shows the possibility of true horror if grace/charity/*xaris* was not given. Romans 9 expresses that God is not only a "superior" or "sovereign" God to all but also the one who establishes all things in His perfect order/creation (*ektisthay* – sequence creation before it happened in time) before they ever happened[11]—and this includes our creation and salvation and every "energy that is!"

---

9. i.e., "we," the saved, his children, the elect, the restored ones (I argue all of us as "the restored under a new name).

10. 543 Strong's concordance: Greek: *apeitheia* – "obstinacy, willful, disobedient. The "alpha privative" or "a-" prefix on "apeitheia" negates the root of the word which is *peitho* – "to obey" or be able to persuade. We find the Hebrew equivalent in the Strong's concordance (Hebrew section number 4508) conveying "rebellion," "defiance"- against God. Paul uses this term that even the unbelieving Greek would understand that *apeitheia* meant a serious breach of Greek social norms and to the Jews as a breach of Jewish social life.

11. Colossians 1:15 "For by Him all things were created *(ektisthay* – "created out of nothing/did not exist before.")"

In Ephesians 1:4–5, 8–9, 11; 2:8; Romans 8:28–31; Isaiah 46:10–11; Romans 13:1ff; Isaiah 45:7; Romans 9:11 we are shown that the kind of "free will" that we will obtain is that "kind" of free will that is "freed up" to "will" those things which are holy and pure and infinitely bound to God. In other words, we will be infinitely released from the shackles of death and the will of the flesh which "chooses" destruction and hell and bound to God's infinite will and love.

Maybe this is hard to comprehend but this kind of "freedom" is the greatest limitation that the carnal mind can apprehend[12]. This kind of free will does not exclude that kind of free will---- that is, the free will" that is "coming to be" in the Lord's masterful plan. This predeterministic premise does, however, eliminate the illusory idea that we can "choose" God from an unregenerate state. It is what I call God's gift of "immediacy" or the "immediate" gratification to feel God's love with yours in our marriage with him. We are released from the grand delusion of self or human "control."

Therefore, the process of predestination goes unto repentance and into the kingdom of God, not only in this life but past the end of time. As Jeremiah 31:18–19 puts it: "You [God] have chastised me—and being chastised, as a bullock unaccustomed to the yoke, you turn me [repent me], O God, and [then] I shall be turned [repented]; for you are the LORD my God. After that [i.e., after God repenting Jeremiah] then I was instructed." So, God turns/repents us, that is, God makes the repentance part happen upon us, and then he instructs us and then, we see our shame, our actions of the flesh, our reproach from our youthful actions. This verse amongst many will I include in this book to show God's process of working that precepted us. We never had a mere "chance" or "opportunity" to repent on our own from our unregenerate natural state that is naturally damned. And for that very reason, we now have the learned lesson from God that his infinite grace is a value that could not have been understood in heavenly bliss. It is here where we suffer unto righteousness where time and space are needed to continue us on a path unto "the fullness of meaning.."

---

12. I use the term "instance" to express eternity as "instantaneous" or "without sequenced-time."

Chapter Nineteen

The Second Noble Truth: The Teleological View – (The Arrival of Meaning)

WE FIND TELOS IN the Greek to mean "summation of meaning." This sense of telos as "achievement" refers to the fulness of the meaning at the end times (*eschaton* – ending) where all things are "filled up" or "fully met." That is, the meaning of all things (*telos*) meets its end (eschaton). *Telos* can also represent a "finalized" action, or series of acts, of a particular thing.

We can find *telos* as an "achievement" mentioned in Aeschylus's "Suppliant Maidens." Aristotle's *telos* as "fulfillment" in his Politics Vl. 8 – pg. 132. 2b, 13. Isocrates" "telos "exein" – "were carried out" — esp. of a motion. Demosthenes's *telos* as "success" in all acts – *telos exthlon ep"ergois* —> (an Orphic Hymn).

Telos as "power," "full power," "the influential" —cf. Thucydides IV. 118, 10 — "*oi*" "*en telei.*"

Josephus's work called "Wars" –cf. I.243; Antiquities 14.302 —> "Those in office." Antiquities II, 6,4 — "decision." Aeschylus, Eum., 243 —> "telos" = "what is valid."

THE USAGE OF *TELOS*

"Completion"

Plato – *Laws* VI. 722 c – telos = "completion" – as a state or condition (i.e., "a state of perfection); Josephus's *Antiquities* 10 – "upper limit" "final step";

Plato *Republic*. VII. 532 "The Supreme Stage";

Isocrates *Orations*. 6, 50, etc. "issue";

Polybius *Istoria*. 61. 2 i. "issue";

Josephus *Vita*. 154 – "issue";

Menander *Fragments*. 276, 16: 287.4.

"To the end"

Josephus's *Antiquities* 17, 185 *telos* – "End of Life"; Josephus *Wars (Bellum)* "Oi Telos Exontes" – "the dead."

"As obligation"

Demosthenes *Orations* 20.19 *telos* "tax" —in the sense of the full accounting.

"Offering to the gods"

Sophocles *Trachinae*, 238; *panxalka telay*, *Antigone* 143; "offering" – *telos*; *telay enkarpa*, *Tracihane* "offering";

Euripides. *Fragments* 327. 6 (TGF, 238) – "the work or acts of the gods;"

Euripedes, *Hippolytus* 25 *megala telay* of initiations – "celebrations" as *telos*— i.e., the "telos" or "initiations" of the purity rites of the gods and the healing of the soul (as in marital consecration; nuptials; sexual congress with the god— the "final" act of the wedding ceremony with the god or person);

Death and marriage are *telos* for men. –Sophocles.

"Military"

Telos as in a "detachment" of ships or a group "sent to battle" cf. Thucydides I. 48. 3; Polybius II.ii.6.

LXX (The Septuagint)

Here we have the LXX/Septuagint or the Old Testament "translated" into Koine Greek giving us "Semitic equivalents" such as the Hebrew *soph* meaning "end" in Daniel 7:26. In 4 BAS (Biblical Archaeological Society) 8:3 and 18:10 *telos* as "constantly." Isaiah 62:6 "*eos telous*" – "fully."

"The time which follows"

Genesis 49: 1, Numbers 24:14, Deuteronomy 31:29, etc.

"The Latter Days:" Jeremiah 48: 47, Jeremiah 49:39, Numbers 24:14, Jeremiah 23:20,

30:24, Ezekiel 38:16 — "End of Years."

The New Testament

1 Timothy 1:5 *telos* as "the goal"; 1 Peter 1:9 The Telos of Faith in Christ is eschatological salvation (*Komzomenoi*/receiving to/the *telos*/outcome *tayce*/of the *pistis*/faith *humon*/of you *soterian*/salvation ψυχον (*pseuchon*)/of your souls.

1 Corinthians 10:11 *telos* as "The Aims" of the times—carried out/fulfilled; *Teleios nayphontayce* – "be fully minded" = "be sober minded."

RECAP

We can somewhat look back in our history of telos to see its stages and developments.

1. "Achievement, execution of resolve, fulfillment, carried out–of a motion, success, power, full powers, the influential, those in office, discharged orders, official power, decision, what is valid."
2. "Completion – as a "state of perfection," upper limit
3. "The Final Step, the supreme stage, goal, maturity, fully, totally,/
4. "Then End of Life, to be dead
5. "Tax," "Accounting"

6. "Offering"
7. "Celebration"
8. "Detachment" as in ships or troops sent to battle
9. "End"/"Fully"
10. "End of Years"
11. "Eschatological Salvation"

My view:

The secular historical study of *telos* has its humble origins. Upon such everyday usages of telos, I find the strength of *telos'* evolution and adaptation into the narrative of intentful salvation. Such evolution[1] brings out the Gospel for me. From some of *telos'* oldest beginning root meanings unto its biblical salvific meanings truly baffle me as to the comparisons of creation, our creation, our lives, our deaths, our resurrection, and to our salvation.

The Gospel hope seems to be built into the "coming to be" of *telos*

Not only is this "coming to be" found in *telos* but its simple roots are unto a resurrection victory. We can therefore see that *telos* operates within the predetermined-apocalyptic (i.e., all-revealed-in-its-purpose) view. Again, such a view shows us that the Noble Truths of predeterminism, The apocalyptic view, and teleology are working in synergy. They show the intent, purpose, meaning, and reason by which God acts upon us.

TELEOLOGICAL BELIEF IS BELIEF DEFINED

If teleology is to be a branch of biblical study it must incorporate, or stick to, a presupposed apocalyptic view. One must believe that telos comes

---

1. Evolution is used here in terms of progress of a word's usage or a heightened sense by which the participant of language both listens and transmits such ideas . . . as compared to 1,000 years ago. This "evolution" is not meant to mean "better" — for our ancient ancestors used their language in a "genius" or "collective consciousness" that we are not fully aware of. Furthermore, our ancient ancestors had to "convey" ideas in a way of limitation with the emphatic nature of survival.

to (or has) its "completion"[2] of meaning. As we have stated in Aristotle's view of telos: An oak tree is the *telos* of an acorn— likewise, revelation requires a trust in the *gestalt* of scripture from Genesis with forward momentum. That is, one must read the scripture as they're "going someplace" meaningful. If I may take Tolkien's idea into theology: one must suspend their disbelief in reading prophecy.[3] Teleology must hold to a belief in the sacrosanct nature of a providential God who can put his narrative together using people to be as the words on the pages.

All of us have interests that require us to already "believe" before we "know" what we want to do. Whether a physicist, evolutionary biologist, archaeologist, etc., we all exercise a "belief" in a *potential* profession. The journey that got you onto the road to make that next "decision" to become an archaeologist was a journey of many prior adventures of the mind and body. Anyone proclaiming "autonomous choice" is deluded.

The journey or path unto anything always has both *eschaton* and *teleon*. The meaning of the "why" is wrapped up in the *teleon*. The objective fact of "ending" point(s) is wrapped in *eschaton*.

The journey or path of a drug addict (if continued) is death if it is in the eschatological sense. This path is a determined path that naturally takes each of your steps (if continued on this journey) to your "concluded" destruction. The Hebrew term, *pasha* conveys this "journey of sin to destruction" sense.

Many heroin addicts have said that heroin is its own predetermined path. Take the path of the embodiment of heroin and it concludes you with its own fate/fatality (eschaton).

Theologically speaking, teleology is an embodiment that cannot be deconstructed from the threads of a biblical and/or secular view. In this sense, teleology is likened to a road map to the apocalyptic view. As we have stated, the "apocalyptic view" means "the purview" by which one can "see" all events as "one" gestalt—i.e., a quantum totality having come to its fullness of meaning.

Eschatology/*Eschatos* demarks the final period and lends itself to the objective "end result" by which the directive and status of salvation, damnation, resurrection, heaven, hell, etc. are complete. To me, it's as

---

2. Plato – Laws VI. 722 c – telos = "*completion*" –as a state or condition (i.e., "a state of perfection); Josephus" Antiquities 10 – "*upper limit*" "*final step*"; Plato Rep. VII. 532 "*The Supreme Stage*"

3. This is a challenge to the "academics" who teach in "Christian universities" holding to agnosticism or atheism.

though eschatology is a colder science to biblical studies. That is, it is a study of the "metrics" of history, judgments, fulfillments of doom, and the end of the world as we know it.

Maybe another approach was to show the difference between these two studies in that "eschaton" means "an ending unto destruction" while "teleos" means an end to an aim, fulfilment, completion, and/or goal.

Teleon:

In Revelation 10:1–7 we read that the final angel (the seventh) instructs John to write no more, for the mystery of God[4] would be fulfilled (*etelesthay* – root: *teleos*) and time (*kronon*) is no longer.

Eschaton:

In Revelation 11:15 we see that the same seventh angel has "sounded" and voices from heaven have announced: "the kingdom of this world (*kosmos*) has become (*egeneto*) the kingdom of our Lord and of his Christ and He shall reign forever and ever." This event is the *eschatos*, the end, the salvation point, which occurs here in the narrative. The angel tells John to "write no more" for it is over (*eschaton*). There are no more words, no more signals, no more narrative to live in for referencing our lives in this earthly paradigm.

Concerning *telos* or *teleos*: think of the acorn becoming the oak tree—that is its *telos*. Contrast that with the death, decay, and disappearance of the oak tree. This is the oak tree's end, or *eschatos*. In *telos*, it is not the physical end of the oak tree but the summation of the tree. Telos is the completion of the process and how the acorn will "come to be" and be known as oak tree. This might give you a hint as to why I tend to value Biblical "teleology"[5] over "eschatology."

What I find in teleology is a gentle compatibility with (1) intentful and loving predeterminism, (2) the apocalyptic view, (3) prophetic view, and (4) universal salvation. All 4 mentionings work well with teleology

---

4. "musterion" – "mist," "secret," once hidden but now revealed in the Gospel or some fact thereof, "of which initiation is necessary, the counsels of God, a redemptive plan to be revealed at a later date, (root: *mueo* – mime; to mime; to signal to something to be understood).

5. teleology: Greek: *teleos/telos* – the summation of the intent, summation of meaning, the goal fulfilled, aim accomplished, fulfilment – as in a plan.

(the fifth mentioning) within a loving plan to unfurl and consummate. The biblical study of teleology extracts meaning, intent, goal, plan, relationship with the intender—that is—if teleology can be understood, it should be understood as "relational" or "marital" quality much as God consummates us to him in the final wedding ceremony.

Teleology as seen in the lowly Archer

A.K.A. The "Toxophilus"/The lover of the bow

As we read of the *toxotayce* (or *toxsotace*) or *toxsotai* we will find that they were the lowest of the low amongst the Greek warriors and class system, yet their name (*onoma*) implies quite a different judgment.

I'd like to start with one of the first recorded treatments of etymologies in Plato's works called Cratylus. In this work, Plato uses the *daemon* or "god-mind" of Socrates (Socrates having passed on ca. 399 BC and Plato's *Cratylus* written ca. 375 BC) to have a mock "dialogue" or "*dialogos*" with Cratylus to elicit meaning through the logos or logic of words and what they truly signal.

Loeb classic, Plato, Cratylus, Plato IV, translated by H.N. Fowler, 420 B:

> Hermogenes: "What is your view about *doxsa* (opinion) and the like?"
>
> Socrates: "*Doxsa* is derived either from the pursuit (*dioxsis*) which the soul carries on as it pursues the knowledge of the nature of things, or from the shooting of the bow (*toxson*); the latter (the shooting of the bow) is more likely; at any rate, "belief (*oiaysis*)" supports this view, for it appears to mean the "motion (*oisis*)" of the soul towards the essential nature of every individual thing, just as *Boulay (intention)* denotes shooting (*bolay*) and *Boulesthai* (wish, desire/bulls-eye), as well as *Boulesuesthai* (plan), denotes aiming at something. All these words seem to follow *doxsa* and to express the idea of shooting, just as *aboulia* (ill-advisedness/evil), on the other hand, appears to be a failure to hit, as if a person did not shoot or hit that which he shot at or wished or planned or desired."
>
> Hermogenes: "I think you are hurrying things a bit, Socrates."
>
> Socrates: "Yes, for I am running the last lap now, But I think I must still explain *anangkay* (compulsion; the goddess of

objectivity and pain) and *ekusion* (voluntary) because they *naturally* come next. Now by the word *ekousin* is expressed the yielding ("yielding to"—as one stops in submission to and *icon/eikon*) and not opposing, but, as I say, yielding to the motion which is in accordance with the will; but the compulsory (to' *anangiaon* [*anankay* (the wife of Chronos—god of hell and time)]) and resistant, being contrary to the will, is associated with error and ignorance; so it is likened to walking through ravines (*angkay*), because they are hard to travers, rough, and rugged, and retard motion; the anangkaion may, then, originate in a comparison with progress through a ravine. But let us not cease to use my strength, so long as it lasts. . . ."

Terms to know:

archery: *toxsobolia*

archers: *toxsotes*

archery range: *perioxsay toxsobolias*

archery bow: *toxso toxsobolias*

archer bow: *toxso toxobolias*

archery club: *lesxsay toxsobolias*

opinion – i.e., "aiming for a target with words as the arrows": *doxsa*

(*dioxsis* possible meaning: the pursuit of the soul as it carries on in the matter of knowing thing: *dioxsis*) but Plato seems to favor this etymon →: *dioxsis*: from the shooting of the bow. I hold both as a "combinatorial term."

belief: *oiaysis* – motion (*oisis*)" *of the soul towards the essential nature of every individual thing*

intention: denotes shooting: *boulay* (intention)

wish, desire: *boulesthai*

plan, denotes aiming at something: *boulesuesthai*

*O*ther vocabulary found here:

Boulesuesthai (plan), *boulay* (intention), *bolay* (shooting), *boulesthai* (wish, desire/bulls-eye), *aboulia* (ill-advisedly/evil/a failure to hit, as if a person did not shoot or hit that which he shot at or wished or planned or desired"), *ekousin* (the yielding ["yielding to" –as one stops in submission to and *icon/eikon*] and not opposing/yielding to the motion which is in accordance with the will), *anangkay* (retards motion; stubborn; obstinate; goes against the will/the flow).

Plato said "all of the above words seem to follow *doxa*."[6]

As Plato said, the archer has the intent to hit the bull's eye (*boulesthai*) and must do so by marrying himself/herself to the ballistics which make the shot "true." Ballistics are defined by the archer's intention plus the factoring to make the shot such as power, velocity, windage, trajectory, projectile weight, etc. "Ballistics" comes from the word, *boule*.

The *boule* or "volley" has a deep and ancient connotation. The word "will" comes from "the will of the gods." It means the "toss" or "volley" or "volition" of the gods. That is, the target or objective of desire for the Greek pantheon of gods. It means the counsel of the gods.

In archery's ancient philosophical-linguistic numinous relations, the greatest expressions are between the gods and the archer.

That is, the *Toxotayce* shows their obedience to the will of the gods which preceded the shooter. The pursuit (*doxsa*) and belief (*oiaysis*) are combined to form *dioxsis*. This term, *dioxsis* means the "motion of the flow into the pursuit of knowledge and naturally avoids retardation of the flow (*ienai/-ania- pain*), or "that which hinders and ill advises (*aboulia* [evil]). So, when the shooter, or *toxotayce*, makes the shot, the *toxotayce* receives the "glory," i.e., the "*doxa*"—hence, "praise."

To add: the will of the gods preceded the *toxotayce* and drew a true line to the target's *boulesthai* (pronounced: *boo-lehs-thai*) or bull's eye. Therefore, the "shot" is done. It already was, is, will be. All one needed to do was to obey and respect the will of the gods.

Beautiful poetic terms come to play within the nomenclature of Greek archery that apply to a theological application. Classical Greek terms such as *rous*, which means, "the flowing river" are implemented in this rich platonic—philosophical explanation of a poetic and scientific art, i.e., the art of archery. To get into the *rous* meant to add the human

---

6. Plato, *Complete Works*.

element of the will (the ballistics) via *poeisis* (sounds like: "poe-ay-siss)" in order to imitate to the conformity of the will of the gods.

Poeisis is where we get the word, poetics. Poeisis means to "not step in the way of the flow but to act in accord with the fluid motion of the river by which the will or desired trajectory is going." Such observant acts of obedience are necessary to "do the will of the gods." The opposite is "diabolical." That is, *dia* = across + *boule* = "cast," "toss," "volley"/so, "to cast across the designation toss" —> i.e., "*to throw to stumble someone* as they are going to the bullseye"—hence, the term, "diablo."

To further the vocabulary of the artist, whether archer, musician, painter, or dancer, the artist was impassioned with *thumea* (thoo-may-uh). *Thumea* is yet another type of will. *Thumea* participates in the family of wills as "intent, desire, passion, etc." In archery, *thumea* is implemented by the true *toxotayce* to "drive" oneself to the will or the *boule* (sounds like: bow-lay) or "ballistics" of the gods as identified as being directed by the gods. Coming to be into the likeness of the gods through the will that already has been shot and demarcated to the bullseye, or *boulesthai* is a mythological idea nearly akin to the New Testament idea of us following God's directed "volley," "ballistics," "shot to the target, etc. The *boulesthai*, etymologically speaking, means "the sticking place (boule/"will" + [suffixial] —"*sthai*"/"standing"/"resting place")."

The shot of the flesh/Hitting the miss

In the etymological treatment for the archer found in Plato's *Cratylus*, we do find the "angst" source for those who do the opposite of the good *toxsatayce* (archer).

We find that those who "shoot" for their own will, self-will, self-desire, eros, etc., do indeed "shoot" into the field of *harmeteia* (har-mah-tay-ah). This is the Christian term used quite often for "sin."

Plato makes it clear that "the shot" of self-desire brings one into the field of *ananke* (ah-nan-kay)[7] as seen in our English word "angst." It is

---

7. In Orphic tradition, Ananke was the goddess of necessity and compulsion. Ananke is the wife of the god of time, Chronos (Xronos). In Plato's *Cratylus*, 420 B, Plato says that Ananke is likened to traversing ravines (Greek: anxay/[p.i.e. – "constricting, painful, anguish/Old French: "ravin" – deep gorge, trench), streams, and/or rivers, . . . i.e., something that flows against or is troublesome). She is compulsory, retards motions, she is resistant and contrary to motion and will. It is interesting to me that the god of this age mentioned in Ephesians 2:1 might have significance to the wife of Cronus/Xronos/Chronos…i.e., Ananke.

defined as the "field of thorns and bramble," but, for sure, applicable to broadly applied terms for "suffering"—i.e., the "field of suffering."

The plethora of terms in the ancient pagan Greek sources gives us such a detailed treatment for Christian doctrine. You read me right.

Yet another aspect: Are you the god who shoots from, by, for yourself? Would this type of ideological archery not be the antithesis of Colossians 1:16,17 (paraphrase: "all things are made for, of and by Jesus Christ who preceded all things")?

This type of "shooting" defines the *one* who "hits the miss" and wills for objective self-desire—that is, one who is motivated to traject by self-will into the fields of pain, anxiety, objectivism, non-meaning.

In my website lectures I speak of "the archer" in the dialogues of *Cratylus* (by Plato) and the etymologies that are used in the "will, trajectory, art or *poesis* of the *toxon* (shooter) and the personal participation of the toxon called the *rous* which allows the shooter to obey only the one thing that hits the bull's eye or *boulesthai*.[8]

The *Paideia* [pie-day-uh] – root for "foot," as *padua* in Greek or "little ones"– *pedos*—"little one") was classical aspect of education given to the early first century Christians to educate ((Latin– *e*-prefix – "exit"/ *ducare* – "darkness") "bring out of darkness") the Christian youth by teaching them the richness of etymologies and analogy. They were taught forensics (art of argumentation) and logic (reason/mainly that of Plato and Aristotle's works) and the classics, for sure, such as Homer's *Iliad* and *Odyssey* (cf. Werner Jaeger's *Early Christianity and Greek Paideia*). Such terms of the *toxon* would have "met" the *padua* as they also would have understood the doctrines of sovereignty written by Paul. The genius of the Jewish ideas fused with the European Greek sense by which Paul understood and wrote to in a Christian worldview, would have been brought to completion by the Holy Spirit who would and does teach all things to their completion.

To recap:

The archers (*toxotai*) are us. The *toxatayce* are the believers in God's Will. Contrariwise, the "archers" that are still hitting the miss are those aiming for worldly objectives. I believe that over time, over the aeons, the world (*kosmokriton* – the world of criticism/judgment) will one day realize

---

8. Jones, "Anatomy of Will."

THE SECOND NOBLE TRUTH

there is no other direction but one. That one direction is to the bullseye. That direction is the will that goes to the bullseye. The shared shot is where the archer (*toxotacye*) participates in the Will of God which takes you to the bullseye.

We, the believers, are reliant upon God to be given the passionate intent, or what the Greeks called, *thumea*, which means "the passionate mind, beyond the mundane, fervor, anger, beyond just rationale." The will to the Classical Greek mind was called *boule*. We get our words: ballistics, bullet, volley, volition, and ball from the word *boule*.

The etymological beauty found in the Classical Greek religions, philosophies, pure pagan rites, etc. gave the Christian world a wealth of words from which these pagan terms saw their fulfillment in.

Did we not see here the absolute loss of meaning for the terms "free" and "will"? That is, do we not see here that the "free will" of the *Toxon* and understanding Christian exegete is not the same as the counterfeit "free will" that is used in churches all across America today?

Do we see the allegory found in Classical Greek archery terminologies/nomenclature[9] with that of the alignment of the council of the gods? Do we see the same mythological Greek idea fulfilled in the reality of the Christian's relationship to Christ? Participation of the Will of God to the bullseye is not a choice, rather, it is a bending of the bow, a yielding of our very being. This participation with God to hit the mark takes absolute submission to his words which are tethered to the Will of the Father. This is not a natural act. Yielding to God's Will is his act upon us. We participate, not choose, by being "yielded" to his perfect shot.

Endcap etymon for *doxa*: *dekomai*: Proto Indo-European root: *dek-* to take with the ten fingers, take, to take, accept, "to seem good," "to be of worth," "a hymn or praise (doxa) to God," –Greek: *doxologos* = "words of praise," "of good opinion but possibly lacking in knowledge," "prized."

Other remarkable P.I.E. related forms of doxa: dek-condign, dainty, decent, decor, decorate, deign, dignify, discipline, docile ([from the Oxford English Dictionary] "ready to receive instruction or orders to submit or take control;" "willing"), doctor, doctrine, dogma, dogmatic, doxology.

All such terms imply an obedience to a thing—and a resulting honor. Just as in the English borrowing from the Latin, *discipula*, we have the

---

9. arrow = *belos*, will = *boule*, bullseye = *boulesthai* [in all vocabulary words, "b" and "l" are the structure for such terms]; *toxotayce* = archer = one of *doxa* or glory ["t" or "d" and "xs" or "x" are the structure for such terms].

founded Greek word, *mathetikon* for "mathematician" meaning one who rightly divides, dissects, discerns, the logos of Christ." Hence, disciple (*dek-*)" of Christ is "one who is compliant" . . . receiving honor though of lowly status, for "humility" is the substance (*hupo-stasis* ["under" + "standing"/"stance" (a.k.a. – "the root")) by which the discipline starts.

Chapter Twenty

Being Halted

ONCE WE ARE NEW creatures in Christ, we begin the process of our *participation unto* inalterability into eternity with God. In our participation with God's Will and our "shadow will," if you will, we demark heavenly paths like a *plumb line* (Amos 7: 7, 8). We participate in the setting "measured judgment" from heaven to earth. The kingdom of God is established in the walk (Hebrew: halakh) of our directed paths[1]. Where we walk is the invisible kingdom of God. For we participate in his accuracy though the world which would tell us we are *walking* the wrong *way*. Our words are his words. Our acts are now his acts. We are now offensive to many due to this. Yet, no one, including ourselves, is found innocent in this measurement. As in Amos 7, God's people, let alone the world, are now under God's judgment by our *fleshly works*. That is, the works of the flesh are a stink to God. These works are not holy and not sustainable in eternity with his holiness.

No one is innocent. No one will get to heaven by their works. You are already condemned by your works, and even now, your mind condemns you. That which is on earth cannot reach the heavens or obtain innocence lest grace be abounding. Only in Christ is this possible. Being now in Christ, we dance as banners, tensile, flags, fanfare, etc. that signify the invisible verb which moves us by his holy hand. That which is holy is holy and that which is ordained of him is holy, even our wickedness.

---

1. This might be confusing if we don't address the ordained evil "set" by God that we participate in . . . in order that we will "walk (*halakah*)" to his designed end and new beginning for us. For, "ordination" of destruction leads us on the path to righteousness. Never forget, "destruction" is an ordained path and we have all participated on that path—that is, we have all sinned.

Our ordained wickedness, if it didn't exist, would never continually teach us how much we need the grace of Jesus Christ. Yet, in Christ's salvation, we are new creatures dancing in his [2]orchestrated verbal motion. We are participating in union with the verb— i.e., Christ, the Father, and the Spirit as it (they) rushes upon us. We see the contrast of our flesh and God's verb daily, hourly, minute by minute. We are guilty, ashamed, and comforted. Thank God we don't have to have our "will's way!"

Our participation in the spiritual archery game tells of the meaning of "free," "will," "participation," "etc.." When the shot of the arrow has been made, the test of trueness begins. If the arrow hits the mark, we know that the archer has applied the rules and stipulations of every aspect of the laws of trajectory, windage, weight, distance, haze, movement, speed of arrow, etc. which are all mandated to the conformity of the will. He or she is a Greek *matheteke* ("mathematician") or disciple (equivalent of the P.I.E. root *dek-*) of the word. One has become "mature" (the Greek: *marturos*, i.e., martyred to their flesh) and bound to the god/God. There should no longer be your fleshly limitations and opinions by which the "math" of the shot works. Rather, only total submission to the rules, logic, LOGOS of archery can be applied to make the bullseye. You are becoming (Greek: *sunmorphe* — "coming to be into the likeness of") an "archer" by way of this process put upon you.

One last thing: how many misses will you have before you make that perfect shot? Many times. A lifetime of missing. So, how can there be judgment on the future *toxotayce* when he or she is "coming to be" in the likeness of the "Will/*boulay*/ballistics" of God? Where is judgement? Where is the accusation? Logically, shouldn't "grace" be the word of choice throughout? I think yes. How can we judge another when they are "coming to be"? They are also not "fully fit." Neither are we.

Terms to repeat

- *Rous* (river/flow)
- *Boulesthai* (bullseye; i.e., the desire or wish obtained)

---

2. Remembering a conversation I had recently with a friend concerning Jesus' mission was to condemn the law and make salvation impossible lest one be reckoned with him. His ministry was condemnatory and salvific without choice. His options were "rude" to those who wanted "freedom of the flesh." One way, one salvation, one God.

- *Boule* (will, desire, cast to, tossed to, volley, wish, desire, counsel of the gods)
- *Toxon* (bow)
- *Toxotayce* (archer)
- *Doxa* (glory, prize, price, praised, value, worth)
- *Sagittarius* ("the archer" [from the Latin: "sagitta" – "arrow"])
- *Arche* (beginning)
- *Eye* (Hebrew: *Ayin*: "Fountain," "Wellspring" [cf. "*iris-*" "*ireini*" -i.e., "bow" as in "rainbow," and "arch"])
- *Harmeteia* (missing the mark/sin [*a-meros* = "without share'])
- *Ananke* (desire, compulsion, need, want—especially ladened with anxiousness – angst, pain, and/or lust)

Chapter Twenty-One

The Third Noble Truth: The Apocalyptic View

The word "apocalypse" is derived from the Greek *apo* = "off" + *calypto* = "a cover," indicating "*that which covers* ("hell" = lit. hole/unseen/con (with) + ceal (closure/hiddenness)/seal/[1]) is taken away and all that was covered is revealed." Hence, *apocalypsis* means the "full disclosure, revelation." *Revelation* (i.e., the biblical apocalypse) means to *see the full picture*, plan, scheme, etc. When the *concealment is uncovered* (a.k.a. *apocalypsis*) we will then see the entirety of the plan, its execution, and the ending of God's creation as a total lump sum.

Thanks to the unveiling[2], we will be able to *see* the beginning (*engeneto/geneas* = "genesis"), middle (coming to be), and ending/destiny (*teleos*) of the physical (*physis*/natural) world (*kosmos* = "orderly arrangement"). We will then be able to *see* that there was nothing out of place, rather, everything led to the fullness (*pleonektes* = "fullness") of meaning.

Ephesians 1:10–11: "In the administration of the fullness of times God [the Father] might gather together in one all things in Christ, both which are in heaven, and things in the earth; even in Him. In whom also we have obtained an inheritance, being predestined ["pre-horizonened"]

---

1. It is interesting to that the etymology for "seal" is "hell." The Proto-Indo-European word for conceal/seal is *Kel V1*— "to hollow, to cover, to hide." The Greek gives us: *khalyptein*, conceal (cf. Calypso, goddess of silence, who held Odysseus for seven of the ten years of his return from Troy in a Germanic tongue, Hel was the goddess of the dead and hell was her domain. Furthered, we got "hole" as "unseen" place. We will finally be in awe of what God has created before creation (predestination) was put into the physical world.

2. *apocalypto*/"apocalypse" —> *apo* = "off" + *calypto* = "concealment," "covering," "hell [cf. Shippey, "hell" in his *Word Origins of the English Language*]

according to the purpose of Him who works all things after the counsel of His own will."

The apocalyptic view "synthesizes" predestination, universal restoration, and teleology. It brings them all together in "total vision." *Telos* (the end result of the plan's predetermined trajectory) *is* revealed as universal salvation if one looks at the game plan for the *"why"* we are all going through what we go through. The apocalyptic view offers the revelation of *now*. Universal salvation is without concealment of meaning as to why, what, and how God's previously unknown intent and Will has been done[3].

For sure, a resting point for the believer in Christ is knowing objective historical events of Jesus on earth. We can know that a legal, societal, philosophical, archaeological, historical, and scientific "reconstruction" exists in support of the four Gospels. The book of Revelation jumps back and forth, seemingly scattered as the Jewish way of writing, but it is not. It is multilayered for us to understand these Five Noble Truths.

The apocalyptic view reveals God's sovereign predestination. In the apocalyptic view, we can see that living in the "immediacy" of time (i.e., the "here and now") was good for applying doctrine, reading, reproving, exhorting others as oneself, etc… as we walked with God's word in time's past. But at the end of time when *all* is revealed we are shown that even our very steps were ordained. Our "experience" of immediacy of times in the past becomes lumped into the universal picture – the apocalyptic. So, even the earthly and illusory understanding of our "free will" that was, is, and will be until *teleos*. The apocalypse will be not only a new way to see the meaning of God's plan but a new evolution into God's Kingdom. The teleological view, the predeterministic view, the apocalyptic view, and the prophetic view all seem to work together to make a more reasonable theology.

When all is revealed, we shall have a "freedom" that can finally be understood. Maybe this is why we could never have understood what and why freedom never made sense before. For telos is an eternal term, in my humble view. We shall have the "freedom" to act on the infinite strings of God. Our flesh, which bound us "from" God, will have been

---

3. The apocalyptic view gives us the vision to use the doctrines of predeterminism, teleology, prophetic view, universal grace as "-ologies" or classifications of studies to collocate and represents that which is not a doctrine, rather, a reality of apocalypse. For, if the "apocalypse" will be a reality, then the model by which it is represented via these 4 distinct categories of study does indeed "conclude," systematically, a "central reference." This, in other words, is much like time travel and beyond time travel.

burned away." All of the *will* of the flesh's natural animosity towards God will die and go away into the "unseen," "the concealed place" ("hell").

WORD STUDY ON "FREE"

beginnings of dispelling "autonomous agency"

Free: Greek – *eleutheros*: "free man/free woman," "unrestrained (to go at pleasure), liberated, unshackled, free to realize one's destiny in Christ (cf. Strong's Concordance # 1658), free from – no longer under obligation to, so that one may now do what was formerly forbidden the person or thing to which he or she was bound" [rooted in "erchomai": to come from one place into another (prepositional in its freedom from one place due to being at another)"; Anglo Saxon: fregon: "love, favor; freond," "friend," freod, (f.) "friendship, peace; frith, (m.) freodu, "peace, safety, refuge," freo (f) "lady," "those most dear in a household," "not the slaves–but the children of the domicile" – "the free ones in the household," "my dear one"; Sanskrit: priya: "dear"; Late Latin: exfridare: "removed from" + "peace/freedom"; French: frere macon: friend – (initially meant "a loved one"); proto Germanic: *friaz* = "beloved"/"not in bondage" Old Saxon: "vri" = free/not in bondage/beloved; Gothic: *frijon* = "to love"; Old English *freod* = affection, friendship, peace"; Gothic: *friga* = "love"; Old Norse: *Frigg* [wife of Odin] = "beloved"/"loving"; German: *freien* = "to woo"; German: *fraulein* = as in "*mein frau*" = "my precious one." "Free" was a marketer's term for selling women on the slave market. If you were "free" from the market you would be "bound" to the master of the house who bought you. To speak "frankly" was a French (Franc) term to mean, "to speak without being bound to a condition, manner or restraint upon the speaker." A worthy and fit *prijatell* = "friend," or "free-one," who is bought "from" a horrid place (a slave market) and brought "into" a loving place, does not usually complain about their limitations to "act" "free from" the master who loves them. When we join the "economy (*oikos* = "household" + *nomos*[4] = "name, authority, law, boundary line, rule,

---

4. *nomos*: "the epitome of what is valid in social dealings." *Nomos*, from early on, maintained its relationship to the Greek cultic forums and veneration of their gods. The ancient denominator of meaning for *nomos* was the "will of the god" and how this "will" held its sway within the *polis*/city. Such "sway" might be seen as the deity's expression under the term, "nomos." But what genius has elicited nomos, meaning more than the Greek dramas such as Antigone and Creon's destruction? I say Paul's addressment to this very issue in Romans 2:14 was even greater. For both the play

lineage," etc.)" we are given the name that entitles honor and "freedom from" slavery or worse. Keep in mind, the purchase of the slave woman on the market was not her will but the purchaser's "adoration" for the "beloved." No longer do we look at "will" and "free" as technical slavery terms but as marital and family terms. "Free" is a prepositional term. One is "free *from*" something or someone.

"Will (*boule*)" means "to traject," "to toss," "to aim," hence "ballistics," are the measurement of the toss. All such terminologies I will cover later in this anatomy of the will. Ballistics, volley, volition, etc. *Boulomai* (*boule*) are strong terms that underline the predetermined (and determined) intention driving the planning, wishing, and/or resolving. While *thelos* (as "will")[5] means desire, wishfulness, etc., esp. within the intent to make an offer. Culturally speaking, the Greeks called this, "*thelo*-offers" which could be rejected. While *boule* or *boulemai* always works out his

---

and Paul's addressment to nomos give rise to the question: if one's *nomos* is equivocal (questionable/ambiguous) how can a democracy exist? By what ontic referent ("being of reference") do we hold to in order to be a society? If we are all our own *nomoi* we do indeed violate each other in our ambiguities as seen in our modern culture without an ontic referent. Therefore, only a holy (Greek: *holos*: "unmixed") God can hold nomos. This forces *nomos* out of our ambiguous natures' grasps. Again, you can't be your own government and apply it to others (as all of us are doing presently). Later, nomos took a juridical sense alone as we find in Aeshylus's *Prometheus Bound*, 150 f, Soph. Oed. Tyr., 865, Pindar. Fr. 169. Only in the fifth cent. BC did *nomos* come to be written down in individual *nomoi*. And here, does this word acquire, in the context of democratic development, the special sense of a "written law." Biblically speaking, *nomos* primarily refers to the Old Testament law which is immovable. That is, God's *nomos* is a reference point to begin theological reasoning. Paul's Asian (Asia Minor/Turkey present day) conclusions made in his epistles (cf. Romans 2:13) "Doers of" the law (*nomos*) link God's own attitude towards man with that of man towards the law. It is precisely at this point that the new message begins, not with criticism of the *nomos* (law) according to its statutes but the hope based on the law by grace. Finally, this is why I conclude that Jesus' ministry was to denounce the illusion of trying to hold on to the keeping of the Torah (law) which only Jesus could fulfill. His fulfillments in word and deed cleared the path for the new ministry of grace that required the absolute fulfillment of the law. Damnation to the law was by Jesus, and the grace that endlessly abounds poignantly started at Jesus' resurrection. Jesus is the point on the timeline of life where meaning can find its roots and its future.

5. *Thel-o* or *thel'-o* in certain tenses we see *thel-eh'-o*, and *etheleo eth-el-eh'-o*, which are otherwise obsolete, are apparently strengthened from the alternate form of *haireomai* ("to take for oneself" –this is an obsolete term); to determine as an active option from subjective impulse; where *boulomai* properly denotes a passive acquiescence in objective considerations. I.e., "to be inclined to" or in the Hebraistic sense: "to delight in," "rather have," "intend," "disposed to," etc. All such inclinations of *boulomai* listed in this paragraph are considering man's *boulomai* and not God's

purpose, especially in conjunction with pre-setting the physical scenes of history.

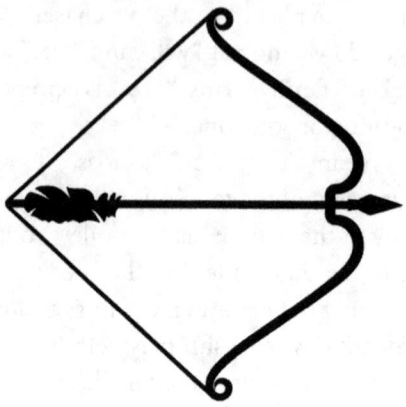

Chapter Twenty-Two

The Fourth Noble Truth: The Prophetic View

(FORETELLING, FOREBODING, DECLARATION, AND PROPHETICAL COMPARATIVE FORMS)

As we have considered the *teleological* view[1], we must now reflect on the utterances[2] of the prophets. Their words hold the validity by which they are revealed in future time, not only by biblical history but secular history and the combination of both. This means that at least from the time a prophet spoke[3] until his or her fulfillment came to pass everything would have had to have been in perfect order to bring about the prophecies's teleology. Thus, prophecy presupposes what we have called predeterminism and teleology.

A "foretelling (*pro-lego*)" of the future is not always understood to be "prophecy." A prophetic "declaration" is another story. In other words, a prophet (Hebrew: *Ne'evi* – "seer"/"prophet") doesn't always "see" the future as a "shared glimpse" —though this most definitely can be the case, hence their name, "seers" or *ne'evim*.

---

1. the explanation of the "ordered system" by which we get "the full summation" of the thing, i.e., the "why."
2. *rhema* – (*rhe-*) "to utter"; "to speak."
3. That "time" that the prophet spoke was indeed "in time." The set up for this time revealed moment, however, must have been contained in the eternal Intent of the Intender. Therefore, prophecy is only a "relay" of something eternally approved, hence, predetermined.

Another kind of "prophecy" – profession:

Many prophets declare *epaggelomai* [4] God's word without question and without praise without sight into the future. In a sense, these are the most noble of the prophets for they share no glory, no satisfaction of seeing the future, etc. as God's chosen mouths to speak. They are alone speaking rhema (utterances) that many consider to be socially insane. In one sense, the prophetic declaration was a "time of suspension" of admonishment for this time, our time, in this world, and the future by which the rhema/utterance of God through his prophets would establish the sustainability of scripture. Furthermore, such prophetic declarations made by the Old Testament prophets made it recognizable as to who Jesus was and why he was here. Jesus' words and deeds could be tied in now. Attributed to the prophet's declarations, Jesus had a social footing by which he could fulfil his Messianic roles. Such a declaration might be likened to the word of God found in Jesus' prophetic declarations concerning his own teleology on earth. I see the value in "prophetic declaration/epaggelomai" still being that which God fulfills without the cognizance of the prophet. This might be one of the greatest expressions of Sovereignty on earth!

As Jesus uttered[5] judgment to his disciples, followers, Pharisees, etc., his "judgments" did not convey a blanket-universal damnation, rather, the "dominion" – a.k.a. the "doom" or "domicile" of the Father by which he shall inherit as the God of grace. As Jesus spoke his Father's eternal truths (for all godly truths are eternal) on earth, he was calling his children to obey while "categorizing" the rest to hark to his words (*rhema*) for there are no other words of salvation from this already condemned world. He spoke as the master of the new kingdom for whom all of his family should take heed –i.e., as a son or daughter "takes heed" to the dominion/house-rule(s) of the father who is the head (archon).

---

4. *epaggelomai*— [sounds like: ep-ang-ge'-lo-mai] literally, "upon a message/a message upon"— idiomatic: say a word/words.

5. utter: "out of," "Middle Dutch – *uteren* – "to turn out," from *uter* = "outer"; — i.e., "to emit/to come out from" — "speak out." Looking at the source by which the "utterance" comes out, I believe that Jesus' "utterances" were relational to the Father, Spirit, and fallen man. Therefore, Jesus' words, being that they were "uttered" from Him, were not limited in their scope, though, humankind's "utterances" are Predestined.

The layering method for the prophetic view

This particular example of the prophetic view[6] consists of only layering three prophets. One of the prophets is considered "pagan," which I refer to in the "a-moral" sense. The other two prophets are "messianic Jews" in the truest sense of that title. All three prophets share a portion of Jesus' character sketch[7].

As I see it, the two messianic prophets[8] that lived before Jesus the Messiah had a specific role. Unlike the Sybil of Cumae (Virgil 70 BC), the messianic prophets were to thread prophecy with the law using prophetic-poetics[9] as the suture.

---

6. I.e., 4 of the Five Noble Truths. The other 4 are: the teleological view, pre-determinative view, apocalyptic view, and universal restorative view (i.e. *apokatastasis/ apokatakaleo*).

7. It is claimed by the Oxford Doyen Dr. Alfred Edersheim that there are at least 456 prophecies from the Old Testament that were fulfilled in Christ Jesus alone. If this is true then the collage" sketch of Christ's life would be more than ample evidence to claim Jesus as the Messiah: "Their (the ancient synagogue) number amounts to upwards of 456 (75 from the Pentateuch, 243 from the prophets, and 138 from the Hagiographa), and their messianic application is supported by more than 558 references to the most ancient rabbinic writings." Edersheim, *Life and Times of Jesus The Messiah*, 2:163.

8. There are, of course, so many prophetic visions that I did not pick. So many of these prophecies bear precision with calendrical accuracy: McClain, "Daniel's Prophecy of the 70 Weeks or *Shavua*," esp. graph on 68 and 69; Machen, "Virgin Birth Of Christ"; Hughes, "Star Of Bethlehem" —an astronomer's confirmation, 50–84; Molnar, "Star of Bethlehem" —the legacy of the Magi; Hoehner, "Chronological Aspects Of The Life Of Christ"; Ladd, "Blessed Hope"; Jones, "Christ of the Zodiac," audio category, "The Vanderbilt Lectures," Lectures 5–10.

9. The Book of Revelation is a "Gospel culmination" of law, prophecy, allusion, allegory, *poetics*, etc.; Koester, *Revelation*, esp. 73: "the glass sea" as the motif within the Canaanite sea god & its religion – Yam – "sea" which plays an important role in Ugaritic Epic poetry (Ford 1975). The possible sharing of symbolism might come into play without insult to the validity of Jewish to Christian symbolism. Such is the case as the Bronze Sea in Solomon's temple: 1 Kings 7:23–26. Dr. Albright, in his *Archaeology and the Religion of Israel*, 148–50 shows the Brazen Sea as a cosmic significance. The word *yam* is similar to the Mesopotamian word "apsu" in meaning which refers to both the fresh water and/or ocean from which all life and all fertility were derived: and to a basin of holy water in the temple. The author of this part of Revelation, because of his interest in liturgy, may have been thinking not only of Solomon's temple but also of the significance of blue in the priestly vestments (Thavapalan 2019); The fresh blue ocean waters are relatable to the Sumerian word *GIN*, the Akkadian *ZAGINNU*, Hittite *KU(wa)NNASH*, Ugaritic *IQNU*, Greek *KUANEOS* —which all relate to the color of lapis lazuli — as we see "the pavement" as lapis lazuli under God's feet in heaven - cf. Exodus 24:9–11.

"The world was not created but only for the Messiah" – Sanhedrin 98 b

"All the prophets prophesied not but of the days of the Messiah" –Sanhedrin 99[10]

Example of layering the prophetic view:

First Prophecy

King David was not just a warrior king but a prophetic voice/medium through which Jesus spoke ca.1,100 years before Jesus walked the earth. Let's take a look at this poetic prophecy in the book of Psalms.

> Psalm 22:13–21 (ca. 1100 BC)
>
> "They gaped upon me with their mouths, as a ravening and roaring lion. (14) I am poured out like water, and all my bones are out of joint; my heart is like wax; it is melted in the midst of my bowels. (15) My strength is dried up like a potsherd; and my tongue cleaveth to my jaws; and thou hast brought me into the dust of death. (16) For dogs have compassed me; the assembly of the wicked have enclosed me; they pierced my hands and my feet. (17) I may tell (Hebrew: *a-sap-per* – "I can count") all my bones; they look and stare upon me. (18) They part my garments among them, and cast lots upon my vesture. (19) But be not thou far from me, O LORD; O my strength haste thee to help me. (20) Deliver my soul from the sword; my darling from the power of the dog. (21) Save me from the lion's mouth; for thou hast heard me from the horns of the unicorns (Hebrew: *qeren* – sharp tooth/teeth within the jaws of a strong beast or horn(s) of a wild beast).

Second Prophecy

The second "prophet[11]" or "prophetess" was amongst the oracles of the Roman Sibyls of Cumae in the early sixth century BC. She has been

---

10. Edersheim, *Life and Times of Jesus the Messiah*, 1.

11. The root of *Nabi* (*Ne'evi*) is *Naba*, meaning, "to bubble forth" like a fountain; *Strong's Concordance* #1301 – NB "flourish, fruit, prophecy, seed inside"; NBB = "hollow" as a container to hold something; NBA = "prophecy [as inside a man not being known of the 5 senses]; N-BYA = "one who brings forth the inner fruit" —cf.

mentioned as the particular crone[12] of notoriety amidst a Greek colonial assembly near Naples, Italy. It was to her that most give credit to 9 initial oracles. There was a particular oracle amongst the remaining three (6 having been burnt by king Tarqin until his belief in her as a true "seer") that Virgil recounts in his work, *Georgics*.[13] This *heathen prophecy* (I use in the a-moral sense) shares with Deutero-Isaiah within a similar time frame in which the Jew's had their three deportations into Babylon (ca. 586 BC). It seems that there were other messianic allusions already in existence at this time but the Sibylline accuracy of the oracle that was loaned into Virgil's hope mentioned in his Georgics supported the prophetic foresight of Deutero Isaiah's prophecy in Isaiah 53:1–12. Such pagan and believing voices rang in exaltation, a *harmony* which arrested my attention, intellect, and heart. With high precision from three very distinct personages, religions, and locations, one can see that Jesus the messiah's life, crucifixion, and resurrection were on prophetic point as the Gospels exhibited their fulfillments.

> Virgil, the pagan poet (ca. 70 – 60 BC)
>
> "Now is come the last age of Cumaean song; the great line of the centuries begins anew. Now the VIRGIN returns, the reign of Saturn (Saturn meaning: renewal, dissolution, abundance, liberation) returns; now a new generation descends from heaven on high. Only do you, pure Lucina (the moon and her gestation period to birth), smile on the BIRTH OF THE CHILD under Whom the Iron Brood (Rome's use of iron smithing for weapons) shall at last cease and a golden race spring up throughout the world! Your own Apollo (Son of Zeus) now is King!"[14])

Strong'sConcordance # 5029 and #5030 and *Brown-Driver-Briggs Hebrew and English Lexicon*, 611 and 612 – #5030. The emphasis of this word and its variants starts with the earliest forms of pictographic Hebrew which phonemes were represented by pictures. Such evidenced inscriptions can be found at Wadi El-Hhol and Serabit El-Khadim in the Sinai Peninsula, dating back to around 2000 BC Cf. Quaknin, "Mysteries of the Alphabet."

12. Crone: Anglo-French: *carogne* – "an insult;" French: *charogne* – "a disagreeable woman."

13. Virgil, *Georgics*.

14. Virgil, «Eclogue 4,» in *Eclogues*. Also cf. Isodore, "Etymologiae" (cont. from above) viii.8.5; Servius, In Aeneida vi.72, 321; Lactantius, Divinae Institutiones i.6.10–11; Solinus, Collectanea rerum memorabilium ii.16, 17, 18.

Third Prophecy

Deutero Isaiah 53 (ca 538 BC)[15]

מִי הֶאֱמִין לִשְׁמֻעָתֵנוּ וּזְרוֹעַ יְהוָה עַל־מִי נִגְלָתָה׃

"Who can believe what we have heard?
Upon whom has the arm of GOD been revealed?

וַיַּעַל כַּיּוֹנֵק לְפָנָיו וְכַשֹּׁרֶשׁ מֵאֶרֶץ צִיָּה לֹא־תֹאַר לוֹ וְלֹא הָדָר וְנִרְאֵהוּ וְלֹא־מַרְאֶה וְנֶחְמְדֵהוּ׃

For He has grown, by God's favor, like a tree crown,
Like a tree trunk out of arid ground.
He had no form or beauty, that we should look at Him:
No charm, that we should find Him pleasing.

נִבְזֶה וַחֲדַל אִישִׁים אִישׁ מַכְאֹבוֹת וִידוּעַ חֹלִי וּכְמַסְתֵּר פָּנִים מִמֶּנּוּ נִבְזֶה וְלֹא חֲשַׁבְנֻהוּ׃

He was despised, shunned by others,
A man of suffering, familiar with disease.
As one who hid His face from us,
He was despised, we held Him of no account.

אָכֵן חֳלָיֵנוּ הוּא נָשָׂא וּמַכְאֹבֵינוּ סְבָלָם וַאֲנַחְנוּ חֲשַׁבְנֻהוּ נָגוּעַ מֻכֵּה אֱלֹהִים וּמְעֻנֶּה׃

Yet it was our sickness that He was bearing,
Our suffering that He endured.
We accounted Him plagued,
Smitten and afflicted by God;

וְהוּא מְחֹלָל מִפְּשָׁעֵנוּ מְדֻכָּא מֵעֲוֺנֹתֵינוּ מוּסַר שְׁלוֹמֵנוּ עָלָיו וּבַחֲבֻרָתוֹ נִרְפָּא־לָנוּ׃

But He was wounded because of our sins,
Crushed because of our iniquities.
He bore the chastisement that made us whole,
And by His bruises we were healed.

כֻּלָּנוּ כַּצֹּאן תָּעִינוּ אִישׁ לְדַרְכּוֹ פָּנִינוּ וַיהוָה הִפְגִּיעַ בּוֹ אֵת עֲוֺן כֻּלָּנוּ׃

We all went astray like sheep,
Each of us going our own way;

---

15. Still debated in certain circles, many scholars suggest a later date than what they would consider the second prophet and evangelist known as Deutero-Isaiah (*secundus propheta et evangelista Esaias*). This beloved prophet, distinguished from the first Isaiah, was to be set in the Babylonian exile, ca. 538 BC These "*argued*" dates still give us at least ca. 560 years before Jesus fulfilled Deutero-Isaiah's "Christ-Character" sketch. My argument stands that the proto-Isaiah was a different prophet than the second Isaiah and not a historical blunder of scripture but a validation of two different authoritative prophets who bore the same shem or "authoritative title-name." I conclude that two distinct prophets under one salvific God bearing the *shem* "Isaiah (Hebrew)": "Yeshayahu" → "Salvation of the Lord." A treasure trove for this topic can be found in Keil & Delitzsch, *Commentary on the Old Testament*, 7:38-42.

And GOD put upon Him
The guilt of all of us."

נִגַּשׂ וְהוּא נַעֲנֶה וְלֹא יִפְתַּח־פִּיו כַּשֶּׂה לַטֶּבַח יוּבָל וּכְרָחֵל לִפְנֵי גֹזְזֶיהָ נֶאֱלָמָה וְלֹא יִפְתַּח פִּיו׃

He was maltreated, yet He was submissive,
He did not open His mouth;
Like a sheep being led to slaughter,
Like an ewe, dumb before those who shear her,
He did not open His mouth.

מֵעֹצֶר וּמִמִּשְׁפָּט לֻקָּח וְאֶת־דּוֹרוֹ מִי יְשׂוֹחֵחַ כִּי נִגְזַר מֵאֶרֶץ חַיִּים מִפֶּשַׁע עַמִּי נֶגַע לָמוֹ׃

By oppressive judgment He was taken away,
Who could describe His abode?
For He was cut off from the land of the living
Through the sin of my people, who deserved the punishment.

וַיִּתֵּן אֶת־רְשָׁעִים קִבְרוֹ וְאֶת־עָשִׁיר בְּמֹתָיו עַל לֹא־חָמָס עָשָׂה וְלֹא מִרְמָה בְּפִיו׃

And His grave was set among the wicked,
And with the rich, in His death—
Though He had done no injustice
And had spoken no falsehood.

וַיהוָה חָפֵץ דַּכְּאוֹ הֶחֱלִי אִם־תָּשִׂים אָשָׁם נַפְשׁוֹ יִרְאֶה זֶרַע יַאֲרִיךְ יָמִים וְחֵפֶץ יְהוָה בְּיָדוֹ יִצְלָח׃

But GOD chose to crush Him,
That, if He made Himself an offering for guilt,
He might see offspring and have long life,
And that through Him GOD's purpose might prosper.

מֵעֲמַל נַפְשׁוֹ יִרְאֶה יִשְׂבָּע בְּדַעְתּוֹ יַצְדִּיק צַדִּיק עַבְדִּי לָרַבִּים וַעֲוֹנֹתָם הוּא יִסְבֹּל׃

Out of his anguish He shall see it;
He shall enjoy it to the full through his devotion.
"My righteous servant makes the many righteous,
It is their punishment that He bears;

לָכֵן אֲחַלֶּק־לוֹ בָרַבִּים וְאֶת־עֲצוּמִים יְחַלֵּק שָׁלָל תַּחַת אֲשֶׁר הֶעֱרָה לַמָּוֶת נַפְשׁוֹ וְאֶת־פֹּשְׁעִים נִמְנָה וְהוּא חֵטְא־רַבִּים נָשָׂא וְלַפֹּשְׁעִים יַפְגִּיעַ׃ (פ)

Assuredly, I will give Him the many as His portion,
He shall receive the multitude as His spoil.
For He exposed Himself to death
And was numbered among the sinners,
Whereas He bore the guilt of the many
And made intercession for sinners."[16]

---

16. As a note to this last passage of Isaiah: I don't remember human sacrifice was sanctioned through the prophets to "save." If the passages are to be of the authorship

Why did I list these three prophets?

God does not discriminate against his own voice, a.k.a., his own prophets

I picked three distinct prophets (seen above) who were removed by time, and for one, their culture. I presented these distinct characters to show that God is not limited by who we think someone is, especially the pagan prophetess at Cumae. As we arrive at chapter 22 in this book concerning prophets, professing, prophesying, seeing, visions, etc., we will come to understand that there are many kinds of "prophecies" and many kinds of "prophets." Some are simply bold sayings of someone who sees sin to be repented of, whether it be their own sin or the sins of a select group. However, isn't it possible that God was behind these "simple bold sayings" all along?

As we shall see in this book nothing is outside the "fullness of meaning" which is orchestrated by God. Other prophecies are poetical visions ladened with ordained judgments holding both warning and recompense. Many times, higher prophecies of this nature call upon prophetic literary devices such as prophetic poetics that deal with events seen as forms and shapes of time, i.e., correlations of "sin unto repentance" as one shape containing many moving pictures. Through the medium of intentional anachronism, we can feel in the high prophetic style a sense of euphony–the musicality of poetical flow with all of its blissful sentiments.

Some of the prophets, such as King David and his son, Solomon, brought us a euphoric musical style (euphony) which was reality based, yet above reality at the same time. Such euphony can be experienced in the prophetic cantos of David's psalms. David's poetical peaks are laden with a combination of supreme agony and supra-a-sexual dispositions which are found in David's words paralleling what Jesus spoke to his Father in Psalms 22:20: "Deliver my soul from the sword; my darling from the power of the dog."

Poetics, without the need for calling them "prophetic (for they simply are prophetic)," can be found in David's son, Solomon.

Let's read Solomon's Song of Songs 1:1

---

of Isaiah, the Jews could not argue against this. Also, the Septuagint had this same prophecy translated to Greek by 200 BC! This means that for any nay-sayer the LXX or Septuagint gives the authority for an earlier prophecy than the event of the Messiah's appearance on earth by at least 200 years prior.

THE FOURTH NOBLE TRUTH

> "Let Him kiss me with His mouth's kisses! Truly, sweeter is your love than wine, Than the smell of your precious oil. Turaq oil is your name. Therefore the girls love You. Draw me after You, let us run! The King brought me to His chambers. We will exalt You and joy in You. We will savor your love above wine. Rightly do they love You."

Other[17] prophetic devices involve *irony* implying a distance between what is said in the corporeal world and what is meant in the metaphysical sense. Irony can be garnered within the context of the prophet's scenario, situation, and figuration of apocalyptic application. Many times, irony is wrapped within euphony, arresting the senses while introducing the sublime. I am in awe of such speech patterns for these were just a few of the prophetic mechanisms by which the prophets used. Through prophet, word, and sometimes "deed," as in prophetic pantomiming, heaven and earth met.

Prophecies that did not fail will always continue unto the eternal sense of total meaning because they are from the eternal being in his eternal abode. That is to say, prophecy thrusts itself back to where it came from, that is, the eternal. Therefore, what greater poetry is there than the eternal poetics of the *Ne'evim* or prophets[18]?!

---

17. A somewhat similar secular poetic style using intentional anachronism might be found in James Joyce's Finnigan's Wake. Though not scriptural, James Joyce's *modus operandi* of writing *Finnigan's Wake* could be compared to John the Revelator writing in his apocalypse. In my mid-twenties I dove into the dream space of Joyce's use of semiotics and dream-speak or "out of time speak" (Campbell, *On James Joyce*; Tindall, *Reader's Guide*). Professor William Tindal quotes James Joyce concerning *Finnegans Wake*: "is about anybody, anywhere, anytime.", or, as Joyce puts it (5981.1) "about every those personal place objects…where soevers (Tindall, *Reader's Guide*, 3])." I bracketed supporting historical and geographical points to show Joyce's references (McHugh, *Annotations*). Such nonlinear sentences from the beginning of his book go as follows: "riverrun, past Eve and Adam's (i.e., beside the river Liffey by a tavern site of the same name and present day shopping center), from swerve of shore to bend of bay (Dublin Bay), brings us by a commodius (Roman Emperor) vicus (i.e., Vico road, Dalkey [see Dalkey Island]/also, a "vicious circle"→ travelling around the island's course with reefs, funneling winds, strong currents, wind over tide conditions, etc.) of recirculation back to Howth Castle (The legendary Sir Tristram, i.e., Malory's Sir Tristram of Howth Castle), and Environs" (Joyce, *Finnegans Wake*) begins the Joyce tome central to Dublin, Ireland. Through Joyce's literary-poetic mechanisms one is allowed to experience several stories/events at the same "eternal" or "a-tempo" "time." Joyce's mastery of languages and history were used to convey the history of man, his fall, Joyce's diatribe against Catholicism, aspects of the Irish funerary wake from its Druidic origins, etc. drawing many timeless points together into one book. To say you get a college education from *Finnegan's Wake* is far reaching but it offers a lifetime of analysis, if you so choose.

18. Other mentionings of prophets, poetical literary devices, anachronism, allusion,

The revered and feared prophets' office was to bring about the inevitable. For sure, they brought "judgment" as was ordained by YHVH. But "judgment" was only the schoolmaster's whip to guide the children of Israel not only in line but to make them recognize the whip was not a sustainable option, therefore, there must be a better way. The prophets presented something far past the whip for children of Israel. They presented a hope past the sting of the whip when the objective "keeping" of legalities of the children of Israel were found wanting. To say that one "kept the law" was a sham. The prophets declared a "hope" of grace above the condemnatory law that would show the law's "failure to acclimate" when compared to our growing relationship with God, becoming more like him in his image (Romans 8:29-31).

The law was at a crux when the messianic prophets came and more than that: when the Messiah came. The believing Jew (who lived among the prophets/*Nevi'im*) held that to reject the prophets would be to reject God's mouth, law, *dabar*, word, etc. The law indicated its own death when held in the face of a messianic hope which forgave sins condemnable by the law.

The Importance of the Law within Prophecy

The prophets were using the law to traject hope, hence, a correlative failure for the law to continue to condemn. The prophets never dismissed the law/Torah (Schurer 1890). The law, in a sense, was the rear sight aperture by which "the aim" was rooted. Though, it had no "leading directive" or frontal sight. What was the law "aiming for?" The prophets were the ones who "aligned" these two sights.

As Jesus said in Matthew 5:17–18: "Think not that I am come to destroy the law, or the prophets" I am not come to destroy, but to fulfill. For verily I say unto you, Till heaven and earth pass, one jot or one tittle (of the law) shall in no wise pass from the law, till all be fulfilled." It is in his grace and his grace by the law that "all in all should be subjected to Christ and submitted back to the Father in Christ (1 Corinthians 15:20–28)."

Imagine a "place" or existence of eternal kindness, treating others as you would have them treat you. Is this not the eternal grace we all seek on earth? The law of the Jews, as used as a device within the poesis of the

---

allegory, etc. can be found in Koester, *Revelation*; Ford, *Revelation*; Pope, *Song of Songs*; Strong and McClintock, *Cyclopedia of Biblical, Theological, and Ecclesiastical Literature*, vol. 8, Pe-Re.

prophets, became allegorical. Not just the prophets but the epistles are filled with mentionings of the law in order to understand grace. Without the law, grace could not be fully understood. In Romans 6:6, Paul says: "Knowing this, that our old man is crucified with Him, that the body of sin might be destroyed, that henceforth we should not serve sin. (7) For he that is dead is freed from sin." This will be one of many passages in scripture that will show that the old man, our old sinful being, who we were naturally is damned but we are saved. See Ephesians 2:1–22 concerning our "old damnable selves that were saved by grace, and not of ourselves or of the law that damned."

The Process from Law, to Prophet, to Jesus

One could call this section "a necessary process" or "evolution of understanding"[19] by which objective thinking (i.e. The Torah) moves forward into the abstract world of prophetic poetics.[20] Then, with a forward march, we move into the objective again but with a twist; the objective is also purely eternal in word and deed. Jesus is the "form" by which we observe eternity in motion in our limited time which creates the ultimate paradox. It was Jesus' messages that baffled even that of Plato's standard of the eternal form as the unalterable.[21] For he, Jesus, abides in the (1) eternal form of divine time (immovable/inalterable), (2) physical time or divisible time (day, night, hour, minute, sec.), and (3) psychological forms of time (past, present, future). All of Jesus' "abodes" would have baffled Plato's "eternal form" and "divisible" time in that Jesus, bearing eternity, participated within time's moving pictures (or "slices" or "divisions") that represent "portions" of eternity.

Lastly

In Revelation 13:8 the Bible makes a proclamation that Jesus was "the Lamb slain from (*apo* – off/of) the foundation of the world." What does that mean for all of the events that would have had to have taken place at creation and throughout its history until the very location, time, situation, reason, etc., for Jesus' crucifixion (and resurrection)? By way of

---

19. Barfield, *Poetic Diction*.
20. Koester, *Revelation*; Ford, *Revelation*.
21. Plato, *Timaeus* 38.

illustration, let us consider all things would need to be in place in just the right way, long in advance of Jesus' ministry, if Jesus was to be the "Lamb slain *from* the foundation of the world."

Calendarists such as Drs. Harold W. Hoehner, Alva J. McClain, and George Eldon Ladd have taken tremendous care to account for special feast days, times, locations, leap years, etc., in order to show us that in Daniel 9:25-27. "going forth to rebuild Jerusalem until the Messiah would be 483 years (69 *Shavua*)[22].

Nehemiah 2:1-8 tells us of the blessing of Artaxerxes to the Jews (Judah/Southern Israel) as he established a decree in Nissan 1st 444 BC (March 5 due to the new crescent moon would have shown itself at ca. 10 p.m.) to support the Jews in agreement what Daniel professed.

In 2 Chronicles 36:21[23] we read of the account of the "sabbaths" or "*shavua*'[24] that were not observed by ancient Judah (Southern Israel). While Ephraim (Northern Israel) had already been deported and been sent away by the Assyrians in 722 BC due to Asherah-fertility goddess worship the southern Jews (Judah) followed in the same religious syncretism. Judah, unlike Ephraim, remained an entity by which prophetic timelines could be made. The prophecy of Ezekiel 37 portents Ephraim and Judah becoming "one stick" at the end of days. Such a "one stick" is Israel. This, of course, happened in 1948.

A *shavua* is an agricultural term for a group of six years tilling, sowing, seeding, and reaping of the crops of one's designated field for cultivation. In the seventh year one is to not till, sow, seed. and reap for biological fact that the nutrients of the field for cultivation be robbed and no more cultivation could occur. The passage concerning the *shavua*s which were not observed goes as follows: "To fulfill the word of the LORD by the mouth of Jeremiah, until the land had enjoyed her "sabbaths," for as long as she lay desolate she kept sabbath, to fulfill three score and ten years [i.e., Judah's seventy years of not keeping the *Shavua*]" (2 Chr 36:21).

---

22. There are various arguments to when Daniel wrote this prophecy. Some say 535 BC, some say 164 BC. One thing for sure is the Messiah came into Jerusalem on the very day that the prophecy said He would. Most importantly, Jesus' entrance was either ca 194 years after Daniel or ca 565 years after the older view of Daniel's writing. My point: Jesus had not "materialized" yet which makes Daniel's prophecy verifiable.

23. The Thompson Chain Reference Bible gives us a date of ca. 610 BC.

24. One interesting point to be made: Sabbath, *Shabboa, Shabbath, Sabbat, Shavua* and even the famous Queen Sheba connote "completion, final, fulfillment of trials, sealed to the fullness, etc."

This last passage in 2 Chronicles 36:21 is multiplied by "seven." In Daniel 9:24 we see it as the final judgment upon Judah and the world that share in the last seven years of this 490–year schemata laid out by God's providential hand.

"Seventy Shavua [seven-year periods = "agricultural weeks'] are determined upon your people and upon your Holy City, to finish the transgressions, and to make an end of sins, and to make reconciliation for iniquity, and to bring everlasting righteousness, and to seal up the vision and prophecy, and to anoint the most Holy." (Dan 9:24).

At what "era" has transgressions "finished." What era has "sin ended"? What era do we find our "reconciliation for iniquity"? What point in this or another *aeon* or era is "everlasting righteousness" a thing? Where in Revelation does it speak of the "sealing up of the vision and prophecy"? Finally, when does the "most holy anointed" appear?

Daniel 9:24 thus speaks of prophecy and the *teleology* of the Bible, that is, the summit of meaning from creation where the lamb was slain for the fullness of the narrative, to the unfurling of the entire "tree of meaning." Prior "events" must be sutured to future "events" in order to have teleological meaning. This hints that our new earth and new heaven (Isa 65:17; 2 Pet 3:13) might be a "conclusion of meaning" to the prior world that we live in now. Not that we will remember this world as it is in time but maybe essence. Revelation 3:7 makes it clear that the entire world will be suffering during this time but that *we* will bear the sufferings that calibrate us to Christ's image. Once experienced, there will be no more tears. Pain and suffering will cease in part because we will need no more "signals" to point us in the direction of God... for we are already there.

But we must return to Hebraic Old Testament prophecy in order to rectify Revelation's first-century Christian figurations of literal fulfillment. Using the moon as the *mene* or "counter" reference for the Jews, 360 days would comprise a year. Multiplying sixty-nine *shavua* ("weeks") or sixty-nine groups of seven years ("weeks'—i.e., with a sabbatical year as the last year of the seven years, or week) gives us 173,880 days = "69 sevens (*Shavua*) = 483 years (if using the moon as "the counter of days—i.e. 360-day years).

The decree was established decades prior by Cyrus to protect the Jews who wanted to go back into Jerusalem and re-establish their worship site. Daniel 9:24–27 had given a decree that sixty-nine *shavua* (sabbatical "years," i.e., seven years, or groups of seven years) or sevens (= 483 years) would be the exact time element until Messiah rode a donkey into Jerusalem as Hosanna.

In ca. 538 BC we find the prophecy of Daniel 9:24-27 as follows:

> Daniel 9:24: "Seventy weeks[25] are determined upon thy people and upon thy holy city, to finish the transgression, and to make an end of sins, and to make reconciliation for iniquity, and to bring in everlasting righteousness, and to seal up the vision and prophecy, and to anoint the most Holy. (Daniel 9:25) Know therefore and understand, that from the going forth of the commandment to restore and to build Jerusalem unto the Messiah the Prince, shall be seven *shavua*,[26] and threescore [sixty] and two weeks:[27] the street shall be built again, and the wall, even in troubled times. (Daniel 9:26) And after threescore and two weeks shall Messiah be cut off, but not for himself: and the people of the prince that shall come shall destroy the city and the sanctuary; and the end thereof shall be with a flood, and unto the end of the war desolations are determined. (Daniel 9:27) And he shall confirm with many the covenant for one week:[28] and in the middle of the seven-year period [*shavua*: "week"] he shall cause the sacrifice and the oblation to cease, and for the overspreading of abominations he shall make it desolate, even until the consummation, and that determined shall be poured upon the desolate."

It was in the era of Achaemenid Persian rule that Cyrus had given his decree in 539 BC and later picked up and enforced by Nehemiah in 444 BC[29] protecting any Jew wanting to go back and re-establish their worship site in Jerusalem.

Looking at the prophetic view we can see the following: It wasn't until 586 BC that three deportations of Judah took place—putting Judah into Babylonian captivity.

Going to secular sources one can find tremendous resources concerning Cyrus' decree to restore Jerusalem in Cyrus' day to Judah.[30] We

---

25. Here we have "weeks" to be understood as *groups of seven years*, i.e., "weeks" = Hebrew *shavua* = seven years with last year not tilling the ground.

26. Here "weeks" = groups of seven years.

27. Or *shavua* = groups of seven years.

28. Seven years.

29. cf. Ezra 1:1-2; 4:1-5, 11-24; 6:1-5, 14-15; 7:11, 20, and 27.

30. One such place online is the Associates for Biblical Research under "The Daniel 9:24–27 Project" (subtitled: "The Framework for Messianic Chronology").

know the Cyrus decree was in 539 BC as we have the timeframe in Nehemiah 2:1–8. Daniel's prophecy of the period from the beginning of Nehemiah's decree until the Messiah specifies 483 years (or sixty-nine *shavua*).

Isaiah 45:1–4

> (1) "Thus saith the LORD to his anointed, Cyrus, "whose right hand I have holden [held], to subdue nations before him; and I will loose the loins of kings, to open before him the two leaved gates; and the gates shall not be shut. (2) I will go before thee, and make the crooked places straight; I will break in pieces the gates of brass, and cut in sunder the bars of iron: (3) And I will give thee the treasures of darkness, and hidden riches of secret places, that thou mayest know that I, the LORD, which call thee by name, am the God of Israel. (4) For Jacob my servant's sake, and Israel mine elect, I have even called thee by thy name: I have surnamed thee, (though) thou hast not known me.

What does this tell us about rectification before repentance? God had already written "the way" by which Judah would be restored, especially, in prophetic/teleological meaning such as the restoration of Israel in 1948. Salvation was appointed unto the pagan Persian king, Cyrus. Cyrus was called "God's anointed." By name, Cyrus would fulfill the *exact* role by which God spoke. He would be God's arm in aiding the Jews to rebuild Jerusalem's temple. This is prophecy, teleology, and predeterminism.

Daniel said that from the time of Cyrus" decree until the Messiah would be sixty-nine *shavua*. The last *shavua* or seven-year period is the tribulation.

We have that limitation of "thousands" established in Jesus' words. Consider: in Matthew 24:3 Jesus' disciples ask Jesus a two-part question: (1) when will the temple be decimated and (2) when will the sign of your coming? (This understands Jesus as the Son of Man coming in the clouds to gather the elect).

Jesus answers them in Mark 13:2 telling his disciples that these buildings and temple at Jerusalem that are seen before them will not have one stone of itself that is not thrown down. It is interesting that Josephus gives an account of this prophecy that was fulfilled in AD 70 The report of Titus's decimation of this fortified resistance palace/temple (along with Jerusalem) on Tisha B'Av, AD 70 say that Jerusalem and its temple were "burned to the ground." Only the citadel was left standing as a memorial for what Titus did to Jerusalem. The reference seems to be less severe because Jesus is referring to the buildings in front of the disciples. Then, Jesus answered the second part of the question. When will the sign of you in the heavens be? Jesus answers them with talk of an international dismay of special magnificence. Jesus gives the criteria that must happen before he is to come in the heavens by his "sign." False christs, wars, rumors of wars, famines, etc., are just the beginning of sorrows. Jesus says that the gospel *must* be "first be published among all nations." He says in Mark 13:12 that "brother shall betray brother; father shall betray son; and children shall rise up against their parents and shall cause the parents to be put to death."

Then, Jesus instructs us to read Daniel's prophecy (which we have just covered). In Mark 13:20 Jesus says that if the days of this tribulation weren't so short no flesh would survive. But, for the sake of God's beloved he has made this a short duration so that we would understand what is happening. Finally, Jesus tells his audience in Mark 13:24 that in "those days," after that (i.e., this tribulation), where his Christians are on the earth, you will see the sun, moon, and stars not give off their light; they shall "fall." Then the sign of the son of man will be seen coming with great power and glory. Then he shall send his angels to gather his elect. Matthew 24:29–30 compliments Mark's passage with "Immediately after this tribulation[31] you will see the heavens shaken and then you will see the sign of the Son of Man in heaven. In a moment, in the twinkling of an eye, at the last trump: for the trumpet shall sound, and the dead shall be raised incorruptible, and we shall be changed" (1 Cor 15:52). Revelation 10:7 makes it clear that the last (seventh) angel is Christ himself, with his new name (authority/role). At his presence, his parousia (physical presence) is seen as follows: "For the Lord himself shall descend from heaven with a shout, with the voice of the archangel, and with the trump of God: and the dead in Christ shall rise first. Then we who are alive and remain shall be caught up together with them in the clouds, to meet the Lord in the air, and so shall we ever be with the Lord." (1 Thess 4:16–17)

First Corinthians 15:52 qualifies this verse to make clear that it refers to the "*last* trump[32]": "In a moment, in the twinkling of an eye, *at the last trump*; for the trumpet shall sound, and the dead shall be raised incorruptible, and we shall be changed."

---

31. Tribulation—the last *shavua*—the seven years of Revelation's plagues.
32. Trumpet/trump – Greek: *salpis* – "a horned instrument."

From here you can at least read Revelation with the understanding that the "seventh" of anything mentioned will be the last of the seven years.

Again, Revelation is not written in standard western paginated order of sequenced events. It is a Jewish system of writing. The timelines always agree with Daniel's last *shavua* as the last seven years of desolation of abomination, each year within the last *shavua* as providing another angel, vial, trumpet, and plague. The scripture is clear in Matthew 24 and Mark 13 that after the tribulation (the last *shavua*) we shall have our reconciliation. "The thousand-year reign" is a horrible translation. It is *Xilia* in Revelation 20 and must fit into the start of Christ's birth, ministry, or death and resurrection and end with the end of this *aeon*. For no other time can be as scripture makes it clear that time is no more: "And swared by Him that Liveth for ever and ever, who created heaven, and the things that therein are, and the earth, and the things that therein are, and the sea, and the things which are therein, that there should be time no longer"[33] (Rev 10:6). So, after the tribulation, how can there be more time? There cannot. This means that from Christ to the end of this age, time, orderly arrangement, until tribulation (the last *shavua*), would fit into the two-thousand-year mark. I say this because Israel has become one nation again. Where do I get this? In Matthew 24:32–34 Jesus makes a parable: "(33) Now learn a parable of the fig tree [= Israel]; When his branch is yet tender, and putteth forth leaves, you know that summer is near. (33) So likewise, when you see these things, know that it is near, even at the doors. (34) Verily I say unto you, this generation shall not pass until all these things are fulfilled." Jesus had just been talking about the end of the age/world/creation as we exist in it. His parable was spoken to nail the timeline in the head. Might I add that the word "generation" is used as the lifetime of a man. It was in 1948 that Israel became a nation again. Could we be in that generation?

This is key if we are to understand that it is the last *shavua* that Jesus is referring to. Otherwise, it would be Jesus' ending mission during the early first century. If this is the case, the scripture becomes inconsistent with prophesied world events, not only Jesus' prophecies but the gamut of major and minor prophets. But if Revelation is the Jewish way of telling of the last *shavua* then we have the panorama of events that Daniel refers to as the last seven years of "sifting."

---

33. Some scholars like to interpret this passage as: "your time is up," "the jig is up."

Reading Revelation can be quite a challenge if one doesn't understand that one chapter is qualifying not just the next chapter but all chapters in a kind of dream anachronism. Revelation 2–3 makes it clear that the seven stars are the seven angels of the seven churches of ending judgment and the first and formative churches. These same seven churches are also the seven lampstands. We see in Revelation 1:1–2 and 9–11 the seven churches in Asia Minor (modern-day Turkey) by their names in Revelation: Ephesus, Smyrna, Pergamum, Thyatira, Sardis, Philadelphia, and Laodicea. From these earliest seven churches we read that the past, present, and future world receives the Gospel's judgments/discretions/reprimands/etc. Arguably, these Gospel judgments are to make law and sin meet their final destination in Revelation. Such an example of an "angel" or "evangelist" over these churches would have been Paul. So, one of the "angels" was Paul in Revelation. Some estimate 14 to 20 churches in all of Paul's overseeing (at least jump starting). For sure, other early churches were in Rome, Corinth, Galatia, Philippi, Colossae, and Thessaloniki as is mentioned in Paul's Epistles in the New Testament.

Revelation is "dimensional" in that times, places, and literal Jewish tabernacle practices were fulfilled as abstract-poetical notions. It is rich. The book of Revelation was written in the Jewish style of staggering and sandwiching the timeline of a vision of events. We can "see" John's apocalypse as a collective whole without time as a governor of events. Rather, placements of time are laid out before us. John's apocalypse (revelation) is the longing before the wedding and the birth pangs of a child being born.

Considering the lifting up of the non-Jew/Christian to bring about God's 5NT plan:

How can we as Christians throw out the idea that God has predestined the outcomes of the major events in the scripture that have affected us in the physical world? Given that these major events were prophesied to happen, how can we "conclude" that all other events in world history didn't have to happen the way they did in order for the prophetic outcome to be the perfect way that it was. Contrariwise, many Christians do not believe that "pagan history" was also predestined. Yet here we have a notable pagan, Cyrus, who fulfills the very act to commission salvation to the Jews and the world! Deutero Isaiah 45 and 46 tell us of a God Who ordained, by name, Cyrus, a pagan monarch to free God's people. God said that he, the LORD, "declared the end from the beginning and called Cyrus by his surname before Cyrus was born."

What's my point in telling you all of this? Not one event in history could be out of place if prophecy is to bring about end time events as they are prophesied to happen[34]. This also means that all things must be determined by God and that the end is the meaningful end of God's plan. And, if all of this is true, which scripture tells us to believe that it is, then there is a complete picture set by God before and from the foundation of the world, and that is apocalyptic or fully revealed in in wholesome picture, set by God's intention before anything happened into creation. For a detailed treatment on current events and prophecy please go to "Prophetic View 1."[35]

---

34. This is my argument for the 5NTs that all of their (the 5NTs) methodological implementations "meet" the totality of the gestalt to the end result.

35. Jones, "Prophetic View 1."

Chapter Twenty-Three

The Fifth and Final Noble Truth: Universal Salvation

(THE CORE OF THE FIVE NOBLE TRUTHS)

Here is a list of a few universal salvation verses. When these verses are looked at as a "sandwiching" or "stacking" of thought we can see that God is working through man's ideas of space and time to understand our outcome to be a glorious one.

> Philippians 2:10–11 "That at the name of Jesus every knee should bow, of things in heaven, and things in earth, and things under the earth; (11) And that every tongue should confess that Jesus Christ is Lord, to the glory of God the Father."
>
> Romans 10:9 "That if[1] thou shalt with thy mouth confess the Lord Jesus and shalt believe in thine heart that God hath raised Him from the dead, thou shalt be saved."

---

1. Greek: *ehan* (root: *ean*): "Conditional particle or conjunction. *Ehan* is used to introduce conditional clauses, often translated as "if" or "whenever" in English. It denotes a condition that is possible or hypothetical, which is most likely based on a futurative contingency. My point to addressing this is that some may say "therefore, based on this verse, salvation is contingent upon one's choice." But, when one looks at the verses concerning the universal call to salvation, one sees there is no choice. The emphasis of volition (will from the redeemed or "choice" from that person who is saved) is negated and is shown to be "conditioned" by the surrounding passages that tell us that God will have literally all saved, all shall confess, all shall profess, all shall be subsumed in Christ and given to the Father as covered in Christ's blood, etc. This conditional volition of the flesh always, without fail, chooses damnation based on its nature as seen in Ephesians 2:1–22. It is very important to understand the mechanics of

THE FIFTH AND FINAL NOBLE TRUTH

Romans 14:11 "For it is written, As I live saith the Lord, every knee shall bow to me, and every tongue shall confess to God."

1 John 1:9 "If we confess our sins He is faithful and just to forgive us our sins, and to cleanse us from all unrighteousness."

2 Corinthians 5:15 "He died for everyone so that those who receive His new life (the all [*panta*]) will no longer live for themselves. Instead, they will live for Christ, who died and was raised for them."

1 Timothy 2:3,4 "For this is good and acceptable in the sight of God our Savior:
   Who will have all (*panta* – every/"everyone") to be saved and to come unto the knowledge of the truth."

1 Timothy 4:10 "Who is the Saviour of all (panta) and especially[2] of those who believe."

1 John 2:2 "He is the expiation for our sins, and not ours only but also for the sins of the whole world."

2 Peter 3:9 "The Lord is not slack concerning His promise, as some men count slackness; but is long-suffering to us-ward, not willing that any should perish, but that all should come to repentance."

As we read these verses, we see the hope that God gives us but the desolation that man gives in his natural state. Man "will choose" damnation and will be destroyed as he is known. The hope is fully in the external force of God's choosing us unto salvation.

Universal salvation, being subsumed under predestination, synthesizes the *apokalypsis* (unveiling). In turn, the "full disclosure" or, "the apocalyptic (*apokalypsis*) view," shows us that the final demarcation for the fruition of meaning (*teleos*) will be all nations, tribes and tongues without number (countless) worshiping God at his throne (Revelation 7:9) and all of the kingdoms of the world becoming the kingdom of God and of his Christ (Rev 11:15). If we go to Revelation 21:24 we find that the nations shall walk in the light of Christ's new kingdom. If *all* nations shall become the kingdom of God and his Christ then where is the *exclusion* of salvation to be found in Revelation 21:24? Exclusion from

---

"wills." God's will and man's "nature" or "will." God's goes up and man's goes down. We will receive new bodies that will "will" good one day, 2 Corinthians 5:1–21.

2. this gives a good conscience to the believers and a great hope to the world as the Gospel.

salvation does not exist in this apocalyptic text. Contrary to the exclusion view, universal inclusion of salvation does exist here.

Colossians 1:16–20 makes it clear that *all* things are made for, by, of, to, from God the Son and that he will "restore back to perfection (*apokatakaleo*) all things—reconciling all things unto himself in love." This qualifies universal salvation under the umbrella of full restoration back to himself. In Romans 11:32 Paul says: "Paul has concluded them all [pagans, Jews, us] as being in *unbelief*, that God might have *mercy* on us all." Verses 33–36 proclaim God's never-ending riches are without understanding to the carnal[3] or physical senses. Could we not grasp this better with the understanding that we were ordained to be engrafted into the kingdom of New Jerusalem? In verse 36 Paul says: "For of *him*, and through *him*, and to *him*, are all things: to *whom* be glory for ever." So, it is Paul who speaks logically throughout Romans leading us to the message of the full reconciliation of the Jews who were dead in their sins and the law, with us joining them. Paul makes it clear that the gentile, or once-outside pagan, is us. It is our joy to know that we are engrafted into this saved kingdom of God. We are not necessarily the Middle Eastern-biological Semitic-Jews but Jews of the heart.

Definition:

Universal salvation (*apokatakalleo/apokatastasis* = full restoration) is the leading of all people to Christ, from Christ, by Christ, of Christ as the willing new king of Grace. Romans 14:11: "For it is written, "As I live, says the Lord, every knee shall bow to me and *every tongue shall confess* to God their allegiance."

The word for confess is *homologeo* which means the "same-ness of words." Therefore, to make a better interpretation here might be to say: We show allegiance to God by saying the words that his Son told the world. In this context of interpretation, we would understand that we should feel the suffering that Jesus did when he spoke and the freedom by which we are released from the shackles of this world.

Another way to see *homologeo* working in this context is in the works that God does in us. The biblical Greek words: "confess" (*homologeo*),

---

3. The Greek term *phusikos* is known to the English language as "physical" but also connotes to the Greek mind as sensual, carnal, objective, etc. I do not believe that Paul is appealing to the "carnal senses" to the believer, rather, Paul is appealing to what the carnal mind that still wars with the spirit cannot conceptualize.

"show" (*phanein*), and "agree" (*sumphoneo*–as in symphony) all exemplify that we are in accord (or have "same-ness"/"with-ness"/) with God. Supporting this idea, we have Philippians 2:13: "For it is *God who* works in you to both *will* and do of *his* good pleasure."

So, we are given in Philippians 2:13 the total sum view[4] (apocalyptic, predeterministic, universalistic, prophetical and teleological) in the *working will* of God in us. This "will" in us that is *working* by *God* to do *his* good pleasure must be the same *will* that makes us fulfill Romans 10:9: "If you declare with your mouth, "Jesus is Lord," and believe in your heart that God raised him from the dead, you *will* be *saved*."

The passage we've all been waiting for

Romans 5:12 – **12)** Wherefore, as by one man sin entered into the world, and death by sin; and so death passed upon all men, for that all have sinned: **13)** For until the law sin was in the world: but sin is not imputed when there is no law. **14)** Nevertheless death reigned from Adam to Moses, even over them that had not sinned after the similitude of Adam's transgression, who is the figure of him that was to come.

15) But not as the offence(s), so also *is* the free gift. For if through the offence of one (person) many be dead, much more the grace of God, and the gift by grace, *which is* by one man, Jesus Christ, hath abounded unto many. **16)** And not as *it was* by one that sinned, *so is* the gift: for the judgment *was* by one to condemnation, but the free gift *is* of many offences unto justification. **17)** For if by one man's offence death reigned by one; much more they which receive abundance of grace and of the gift of righteousness shall reign in life by one, Jesus Christ.

18) Therefore as by the offence of one *judgment came* upon all men to condemnation; even so by the righteousness of one *the free gift came* upon all men unto justification of life. **19)** For as by one man's disobedience many were made sinners, so by the obedience of one shall many be made righteous. **20)** Moreover the law entered, that the offence might abound. But where sin abounded, grace did much more abound: **21)**

---

4. "apocalypse" – *apo* = "remove" + *kalupto* = "cover" (Proto-Indo-European: *KEL/Hell/Seal/– "conceal") Therefore, when the "hell" (*khaluptein*) is taken away (*apo* – "off/of/away" (+ *khaluptein* – hell)) we shall see ALL things for what they are without limitations of space and time to "limit" us. Hence, "eternal-instancy" is necessary. Cf. Shipley, *Dictionary of Word Origins* for *KEL —con-ceal, hell, hole, cellar, hide, hidden, heal/save – as in "protect by covering."

That as sin hath reigned unto death, even so might grace reign through righteousness unto eternal life by Jesus Christ our Lord.

Robin Parry and Christopher Partridge:

> For in 5:12 (Romans) Paul identified the group or class he had in mind with great clarity; it is, he said, all human beings, or more accurately, all humans who have sinned. Then in verse 15 he distinguished within that single group or class between "the one" and "the many" – "the one" being Adam himself, who first sinned, and "the many" being those who died as a result of Adam's sin. As John Murray has pointed out:
>> "When Paul uses the expression "the many," he is not intending to delimit the denotation. The scope of "the many" must be the same as the "all men" of verses 12 and 18. He uses "the many" here, as in verse 19, for the purpose of contrasting more effectively "the one" and "the many," singularity and plurality—it was the trespass of "the one..." "the many" died as a result."[5]

---

5. Murray, *Oxford English Dictionary*, 192–93.

SECTION II

Chapter Twenty-Four

"Born in Memphis" (the "coming to be" of me and why I know there's hope for you and for everyone)

My preface is really the honest and humble beginnings of a stuttering kid who felt a desire for Jesus from as early as I can remember. Through the rebus of my earlier formative years, I can pull back now and see that each particular event that seemed so emotionally disconnected to a logical way of thinking was indeed a bead on an infinite stringed system that bore the name *logos*, or what I might call God's ordered system.

MY FORMATIVE YEARS

I was born on July 18, 1967 and raised in Memphis, Tennessee until I was ten years old. My recollection of fifty years ago captures that of a holy and magical time. That holy and magical hub was in Memphis, Tennessee. I can never forget the particulars, such as my address, zip code, phone number, and layout of my home at 3351 Joselyn Street, zip code 38128, phone number 388-5193. In the 70s, kids rode their bikes everywhere until ca. 6 p.m. when dinner was usually served around our block. It was kind of understood as a "standard time" to eat dinner in my generation. Sometimes, I think the parents had dinner synchronized somehow so that we could all have our "heaven" to look forward to, that is, our bellies filled. Looking back, I have a great respect for our parents' combined efforts in providing us kids with our little haven of joy. What I remember vividly is the acceptance factor in our youth. Each kid on the block had their idiosyncrasies and was accepted for who they were. For the most part we all got along in our younger years and little to no judgment was ever sensed.

My school was the other source of my friends. I went to Messiah Lutheran which was located right off Austin Peay Highway and about a mile up the street from my dad's work. Messiah Lutheran still stands as a strong Lutheran school and church today. Terry Hewlit, the Head Director of Messiah Lutheran, has become a good friend of mine through the internet and phone calls. He has sent me several of my old year books, articles, and report cards of my grades that weren't at all as bad as I remembered them to be. He keeps me up on what goes on currently with my old school and some of my old friends. I am truly indebted.

This same highway that Messiah Lutheran was located on also ran directly across my dad's business just a mile up the street. His business was joined to a franchise paint company called Sherwin Williams that still thrives today. His personal business that he combined with Sherwin Williams was called Raleigh Home Decorating Company from which Raleigh was a subdivision of Memphis, Tennessee. At my dad's place of business, he would save both silver dollars and half dollars for me in a large plastic see-through bag. I know he did this so that I could watch it accumulate. This visual was dad's plan to give me hope that I would "one day" be able to buy a better drum set than the one I had.

I would always scuttle to the art supplies section in dad's office building by which I wished to express my graphic arts side on any given day. Dad was quick to grant me any art supply I wanted or needed. Dad carried the finest art supplies in town which inspired me to draw. Such tactile attributes of fresh sketch pads, charcoal pencils, high grade gum erasers, etc. only supported the skills that I acquired by watching dad draw for me while indirectly teaching me. This too was a gift that my dad had given me of many. Dad also taught me how to play chess. He built an elaborate chess table for me. I cannot express how beautifully handcrafted this table is. This table still stands the test of time as I still use it mostly to study theology and write this book on. Even now the memory all of our chess matches that we played so many decades ago still tugs at my heart with echoes of my father's spirit.

Mom was the dreamer and the abstract artist in the household. She was so beautiful, undeniably beautiful. Her views of life came from an old Scottish heritage, the Weston clan from the Orkney Isles. She was a North Carolinian who was raised on a few hundred acres of both farmland and a mysterious pine tree filled out skirting woodland. I would stay at her old home with her mom, my "Granny" in the summertime while dad would paint, fix, build, rearrange our Memphis home to our amazement every summer. She imbued the spirit of magic in our home. She inspired all of us through each season with an overwhelming sense of color correlative to their festivities that were associated with them. She made haunted houses out of boxes for me around the first of October so that I could feel the lead up to Halloween throughout October. Thanksgiving was another beautifully themed season in our home for it filled the gap between Halloween and Christmas with mom's fall-time recipes, scented candles, clothing to match the outside colors, etc. Finally, in our home, Christmas was the pinnacle of the three months of magic. Elves and Santa were constantly spoken of, though as a whisper as not to lose their spirit. Most importantly, Jesus Christ was talked about as the only hope that we all have and the joy which he brings to us both in the incarnation and resurrection. She is the reason I have such a mythological bent.

If dad was the "*sketch*" of my life's formative years, then mom was the *color*.

At my school I took for granted that most of the kids believed that Jesus was Lord and though we might "act out" on occasion we had a spiritual compass by which we could gauge our thoughts, feelings, actions, etc., with one another. In the 1970s at Messiah Lutheran, one was expected to respect one's elders, parents, teachers, leaders within the church, and everyone in the paradigm of a Christian life. This simply was the way it was, no matter what the current opinion is—all of which I didn't really know until later.

I'll never forget the Lutheran mosaic windows, purple, white, red candles, and cathedral ceiling, which was very much like most Roman Catholic church buildings. The sun's light would illuminate us with hues of purple, red, green, yellow, etc., when we started each day of school at the chapel. I mostly sensed the overwhelming presence of the purple and red combination that were exclaimed at Christmas time. The purple representing the Kings of Kings and the red representing the blood that Christ shed for us. These colors still beautifully haunt me around Christmas time. The regal sense by which liturgy was recognized without making it a theologically challenged thing. Simply put, the icons of the church, the seasonal associations by which we liturgically expressed them, and all of the somewhat historically the pre-Christian festivities that went with them simply exemplified Christ's beauty to me. Yes, an "amoral" pagan's

Christ! Nonetheless, Christ, the creator of all of creation, both invisible and visible with all supreme power and energy. A central focal point was what I had and now have again. But hardships came to challenge these foundational beliefs. My childlike love for God and his creation would be shaken to the core.

Chapter Twenty-Five

Suffering Has Meaning: (A Word about Suffering and God's Providence)

IF YOU ARE A believer in Christ, you will inevitably experience tragedy. You will inevitably experience hardships, possibly daily. It can be easy to conclude that you are the only one who has ever gone through *specifically* this or that. We can also conclude through tragedy that joy and revelation come out of this contiguum.

I would probably agree with you if you told me that. Some of us might find it embarrassing to feel that way so we remain silent and internalize a kind of specialness in our sufferings. We wait for a logic that can come from such a suffering of uniqueness not found in an idea about God's sovereignty "because God wouldn't cause harm to us."

If we embrace the narrative that God wouldn't cause suffering then we illogically weaponize our special sufferings and suspend our beliefs in an invisible-sovereign God resulting in a blockage of human intercourse with God.

UNHEALTHY "SPECIALNESS "

February 12, 1950

Dear Dr. Marcus:

A human being is a part of the whole, called by us "Universe," a part limited in time and space. He experiences himself, his thoughts and feelings, as something separated from the rest – a kind of optical delusion of his consciousness. This delusion is a kind of prison for us, restricting us to our personal desires and to affection for a few persons nearest to us. Our task must be to free ourselves from this prison by widening our circle of compassion to embrace all living creatures and the whole nature in its beauty. Nobody is able to achieve this completely, but the striving for such achievement is in itself a part of liberation and a foundation for inner security.

With my best wishes,
sincerely yours,

Albert Einstein
Dr. Robert S. Marcus
World Jewish Congress
1834 Broadway
New York 23, N.Y.

Someone thinking, "Only I have suffered like this, therefore, I have some kind of claim on this type of suffering" might find their "specialness" not only in the uniqueness of their suffering but their justifications for acting out, having self-pity, self-loathing, etc..... which are all by-products of a free agency mentality, a rogue of sorts, that can tell you that "no one has suffered like me." This "specialness" can be argued away through scripture. Here, we are at the crux of the verse: "For by him [Christ] all things were created: things in heaven and on earth, visible and invisible, whether it be thrones or powers or rulers or authorities; all things were created by him and for him" (Colossians 1:16).

These above passages apply to "political" powers, since *thronoi* (thrones), *kyriotaytes* (lords/magistrates), *arxai* (rulers), and *exousiai* (authorities) were used. Maybe one could say that these invisible and visible powers are heads in heaven, earth and hell.

Here's a look at *invisible existent powers (aorates hyperchouses dynameis)* that run their predeterminate courses:

> "Now listen here! — those who say, "Today or tomorrow we will go to this or that city, spend a year there, carry on *aorates hyperchouses dynameis* and make money." You don't even know what will happen tomorrow! Who are you/what is your life? You are a mist that appears for a short duration and then vanishes. What you should say is this: "If it is the Lord's will, we should even live and do this or that." As it is, you boast and brag. All such boasting is *evil* (Greek *ponera* – inevitably painful; burdensome; weighty; hard to move; evil)."
> (James 4:13)

Just think about this last verse for a moment. There is a *natural evil will* (of boasting and bragging of "what we are going to do tomorrow") that is going on while we are *perceiving* in the flesh that we are doing something. Evil is definitively here, as we speak, as though we can do something at all. The illusory "free will" that James addresses is considered evil by James. James calls this kind of evil "bragging." Our apostle James wants us to understand it this way: "*if God wills* that we should live then we should live (or die)." How far have we come from this in our daily church thinking, planning, organizing, preaching, teaching, etc.? Today we have become Christians in a secular society *laden with a language* that does not exalt God and *his Will* in our lives. Many of us simply do not have discernment in these matters. Sin speaks true and consistently as to what "freedom from" God's righteousness is. In this view, sin doesn't lie.

The main point that I am conveying from this is that *even our sufferings* are integrated into God's Will. All of the "powers that be" are ordained unto your joy and suffering. There's no way to de-thread this fabric that God has woven before the world began. It is God who has a predetermined plan that requires our suffering. There needs to be more acknowledgment to this if we are to have a sober church. If our theology is not consistent, we revert to randomness, dualism, auto-deism (i.e., "free-will"/"self-will worship"), fatalism, and nihilism. Predestination of our sufferings is a big part of the union that we share with Christ's sufferings. Then *why* are we here at a point in time that even the ministers in the churches say, "God wouldn't cause cancer, car wrecks, rape, murder, incest, etc." Our fear of ministers expresses, to me for sure, that the truth is too hard and that for many ministers it is easier to promulgate an incoherent theology versus a systematic, coherent, cohesive theology that hurts "the flesh" to hear initially.

Chapter Twenty-Six

Leaving My Eden[1]: (what happens when such a beautiful childhood paradigm is shattered?)

WE HAVE LED UP to this point with a lot of information, and hopefully, some applicable information but maybe you're not knowing where I am leading to. I hope to convey to you through this next personal testimony *why* I wrote this book. With all of my humanness exposed to you I commence this next section.

MEMPHIS, TENNESSEE

My family left Memphis in 1979 due to a nearly instantaneous vaulting crime wave. We moved to Hendersonville, Tennessee (about ten miles north of Nashville, Tennessee). I turned eleven that summer. I entered sixth grade and began attending a public school that was not focused on God. The teachers were careful with me to talk about God, or as they called it, "religion." Such an idea was so foreign to me because I never thought that a relationship with a community of people who loved God would be called "religious."

    Instead of reverence, as I understood the meaning to be in my youngest years, I heard and witnessed some of the kids talk about every possible kind of disrespect toward the opposite sex, blaspheming God's name in every possible way, and drugs and alcohol were already accepted

---

1. We had no idea that Memphis would continue in its collapse. Memphis ranks presently (2025) as the number one city for violent crimes in the nation.

as a norm for children who were only ten and eleven. Even children younger than ten had, I heard, boasted of already doing drugs. It was beyond my capacity to mentally, morally, and emotionally compute this. I can still remember the emotion of this hurting me for them and feeling the absolute loss of the kingdom of God for their sakes. I remember not judging them but rather agonizing in my heart for them. I remember crying for them.

There were, of course, kids who opposed that way of thinking. Though, as the years passed, we integrated day after day and inevitably we started to act and think somewhat alike.

It was in sixth grade in my new school, new home, new neighborhood, and new life that I obtained a stutter. My stutter destroyed any sense of strength—should I say "will power'—to fit in anywhere. I didn't have the ability to be cool anymore, a commodity that was priceless in school. I asked God *why would I not be able to share in the freedom to speak like everyone else?* The ridicule of my stutter increased. My stutter mentally and emotionally crippled me. For the first time in my life, I didn't want to go to school. I didn't want to socialize. The horror of speaking up in class, answering a question directed at me, reading aloud, etc., was enough to end me. I didn't want to study or do schoolwork. I didn't want to go to school. I asked my Mom to allow me to skip school on days when I knew we had to read aloud or do oral book reports in front of the class.

During this time my dad had taken on a corporate job which took him away from home. Sometimes, he wouldn't come home. I'll never forget the summer of 1980 when my dad brought his corporate boss to my home where my mom made a tremendous dinner for us all. Mr. Hillman Cagle was dad's boss's name. Hillman Cagle is one of the particular people in my memory that I consider poetically pivotal. He treated my mom like dirt. He wanted to show off his position, I guess to impress my dad. He talked down to her. Dad didn't say anything about it. Even then, I believed it was to save his job. I still had the ethical mind of a child to want to tell this dragon to get out of our home but could feel the stress upon my dad. I could empathize with him. After this most memorable and horrible evening the following years of my life became more and more clouded. Every day I practiced numbing myself mentally and emotionally to not "take in" the day's particulars (events) nor what life meant anymore.

From 1979 to 1982 one of the countless events of my remembrances concerned our neighbors, the Lancasters. They had brought so much grief to my family with their drunken nights and coming over to our yard to trash it. One night, in a drunken fit, Mr. Lancaster threatened my dad's life. His son had thrown dog poop on my mom over the fence. My dad threw back their beer bottles that they had thrown onto our yard.

All of this torture from the Lancasters had lasted for nearly three years, which took its toll on all of us. Their youngest son tortured me with words as well as throwing objects at me on the bus every day, only to threaten me with his much older and bigger brother, who, he said, would beat me up if I challenged him back. Not just this, but every day I experience a new lie that he created about me and my family that I would attempt to debunk while stuttering. I wanted to die. I wanted to commit suicide. Eventually, my dad got an attorney and because of the severity of the threats made against my dad and my family, they were forced to move a long distance from our home. They had a restraining order set and I never heard from them again. Nonetheless, the trauma was instilled in all of us.

Chapter Twenty-Seven

Jumping Forward: (Being Torn from Innocence)

Around 1982, my dad showed signs of pressure to fit into the corporate world of business. He joined the Lion's club and stayed out late. He was influenced by Hillman Cagle to be more "social." My dad and Hillman Cagle would go out drinking. Later, I found out that they went to different clubs with not the best of intentions. Mom eventually found napkins with lipstick on them that weren't hers in dad's car. Mom kept it together, for the sake of the family and, I'm sure, also out of fear. She did challenge dad later. She knew this would be bad, but she couldn't allow this behavior to go on in front of me, as a budding teen, nor in front of her, as a wife who deserved a faithful husband. Dad had begun drinking heavily during this time. His rages met his drinking sprees. I'll never forget the day when she addressed him on his infidelity and alcoholism. She asked, "What has happened to you? Have I not always been faithfully yours? Have I always not been here for you?" My dad's rage ended in him throwing a whiskey bottle at her and driving off. He didn't come back until we acted on faith a while later.

In 1985 I joined the Marines. I finished boot camp at Parris Island and I.T.S. (Infantry Training) at Camp Lejeune by January 1986. My dad was gone during this time. He had left my Mom and me and was living with an assumed girlfriend. Though I was in the military I felt the agony of my mom being alone with only an eighth grade education living in a very expensive home in one of the wealthiest neighborhoods in Hendersonville. Not only did I have my challenges in some of the toughest training in the world, I was thinking of my mom constantly. At one point

I even sent her home money from my military base. This money (which was called "chits") was a government coupon and not civilian money. I thought it would help mom. In my naivete I thought she could pay the mortgage with this. Well, she couldn't. Also, I couldn't afford to purchase the necessary things for myself through training once I had sent this government tender home. This got me into a whole lot of trouble. Eventually, the commanding officer of our company saw this as a "noble act'—albeit a stupid one—and I was exonerated from any wrongdoing.

While it may seem strange, all of these horrors that were happening at home made me feel like *I* should carry guilt for it. After all, in my teens I finally stood up against my dad for yelling and screaming at my mom and me, and this act, I believed, had *caused* dad to leave. It's all *my* fault, I thought. Thus, I carried the guilt of protecting my mom's heart and body. Knowing what I know now, my dad was nothing more than a fallen sinner like all of us. He needed Christ like all of us need Christ.

Then, a new challenge came. Eventually in 1986 my dad attempted suicide. Hillman Cagle, of all people, called me and said that my dad was in the hospital and that my dad's condition was bad. He said that I needed to handle it like a man and "get over it." This is the last I ever heard of Hillman Cagle. It was as though Hillman wanted me to "get over" sadness, remorse, brokenness, and humiliation through "being a man." It was Hillman Cagle, "the man," who led my dad into alcoholism, fraternizing, and disrespecting my mom. These were words of a devil to me. I hated Hillman. Yet, I had a situation handed to me. I had to be something more than an "idea" of a man.

This was the pivotal time in my life and my mom's life. If we were to handle this beyond what Hillman would do, the only way to handle this situation is to do what Jesus would do.

So, here we are before God, my dad lying in a hospital bed, and my Mom distraught from all the years and their culmination set before her. I later thought about the cliche "What Would Jesus Do?" wristbands as to how we simply handled this situation. At the hospital, my Mom asked me what we should do now, Kyle? Dad left me for another woman; he has been excessively violent, and more. What should we do?" Maybe it was the only recourse I had but thank God that it was: I replied: "What would Jesus do, Mom?"

So, we took him home. We eventually lost that home due to the mismanagement of finances by my dad's lifestyle and mom's inability to fight back. I understand them both now without judgment for their actions.

I filed for a line 7 in the Marines and was honorably discharged finally in 1988. My family finally regrouped. Dad came to the Lord. We became a God-fearing family. Remembering all of my childhood, I desired to start that all over again with my renewed Family. For the next twenty-four years I was blessed to have them both in my life. We had challenges for sure, but we recognized God as the supreme leader of our family. We eventually created a nursing home on a private level and paid off all of our debts. We bought a home together and eventually I purchased my own home.

Chapter Twenty-Eight

Continued Pain: (Trying To Get A Life)

I GOT MARRIED IN 2000. My wife at the time, who had been a scientist in China, moved from China to the U.S., getting her master's in business, with English as a second language. She had been in the Red Army and had served the state. Perhaps unsurprisingly, given her background, she was an unbeliever in God. She came from poverty and fear in her youth. Her bedroom window in China was backed up to the public waste alley, so she smelled feces all through her youth. Her background instilled in her a strong desire to leave all the poverty behind and never return. The hope of an ordered system that she could grasp ahold of to save her from poverty unto death was somewhat satisfied for her within the Chinese communist paradigm. However, with many pitfalls in this system she decided to leave China. When she moved to the U.S., she carried with her the attributes of what communism did and did not do for her as a living soul. Eventually, she became a Christian following the many theological discussions that we had.

I raised her only daughter, Alicia, as my own. I eventually home schooled her due to her busy schedule as an ice figure skater, which she went on to place in the nationals. She had great coaches and was even coached on occasion by Scott Hamilton, once by Michelle Kwan, and by other recognizable skaters.

I found once again a *magical* and *holy* place in this world. A world that I hadn't experienced since I was very young in Memphis. My responsibilities were considerable, being both a family man and a joint income-provider. My wife trusted what I did to teach and father Alicia. I spent pretty much every waking hour with Alicia as a homeschool parent and best friend/father. My wife spent time with Alicia as well as working at the ice-skating facility. This was where Alicia trained, and my wife's job benefited us with some discounts and benefits. The only times I wasn't with her or around my wife were when I taught music privately or played concerts.

As Alicia, my daughter, was entering Columbia Junior College at fifteen years old with supervision as a minor and with just a few more high school credits to go, she exhibited a high academic ability for languages and science. I must always give credit to her mother for teaching her the sciences and higher math, for which I would never have been equipped to have done. So, the science learned from her mother and the saturation of proto-Indo-European languages (especially Greek) and Hebrew from me completed Alicia in the areas of languages and science. Alicia had become fully fit to receive knowledge with a categorizing mind.

Alicia and I had studied Greek, Hebrew, Latin, and proto-Indo-European linguistics together since she was ten. I had her analyzing Shakespeare at an even earlier age. She understood Anglo Saxon roots as well. She linked etymologies to biblical studies. She found truths of how the biblical languages exemplified the classical languages of the old world. She found a "collective logos" through this genius of language studies, showing a richness and more importantly a hope fulfilled from the authors who wrote in ancient Greek, Assyrian, Akkadian, Sumerian, etc. She saw how Christ was the answer for all that the ancients were reaching for without the fleshly conclusion found in Jesus' life and death. She began to be able to break down any word and follow its etiology and etymology. This beautiful gift followed into her scientific studies as well.

Our lives were without question seemingly "successful." All was well, or so I thought. During that time, while Alicia would be training, I began working on theological lectures that I put to audio recording and text. This gave me even more fulfillment. I was able to process the events of my life with God's works upon my family's. This was the era upon which I began a foundation of theological thought that has continued to the present day.

ARTISTIC BREAK

This is my graphic art piece called "Hero vs. Messiah." It was my first sketch and watercolor attempt to complement my lecture called, "Hero vs. Messiah." This graphic will recur and be explained in chapter 52.

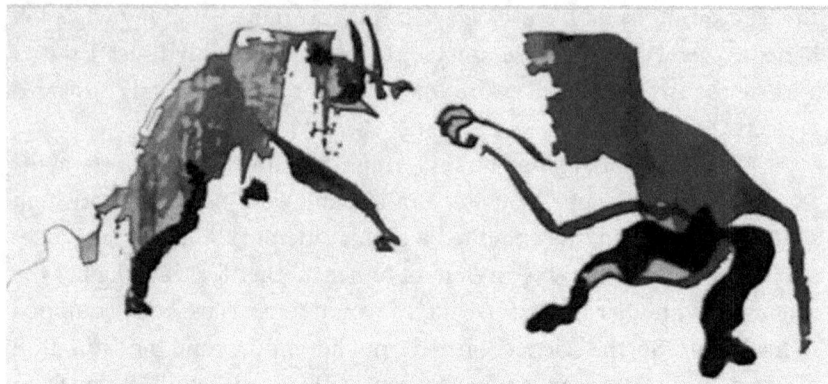

Seen below is my "*Shadow Sketch*" called, "The March of the Shadows." It represents, to me, the march of shadow logic when truth is not seen as a worthy component in a culture.

I was expressing the Hero as to what he was in the face of the Messiah. The Hero can waffle with trueness mixed with lies. He can pretend one minute to be "as" a Messiah, the next, an anti-hero for convenience's sake. In the March of the Shadows, I expressed pure dark reason in procession. The Shadows are what they are until light/truth exposes them. They are "true" in their non-sustainability marching in an order *unto* destruction.

Chapter Twenty-Nine

My parents" "sketch" and "color": (reaching back to the ghost of innocence)

I REVIVED THAT SAME exact spirit during these times that my mom and dad had nurtured with me, concerning the holidays, times and seasons of the year, and such things. At night, to put us to sleep, Alicia and I would watch *Harry Potter* and the *Lord of the Rings* together. We watched all the Jesus movies ever made. All such entertainment gave us a gentle hand in putting us to sleep. All was seemingly well with us.

My wife at the time worked with me to get out of any debt, something that she was adamant about. I absolutely concurred. We were debt-free at the prime of our lives. House paid for, cars paid for, no debts, save for food, electricity, and insurance.

During my time with Alicia and my first wife, I would begin building "haunted houses" in my backyard around August. The process of planning and executing these projects every year was one of my biggest joys. It would take on average three months to build each one of these and at least that much time to break them down. By the last week in October we would have our two nights, sometimes three, with outside black-and-white silent Dracula (Nosferatu) movies, people reading Edgar Allen Poe, entertainment such as Steppenwolf's guitarist, Bobby Cochran, singing Halloween songs, while ca. forty actors in the haunted house would terrify anyone who dared to enter this "maze of death." We also had food cooking on the grills with all of the associated smells of joy and the sounds of people ecstatically screaming in the haunted house. Cars parked for blocks down the street, etc. It was like the spirit of the 1970s had visited the new millennium. With our Bose sound system and

DOES GRACE HAVE A CEILING?

fifty smoke machines roaring no one could miss this monstrosity for miles.

The haunted house would take up half an acre alone, not to mention all of the other activities taking up the rest of the back yard. Some eighty to one hundred rooms comprised these haunted houses that I built for Alicia for nearly thirteen years. I didn't care about the work or money (at the time we had no debt, house paid for, cars paid for, built in insurance with Susan's job, etc.) because of the joy it brought Alicia.

Despite all of the "collective joy" of being debt free, me being a dedicated father and husband, it only made my wife happy if we made *more* money including profits off the haunted houses that brought us such joy. I wanted there to be some joy in having something other than money as a focus. I did, however, charge enough to recover from the cost of the materials (and did get it). I put all of the profits into my wife's hands every year and said that we have a little more than what we put into it. But she was never satisfied with "a little more." Though everyone loved it and everyone came to it each year, it was obvious that abundant profit was all that she cared about concerning these joyful endeavors. We were debt-free and making close to $100,000 per year at the time (which is roughly equivalent to $165,000 in 2025). What did it matter? We were thankful, joyful, happy, at peace—I thought.

My wife's lack of emotional sharing became evident to me more and more as our marriage continued. Intimacy in every way became nil from her side. I asked my wife, "Could we have a child together?" She said to me, "You are not worth having a child with, you don't make enough money." She began to only talk about money, even though we were better off than ever financially. I thought that if I worked harder for whatever reason she would be more secure and joyful. That never happened. I put everything into Alicia to show my wife that I am "worthy" to be a father and husband. I put every bit of compassion and kindness that I had in me to my wife. I worked harder than ever. I thought my efforts and will could hold this marriage together. I thought that though skating bills were astronomical it never hurt us because we made enough and were debt-free. Shouldn't this make her happy? It was still not enough.

During Alicia's first year of college both of my parent's health began to fail. I had always loved my parents beyond the stars. No matter what had happened in the past, Christ's love had healed us all. I was the first to forgive, because I always felt the most guilt. I think that I felt this guilt because I reasoned that it was *my responsibility* to hold it all together. My bond with them was as a child's love for their parents. Now, with both my parents dying and needing extra financial resources and with more bills coming in for college, I needed my wife's emotional support more than ever. I thought that my wife would be there for me. Instead, she told me as we were driving to the hospital for the last time that if I made more money my parents wouldn't be dying.

My parent's pre-existing conditions trajected exactly as they should have to these times and dates of devastation.

Chapter Thirty

Enters the Holy Ghost:
(loss and gain in this world have a purpose)

With my mom dying on June 30, 2011 at 3:30 pm and my dad dying on November 10, 2011 at 7:45 pm they had left me on this earth with a void that was filled by God. I still tried to create hope in this world with my wife. The lack of intimacy, the blame for what I couldn't have stopped concerning my parent's death, the violent challenges of "why don't we just get a divorce" anytime we had an argument, and the self-preservatory fear of losing my home (which I had paid off long before I met my wife) were all of a sudden caught up into a ball of grace. The Holy Spirit comforted me and directed me to go to her and say, "I want a divorce." That same year I went on to win an Emmy Award, and the legendary Bluegrass musician Ricky Skaggs hired me as his percussionist. It was like God was telling me to trust him and that I would not falter. There were many other legendary musicians that I had played with, did play with, and have since played with. I think all of this is to say, God was reassuring me that I had worth in this world but all of these awards and semi star-dom were not the point. The key point was something God would continue to teach me.

There were still residual effects from my divorce that cost me more than I can explain here. Such effects threw me into bankruptcy years later after fighting financial devastation and failure to recover. Yet, a "bank" was eventually filled with God's gold, that is to say, with a second loving wife who came along after my devastating divorce and cared for me. She gave me a beautiful child named Eden and two beautiful stepchildren.

So much good has happened in between all these events but I have only listed a few things. Trials are *never* over. What I began to learn (and am still learning) is that God not only knows but *ordains* your joy and your sufferings to make you understand God's value and your own value.

FINAL STATEMENTS

I would like to mention that my daughter, Alicia, transferred to Belmont University. She studied biology obtaining a 3.8 G.P.A. and achieving awards for academic and leadership excellence. She went to medical school at E.T.S.U. where she matriculated ranking high in her grades. She presently is a practicing M.D. having finished her residency and is doing her fellowship as I type. As I am typing, Alicia has finished her residency and is her fellowship. Not only Alicia, but all of my inherited step kids are honor students thriving with brilliant inquisitive minds. My 10-year-old, Eden, is learning the Greek New Testament and figuring out etymologies with the fervor for truth like all of my other children. Eden is also teaching chess at the local library (she started teaching chess when she was 7). Alicia, Ethan, Fiona, Eden, and my wife, Samantha, are a gift beyond comprehension.

REFLECTIONS AND GRATITUDE

I would also like to go back in time to 1986 when I first came back from the Marines to see my Dad at the hospital. A time when I needed a spiritual guide. Here, I would like to mention Jim, a hardline Calvanist minister from Texas, who addressed me with the idea of predestination after dad had attempted suicide. Jim also imbued me with the importance of knowing the Greek and Hebrew text of the Bible. For this, I will always be grateful to God for Jim. Because of Jim's influence, I enrolled in college to study Greek and Hebrew. If it hadn't been for this agent of God's knowledge I don't know where I would be. Keep this in mind: we are all agents, whether "unsaved" or "saved." Here, I must qualify my statement: (I) we're *all* on a journey to God and (II) I have been part of the "unsaved" being saved. This will be addressed later.

I would like to also mention my dad for keeping my interest in drumming all those years. I would like to mention my mom for inspiring me to be different, abstract sometimes, and fill the air with new worlds for all to enjoy. Between these two angels, I was given flight for where I needed to go, no matter how much the pain.

SECTION III

Chapter Thirty-One

Theology: (using a theology to escape bad ideologies and failed orthodoxies)

IN MY EARLY TWENTIES I believe that God deemed it necessary that I study under a man who had drawn a hard line with "his theology." Jim (I will leave his last name excluded) was my first encounter with what *seemed to be* irrefutable evidence found in scripture that I had not been aware of in all of my Christian life. He directed me to the histories of the Babylonians, Persians, Greeks, Romans and the early first century church. This excited me since secular history could "meet" and "support" a real Jewish and Christian history. He taught me about what paganism meant to the Early Israelites and how that they were taken captive for synthesizing their beliefs in YHVH with that of Ashtaroth (and early Mesopotamian goddesses) and Baal. Jim taught me that Christmas and Easter had Babylonian-pagan origins and that one should abstain from such pagan practices. These were topics that I had had no idea of in my youth and somehow infuriated me as to why no one had told me about. He taught me that predestination binds the Bible together. He taught me about the timelines concerning the end of the age of this world (for whatever view you take I am fine with) ties in with Daniel's prophecy concerning Judah's migration back into Jerusalem under Nehemiah (Nehemiah having the courage to enforce Cyrus" decree (537 BC) nearly 80 years prior, ca. 444 BC). He proposed that free will, as we understand it as "free agency" cannot exist separate from God's Will. He taught me that most humans will be damned for God did not predestinate them unto salvation. He taught me about Calvinism. He taught me to be exclusive from the world, including my best friends and family. He taught me that

God creates evil and good. Etc. etc. For whatever offense these topics might be to some, he told me facts if not truths about much of what I just mentioned and many allurements "within the lines" of these topics that took me out to sea without help. Whatever be my views of Jim, I now have none other thanks to God for whatever Jim taught me. I realize that I, as well as Jim, were, are, and will be on our journey with God of coming to be who we are lovingly supposed to be.

My reason for telling you about Jim is that my book represents a massive effort of over 35 years of study to get out of cults' misdirected theologies which can take the form of the High Churches all the way to seemingly harmless churches that act within a vacuum.

Jim was the first man to talk to me about God with a challenge to who I really am in this life. I took hold of what he taught/showed me and went out into the world with these topics as an arsenal. Full of my limitations to what surrounded each topic and having older church elders to avoid or condemn me, Jim's self-proclaimed prophecy that "the world would condemn you, saying all manner of evil about you" supported my belief in Jim's teaching and later his founded church upon me, his wife, and sometimes stepson. Later, Jim would have more followers that found themselves in the same situations as me, excluded from the world and filled with anxiousness. Jim's church became "the respite" by which the "elect" would congregate. Over time, whether by implication or overtly telling us, Jim would put thoughts into the congregation's minds as being "*possibly* the only place left on earth to worship and be taught correctly the word of God."

Finally, the efforts which brought me here to you have also been directed by God's graceful sovereignty for I have no judgment against any man or system of thought. We are all fallen and placed where we are supposed to be. At the same time, let no one own your mind and halt your journey from the freedom that is in Christ. I only say this as a man looking through time and not as a whole thought. Therefore, this book represents my fight out of darkness and into bliss. I no longer study and produce Christian works such as podcasts, books, websites, classes, etc. for the sake of "reaction" or "responding" for the most part, rather, the joy of God's infinite freedom and bliss offered to us which the world cannot offer.

Chapter Thirty-Two

What Predestination Is and Not: (Examples of Predestination in the Old Testament)

"That which has been is what will be
That which is done is what will be done
And there is nothing new under the sun.
Is there anything of which it may be said,
"See, this is new?"" (Ecclesiastes 1:9)

"That which is has already been,
And what is to be has already been
And God requires an account of what is past." (Ecclesiastes 3:15)

"Declaring the end from the beginning,
And from ancient times things that are not yet done;
Saying, "My counsel shall stand,
And I will do all My pleasure." (Isaiah 46:10)

"I form the light, and create darkness;
I make peace and create *evil*;[1]
I the LORD do all these things." (Isaiah 45:7)

---

1. "Evil" is the English translation from the Hebrew *ra'ah*, meaning destruction, devastation, ruin of all kinds. This is not saying that God is immoral or evil, rather, God brings destruction for the greater plan (i.e., "ordained" destruction). We all have had devastation or a "destruction" of sorts in our lives. It is God who ordained evil in order for us to grow closer to him in his overall beneficial (*tov*/"good") plan. It is the destruction of our flesh that pulls us closer to him and not an angry God who loves to destroy us (his children). Gottfried Wilhelm, Baron von Leibnitz ([1646-1716] philosopher, theologian, mechanician, naturalist, and votary of all arts and all sciences was a most brilliant scholar and precursor to Immanuel Kant) who explored the nature of creation as a unified agreement. His theodicy was that "evil" played within the bigger more beneficial plan. He believed that God created the best possible world, which is why it's harmonious and why things happen the way they do.

The verses of Ecclesiastes and Isaiah declare *that nothing was before God*. These verses declare a prime force that causes all energies to "happen" or "exist." In other words, these two writers express that God is the originating and causative force of all past, present, and future events.

The New Testament gets very personal with us concerning this great predetermining force. We can read in scripture that our salvation is wrapped up in his great predeterminate intention as we see in Ephesians.

In Ephesians 1:4–23 we see both full restoration of all things (cf. parallel restorations in passages Colossians 1:14–17; I Corinthians 15:28) and predestination as being the driving force being such a restoration:

> Ephesians 1:4-14 (King James Version)
>
> "According as he hath chosen us in him before the foundation of the world, that we should be holy and without blame before him in love: Having predestined us unto the adoption of children by Jesus Christ to himself, according to the good pleasure of his will, To the praise of the glory of his grace, wherein he hath made us accepted in the beloved. In whom we have redemption through his blood, the forgiveness of sins, according to the riches of his grace; Wherein he hath abounded toward us in all wisdom and prudence; Having made known unto us the mystery of his will, according to his good pleasure which he hath purposed in himself: That in the dispensation of the fulness of times he might gather together in one all things in Christ, both which are in heaven, and which are on earth; even in him: In whom also we have obtained an inheritance, being predestined according to the purpose of him who worketh all things after the counsel of his own will: That we should be to the praise of his glory, who first trusted in Christ. In whom ye also trusted, after that ye heard the word of truth, the gospel of your salvation: in whom also after that ye believed, ye were sealed with that holy Spirit of promise, Which is the earnestness of our inheritance until the redemption of the purchased possession, unto the praise of his glory."

THE INTENTIONAL INTENDER

> "For whom he [God] did foreknow, he also did predestinate to be conformed to the image of his Son, that he [Christ] might be the firstborn among many brothers. Moreover, whom he [God]

did predestinate, whom he also called, whom he also justified: and whom he justified, whom he also glorified. What shall we say then to these things? If God be for us, who can be against us?" (Romans 8:29–31)

This passage from Romans makes it clear that God "foreknew (*pro-ginosko* = "pro-gnosis"/"pre-knowledge")" and also did "predestinate (*pro-horidzo* = "pre" or "before" + "the horizon")" our salvation.

We can put the Old Testament with the New Testament now:

Our salvation came out of the *"what is to be has already been"* of Ecclesiastes 3:15. This would mean that our salvation was going to happen anyway. So, is this salvific act "determinism" or "predeterminism"? Ephesians 1:4 states that God "chose *us* in him [i.e., Christ] *before* the foundation of the cosmos." Ephesians continues in this predeterministic relationship from God to us by saying in Ephesians 1:5 that God predestined us unto the adoption of his sons[2] according to the purpose of his will.

Calvinism poses an impasse for true biblical predestination in many Christian camps. Even top scholars in their day such as Professors Strong and McClintock were tainted with a mixture of biblical and T.U.L.I.P. Calvinism.

As presented below, it seems that we have not advanced our understanding of biblical predestination without the crutch of T.U.L.I.P. Calvinism. Furthermore, we have solidified within the blend of these errors creating diversions from what predestination truly is.

Let's look at what it is not, though, very close indeed: *Predestination* defined ca. 150 years ago from Professors John McClintock and James Strong in their *Cyclopedia of Biblical, Theological, and Ecclesiastical Literature* first print 1867–1887 [from this edition I quote]; volume VIII (Pet-Re):

> "Predestination, a doctrine upon which great division of opinion prevails among Christians. 1.) Definition: – The word

---

2. We know that in "biblical speak" the term "sons" (Hebrew: *ben*) means those who "carry on the name" or *onoma* – i.e., "authority, fame, reputation, identity." This does not have to apply to gender. The Greek *onoma* and the Hebrew *shem* mean: authority, genealogy, lineage, house, proprietorship, etc. Therefore, Ruth and Esther are good examples of "sons" in the sense of *shem* for they are those who carry the *name* onward (a kind of perpetuity handed from God to his "*Bar*" – "sons" – "carriers of the inheritance"). If I may use Job as a perfect example of the two separate forms of belief: The "nature" of the illusory doctrines of "determinism" as a replacement theology for predeterminism led by Job's "fatalistic" then "nihilistic" ideology.

> predestinate properly signifies to destine (i.e., to set apart, or devote to a particular use, condition, or end) beforehand. It therefore denotes a mere act of the will, and should be carefully distinguished from that exercise of power by which volitions are actualized or carried into effect (i.e., human will). Etymologically it would be proper to say that God before the foundation of the world predestined the sun to be luminous, lodestone (more than likely the "gravitational pull with the moon") to attract the atmosphere to perform its varied ministries . . . etc." (VI) Connection of Predestination with other Doctrines. – Much confusion and obscurity has arisen in the progress of the predestinarian controversy from failing to keep the real issue always distinctly in view (as I have mentioned earlier). The point in controversy is not whether or not God had a plan when He entered upon creation (cf. Foreknowledge and Providence for a distinct study of topics). Neither is it whether or not that plan embraced a positive pre appointment of every individual event in the whole range of futurity. Nor yet is it whether or not an exercise of divine energy is inseparably connected with any or all of God's predeterminations so that they are "effectual" decree (See "Calling; Grace"). The real question is: Has God by an immutable and eternal decree predestinated some of the human family unto eternal life, and all the others unto everlasting perdition without any reference whatever to the use they may make of their moral agency? This the Calvinist affirms, usually basing his affirmation solely on what he regards a Scripture authority, and often admitting that the human mind cannot reconcile it with the character of God or the dictates of human reason."

So, we just read the final conclusive question: "*The real question is: Has God by an immutable and eternal decree predestinated some of the human family unto eternal life, and all the others unto everlasting perdition without any reference whatever to the use they may make of their moral agency?*"

First, I'll address this with an etymological answer: *Prohoridzo* as in "pre-horizon" is a "divine" place where God dwells in his eternal abode. This "place" is before, pre-, prior, etc. the boundary line that enters into time (Chronos" abode, the place of entropy). This pre-horizon "place" does not mean "pre-selection," rather, it means "before the horizon of creation," i.e., a place where we *were*[3] with him in eternity/pre-time.

---

3. I use the term "were" being fully aware that eternity has no tense. This term, "*were*," is for us for now.

The beauty of this common example of "missing the point" is that their "missing the point" explains clearly that biblical predeterminism is apocalyptic universal salvation set "before" the foundation of the world. Within this view there can be no pre-emptive damnation unto never ending fire if all of creation is to be restored back into Christ (I Corinthians 15: 22; I Corinthians 15:28; 2 Corinthians 5: 14, 15). Furthermore, "the boundary" which divides time from the never-ending abode with Christ should be factored in when one is either reading about the judgments upon *all* flesh or the salvation of *all* souls. It is the ultimate play of meaning for both sides of the boundary line.

For now, I claim that "predestination" is to be distinguished from an act of determining from the foundation of the world—i.e., to cause *something* before that same *something* happens (as an idea precedes a consequence(s)). Predestination, distinguished from "determining" especially in the sense of *the place that is determined or ordained "from"* (i.e. the foundation of the world [a physical and time-bound place]). Biblically (and etymologically justifiable), predestination is the divine-eternal-place [without time's constraints] *where* we will ALL abide in our marriage with Christ *in* his new name (or authority). This place is in his new title/name/"onoma."

Chapter Thirty-Three

Determinism is not Predeterminism

Here's a look into Job's "determined" suffering *from* and *to* a "predetermined" outcome.

In the book of Job, the first two chapters set us up for knowing Job's faith. What did Job believe in? He believed in sovereignty. That is, Job believed that God did both acts of "building up" and "tearing down"—a.k.a., "Good and Evil" (please read Job 1 and 2).

In the last 3 verses of chapter 2 we see Job in verse 20 being wracked with pain, shaving his head, ripping his mantle, and falling down to the ground worshipping God! In verse 21 of chapter 2 Job says that "God gives and takes away; blessed be the name of the LORD." Finally, chapter 2 vs. 22 says that "in all this (expressions of agony) Job sinned not, nor (did he) charge God foolishly."

This, for sure, gives us a theological lesson: God can take everything you "own," and still, he is to be praised. This flies in the face of many modern cultural ideas about God's "benevolence," "kindness," "gentleness," "gracefulness," etc.—yet, does God not have all of those attributes? Yes, he does. The onus is on us to understand what "benevolence," "kindness," "gentleness," and "gracefulness" mean within the *context* of God's sovereign predeterminism and teleological plan.

In Job 3, we find the nearly perfect man (Job) in the LOGOS stretched beyond his capabilities to cope with such an onslaught of torture sent from the LOGOS as Job expresses in Chapters 6 through the last chapter (42). By the time we get to chapter 6 we can see Job in a slow ascension out of the kind of mental/spiritual hell that he was in.

But my real focus of Job chapter 3 is to observe that pure "satanism" can only speak within the boundaries of God's sovereignty" (as we find in chapter 3). I hope to dispel the idea of dualism in this chapter and show that any "kind" of *satan* or *adversary* we encounter in scripture or in our lives must be understood as a tool used by God to "score" or "calibrate" his people into what God desires in his sovereign loving plan.

In Job chapter 3 we find in Job's soliloquy a stark contrast to his former views in relation with God, i.e., Job's belief in God's sovereign predetermined plan in all things. We will now cover Job's expressing his illusory "natural plight" (or "fatalistic view") after having lost nearly everything and having "gone past" Job's reason of God's predeterminism, if only for a moment — which is true hell.

Job 3:1–26

1 After this Job opened his mouth, and cursed his day.

2 And Job spoke, and said,

3 Let the day perish wherein I was born, and the night in which it was said, There is a man child conceived.

4 Let that day be darkness; let not God regard it from above, neither let the light shine upon it.

5 Let darkness and the shadow of death stain it; let a cloud dwell upon it; let the blackness of the day terrify it.

6 As for that night, let darkness seize upon it; let it not be joined unto the days of the year, let it not come into the number of the months.

7 Lo, let that night be solitary, let no joyful voice come therein.

8 Let them curse it (i.e., the day Job was born) that curse the day, who are ready to raise up their mourning.

9 Let the stars of the twilight thereof be dark; let it look for light, but have none; neither let it see the dawning of the day:

10 Because it did not shut the doors of my mother's womb, nor hid sorrow from mine eyes.

11 Why did I not die from the womb? why did I not give up the ghost when I came out of the belly?

12 Why did the knees prevent me? or why the breasts that I should suck?

13 For now should I have lain still and been quiet, I should have slept: then had I been at rest,

14 With kings and counselors of the earth, which built desolate places for themselves;

15 Or with princes that had gold, who filled their houses with silver:

16 Or as an hidden untimely birth I had not been; as infants which never saw light.

17 There the wicked cease from troubling; and there the weary be at rest.

18 There the prisoners rest together; they hear not the voice of the oppressor.

19 The small and great are there; and the servant is free from his master.

20 Wherefore is light given to him that is in misery, and life unto the bitter in soul;

21 Which long for death, but it cometh not; and dig for it more than for hid treasures;

22 Which rejoice exceedingly, and are glad, when they can find the grave?

23 Why is light given to a man whose way is hid, and whom God hath hedged in?

24 For my sighing cometh before I eat, and my roarings are poured out like the waters.

25 For the thing which I greatly feared has come upon me, and that which I was afraid of has come unto me.

26 I was not in safety, neither had I rested, nor was I quiet; yet trouble came.

From my take on Job's case in Job 3: 1-26, I do not see that Job had sinned in his temporary loss of sanity. Though we're dealing with a different condition of Job in chapter 3 from that of Job 2 (i.e., "*Job sinned not*" in chapter 2: 22), Job, in Job 3, is in his full expression of his newly found *limitations*. That is, Job "acts"/"speaks" from the limitations of his abject torture. Still, Job acts within the lines of integrity in his delusion, i.e., Job is an honest "journalist" in his descent, of sorts.

The parallel between the satan figure's *limitations* under God's command in chapter one and the *limitations* by which Job spoke through in chapter 3 bear a "range" by which freedom is not possible outside the boundaries of the beset office of the satan for Job was *hedged in* (to use the satan's words) to the idea of fatalism. Job was bound to the reason of "immediacy" or the *"immediate now."* This is an aspect of "fatalism"

WHAT PREDESTINATION IS AND NOT

in the sense of "plight" vs. sovereignty — which was Job's past faith "in God's will alone" (*in sola Dei Voluntate*). This tells me that the world of objectivity is all that Job could see. It may be interesting to note that in the Greek myths the goddess of "objectivity," Ananke, was also considered the goddess of pain, tearing, angst, going against the stream or flow etc. while her husband was the god Chronos. Chronos in Greek myth is the god of time, the "divider" who consumes all things. Chronos is sometimes depicted as "the horned one." If there could be a parallel here, Job momentarily left his faith in the God of eternity for the god of time.

We find through Job's "descent," another similar belief system (ultimately related to Chronos and Ananke). It is one of Fate-faith. Though "Fates" did not exist in Job's day known as "Fates" (as they would later be known in Norse mythology as Nornir), it was a "natural default" to become *fatalistic* when one's belief in the sovereignty of God is dismissed. To add, did not Satan act as a "Fate" with Eve in offering gifts if she partook of an illegal act? She was told by Satan that she would be "allotted" eyes to see as a god. It is this "satan" that is mentioned in scripture as "god," "ruler," "prince of the power of the air," as seen in Ephesians 2:2; John 12: 31; 1 John 5:19; 1 Timothy 4:1, etc.[1]

If I may turn my explanation to an interpretation of the storyline of Job 42 for a moment. We read in the last chapter of the book of Job *that God sent this evil upon Job*. So, it wasn't "the satan" (the adversity/the adversary) that was in charge, rather it was God. It is God who placed Job in *Abad* (Hebrew: *Abaddon* – "place of perishing") without dying. In a sense, Job was a journalist who was placed into the world of nonsense (a place of "no-signage;" "no-significance") which generated an infinite regress (one action leading to another without resolve or significance). This *Abad* (place of no "signaling") took its toll upon Job's critical thinking and emotional well-being. Nonetheless, Job remained consistently truthful to his "report" within his shadow logic even when he spoke *through* "the limitations of satan" in his hell. For sure, Job was an archetype of Jesus.

---

1. One might find *doctrines of devils* within the historical accounts of the Djinns, Metod (The Anglo-Saxon god of "measure out"/"to meet out"), and witches pertaining to dispensing of riches and the debt and repayment (*owing*) of the thing gained—just to name a few.

The "ordained" hand of darkness

I believe that honesty can be spoken through darkness. Job's complaint was a complex mesh of his heart still bound to God's sovereignty while his complaints *sounded off* the highly calibrated limitations of Satan's sifting. I always felt that the few times Satan spoke in the Bible he was "bound to" a *circuit* of action, a kind of dark "moor[2]" by which he *traversed*.

Job enters into the field of the satan.

THE DESCENT OF JOB

archetypes of Christ

Let's analyze Job's *descent* as he "leaves" his mind and faith from the solace of YHVH's predeterminism and enters into a nihilistic free fall. Passing through the *monstra*: the divine omens of afflictions from the dark hand of God. His "journey" is well documented through his afflictions.

Job's Monsters

> Job 3:3–5
> **3** Damn the Day I was born
> The night that said, "a boy was begot'
> **4** That Day –let it be darkness.
> God above ignore it.
> No light break upon it
> **5** Darkness and gloom claim it,
> Cloud settle over it
> Eclipse terrify it.

In Job 3:3, Job says, "Damn the Day." In the Hebrew text of Job 3:3 – we read: *ya-abad-yom* (*Qal* imperfect – "let perish the Day").

---

2. *Waes se grimma gaest Grendel haten, maere mercstappa, se dhe moras heold, fen ond faesten; fifelcynnes eard wonsaeli wer weardode hwile.* (Beowulf: ll 102–5)
Grendelkin (Grendel), like Cain, is forced to *tread the paths of exile (1352)*. Grendel is called "rinc man (720) bereft of joys (721, 1275)." Grendel, the *rinc man* or "border walker," *gives* us the modus operandi to Grendel's "loop" by which he treads. The "ring" myth, as a cursed "loop" that can be understood in J.R.R. Tolkien's, *The Lord of the Rings*, conveyed this same idea as the "curse" of man's endless cyclical pursuit for power that can only end in one's destruction.

In this statement, Job assigns no deity to damn the day in the Hebrew. So, I ask the question: by what "agency" is Job referring to? That is, who would "Damn the Day" if there is no God?

The Integrity of error

Job declines from his sound doctrinal stance with God yet does not sin because he is still saying the truth from the perspective of his worlview. That is, Job is consistently honest with his new participation inside shadow logic.

The MISS

Job spoke for agony as though it was reason. Still, in Job's shadow logic, Job never attributed power or causality to another deity other than YHVH. Even in the words of Job's shadow logic, Job reasoned the "impossibility" of another deity other than YHVH. Though constantly not mentioning YHVH, the spoken words from shadow logic seemed to "give way" to YHVH. That is, Job's words were shown to be governed by a specified "blindness" of THE CAUSAL AGENCY—(God blinds, gives sight, gives reason, takes reason away, etc.) first seen in Job 3:3 as Job's failure to assign in "Damning the Day." To me, this failure to assign causality was an obvious "aporia" or *irresolvable internal contradiction*, i.e., a logical disjunction in a theory if applied to the illusory doctrines of fatalism that leads to nihilism.

Again, fate cannot hold the title of *non-agency of causality* and then acclaim *causality*. Though nature and fate might seemingly *bring about* new conditions, they both share an office via determinism. That is, nature and fate are recipients of a higher order. "Mother nature" has been accused of being "fatal" in the sense of "bringing about" death and life but we realize "mother nature" as anthropomorphic, not literal.

Recalling the interview with Joseph Campbell and Bill Moyers. Joseph, one of the world's highest acclaimed mythologists, was asked by Bill Moyers: "Joseph, knowing all that you know, travelling to hundreds of remote villages, countries, islands, etc., and studying their languages, religions, beliefs, taboos, etc., what have you personally concluded to be the meaning of Life?" . . . Joseph answered: *"There is no meaning to life."* Bill Moyers, being a good-natured and very liberal ordained Baptist minister reacted, "this is ludicrous!" "You mean to tell me that in all the knowledge you have acquired you have concluded this?"

Ha. If I may take away from this an insight to Joseph. Knowing all of Joseph's works, Joseph was saying (with my paraphrase): "meaning is derived from what is meaningful . . . the chess board is Life—that is, the board of laws, rules, etc., i.e., *how nature works*. We, the people at the board, are the pieces by which our degrees are respectively played out on the board of rules. This is still not a meaning as of yet. Meaning comes from the *intent* by the *intender* who plays both sides and signifies *its* authority by the intangible act upon the tangible board as magistrate. Meaning is intent fully met in all of its corporal instances.

Job's actions thus far have led me to conclude that Job was arrested with what I will call, shadow logic.

Let's look at Job 3:3–5 again as:

Job the Mythologer

> Job 3:3–5
> **3** Damn the Day I was born
> The night that said, "a boy was begot'
> **4** That Day –let it be darkness.
> God above ignore it.
> No light break upon it
> **5** Darkness and gloom claim it,
> Cloud settle over it
> Eclipse terrify it.

Here we have Job's convolution of commanding particular elements of creation to "act" (or "fate" something) -- which, in Job's abandoned worldview, were all under God's sovereign rule regardless of the state of mind that Job was in. Job even denied the doctrines of old-world Heathenism, which gave the Fates power over the gods. Seems Job would have stuck to something, but, being sifted as Job was, God restrained all immediate comfort except for the future resolve that God had for him. A true lesson in faith.

Job can be assessed as follows within his contradictions:

a. using nonce intermediary compliant forces to "damn" the day at first

b. Tells God to "ignore" it (the only time Job refers to God in his delusion)

c. assuming that he, Job, is in command to speak into existence "a reality" that reality might be subsumed

Job "hides himself" from God in the illusory doctrines of fatalism via a "doctrine of shadows" and not a reality

Job damns the day that "a boy (i.e., Job) is begotten" and subscribes to this fate as day/day as fate.

I believe that Satan appears (*emphanistayke*) in the following points:

a. Satan as an "objective (seen, heard, experienced in the physical world) literary mechanism" which talked to YHVH in the first two chapters

b. Satan through the words of Job's wife's mouth: "Curse God and Die (for your loss)."

c. Satan as a Prophet of Shadows for "the" satan's own demise

Does Job not prophesy from the Devil's perspective? Such a Miltonian theme here! "Damn the *night* that a Boy (Job/Jesus Christ) was begotten." Moreover! —A Pre-Mosaic-Mesopotamian (i.e., Job/Jobab) who held a satanic prophecy of the Christ to come while cursing his own fate (Job's own fate). I see this as a *poetic mechanism* producing, by its nature, both (1) "shadow sketch of fatalism" and (2) death's portent of Messiah. Please refer to my video lecture on "Job and Macbeth, a comparative analysis" on my website.

There are many Christ typologies in Job. Job was righteous in all of his ways. The Lex Talionis/Codex Hammurabi (composed 1755–1750 BC) was the contemporary law code during Job's day. The Ludlul-Bel-Nemeqi (ca. 1,700 BC) was a Sumerian poem concerning "the man of suffering"(Hebrew: *Iyyob*). Yet, no infraction. Job was clean, pure, above the law of retribution . . . and still, God caused the calamity upon Job (as accepted in Job 1 and 2 as coming from GOD's causal act. Job was not indebted to the law but a keeper of the law. Job was stated as righteous in this way which answers to the later false claims of his "friends" who "comfort-indicted" him as having done something to incur a punishment from God. We will find that "The Satan" is the one, in his jurisdiction, to act in speech through these "friends." In the flesh, Job, we will find, was in hell for a few days, "cut off from God" via the beliefs of fatalism, infinite regress, dualism, doctrines of rogue agency-free will, and retributive ideas that have nothing to do with grace.

Job has not sinned here in his sheol, or hell. He is speaking from sheol with the words of "the Satan" —as did Peter, the cornerstone of the true Christian Church.

Even Peter was called, "Satan," when Peter told Jesus that Jesus wouldn't "suffer unto death" (T Cup). Though, Peter was sawn asunder for the sake of Christ.

Even Jesus asked his Father in the garden of Gethsemane to "let this cup pass, *nonetheless*, your Will be done!"

In all of this, Jesus did not sin, regardless of his flesh "wishing" and "desiring" to dismiss the cup unto death. Both Peter and Jesus said words that would have alleviated pain, suffering, death, *calamity* to "have passed." Peter held to the uncommitted and unfounded prophecy that substantiates The *Messiah* as Jesus. To deny *this* death is to deny Jesus for who he was and *is*.

Job 3:4 – "That Day--let it be darkness, God above ignore it (Sheol – out of sight) No light break upon it (--also, "it" is "the Fated Day- supervening fates implied under the speech of "the Shadows" of dark allotments/doom/—as Tolkien might say, "in the Land of Mordor where the Shadows lie").

Job 3:5 – "Darkness (as Fate) and Gloom (as Fate) claim it, Cloud (as Fate) settle over it" contains a dark-brilliance in Job's blind but honest poesis.

I found 7 points within the Field of Job's "fatalism" which led to infinite regression/nihilism:

1. Job's attribution to "the plight" as a "replacement Theology" for Job's past beliefs and doctrine within God's sovereign intent. This "replacement theology" is laden with inconsistent and antithetical motifs to an intentful sovereign God. These inconsistent and antithetical motifs verify their own laws of "infinite regress"
2. "Plight" is a nonsense word- or "nonce" word as a "false signal'
3. The "bru-ha-ha" of war/devastation/riot/eats its own tail only to return again
4. There is no "direction" other than reaction and muddled self-referencing (equivocation).

5. The "field of fatalism" is the board of no rule containment; the field of fatalism is without loving intent; the field of fatalism is the field of "blankets" of allotments to debts which are deaths. The field of fatalism is the field by which the only signals are those leading to your death. The field of fatalism's "belief" is limited and finite: "hold on to your goods, riches, stuff and things until that day by which "fate" comes upon you and signals all things to--i.e., your death; your debt.

6. A failed "theodicy" is an invention to believe that God is placed within the field of bru-ha ha/--a land of no signals, a land of "evil" – where God has *no* part to take from this "field of evil," "field of calamity." As an example: many "nicer" Christians try to implement various theodicies to argue out God's responsibility of any evil in this world —moral or physical. Such thinking leads inevitably to "dualism."

7. God's *intent* is taken out of the illusory belief in Job's archaic theodicy, because Job only address "calamity" as "evil" and "evil" as "plight" and "the day" as the bringer of the "plight" and the day to be darkened out and "not have ever been." This is nihilism. Nihilism, in fact, is the result of infinite regressive thinking—though an infinite regressive wouldn't tell you that, initially.

JOB CHAPTERS 1 AND 2

Satan: The Antagonist

Though the antagonist's identity is subsumed in the satan figure, we will later see that "the satan" or "sifter" is revealed as the hand of God, or the evil that the LORD had brought upon Job (Job 42:11). Job spoke through the mouth of the satan's limitations in Chapter 3. In chapter 6 we begin Job's "reckoning" and his slow "ascent" out of the darkness or "hell" from whence God placed him. In all that happened to Job, Job said to God, "I know that you can do all things; no purpose of yours can be thwarted." (Job 42:2, NIV) After physically seeing God, Job says, "But now my own eye has seen you so I recant and repent in dust and ashes" (Job 42:5–6).

Good and calamity are revealed as the "Will of God" – though not yet revealed until later. That is: God creates good (Hebrew: *Tov* – fortune, building up) and calamity (Hebrew: *Ra'ah* – "evil": breaking down)> Job's wife's words denote her following a satanic alliance —i.e., "wealth and health" are "good," therefore, loss of wealth and health is the negation of good > Job acts as a prophet of God's divine will by what Job does not/cannot say—being that Job's role is "fixed" to fatalism, nihilism, infinite regress" *from* the of divine will >Job, speaking as the voice of Satan, still prophesied the "boy begotten" as a cursed day within the context of nihilism's rule— THIS is possibly the satanic prophecy of the coming of the Messiah and the despair of nihilism's rule.

"The Day, let it be darkness—" is not completed. This is Job's fallen nature. To say, "The Day—let it be darkness and Darkness, let it be Day" < this is a literary mechanism used in Shakespeare's *Macbeth* (which the "opposites" still have direction to go in). Job's "direction" goes into the illusory notion of "just ending."

Job doesn't say, "tables turned" in my "plight" as do the witches in Macbeth. What Job is saying is: "let the Light (acknowledging light) become Black (knowing black because he knows light)" and *nothing else*.

Job's hidden "true north" must be known to him for if all things go forward to God's good plan/teleon, then, the unreality of a plan being an "opposite" of God's sovereignty is all Job had to go on in his illusory plight of nihilism.

There are no other tools or devices by which Job could use to "reason," whether the "reason" was sane or insane. Sovereignty was the only solution and it was the only thing that Job and his wife did not acknowledge when they spoke for the unreason of satan.

This elicitation of truth percolates through Job's torture. Job only mimics the satan (which tells me "satan" is tortured, regardless of satan's existence). Job's natural rejection and natural blindness of Supernatural Autonomy is all too natural. "Let the darkness rule and no light be used." Job exclaims (by not mentioning God's sovereign Will as he clearly did in the first 3 chapters of Job) that which he does not truly believe meanwhile being stripped of his belief for the moment. Job extols the picture negative of God—hence acknowledging God wholly, yet "wholly-indirect."

Therefore, I believe Job is the perfect example of a pure man "as" the mouth of God and the satan. I believe this narrative also tells me that Job is not sinning when he is being honest within his reason of "plight" vs. God's sovereignty.

The plight: that Job only sees creation as if it were possible without God –and the justification that there can't be an employed "sense, prime cause, intent, resolve, etc.—hence, Job is without a "will," bound to pure nihilism, yet a believer against his "plight-filled-will."

Still, Job is tested by being "detached" from God solely against Job's desire to love and be at peace with God. In the same fashion, Jesus, as he hung dying on a cross, was abandoned (Lama, Sabachthani – My God My God, why have you forsaken me) as was Job—though, Christ Jesus was human and God having the power of God Father to "understand" why his suffering must happen. Maybe this is the biggest lesson, i.e., we are to conform to Jesus' image through great suffering. Job's story also teaches me that being in the Will of God means that we are coming to a point that we will understand we are no longer bound to darkness or the illusion of "free-autonomous-will."[3]

---

3. Please see Jones, "Shadows of Job," for two other possible treatments on the "descent of Job" that I kept out.

Chapter Thirty-Four

Terminologies

Looking at the more natural elements that have "professed" Jesus over time:

The origin of words can be found from their objective usages such as "rock, tree, river, wheel, day, etc."

Words in their earliest forms also represented an associative nature by which the observer related themselves to the observed.

Let's take the aforementioned objective (or "objects") terms: "rock, tree, river, wheel, and day" from their root forms to their abstractions.

Rock

The Hebrew words for stone were a few. One of them was *dabar*. *Dabar* could be used to mean *logos* in the Greek language. Nonetheless, *dabar* and *logos* had their differences which I will not treat here. *Dabar* also meant "stone of order, a stone for reference while dancing around (the *Hag*). *Dabar* also meant "judgment," "bee," "prophet," "speech of delineation," and "reference point." Thorlief Boman gave a wonderful case study for *dabar* by saying that *dabar*, the Hebrew equivalent of LOGOS, was known as the "driving force behind words that follow one another or to drive forward that which is behind." Thus, *dabar* meant "a function of speaking and deed." Such cases of "word" and "deed" as the same thing can be found in Genesis 24:66, 1 Kings 11:41 and John 1:1.

Tree

Our Proto Indo-European root says it all: "*drew-o-* = "be firm, solid, steadfast, etc." from where the abstract concept of "true" comes from. I have had on multiple occasions run upon the "abstract" of "root, stem, and branches" for the equivalent of "truth." That is to say, "to speak the full thing, from beginning to the end of the thing." I can have no argument against this "abstraction" to be the best answer for "what is true?" Jesus is the "root" of Jesse (cf. Isaiah 11: 10; Romans 15:12). He is the Arm (*Zimach* – "the Branch" of the Lord/"the extension") of the Lord (Isaiah 59:1). Though not a "tree," per se, John 15:5 Jesus said, "I am the vine and you are the branches." Jesus makes it clear that he is the vine or Greek *ampelos* meaning the "root coil" of the vine from which the branches (*klaymata*) abide.

River

No one has given me a better definition of "river" than Plato in his dialogues of Cratylus. *Rous* or "river" means the uninterrupted flowing thing. Plato took this objective form to the mental. Plato teaches us that the *rous* or river is likened to "uninterrupted thought" or "flow of thought without impedance" which is also referred to as *poiesis* or poetics.

Plato continued in his Cratylus dialogue by saying that in contrast to the "flow," "river," *rous*, or *poiesis* —anything that halts or goes against the flow, river, or *rous* of divine motion in a man was based on idolatry. When we lust for an objective form that is not in the context of the divine flow we commit idolatry. Therefore, if we set our *eyes* or sights (*eido*) to serve (*latreia*) another thing we *go out of the rous/river*. Hence, eido + latreia = "idolatry" —> the traversing of the flow causing a pathology.

Wheel

P.I.E. *kw(e)-kwl-o-/root: *owk* = wheel,circle."

Cycle, revolve, round, move, sojourn, …. that which turns.

Greek: *kuklops*, round-eye (*kukl* – "round"/*ops* – "eye"), bounding circle, limit, divide, separate, landmark (sometimes marked with stones).

Latin: "Chorus" – a dance in a circle – such persons singing and dancing.

Bulgarian: *Horo* – a processional dance in a circle.

The Greek also holds to the cognate: *Khoros* which means round dance; dancing place; enclosed dancing floor.

The limitation by which one can move.

Day

P.I.E. root: *agh – "a day" which initially meant "the eye of the deity." The P.I.E. word for "to shine" is *dyeu-. Sanskrit: *Dyaus*– god of the sky. Many scholars hold that the Germanic prefix "d-" was added from the *dyeu-* (originally: *agh-*) making the Germanic, Norse, and Gothic "day": *dag, dagr, tag*, etc. which finally resulted in our English "day." This word also held a theological connotation as the "eye" of God or God himself. All such a treatment can be found in the thoroughly exhaustive work on "Day" by Dr. Anna Meshki's *Kartvelian Linguo-Culturology*.

Mountain

Horos: that *place* where heaven and earth meet. The place of "cutting off." Eternity seems to be implied as being "past" this abode of the gods who live on the top of the mountain, at least, that is where the gods walk (either within or without our sight).

All of this to say, our origins of language have a linkage to not only God but his abode, movement, his attributes, and force by which all other sequences are caused. This is an endless pursuit and one by which I will continue until that which is greater comes to complete us all.

THE MEDIEVAL SKETCH

Medieval words as representations of ordered society

Words such as "villain" – "villager," though villain can carry a bad connotation; pagan (*paein*/the "ones who lived past the peg"); pedestrian (the *podos/paedos* – little ones/little footers), infantry (*feda* – Old English: "infants")"; heathen (*heath + -an*) – "one who lives in the uncultivated areas" – a.k.a., the heath; "doom" – judgment – domicile (house of judgment/*dom*/doom/dominion, judgment house/place where rules are made and followed—hence, "dominion, domicile, dominate, domestic, etc." Cf. Old English: *Faeder* – faith, trust, abide in —the "federal" laws, house, dominion, etc.

We can see how a linguistically-ordered world did indeed exist for millennia! What happened to that world? My answer is simple: we came from unyielding word-priority societies. Our lives depended upon communication. There was no room to "play with words" – so to speak. As "abstractions" from the objective forms occurred it seems that they occurred with reverence to make "higher sense" of our existence. These word abstractions were "word-attempts" to make sense of the "higher expressions" that humans wanted to make. These apprehensions are why we are a higher species than basic neanderthal man. Language is nearly everything.

My contention has always been that the "bastardization" of words (i.e., the extrapolation and disenfranchisement of indigenously used words from their correlative cultures by which they were used to signal meaning) creates a weaker society because their language becomes riddled with linguistic incoherencies (etymological aporias) without the gold in the bank to back it up. For the "new words" begin a new without primitive objective ties.

Then, we must address that many words that were stripped from their "natural" or "pagan" usage[1] and "moralized" to "fit" later Latin church doctrines of "damnation." Funny enough, there are at least 4

---

1. I would have used the word "endonymics" here but for the sake of keeping it less complicated throughout the book I placed it here in my footnotes describing the study of "indigenous languages used by a particular group, class, tribe, etc. that bind one to another socially, religiously, anthropologically, etc. to each other by the very language they use. Another way to say it: the reference or "signage" language of the tribe is the glue to the culture—a.k.a.: "semiotics." And in this cultural-linguistic-glue I argue that the importance of linguistics, morphologies of language, etymologies and philology is of the utmost importance if one is to make "sense (semion/sign)" of our history. Linguistics are handed to us to study and learn from therefore I reject any argument against studying any branch of linguistics and consider it academic/intellectual suicide to dismiss linguistics on any level. As a side note: It might be of interest that Genesis 11 accounts for a biblical character (most believe it was Nimrod/Enmerker) who built the Tower of Babel attempted to create a man-made endonymic language, i.e., His own Shem (Hebrew: *Shem* – "language, law, boundary line"). Subsequently, as the Bible tells us, Nimrod experienced the collapse of his kingdom and tower. I further this event of Babel by concerning the 4 very distinct Hebrew words for "language" that the English only uses as "language." These 4 distinct terms in the Hebrew for "language" are treated in my video lectures in Jones, "National Monuments Started in Genesis 11."

different usages that I found for "damn²" in Latin found in the legal verbiage of Seneca and in the magnum opus Oxford Latin Dictionary by Lewis and Short which only one of the 4 four forms of "damn" means to a "place of endless retribution" or "condemnation." This shows that unless the choice to have the proper declensional form of Latin's "damn-" translationally match that of the Greek for its *kollosin* – i.e., "judgment unto repentance," then what had been chosen for the Latin Vulgate's "damn" did not indeed not match that of *kollosin*, or "condemned to repentance."

Consider the following words and their roots:

- Good: (Greek: agathos = "good;" "that which is beneficial"/Hebrew Tov = agathos).
- Evil: Proto Indo-European: *upelo* = *hyper* = over and exceeding, missing the mark (due to excessiveness); Proto Germanic: *ubilaz* = unable, *not skilled*, not able (to bring good), etc.; Greek: "aboulia" = "not" + "directed'--> "ill-advised."
- Holy: *hagios* = unmixed, without blend, pure.
- God: *Gud* = Proto Indo-European = a cheese sack made of a cow's stomach; that which holds "goodness;" the "Holy Sack."
- Nature: phusis: natural, goes with nature to its teleology, i.e., its "fate/fatality" – death, rot, decay.
- Faith: (Greek: pistis) – resting in something *that is not seen* in its fullness yet yields goodness. Proto Indo-European: Faith: "Bheidh"- a place to have rest, abiding, … to have respite in what one has.
- Sin: harmeteia – "missing the mark" — "going outside the circle, bounds, eye."
- Free: Anglo Saxon: *Freod* = the freed ones; ones of the household; *a wife bought from the slave market.* Fre – Middle English: "generous" (as used in Chaucer's day. Status: "Not bound as a slave."
- Baptism: see my treatment on the seven distinct forms of baptism: *bapto, bapteisin, baptizomai, tingere, tauraboulim,* washing, *baptismos*, etc. The range of "baptisms" go from "sprinkled" to "immersed without cessation"—such as the fire of the Holy Spirit in us to witness to many of the Gospel of Jesus.

2. *damnaverit* as used in an inheritance from one who has passed on to another; *damnosus* as used in "full of injury" or "having received injury;" *damnum* – a penalty; *damnas* – obligated to make a gift for someone; *damnaticius* – condemned

TERMINOLOGIES

- Earth: Anglo Saxon: *arda* = Land; Hebrew: *erotz*: a piece of potsherd from the bigger pot or vessel. Akkadian: *erets* – "earth," Sumerian: cf. Aratta: i.e., the shiny mountain; land of myth; "praiseworthy," "the temple of Kes (Cush?)'--i.e., central site of the nation, praiseworthy furious bull, etc. [cf. page 105 "An Annotated Sumerian Dictionary].

- Tongues: Greek: *glossa* = intelligent language (as in "glossary" vs. "glossolalia" = "to babble" or "utter chaotic sounds").

- Communion: Greek: *koinonia* = to share that which is "in common" with others (not a liturgical practice originally).

- Martyr: Greek: *martyros* = used for those who are (or one who is) "mature"/of age to do the complete job, etc.

Chapter Thirty-Five

The Rocks Would Cry Out

Luke 19: 29 – 40

29 And it came to pass, when he was come nigh to Bethphage and Bethany, at the mount called the mount of Olives, he sent two of his disciples,

30 Saying, Go ye into the village over against you; in the which at your entering ye shall find a colt tied, whereon yet never man sat: loose him, and bring him hither.

31 And if any man asks you, Why do ye loose him? thus shall ye say unto him, Because the Lord hath need of him.

32 And they that were sent went their way, and found even as he had said unto them.

33 And as they were loosing the colt, the owners thereof said unto them, Why loose ye the colt?

34 And they said, The Lord hath need of him.

35 And they brought him to Jesus: and they cast their garments upon the colt, and they set Jesus thereon.

36 And as he went, they spread their clothes in the way.

37 And when He was come nigh, even now at the descent of the mount of Olives, the whole multitude of the disciples began to rejoice and praise God with a loud voice for all the mighty works that they had seen;

38 Saying, Blessed be the King that cometh in the name of the Lord: peace in heaven, and glory in the highest.

39 And some of the Pharisees from among the multitude said unto him, Master, rebuke thy disciples.

40 And He answered and said unto them, I tell you that, if they should hold their peace, the stones would immediately cry out.

COMMENTARY

A whole crowd of disciples (*matheton*) began their *hallal* (or praises) for all of the miracles (*dynameon*, "evidence(s) of spiritual power") they had seen. These *matheton*/disciples began to ecstatically praise Jesus knowing Zechariah 9:9: "Rejoice greatly, Daughter Zion! Shout, Daughter Jerusalem! See, your king comes to you, righteous and victorious, lowly and riding on a donkey, on a colt, the foal of a donkey."

Luke 19: 39-40 states (by Jesus) a contingency of profession: "if" they (the human witnesses) don't witness for me (Jesus)/"then" nature (the stones in this case) will. Jesus reverts to nature professing the Gospel saying that if it was possible that the human will (still being governed to its nature) would/could reject[1] its profession of Jesus, then, the "overwhelming necessity"[2] of the creative act of the Will of the Father would have already caused the inevitable to arise, that is, a "witness" to his son's messianic import. Hence, never was there a "counter – act" to the Will of the Father and the proclamation of his Son!

A BRIEF EXEGESIS

In verse 39, we see a "select few" of the Pharisees: *tines ton Pharisaion*. There is a sense that these "select few Pharisees" were in the procession within the mix of the mob. John 12:19 speaks of a group of Pharisees that stood off from the procession and blamed each other for the victories of Jesus. The Pharisees that were brazen enough to tell Jesus to rebuke his disciples were probably not of the same order as the Pharisees that stood back. Regardless, Jesus tells these aggressive Pharisees, "If these (his diciples) shall hold their peace the stones would cry out (Greek: *ean houtoi siopesoisin hoi lithoi kraxousin*)."

---

1. Jesus' stating of the ludicrous for "effect." In other words: "if the impossible would arise, then, the inevitable would become.
2. as the French goes: "*necessite imperieuse*" —> "overwhelming necessity"

If these shall hold their peace = This is what is called "a condition of the first class – deemed as determinately fulfilled. *Ean* ("if these") is used instead of *ei* because it "cuts no figure in the case (cf. Acts 8:31[cf. "a" at bottom]; I Thessalonians 3:8 [cf. b below]; I John 5:15 [cf.c below])." The kind of condition is determined by the mode which is here indicative. The future tense by its very nature does approximate the aorist subjunctive, but after all it is the indicative. The stones will cry out: — *hoi lithoi kraxousin*. Such a case for the impossible happening.

a. And he said, "How can I, *except someone* should guide me"?
b. "For now we live, *if you* stand fast in the Lord."
c. "And *if we* know that he hears us in whatever we ask, we know that we already possess what we have asked of him."

MY SENTIMENTS

Here we see Zechariah's prophecy being fulfilled with Christ riding into Jerusalem on a donkey as Messiah. We see Jesus making it clear that inanimate objects (in this case, the Lithos-stones) would "animate" and proclaim Jesus as Messiah if his disciples didn't. Yet, the Pharisees were there to taunt. Still, the Messiah was there fulfilling the prophecy that must be fulfilled in order to complete the plan of the Father. Furthermore, Jesus laid out another prophecy here. Jesus said if "those" who are praising/announcing the Messiah *could be halted* (i.e., an impossibility by prophecy and its predetermined course) then these stones would praise me. As such happened, the stones of the temple at Jerusalem were all turned over in AD 70 to confirm Jesus' validation as a prophet and Messiah. For his message was that he was the Messiah with the validity of a prophet unlike any other prophet. For no true prophet would claim themselves as the Messiah except for Jesus.

I believe that *all things* (matter, anti-matter, quarks, electrons, bosons, etc.) are bound to a "creed" which holds to the integrity of the Gospel of Jesus Christ. I believe that the evolution of the creation within the physical, psychical, emotional, and intellectual aspects *expressed in total sum* (from creation to teleon/eschaton) is an "indicative motion" signaling or heralding the Messiah.

Chapter Thirty-Six

The Intangible that Naturally Cries Out

All such words (plus our entire English language) have beautiful histories in antiquity answering for us. Yet so many perplexing questions have been created through the "disenfranchisement" of their pagan or natural usage.[1] Several of these listed words must go back further than Greek or Hebrew to see how they naturally and supernaturally came to be in the containment of the Father's intention and the math of the logos' order. "Good" links to "God" which is linked to *guda*, literally "cheese" formed from curdled milk.[2] "Faith" is Proto Indo-European: *bheidh*—a place to settle in and launch from, a kind of bed, either mental or physical or both.

I am not only referring to words, but the liturgies that became so sacrosanct that you would be damned by men's hands to challenge a man-made idea of God. Hence, the accepted language that would support the liturgy. Consider the medieval damnation language in Latin and its cognates, which in turn bastardized the English terms for judgment in the King James Bible. We have numerous terms for "damn" and "judge" that were mishandled and shaped into the singular meaning of "judgment

---

1. By pagan/natural, I mean the usage that was established throughout the ages in a non-religious way, which has subsequently become a "moralized," "utilitarian," "modern" and/or practical" yielding its force to a "connotation" that might or might not be philogically sound. This filtering out of the primal sense of the words has left us without the force to the original sense by which it was intended. Worse yet, I believe that we, at present time, have secularized our words by turning our "language" to the trend of the day to fit our relative position of how we want to use language. This is the death of a language and the birth of the overtaking of a culture with relativism. Our American culture is proud to do this. Many Americans boldly say that "etymologies are useless, just use what you need to convey what 'needs to be said.'"

2. Jones, "Holy Cheese."

in hell" as many believe even today. In reality, there were different Latin meanings for "damn" or "judge," such as "to see which one you want," "to scrutinize as less or more," "to disqualify," "to send to prison," "to send to hell." Such "moralizing" terms for judgment in the book of Revelation divert us from the coherence[3] of "leading to grace from the penitentiary" (i.e., Greek *kolosos* as opposed to Greek *krinos*, which means, "a crime which is to be addressed by law'—ending there with punishment and the lack of a "leading to a betterment or better place"). Much like Greek *telos*, it gives us a stative form and nothing more. Living words, to me, are obvious in that they are not "stative." That is, they are still moving forward, taking us on a journey, taking us to a place where we will finally understand, directing us to a future destination, a hope.

I also refer to the "modernization" and adaptation of current cultural flows which "influence" the verbiage of the New Testament as presented in English. Such displacements of the original Greek have crept into our modern "baptisms" of the modern "church." We think of "baptism" as one thing. We do not look at its force throughout history, its allegory, its directional indication to the Messiah, etc. Such is the case for the six baptisms that I can recollect from Dr. Walter Dale's 5 volume treatment on various baptisms: 1) the *tauraboolum* or bull's blood baptism poured out upon warriors and gladiators before a fight; (2) ritual washings in the "brazen sea" for the Levites before the high priest would enter the most holy part of the temple; (3) ordinance baptism for anyone entering Jerusalem from the "heathen's land;" (4) Johannine baptism where John the Baptist (as prophet) symbolically poured out water upon Jesus to announce Jesus as the Messiah; (5) early Christian baptism to announce one's "coming to be" in the regards of ordinance and respect Jewish law as a follower of Jesus; finally, (6) Ephesians 4's *baptisma*, which is an odd "baptism." *Baptisma* means a "result," "total submersion," "absolute change," "sunk into." This is not "as" a one-time dipping or dunking but the "result" of an agent of change put on the one receiving *baptisma*. The prophet John the Baptist was doing a prophetical pantomime and John let it be known that his act of water baptism was necessary for that moment but that the Messiah would come later and baptize (*baptisei*) with the Holy Spirit and with fire. So, here we see Jesus not baptizing at all with water but with the Holy Spirit. Not once was Jesus mentioned to have "baptized" with water in the Gospels. It also makes sense that this kind

---

3. that is, of what I believe to be a coherent biblical narrative.

of fiery Spirit "baptism" would be *the* agent of change upon the recipient. We can see the evolutions of water to spirit-and-fire baptisms if we can understand the cultural paradigms by which our ancestors acted upon[4]. There can be no judgment to these evolutions that lead to the Messiah and the Holy Spirit. But, how can we return to ordinances made by man's hands if the Messiah is the *telos* of these older watery acts of hope?! How can we do the pagan's *tauraboolum* which was the natural starter for the allegory to "blood sacrifice" that would be fulfilled in Christ (i.e., the pagan's classic baptism of animal blood sprinkling)?!? Or, how can we return to a high priest's washing (Judaic baptism of water washing) in order to enter a "most high" temple when we ourselves are the temple of God[5]? How can we return to John the Baptist when his pantomiming of the greater act of spirit baptism (Johannic baptism/prophetical/pant omime enactment) is fulfilled in the incarnate Christ? The last and *only* Christ sanctified "baptism" was the continuance of the Holy Ghost and fire[6]. Do we not have that daily? Do we not have fiery trials daily? Do we not have the comforter to guide us when we pray? If we hold to a perpetual ordinance of water baptisms in the churches and hold that there is an "alive baptism" of the spirit of God upon us in perpetuity we should therefore have two baptisms. But this is not biblical!

Paul makes it clear that there is one baptism. Paul brought us from the "foundations" of our understanding to this glorious "baptism" found in Ephesians 2, 3, and ending in Ephesians 4:5—

> Ephesians 4:5
> "There is now one Lord, one faith, and one baptism (*baptisma*: noun/singular/neuter)."

This "baptism" was in the nominative (noun) state, yet *bapto* in its root form is an active verb. What does this mean?! It means that the verb "baptism" has taken on a state-of-continuity – i.e., a gerundive)[7].

---

4. cf. Dr. Walter Dale's 5 incredible treatments on the very distinct baptisms: *Classic Baptism* (which is a look into pagan rites and rituals such as the taurobolium or bull's blood baptism and other pagan "baptisms"); *Judaic Baptism*, *Johannic Baptism*, *Christic Baptism*, and *Patristic Baptism*.

5. I Corinthians 3:16–17 – "Do you not know that you are God's temple and that God's Spirit dwells in you?"

6. The early church fathers (Ante-Nicene AD 30s to 350), prior to Constantine's Roman Catholic institution (Council of Nicaea/Nicene/Post-Nicene – ca. AD 350) did not hold to the doctrines of water baptism. Such early church fathers Gregory of Nazianzen, Alexander Didymus, Ambrose.

7. much like adding "-ing" to a verb like "travel" – to "traveling." Baptisma is used in

Baptisma (as used as the one baptism in Eph. 4:5) is not a "one-time-washing, sprinkling, dipping, etc." As Gregory of Nazianzen says, "*Baptisma* is not a type (Greek: *tupixou*) but rather a reality (Greek: *alaythinou*) that purifies the depths of our soul."[8] Baptism(a) is active, it is continual. It is eternally coming to be upon you. Therefore, if water was employed in this "state" of baptism, we would continually be submerged, therefore, drowned. And, "drowned unto what? When the Bible uses *bapto* (fully submerged), an enactment of the water ritual was exemplified. Neither is the case found in Ephesians 4:5. So, if there is only one baptism(a), that of the spirit which purges us, then this baptism(a) must be the same baptism that Jesus talked about: "Ye shall be baptized with the baptism that I am baptized with." John the Baptist made it clear of the distinct nature of his portentous washing of the coming one (who was before John in the flesh) and the baptism of fire that Jesus would baptize with (and be baptized with). So, with all of this said, there can be only one baptism. It must be the one by the Holy Spirit (which is joined with fire). This is the burning, the purging, the fire of God that cleans us from our sins. Have we been so blind for so long that we can't accept this? —that is, that God does the purging of our sins through fire.

Of course, the study of baptism takes us further than even this, but just one example of how easy it is to overlook the social, religious, linguistic, and endonymic usages for such a thing as "baptism."

I also place this portion (baptisms) of my book under the noble truth of the apocalyptic **view** because it gives us a bigger "vision" for the perspective of God acting upon us.

Quantum thinking

Take for example our Proto Indo-European (P.I.E.) root meaning for "unfurl, unfold, roll out," etc. We have the P.I.E. root word *dran*. *Dran* is the root word for "drama" and "trauma." They mean the same thing under the etymological "jurisprudence" of *dran*. Such a word might depict "to roll out" or "unfold" (P.I.E. *dran* > tran, tram—trauma/"drama" = to watch the full act unfurl/"to watch the quantum-gestalt of the thing[9]."

Ephesians 4:5 as "baptize + -ing." Therefore, in the "continual sense."

8. Dale, *Christic Baptism and Patristic Baptism*, 342.

9. (Skeat, *Concise Dictionary of English Etymology*, 504) "Thing": Old English: "thing, thingc, as in *"meeting, assembly, council, discussion,"* also *"action, deed to be done."* In late Old English, *"concrete inanimate object; that which exists by itself; entity,*

From the linguistic amoral-pagan-secular and/or heathen's usage of such a word, we would have a "secular-faith-based" word. It would mean that there was a beginning and end and connective tissue to the events from beginning to end.

We, as Christians (if we do believe in God's predeterminism), should have no judgment in taking a *pagan*[10] term as "predetermined" as ultimate in its meaning (in every era) and understand and believe that God has brought us to a more evolved sense to "see" that we are in the fullness of time and are allowed to see such truths—that is, if God predestined *all* things, then, the "trauma," "drama," "unfurling" *is* the *will* of God—just as Ecclesiastes has said! But, we want to eradicate such "traumas" and "dramas" from our memory as being "evil" through neo-designer psychology and failed nouthetic counseling of only "theologies" and "neo-christian-based ideologies." Then, we have the *demonic*[11] already telling us how to think. Such is the case of the health and wealth prosperity movement (*daomidzo*) as well which condemns the God who brings "trauma" to someone's life. Have we not learned anything from the book of Job?

Again, in Job 1:21, Job had just lost all of his possessions and family, save that of his wife. Job said, "God gives and takes away. Blessed be the name of the LORD." I wonder what the literal "daemonic" prosperity preachers would say to this? Wasn't Job blessed? Wasn't Job in the "trauma"/"drama" of God? Wasn't Job written in the unfurling of the plan of God?! Then, *why* would anyone who knows their Bible condemn the

---

being, creature;" also "event." The sense evolution probably is from the notion of the "matter" or *subject of deliberation in an assembly.* Compare French *chose,* Spanish *cosa* "thing," from Latin *causa "judicial process, lawsuit, case"* (see *cause* (n.)); Latin *res:* «affair, thing," also "case at law, cause." It is reconstructed to be from Proto-Germanic *thinga-* "assembly" (source also of Old Frisian *thing* "assembly, council, suit, matter, thing," Middle Dutch *dinc* «court-day, suit, plea, concern, affair, thing," Dutch *ding* "thing," Old High German *ding* «public assembly for judgment and business, lawsuit," German *Ding* "affair, matter, thing," Old Norse/Icelandic: thing. Þing "public assembly." The Germanic word is perhaps (Watkins, Boutkan) literally "appointed time," from a PIE *tenk-* (1), from root *ten-* «stretch," perhaps on the notion of *"stretch of time for a meeting or assembly,"* A.S. thing – thnc.

10. Skeat, Dr. Walter, "A Concise Dictionary of English Etymology": "a *countryman*"; *"villager"*; *"common folk,"* Latin: *paganus,* (1) a village, (2) a pagan, because the rustic people remained rustic – Latin: *pagus, a village, district, canton.* Supposed to be from *"pag,"* base of *"pangere"* to *"fasten"*; as *being marked out by fixed limits*; cf. "Pact."

11. demon: *dao* = "to dispense" + *midzo* = "riches"/"abundance" = *daomidzo* = "demon."

logical acts that are leading to a logical conclusion from a logical starting point?!? Aren't all things God intended?

If God wanted to, not being bound to time, could he erase you and me right now? As an author of a book, could a writer not say, "this is not worthy to be here"? But thankfully, God is *intent* on what he does and he does not make mistakes. Physics doesn't make mistakes when applied properly. Nature is an expression that doesn't lie. Nature is God's nomos – expression. True expression has true intention—and mostly, the truest of all must be the intender, the author, the causer, the motivator, the holder, the verb, the existing one, YHVH— "the one who holds all, the one who causes all, the verb, none other."

We blame others and ourselves for the destruction of our plans, other's outcomes, wealth, lack of wealth. We complain at the breakdown of our moral situations on a global or nationalistic level. We complain when the president not of your choice is elected—shamefully, sometimes through their entire term vs. praying for their souls. We say, "it's not like it used to be."

Show me, please, where chaos (exemplified entropic "progression") makes a mistake. It doesn't. Complex, yes— orderly-disorder, yes— predetermined, yes— final expression of thermodynamics, yes— all energies required from the point of origin to make a predeterministic expression from beginning to end without flaw of expressed formula, yes— the end needing the beginning and middle of events, yes! Hence, our first maxims from Ecclesiastes 1:9, 10; 3:15; and Isaiah 45:7 – ff, Isaiah 48.

Finally, if all that I am presenting is fiction, fantasy, folklore, or myth, you'd still have hope. However, I believe that this is not the case. We have rules regardless of what we think. We claim to be free in our wills but free from what? "Free" is a relative or relational word as I have said. "Free" means *to will without the shackles of one thing but shackled to another*. Being "free" means *freedom from something because you are bound to something else*. Being bound to something or someone, such as a good wife or good husband, is often used as an expression of being committed to one person and "free from" the insanity of the dating game or a bad partner.

Chapter Thirty-Seven

A Return to the Reason of Universal Salvation

HAVING DISCUSSED "FREE" AS "free from"—we have a "prepositional stance" with our Lord to be bound to him. Let's look at other prepositions relating to Christ and us that support this kind of freedom "from" the natural world.

The prepositions of Christ

Colossians 1:16–20, speaking of Christ, says:

> **16** For *by* Him were all things created, that are *in* heaven, and that are *in* earth, visible and invisible, whether they be thrones, or dominions, or principalities, or powers: all things were created *by* Him, and *for* Him.
> **17** And He is *before* all things, and *by* Him all things consist.
> **18** And He is the head of the body, the church: Who is the *beginning*, the firstborn *from* the dead; that *in* all things He might have the preeminence.
> **19** For it pleased the Father that *in* Him should all fullness dwell;
> **20** And, having made peace through the blood of His cross, *by* Him to *reconcile all things unto* Himself, by Him, I say, whether they be things *in* earth, or things *in* heaven.

Focusing on these prepositions allows us to see that this passage focuses both on creation and redemption in, by, of, out from, at, and through Christ. Christ precedes all things in time and everything is created through him–including our salvation. Everything (Colossians 1:20) is reconciled through him. "By" means of Christ's blood shed on the cross— *all things will be fully restored unto God.* Just look at the language used in the verses in Colossians 1:16-20. "Reconcile" translates from the Greek *apokatallassó* to mean "fully restore;" "bring back to new;" "bring back to harmony." "All things" translates *ta panta* which means "everything;" "all;" "every;" "without loss of anything."

How does all of this theology and language study relate to me?

Whether or not you are a believer in Christ you will inevitably experience tragedy. You will inevitably experience hardships, possibly on a daily basis. It can be easy to conclude that you are the only one who has ever gone through *specifically* this or that tragedy or hardship. We are in a sense prisms that reflect any kind of input differently. Therefore, it is easy to default to the reason that "only we have experienced trauma in such and such a way. There is without a doubt truth in that. Nonetheless, we can also conclude through tragedy that joy and revelation come out of this contiguum of tragedies with a reasonable outcome. Such an outcome can still be "rationalized" as "just another hardship." But I ask to what end? If one "reasons" that there is no meaning behind the suffering then nihilism is the definition of "the reason."

Some Christians and Jews are left feeling a hint of nihilism based on what we are told in Church: "God wouldn't have us suffer." So, we remain silent and internalize a kind of "disconnect" during these times of suffering. We wait for a logic that can come from such a suffering of uniqueness not found in an idea about God's sovereignty because we are told to "rationalize" that surely God wouldn't cause harm to us. Yet, it is this very thing that is most important — this is the time to grow through our pain and realize that God has ordained these sufferings for our betterment. If we claim the narrative that God wouldn't cause suffering then we illogically weaponize our special sufferings and suspend our beliefs in God into a fantasy world where God is not fully sovereign. This is the definition of theological fantasy if one takes the scripture to be coherent due to predeterminism. Such a fantasy is a blockage of human intercourse with God[1].

1. I'd like to keep consistency with my thesis here by saying that the "blockage" is on our side of the fence, not God's. With that said, we are still on our journey towards God in our darkest of times with blindness and all. i.e., we are "coming to be" children of God regardless of ourselves. Finally, there is still only "one choice" that we will be "concluded to," that is, God himself is choosing for you, God himself is willing in you, God Himself is working in you to do His good pleasure: Jeremiah 31:19; Philippians 2:13

Remembering "unhealthy specialness"

One might say: "Only I have suffered like this, *therefore*, I have some kind of claim on this type of suffering." Thinking like this, someone might find their specialness not only in their uniqueness of suffering but their justifications for acting as a free agent, a rogue of sorts, who can tell you that "no one has suffered like me."

This "specialness" can be argued away through scripture. Here, we are at the crux of the verse that you just read: "For by him were all things created: things in heaven and on earth, visible and invisible, whether it be thrones or powers or rulers or authorities; all things were created by him and for him" (Colossians 1:16). One might also refer to our discussion on Romans 13:1–14 concerning these same "powers."

With the above scripture (Colossians 1:16), we can make the argument that it applies to political powers since the words *thronoi* (thrones), *kyriotaytes* (lords/magistrates), *arxai* (rulers), and *exousiai* (authorities) were used. Maybe one could say that these invisible and visible powers are heads in heaven, earth, and hell: *aorates* ("a" = without/"orates" = sight/invisible), *hyparchouses* (archons/heads/leaders), *dynameis* ((with) power).

Powers surround us and rule us. There are existing powers that guide us (beyond the visible archons in the political arenas – such as quarks[2]) are tactfully ordained by God through his predeterminate counsel.

What better biblical passage could I find for this case:

> 1 Peter 4:1
> "(Since) therefore Christ suffered in the flesh, are yourselves with the same way of thinking, for whoever has suffered in the flesh has ceased from sin, so as to live for the rest of the time in the flesh no longer for human passions but for the will of God."

The hardest saying might be the best saying,

> Romans 13:1 – "Let every person be subject to the governing authorities. For there is no authority except from God, and those that exist have been instituted by God" (cf footnote #36 for exegesis of this passage.)

---

2. A quark is an elementary particle and a fundamental constituent of matter. Quarks combine to form composite particles called hadrons, the most stable of which are protons and neutrons, the components of atomic nuclei.

Paul's words here may offend if one is "partisan" —i.e., those who "part" from others because of their political views.

It is one thing to agree on a few things with one partisan leader and to agree with another partisan leader on other topics. It is another thing to hold no higher notion of "the powers that be" than that of a political sect.

In Romans 13:1 Paul addresses this political division by bypassing the very partisan politics which have been causing societal subterfuge for eons and replaces "partisan politics" with the belief in God's sovereignty.

In Romans 13:1 Paul doesn't just give credence to God as "a power" by which one can "wield" or "use (illusively speaking[3])" via "praying for the political party's" victory. Rather, Paul states that "all" existing leaders are solely appointed by the self existing God—the I AM.

Nonetheless, such confusion from Paul's time continues to this day. Paul's political and theological understanding, if adhered to "in mass." would divert us from the political anarchies which have brought many countries to civil war to a rest in God's sovereignty which, if believed by a body of believers, would give rest to the "will of the flesh" or "false might" that is believed to "win" elections and pass bills.

What Paul desires is our apprehending the idea of a non-partisan theocracy of the heart under Jesus—and a letting go of political "constructs" that would *replace* such a direct relationship to God.

Paul (in Romans 13:1) is not establishing man's authority over man, rather submission to God on all parties to recognize that God sovereignly placed our leaders in power for God's purposes and that we are to give to God the things that are God's and give those things which are Caesar's.... even unto our death, as Paul and Jesus displayed. That's right, a spiritual submission to a political construct to whomever is in "power." Paul did it, Jesus did it, why can't we?

With that said: Coming to a truth will usually require "niceties"[4] to leave. Not only does "good"[5] rule[6] but "bad"[7] rules too—but they "rule"

---

3. that is, if we thought we actually could do so and so in our fantasies but not in reality.
4. "nice: ne-scere: natal, ignorant, as a baby, foolish, stupid."
5. "beneficial," "advantageous" (Greek -agathos/Hebrew -tov.
6. Greek: arche -rule as leader; exousia-exist – appointed as a power "that be."
7. Hebrew: "Ra'ah" – destruction, pestilence, "evil" – either moral or physical.

as "appointed" by God[8] if one is to adhere to the scripture. That is, these archons are in obedience to a higher power.

Sometimes, for utilitarian meaning, I use the term "good" from the modern vernacular English to express something that is "meeting the standard," "wholesome" or "beneficial." One can take the opposite of good to mean "under the standard," "not wholesome," or "not beneficial." The problem arises when we give these adjectives (such as "good" or "bad") a "power of agency" or "action" where *good* battles *bad*. Such a light or simple meaning for "good" might be perverted to the illusory world of dualism[9]. Dangerously, we wield words for our own sense perception. Words can become utensils for our thoughts rather than guidelines by which we should live, breathe, and think. I say this in order that we may once again be pulled out of our sense perceptions and back into a coherent theology. We might even disband the sense that we "have done" good or "have done" bad/evil of our own "free will."

> Ecclesiastes 1:9
> "The things that hath been, it is that which shall be; and that which is done is that which shall; and there is no new thing under the sun."

> Ecclesiastes 3:15
> "That which is has already been; that which is to be has already been."

If you remember earlier, we discussed this passage to our salvation. We are now challenged with the age-old dilemma of "evil." If we, as believers in Christ or as believing Jews, take into account the Ecclesiastical writer's words (Eccl. 1:9; Eccl. 3:15) then the future had already been set from the past. All crime, all love, murder, rape, incest, birthdays, births, marriages, etc. . . . must be acknowledged as a "past event" in the mind of God (and not attributed to man's will[10], effort, doing) that would unfurl at some exacting future point in time. These future events would be a

---

8. Romans 13:1 Let every person be subject (hupotassestho – "placed under") to the governing (huperexousais) authorities (exousias-existing powers, existing authorities). For there is no authority (exousia) except *from* God, and those that exist (ousia) have *been instituted* (tetagmena ("tactfully placed" + eisin (have been)) by God."
9. I speak of "light and simple" as damnable when the "illusory" are born from them.
10. "Will" as in the Greek: *boule*: "to toss, cast, volley, etc." versus the Greek *thelema* meaning passions of the heart/motivation/drive/impulse.

part of the entire cosmos (Greek: "cosmos:" "orderly arrangement"[11]). For consistency of reading scripture, we would then need to acknowledge the apocalyptic[12] (the "seal" or "cover" is "taken off") view that all things are connected and will be viewed as such at the poignant teleological end. This "apocalyptic view," therefore, reasons that Hitler and his third Reich were a necessary movement which included the devastation on the Jews. The apocalyptic view includes that all devastation and beauty would be answerable to one force/one God/one intent/one predeterminer. There is positively no other answer "theologically" but that a truly sovereign God with consistency in its thinking[13] would cause all natural "effects" to

11. Though an argument might arise on the concept of "chaos" as "un-orderly" or "random." Modern astrophysicists have discovered that "black matter" operates on entirely different principles than Einstein's relativity and/or Newtonian physics. In Genesis 1:1-2 we see the idea of black matter in the word "mayim" which is biblically described as "void," "emptiness," "vacuous," "shapeless," etc., all of which God hovered over and called out of (the mayim) creation itself. Anti-matter and matter could also be addressed here as agreeing fields of study with this idea of "coming into being'---a.k.a. "creation."

12. I further my definition of the "apocalyptic view" by displaying that God's "revealed" plan (as mentioned in the book of Revelation) was what God ordained for us in this life, this world, this cosmos. That all "evil" and "good" ideas that we vacillated to and fro with would all be shown in the *fullness of time* (at the final "teleological point" of our existence) as the quantum equation of God's expression of His love for us. That is, the "fullness of meaning" will be displayed with our eyes able to "see" fully and finally that God has planned ALL things for the benefit of us all in time.

13. It is here that, much like a magnet, most "natural thinking persons" would condemn the idea that God would kill off millions of Jews or commit any genocide. Yet, all other answers fall short and are incomplete with less rationale and less comfort. Such examples of natural "rationale" might be as follows: luck, fate, randomness, nature, etc. "Luck" only denotes "allotment" by its very etymon, so, "luck" is a name for a "force which gives" or "a space within the receiving." Though we have disenfranchised "luck" from its root we must dig deep to see its original sentiment. Fate is nothing more than a "destiny" masked as a throw away fairy tale or myth at best. The Norns, Fatua, Graces, Parcae, and Morai were all the same in their respective myths and conveyed at best the idea of "fate" which meant "ending allotments unto death — hence, "fatality" or "fate" as the final allotment ("luck"). Randomness finds its meaning in the Middle English *randoun/randon*, which means to "go fast." Taken to its connotative meaning: "haphazard"; "impetuous," "rant," "running," "to flow/to run out," etc. Yet, when applied to a "random nature" found in someone we see that it means a person who "goes around and around without meaning or a sticking point to return to." So, I am convinced that any consistent law that holds "nature" (as we see in relativity, Newtonian physics, string theory) in an orderly motion (a math to its destruction: "entropy") to its fatality could not be "random." Therefore, "random," when used as a "force" or "impetus" or "continuing act" upon "nature" is a totally disenfranchised idea from what the word means. If I were not a theist/Christian I would say that nature gives us the only "rational" answer if we ONLY look at the "nature" of people giving and receiving and not the intellect by which all things are constituted. Via man's imagination – "nature" can be

occur. This theological relation between prime cause and effect of nature holds theological consistency which spares no one's feelings for the here and now. This theological approach is exactly what is lacking in most churches and is exactly the Christians number one problem today – i.e., a realization that comfort can only come if one believes that all things have meaning. Hence the term "meaningful."

Yet, there is much more accounting for mass murder, brutality, rape, cruelties of all kinds. The Old Testament is filled with accounts of Israel being slaughtered, taken captive, cannibalized by their own, daughters of men being raped by fallen angels, brothers raping sisters, incest among families in orgiastic parties, etc. Simply put, sin is the thing that is ordained by God to bring us home. Sin brought Northern Israel and Judah captive in 722 BC and 586 BC (respectively). Yet, this sin brought their prophetic restoration known to us in the twentieth century AD! Arguably the oldest account in the Bible comes to us in the book of Job where we read of horrible acts upon Job where he seemingly did not deserve them. He was more righteous of a man than most of us reading this. At the last chapter of Job (Job 42:11) we read that Job was recovering from *all of the evil that the Lord had brought upon him.*

Another example of being "placed under the judgment" or "dismissal" of God for a season is found in Romans 9. Paul states in Romans 9:11: "Before the children being not yet born, neither having done any "good or evil," that the purpose of election might stand, *not of works*, but of HIM Who calleth. (12) It was said unto her, "the elder shall serve the younger. (13) As it is written, Jacob have I loved and Esau have I

---

deified or anthropomorphized into a "causality goddess" – i.e., "gaia" – "mother earth" but "nature" only gives what she obeys. "She" is in the a accusative case, i.e., "in the receiving." "She" "receives" as the woman is penetrated by the masculine "genitive." Even Greek grammar must follow order to express motions in the universe. Therefore, the "obedience" to laws of our objective world (*phusis*–natural objects and *kosmokriton*–the prince of this world and the prince of the "trending nature" of this world) is what nature is. *Phusis* – "natural" is actually a condemnable word in scripture though we, as a secular society for the most part, have deemed praiseworthy the savage, the nature child, the earth spirit gatherings as something "other than" and "better than." What is worshiped is something "in the receiving" that cannot be the ultimate causality, rather, a servant. The "natural man" as addressed in 1 Corinthians 2:14; 15:46 is unregenerate and not amenable to God and the things of God. Paul says the acts of "natural man" are foolish. This means that the "natural man" acts upon the objective reason, the satisfying of the eyes and the lusts of the flesh. The "natural man" wants what is objectively here in the concrete world and is not of a spiritual mind. The natural man cannot, by its nature, follow the God that cannot be expressed in immediate time or space. Belief is not in the "natural man's" vocabulary.

hated." I must admit that this has been one of the hardest sayings in the English Bible until I understood the context of the Greek interpretation and translation of "hate." The Greek word for "hate" found in this passage is the word *emiseysa* which means "to dismiss from a classroom, player-stage or acting (that is, the removal or "killing of" of the actor [the acting of" killing of" for the meaning of the play), sending a child to their room until they repent of their actions, esteem less, detest, love less, to hate, denounce, to renounce one choice in favor of another, being rejected by a clique, etc."

But with all of the English "translations" of Romans 9: 13 the context of "hating Esau" is not the "hate" in the English sense. We see in the book of Revelation that God promises a restoration of every tribe, nation and tongue. Some of my best friends are Christian Arabs and Coptic Egyptians (Christian Egyptians) that would be considered the "sons of Esau." If one reads the story of Jacob and Esau, we find that Esau was more righteous than Jacob – "the scoundrel." So, what is left is this: the narrative by which Jacob remains in the story line trails itself over time to the Christ figure while Esau was not "written in the storyline leading to the Christ." Esau was "written out" of the story line. But it is in this religious-social context that most Arabs (a.k.a. "Esau") would be "written into the Quran" if we are to take the semantic reason of *emiseysa, miseo*, "dismissal" or "hatred."

Now that we have established what "hate" really means we can now understand the sovereignty in why God cannot have reactionary "hate" for he is the one who ordained the story of us all, including the Bible. He is outside the field of "aleatory" or "response driven reactions." Therefore, in the biblical context we are left with God's "hate" or *emiseysa*, from its root form: "miseo" as something "other than" the humanistic natural reaction of loathing another. What we are left with in the biblical context of "hate" is the word "dismiss" (Greek root "miseo" – emiseya). With this said, I feel this word is best found in the "interpretation" of context over the millennia. Hence, this biblical passage is to mean that "Esau was dismissed from the narrative of the line of Israel unto the Messiah[14]."

---

14. Which is exactly what happened. The Arabs did not bring the "line" of the Messiah. It was the 2,000-year-journey from Abraham to Jesus which fulfilled the "blessed hope" of Israel. There was no Davidic line in the Arabic world, nor archetypical laws, feast days, festivals, ordinances, etc. that found their fulfillment in the sacrificial lamb – Jesus, the Messiah. It is more than enough for an individual to proclaim their allegiance to any faith and physically die to it. Conversely, it was/is of utmost importance that Jesus emotionally, economically, socially, and physically die because he was/is the

In our past natural state, none of us were "leading to Christ" by our natures[15.] Nonetheless, God was "leading us" to him – even with our "necessary damnable natures." We find the "necessary damnable nature" of us all in Ephesians 2 where we once were all children of disobedience which if we continued "naturally" in that direction we would be damnable. But we were saved by grace in order to see the juxtaposition of our "natures" of damnable vs. salvageable. Therefore, does nature remain "justified" if humankind is "natural"? Absolutely not.

Another view of "natural"

If we claim (with hopes of being a "civil society") that such heinous acts as murder and rape are not "civil" then what are they? Are they "other than natural." Are these "acts" subnatural, supernatural, metanatural? How are these, if any, "natures" condemned or justified? —and by what court of law (if we are incapable of differentiating "natural" from "other than natural") do we make judgment upon another's actions? Where is the moral law centered? Worse yet, if all heinous acts are natural then who are we as atheists, agnostics, God haters, etc. to place judgment or doom upon another? San Quentin shows "a justice" within the prison colony. It is brutal and all who are sent there will find out that what is "right" is not necessarily aligned with a moral code.... only a code of sorts.

If this is unanswerable maybe one could ask: by whom are "uncivil acts" justified? If one rejects the kinds of "natural" heinous acts as "immoral" then why does morality exist and by what standard does it hold? Yet, if one rejects the idea of a God then by whom or what would cause a Holocaust so great as Hitler's against the Jews? If we claim that the

---

Messiah. His life and death are cleanly laid out in Isaiah 53:1–12. This passage gives the check marks for everything the Jewish Messiah must fulfill. For an in-depth study of the archetypes that Jesus had to fulfill one might refer to Alfred Edersheim in his magna opera: *Jesus the Messiah, A Sketch of the Jewish Social Life,* and *The Temple.*

15. Ephesians 2:1 "As for you (Ephesians/all Christians), you were dead in your transgressions and sins, (2) in which you used to live when you followed the ways of this world (*tou kosmou*) and of the ruler (*archon* (as we have defined "archons" as "those whom God appointed – Romans 3:31)) of the kingdom of the air (the exousias of the air-the "trending," "fashion," "popularity," "zeitgeist," "social persuasions," "peer pressures," etc.), the spirit which is now at work in those who are disobedient (Greek: *uiois* (sons) + *tayce* (definite article – "the" genitive – "of" – feminine – "in the receiving" + *apatheias* = "apathetic" – "not caring," "past feeling"). note: please continue to read the next few verses to see just how we were as "natural" – *phusikos* beings and how that God saved us from continuing in the direction of the "will of the *phusikos*."

"nature" of a single man, namely Hitler, is the same as us – i.e., "natural" – then we must discount morality for we associate "natural" as the highest law to abide by. We are left to default to a code under a madman like Hitler in order to survive. If we were Germans living in the days of Hitler, would we be naturally or unnaturally imposed upon to give allegiance to him and to hate the Jews? This zeitgeist became seemingly unstoppable for a time.

If we claim a "supernatural" event took place as Hitler or through him then we must admit there is another world of "nature" inconceivable to most of us. We are by reason forced to look at the possibilities of "something other" than innocence in the sense of nature. Or, we could look at Hitler's heinous act from a predetermination perspective caused by string theory which sees that all events are preceded by past and future. If so, then genocide is a metanatural act not accountable to morality which would simply be unstoppable by any laws established by natural man. If we take the biblical view, then, by God's determination upon the field of nature meshed in time a Holocaust happened by intention. I return continually to Isaiah 45:7 – ff "I create "evil" and make peace." Paul answers us in Romans 9:11–33 "Is there unrighteousness with God?" Even if this "dismissal" is a predetermined path unto the Holocaust, it can be argued in a coherent theological argument that "All things are ordained at the sovereign counsel of his Will." Again, if this is true, and if it is the ONLY way then we are also given another very unnatural view: that we will all be with God IMMEDIATELY upon our passing. Every nation, tribe, tongue, religious background, etc.… we will ALL bow to Christ as our redeemer at our meeting him. Why would we argue against this? Simply put: our "natural man" cannot conceive that God would kill. Yet this same "nature" says that God could not predetermine our salvation.

Well, I'm done with my "nature." My "nature" has only caused me my blindness to the beauty set before me with my heaven on earth and with my Christ at a later appointed time.

The ergative relationship: God and us

We find in Philippians 2:13 "For it is God which worketh in you both to will and to do of His good pleasure." God is the verb acting upon us. We are the dead noun–the object– in this ergative relationship, bringing us to life in him.

THE REASON OF UNIVERSAL SALVATION

The flesh or *phusikos* is called the "natural man" in Ephesians 2. The entire chapter gives sway to the ordained path by which we never had a choice to do evil or good but that God, by taking this fallen clay, shapes us over time using our temptation, suffering, sickness, death, etc. to calibrate our flesh over time in order that we may "see" that it is God who is in control. We must not waffle with this idea. We must hold steadfast to this idea if we are to have a solid understanding of sovereignty in its true sense.

With this understanding, let's apply apokatastasis or "full restoration" in the next few paragraphs. Can we get back to God from where we came from? Can we be "born again" – *anothen* or "anew"- where all is restored, forgiven, released from the bondage of the flesh, and released from the wages of sin (the body's natural choice), i.e., death?

We know that Romans 13:1 – ff. says that God established the *exousia* (leaders-pagan/non-pagan), *archons* (*arxontayce*: heads of nations/states/), *diatagay* (ordinances est. by secular rule and/or theocratic). Paul instructed the early church at Rome to obey such Roman officials, laws, ordinances, etc. Knowing this we must be aware that Rome also executed Christians–including Paul. Paul was "consenting" here that in the fullness of his time, he, himself, would be executed. Paul's instruction in Romans 13:1–14 signed his "authority" off to the "powers of Rome" for whom they were subject to the only power–God. Likened to this "justification" of human executions for the sake of the witness of our belief in God's sovereignty, we look to the Nazi *Zeitgeist* by this mass executions took place.

If we are consistent in our views that God ordained even his own Son to be brutally executed for the glory of faith, predetermined salvation, overcoming this world, etc., then we must justify that the horrid executions of Jewish victims in WW2 under Hitler would be justified in universal salvation by which they, the Jews, went to God immediately as did the thief on the cross with Jesus. Hard to swallow? Will we all not die in some way that we do not take pleasure in if we could look into the future?

Look at scripture. It is obvious that Revelation 13:18 says that Jesus was the lamb slain *from the Foundation of the world*. Is this not a plan by God prior to time's consumption of us all? Revelation 13:8 tells us that we will all worship (confess/homologeo) him: "And all that dwell on the earth shall worship Him, whose names are not written in the book of

Life."¹⁶ The "ALL" can't be used both ways for damnation or salvation. The "ALL" must be answering to the natural man in the damnable state and the ALL must refer to us ALL in the "born-again state—after the purging of hell on us is no longer needed.

In Luke 23:34 – Jesus refers to all (rapacious Roman centurions, Jewish haters of Christ, Pharisees, mass hysterical crowds, etc.) when he says to his Father while he is on the cross, "Father, forgive them; for they know not what they do." Of course, we know that *right after* Jesus told his Father this the Romans rent Jesus' clothes and cast lots for it. *Still, the Romans mocked him. Yet*, Jesus told his Father to forgive them. Did Jesus not know what they would do minutes, hours, days, years, after he died and resurrected? *Yet*, in all of the barbarity, Jesus looked to the one malefactor being hung with Jesus telling him that he should be with Jesus that very day. This "immediacy" of translation from this physical life to everlasting is expressed by Jesus and makes perfect sense when one can distinguish the spirit from the body. For this sake, the "immediacy" of spirit life would answer physicality into a new "type" of body capable of living forever. It was Jesus who was with the malefactor then and there at the malefactor's death and resurrection. Yet, the "tempo" by which Jesus entered into his old body was different. His spirit was immediate with the malefactor, and yet he transcended our time, choosing his terms by which he made his new body an epiphany to his disciples with especial emphasis to the women who were the first witnesses—for his new body was not distinguishable at first to his followers.

So, resurrection is a physical thing. It is our only hope from the physical perspective. It seems rational (to me) that resurrection would be a hope for all of us. All of humankind up to the turn of the nineteenth century are more than likely dead. What is their hope? If there are those who feign to *not need hope* then I will gladly leave that alone for them to work that out. But what did it matter to Stephen, the first Christian

---

16. Job 14:16–19 (especially of vs. 17) presents the case for "The book (*TseRor* – "bundle"/"book"/papyrus scroll) of Life" in which the earliest-pre-Mosaic biblical attestation gives us salvation as our sins are put into the book of Life along with the words of God. That our sins (that is, the sins of the God believers in the days of Job until the end of the world) were accounted for and held eternally from us with wax and string as the prescribed priestly acts displayed. The book of Life is a reference to great antiquity then as John wrote the Revelation spanning an "answer to" metaphor and reality. If Christ is the forever priest, then he will be the word which seals away sin and is worshiped eternally. Job 14:17 – "My transgression is sealed up in a tied document (*tseror*), and Thou (God) daubest over mine iniquity" – i.e., "you will cover over my sins." cf Tur Sinai's "The Book of Job" pages 240–41.

THE REASON OF UNIVERSAL SALVATION

martyr and young man who was so filled with the Holy Spirit that the Pharisees stoned him to death. Yet, Stephen saw the trinity through the opening of the heavens right prior to his stoning. He was given "the glimpse" of eternal glory. It would surprise me, with the continuity of the biblical text to tell me that Stephen went to be with God immediately. I believe this is the case not just for those who are not just "good." Romans 3:10 makes it clear that "none are good, not one, all go astray and seek their own." *That is, the nature of all of us is evil in the presence of God.* Furthermore, "we see" the relativity of evil from our perspective, not God the Father. He cannot look at us for he is holy. God the Father is the one who will forgive us—only in the covering of his Son, Jesus Christ.

> Acts 2:22:
> "Ye men of Israel, hear these words; Jesus of Nazareth, a man approved of God among you by miracles and wonders and signs, which God (The Father) did by Him in the midst of you, as ye yourselves also know; (23 Him (Jesus), being delivered by the determinate counsel and foreknowledge of God, ye have taken, and by wicked hands have crucified and slain; (24 Whom God hath raised up, having loosed the pains of death; because it was not possible that He should be holden of it."

This predeterminate counsel by which God the Father was the predestined choice, will, intent, decision of God the Father upon his Son, to execute his Son in order.

Acts 2:22–24 is just another example of "loosing" and "binding" for what men cannot do but God does. Loosing and binding are for the correlation between Father God and his Son. That is, the Father ordained the Son's death and resurrection and the Son "participated" of the "toxsotayce," the glorified one who fulfilled the "shot" to the bullseye of prophecy (the "glimpse" of eternity into the realities of this connected universe (i.e., the "quantum entanglement"). The 3 years of ministry, the fulfillment of all archetypical messianic allusions, the fulfillment of all of the prophets, the final acts of death and resurrection of Jesus is the meaning of life! This is the explanation of this universe's meaning, i.e., "evil, resurrection, story, plot, known outcome through the prophets, the apocalypse's meaning throughout the story via prophecy and the final hope of Jesus' return to restore of all back to him is the full narrative, the book complete.

Chapter Thirty-Eight

Harder Sayings that Connect the Dots

PHYSICAL AND MORAL EVIL both fall under the Hebrew term, *ra'ah* (destruction, calamity, pestilence, disease, violence, etc.). According to Romans 3:10 and Colossians 1:16, Adolf Hitler was an ordained *archon* (or ruler) by God. Politically speaking, without Adolf as an agent of "evil"[1], the Jews would have never rallied to be a nation to protect themselves in 1948. Apocalyptically speaking, we can now see that (what people during Ezekiel's day could not. Without this agent of evil (Adolf) there would have been no fear for the Jews to rally in defense. Therefore, Ezekiel 37 and Matthew 24's prophecy concerning the return of the Jews would never have come to pass. Adolf was either (1) put in power by himself, (2) Satan or (3) God. If Hitler put himself in power causing the change of historical tides which led Israel to become a nation, then Ezekiel was only a foreseer without God's providential plan in play. If Hitler was put in power by Satan, then God wasn't in control of the devastation that Satan laid out. For that matter, why would Satan (if a true rogue) ever bother to bring about events that would bring about our Lord's second coming? If prophecy is real, then, the secular/historical timeline of Ezekiel 37 unto Ezekiel 38 must be real. Jesus' words concerning the fig tree in its own land again must be real since he was not in disagreement with the prophets. He was in agreement with his Father and the prophets by his words and deeds. Nothing was out of place with Jesus and the words of

---

1. As for the discussion of evil here I conclude that the Hebrew "ra'á" means to "break down" vs. "building up." When God says in Isaiah 45:7 "I, YHVH, make (*asha*) peace (*shalom*) and (*I*) create (borah) calamity (*ra'a*)—these things – all – I do (*asha*)" the meaning for "evil" or "calamity" is not necessarily used as a moral term. Though, in our "nearsighted" view (due to the fall) we vacillate from "good" to "evil" as if there is no higher resolve but the human moral reference.

the law and the prophets. His life was the segway for us all. He prepared us to see him in his full glory as "The Son of Man and the Son of God" at the fullness of time (telos).

Well, we have witnessed this prophecy in the past 77 years on May 14, 1948 when David Ben Gurion[2] proclaimed the establishment of the State of Israel. Alongside David Ben Gurion was U.S. President Harry S. Truman who recognized Israel as a new nation on the same day. Israel became a nation again in 1948 after many events that would have signaled to the worldly and Jewish eye that Israel would have never returned as one state back into their original biblical homeland.

The first thought of hopelessness for the Jews occurred in 722 BC and the second in 586 BC with Judah (Southern Israel). Israel's captivity and annihilation as a nation in 722 BC and Judah's deportation into Babylonian captivity in 586 BC was for sure a despairing time for any hope left for North Israel or Southern Judah to become a nation under God again.

But there was hope in Ezekiel's words. Ezekiel and Daniel gave us markers to know that not only will Israel become a nation but will be joined as "one stick"[3] with Judah. Ezekiel tells us in the next chapter (Ezekiel 38) that when these two nations (Ephraim —Israel and Judah) are joined we must then look to Gog (Russia) and Persia (Iran) (aligned with other armies) in the last half of the last seven years of Daniel's prophecy. Such a "last seven years" was the "last *shavua*" or sabbatical "week" would have Russia and Iran to lead most of the Middle East and Far East against Israel in a final war at the hill of Megiddo (Harmageddo/Armageddon) at the final days leading up to the return of the Messiah.

Matthew 24, Mark 13, and Luke 21 are Jesus' words complimenting this same prophecy that when the "fig tree (Israel)" comes back into its own land again know that in that generation shall all things come to pass. Jesus' words refer to the "generation" from Israel's coming back (1948) to

---

2. the modern founder of the Nation of Israel and the first prime minister of the State of Israel.

3. Ezekiel 37:15–17: (God talking to Ezekiel) "Son of man; take a stick and write on it, "For Judah, with his Israelite companions." Then take another stick and write on it, "for Joseph – Ephraim's stick, together with all his Israelite companions." Then tie the two sticks together so that you're holding one stick" —37:20 – ff: "......I'm taking the Israelites out of the nations in which they've been exiled. I'll gather them from all directions and bring them back home. I'll make them ONE NATION IN THE LAND, on the mountains of Israel, and give them one King (Melek – ruler) – *one King over them all. Never again will they be divided.*" How ironic is it that "David" ben Gurion brought this about —as God's agent?

this last Shavua as the last-time indicators for the end of this aeon/world/age. God tells us through Ezekiel 38 that God will halt Gog and all of his armies aligned at Har-Meggido (The Hill of Meggido/"Armageddon") and at that same moment time will be no more.

Jesus continues to graphically express what will happen in "that generation" of apostasy (Matthew 24, Mark 13, and Luke 21) unto its eschaton (complete destruction) and the fullness of its meaning (teleology). Jesus tells us in Matthew 24 that "Immediately at the end of the tribulation shall we *see* the Son of Man." This epiphany will be at the last of the seven years and the last of the seventh year. Past these last events we will have no more destruction but peace. This is the ending point of the eschaton.

But while we are on earth, the final *shavua* (or seven years of tribulation) seems to be cut up into a series of 7 main events found in the 7 events of the book of Revelation. These sections are signaled by the 7 trumpets being metaphorically understood as the sounding of the 7 angels of judgment and known as well as the 7 "vials of wrath." This "wrath" is not the final "judgment" but rather signals unto the messianic return through tribulation upon the earth. If we think about it, the greater the tribulation the greater the signal. This applies to our personal lives as well as the messianic portent.

This *shavua* (last seven-year period) will also be a decimation of most of the people who dwell on this earth. How could a "good God" do this? The only answer is that God predetermined the perfect story that we should be conformed to God's image through the perfection of calibrating us in the carving away of our flesh, be it spiritual "flesh," physical flesh, or both. We must suffer to grow, even unto death.

Only through calibrated suffering bestowed upon us by God will we come to know and understand the value of God, his mercy, his forgiveness, especially towards those who victimized us[4] . This realization is the apocalypse[5] or revealing as to why. Oh, such beautiful grace there is! There is endless grace which shows itself to us as a contrast to being "judged" by our works. I couldn't face what I've really done in this life in

---

4. that is, "those" who were the "agents" by which God used to carve us into the shape that God so desired.

5. keep in mind, "apocalypse" means "off" + "cover"/"concealment"/"hell." Therefore, "apocalypse" can occur in your life as God "reveals" things. Apocalypse most definitely refers to the exposure of ALL things for what they were — when we are no longer in time.

my sin. Could you? Could you play out on a movie for your family of all the heinous lies and derelictions you have done in front of your innocent children? I say no . . . maybe I'm wrong.

His grace is fixed in the judgment seat/the *thronoi* and is in the same place where judgment against our flesh dies off and is no more. This, therefore, is the judgment seat that exists now, i.e., grace and the king of grace who sits upon his throne. Grace is the judgment. Grace is the verdict if we are to live, otherwise we all burn in hell.

We have already been resurrected in him. Through our death to be self-imposed by him which is likened to his sufferings on this earth we share in his afflictions. We begin to know him more this way. His sufferings bear his name upon us while our sufferings share in the community of the kingdom of God here on earth.

We resurrect daily and will forever more resurrect at the throne of God where we shall dwell with him and worship him night and day. We will physically be with him (Jesus), the Father and Holy Spirit when this physical world is no more. We will experience the holy trinity in our new bodies. Likened to what Christ told the thief on the cross, "this day you will be with me in heaven," we shall share this grace.

There is a heaven that transcends the first and second day of Christ's physical death in the early first century AD. The domicile of Christ resides in us as we understand in part what it means to us to be in this kingdom or dominion. There is no dominion of time here—only eternal truths that never contradict though the world waffles daily to apprehend the "meaning of life" outside Christ and his death to self.

Our flesh still conceals[6] us from the bliss that is to come and agony, oppression, being hated on, rejection, etc. are all real experiences that will continue to wear down the flesh until its will is tired. The flesh is judged as evil/damnable while our spirits are judged forgiven. Our flesh will die off and our spirits (spiritos) will rise into new bodies (neo-sarx) that will be befitting of our souls (pseuxay/i.e., spirit and body as one). God has already made our new bodies for infinite joy. It would be wonderful to understand this on a daily basis.

So, how do we approach these two kingdoms – one of the earth and one of heaven's abode?

Recalling the reference I made earlier to "doom," "judgment," "domicile," "king-*dom*," "domesticity," "dominion," etc. we now have a new

---

6. con = with + ceal (KEL4– Proto-Indo-European/I.E. – "hell"; "that which is cut off; hidden").

look at what "judgment" or "doom" means. Simply, judgment means the "house by which order is." Isn't that place called the king's dominion/domicile of God? Isn't this where we should want (Greek: "thumeia" – "desire") to dwell? Where should we walk but on the paths of God's righteousness?

I remember C.S. Lewis's treatment of the word "free" in his "study of words" book. C.S. said that the child of the king or head of the manor is *free from* talking as the peasants. Likewise, the peasants are *free from* talking as the children of the King.

So much is implied here by C.S. Lewis" treatment on "free." Yet, it goes without saying that peasants, children of the king, and the king all abide together under one domicile, doom, dominion, rule, dominate, etc. It seems fitting that I would mention the apocalyptic vision of John in Revelation 7:9 here: "After this I looked, and there before me was a great multitude that no one could count, from every nation, tribe, people and language, standing before the throne and before the Lamb. They were wearing white robes and were holding palm branches in their hands."

Well, we currently would have to admit that if every nation, tribe and tongue were praising the Christ, then we would have to include "those" that were Muslim, Jewish, Hindu, Jain, Buddhist, etc. "Before the throne and before the Lamb" they were. I can't think of a better house to be in personally. Is this not a hint of universal salvation?

I was asked by a dear friend of mine who has been a theological skeptic and "rational" medical doctor (funnily enough all of our conversations end up in hours of theological discussions) what "universalism" is. I told him. He said, "Well, if all people are going to be saved by Christ in the end, why can't we just do whatever we want? I answered: 'there are two "kingdoms" of thought going on here. One kingdom of thought is ruled by hedonism – "pleasure seeking" – a.k.a. "fulfilling the desires of the *phusikos*." Such a "kingdom" would only ask such a question. The other "kingdom" is that of eternal thanks to who saved us from eternal damnation. Jesus presents his love and salvation and abolishes conflict within his spiritual kingdom; he does not present fear. His life on earth was a sacrifice for us all. He was as a gentle lamb not defending himself but promoting the kingdom of God where no pride, anger, lust, murder, etc. exists. No man lived like him. No man was prophesied to do what he did but him. No man was capable of continuing this grace unto eternal life. No one died in the fashion that he did. If you were before his throne in your heart, you would understand that there is no question to why we should not tell the world. The answer is simple to those who have already been repented by him. The answer is "we have no other recourse but to praise him for it is endless joy to be with him in part (for now) in his kingdom and the hope of life eternal with him."

There's always another way to look at life but it's not as optimal or based in the universal salvation reality of ultimate forgiveness. Anger, judgment, vengeance, etc. (if one could speak of these as "values") discounts grace, forgiveness, understanding universal salvation, predestination (i.e., the idea that God does all things), and the understanding of where we are headed (teleon). Lust in anger or sexual lust for another discounts the care for *telos* or the end result and wants the immediate-now-gratification[7]. You see, the *logos* or grand *logic* shows us that one value will dismiss the other. That is, understanding (1) predestination + (2) universal salvation + (3) the apocalyptic view (the revelation of the total meaning of the narrative of God) + (4) teleology (where you are headed via God's will) and the (5) prophet's declaration of the end sets us cleanly on a consistent path that does not contradict itself. Every one of these five values requires the other four.

---

7. See my website: "The Fullness of Meaning Christian Ministries, com. and go to the audio lecture "Satis and Kob" or "happy and sad." Here you will bind that "happy" meant "to fulfill the immediate want" while "satis" meant "weight, fullness, heaviness from fulfilling the immediate desire" . . . Therefore, "happy-sad" work together to "rend" oneself apart.

Chapter Thirty-Nine

The Pagan's Prophet

In this chapter I will attempt to show you the LOGOS by which Plato was so close to apprehending the eternal form of the LOGOS. Plato was a "signal" to the pagan (amoral) world of something much higher than the objective/natural form. By "logic," Plato shows us that "apprehending" the metaphysical means to be (if you will) "meta" – from the physical. As for pagan prophets I thought I would give you another artistic break. On the next page I drew a "messenger" from the "old world." Laden with Shamanistic motifs, this drawing/watercolor attempts to convey what we might fear – something "devilish" but still carrying the wisdom of the gods. Only that of some of the earliest Indians might carry the weight of its history in support of this theme that I'm only attempting to convey. Maybe Quetzacoatl is the "carry over" of this remote god of antiquity. On the darkest side of this art piece, I imagined the Satan of Genesis and *Melek Taus*, the Yazidi Shaitan south of Tabriz in the Zagros mountains. The Yazidis still, to this day, worship this archangel-Shaitan. They call him *Melek -Taus*, the great peacock-god, or the god/archangel of "many colors."

Both Plato and scripture tell us that the WORD is the agent by which eternity fills itself into chronos or time. This defies reason when these two distinct properties (eternal – logos and limitation – chronons) would meet. The Gospels are the case in point for such a juncture. Jesus is the word which came from eternity and into our naturally observed world by filling it up with a supernatural kingdom via his Gospels and deeds.

In a symbolic sense, the "horned-one" has always been a picture of power throughout the entire world. Cave paintings have depicted the grandeur of the horned animals such as bison, aurochs, rams, oxen, ox

– which God is depicted as the great "*AL*" or "the first" – The Aleph or "ox" – i.e., the leading horned one who leads in pulling the plough. Other gods were depicted as having horns. In the anthropomorphic/analogous[1] sense, the transient and moveable Chronos was the god of eating time/god of consumption. He was depicted with a horn for a crown, hence the etymon – "crown" = *corona* = *chronos*. The Hebrew gives us "*Qeren* (QRN)" from which we see an ancient cognate tie in with the Indo-European root for crown (*krn/crn/hrn* [as in the celtic god, Hern, the "horned one"]). Over time these "horns" became the holders of the cap atop the "crown." As seen in the Daimyo of Japan, Mongol Turkic warriors, English Kings, etc. all royalty has some form of "horned" headdress by which they showed dominance. Many of the American Indians, for sure the chief, wore horns to show the powerful animal spirit shared with the chief such as the Bisons. So, horns were worldwide symbols of power and dominance over the village, tribe, nation, etc. for eons. It shouldn't surprise you that we have images of the Devil and Satan with horns. It is an interesting study if one wants to research the origins of the icons of the Devil's horns.

Biblically speaking, we look at Chronos as a representative worldly archon. We see that Chronos/Satan/thee Devil is *durationally* being subsumed into LOGOS. Chronos is being "categorized out" (*Krino*/"judged") as an *archon* or visual "ruler" of sorts and is being ordered into completion (teleon and eschaton[2]) by the divine architect. When Chronos's function is over, time is over, and all that ever consumed us daily will be over. All that will remain is the immovable kingdom of the eternal WORD/LOGOS.

We, as eternal forms in Chronos's finite dominion, will be torn from this world-soul (nous-monde) and brought into Christ's kingdom. Though, for now, we experience this calibrated tearing away from Chronos dominion. We are being "set apart" as "heretical" to the secular eye. We are the Greek *marturos*, i.e., the "mature ones, the martyrs, the ones

---

1. anthropomorphic/analogous (a./a.) is used here to show an "anthropomorphized" reality. The Greeks sought higher meaning sometimes in using anthropomorphism/analogy to convey a mass movement/mass mind/*pneuma*/*anima*, etc… Such a./a. that blanketed us was called by a single name. Much like the "whore of Babylon," we know that "she" doesn't exist in the physical form alone nor could have single-handedly caused the wreckage upon the world in biblical proportions like she did. Rather, "she" was relegated to the "fantastic" by which she is known biblically.

2. for "teleon" is about the ultimate final meaning and "eschaton" is about the final destruction of all things physical.

who account for the eternal words and deeds by which we act upon." We are the "rememberers of the words." Therefore, if the WORD is supervening and preceding all of time past, present, and future, then, The WORD is the memory of all. We partake daily of his time-filled portion; this is one of the noble truths that I present: the apocalyptic truth.

Even Lewis Carrol said of "memory:" "It's a poor memory that only works backward." Since Lewis Carrol was a mathematician and dear friend to the great Christian universalists and predestinarian, George MacDonald, I could assume he was referring to the "limitless place of immovability" and the "coming to be by the future meeting the me" idea. That is, predeterminism has already been before time (*Chronos*) started his consumption of all things and we shall see the architect of the archetype of the eternal which is outside the utmost boundaries of chronos. Words that can be used in the eternal sense are[3]: Hebrew: *olam*, Greek: *io'nios*, and Greek: *aidios* represent such a place of indivisibility. As to the eternal words of Christ, our mindfulness in the here and now should be in *remembering* the eternal words of Christ spoken ca 2,000 years ago. This is a divine and eternal act.

We are immovable (eternal/outside of natural movement) when we are in the word at the expense of our flesh via our ridicule from others. We suffer greatly. We are the fools in the eyes of those who move like lightning all around us, showing their speed and abilities and their "self-referential judgments" thrown with self-entitled justifications.

In the *apocalyptic perspective* (one of the Five Noble Truths), we can "now see"/"know" (*gnoia*) how the world is governed unto entropy. The world changes with trends and sensual appeals unto its mathematically designed ending. Though, the kingdom of God does not move under the laws of nature/entropy/popularity/trending, the kingdom of God is the ontic reference by which we "see" the juxtaposing natures of "nature" vs. "The kingdom of God."

Those who "act" within the peaceful nature of God in his kingdom (in the here and now) do suffer amongst the powers that exist in the spirit of antiChrist. For now, the weary exegete of the Bible, i.e., *mathetikon*– follower of the LOGOS can surely see his presence coming soon, for there can be little time (chronos) left before Chronos eats itself into entropy.

3. I am very careful in saying in an altruistic sense that these 3 words are expressed only in the eternal sense. The "identifying" nature of these words is more semiotically sound in saying, "*unquantifiable time*" and/or (for the Hebrew especially) "*out of sight/ out of reference.*"

As we can see, the kingdom of God meets the earth as is seen in the apocalyptic view (described above). We can also see how Jesus answered to the Pagan's hope concerning this same logic in studying the philosophers of ancient Greece.

An example of God using the *heathen* or *pagan*[4] to "complete" the thought for which the pagan could never have come to without the LOGOS (or "logic" of Christ) can be seen in the philosophical treatment of Plato's cave added with the theological treatment of the condescension of God as a man (i.e., an eternal/out of time being *expressed* in "sequenced" acts).

Plato's Cave

sensory world: the cave

Images: representation (Greek: *eikasia*)

Physical things: belief (Greek: *pisitis*)

Intelligible world (Greek: noitos kosmos)

Thinking (*dianoia* = mathematical reasoning)

Forms or ideas: intellection (Greek: *noesis* = philosophical thinking/dialectic)

Plato, in his work, Timaeus, said that "our world with all of the objects it contains are copies of forms or ideas that are located somewhere else outside the cave where we are living." Plato expresses it somewhat like this: "The four elements (earth, fire, air and water) are based on different regular (stable/immovable/eternal) polyhedrons and this explains their different qualities. All we can see is that which is reducible to two types of triangles and rectangles. It is the "world soul (nous monde)" which has the armillary sphere. This is enough to see that mathematics and philosophy are complementary. Such stands true to this day.

Plato brilliantly says, "Time is a moving image of eternity (Timaeus 38)." Plato holds that time is a representation of the greater form, eternity, as does the Hebrew text of Genesis chapter one versus Genesis chapter 2 imply. Plato said, "When God, the Demiurge, made the world, simultaneously HE made an image (icon) of eternity progressing in number

---

4. both terms I use in the "amoral" sense as I have defined throughout this book.

while *eternity is unmovable*. Both, image and progressing number are still qualities of being in the cave.

Onto the intelligible world:

Moving out of the cave

"Time," in the English usage, has been used in place of *Chronos* unless I state otherwise. We call eternity in motion "time." Time is an "image." Time can be divided into days, nights, months, and years; all these are sections or divisions of time. The "past," "present," and "future" are merely forms of time.

Plato categorizes between physical and psychological time(s) by saying that sectional time is physical time and the other(s) such as present, past, and future times are psychological categories.

Yet, both physical and psychological time(s) belong to the sensible and transitory world in the same way as physical (chronos) and eternal time (divine time) work together. Chronos calls for its bounded (or Hebrew – *ta'avah*: "boundary") sense to make sense of itself relative to eternal time which "spatially surrounds" it, lest it would be psychologically infinite.

The reference of an "era" is uncountable but psychologically speaking, "era"- psychological-time is in its Greek root word *horo* meaning "circle or cycle." Likewise, the Hebrew gives us *chagag* to mean the "cycle of festivals." Many of the vain pagan cycles were called out by the prophets Isaiah and Jeremiah to have Juday abolish them as they would return every year (cycle) to do.

We have another time called divine time. Divine time is the archetype of time called "eternity." Both can be used as a reference for reason or illogic. Nonetheless, both can be "spoken at, for, to, in the sense of." Reasonably, there must be a form similar between eternity and time as between the original and a reflection. That is, there must be a difference between a perfect type of time and an imitation of time for one cannot be the other in two different worlds, i.e., the physical and the eternal.

One can see how spatiality is addressed here by Plato, for time is only images of moving pictures representing unalterable-unmovable eternity. That is, eternity is self-referencing, needing nothing else, perfection.

We must make sure to understand the differentiations of *chronos*, both in the mytho-religious perspective and metrical-physical perspective.⁵ We are dealing with measurements of physical space. Plato categorized different parts of time and different forms of time. Also, Plato says that if "time" is illustrated in the form of an "image," it must be conceived of as moving.

Plato brilliantly looked at eternity as not "boundless time (aeonos chronos)," but rather the "divine" in accord with eternity; hence, Plato looked at eternity as "a time" that was divinely filled. Hence, the immovable-perfect-indivisible-unchangeable time. This time was obviously not chronos. And, if Plato sought eternity within chronos, the movements would have to stop where divinity was. With the notion of becoming photons that $E=mc^2$ limited us to, allows this to be a metaphysical possibility. This would explain the *neo – soma* ("new bodies") of each resurrected soul that was limited in their "flesh cage" (i.e., *soma*) yet acts with perfection in the "new heaven and new earth (*Kainos Ouranos kai Kainos Gaia*).

In a most similar comparison of eternity, we find the same "filling up" in Isaiah 46:10 and 11: "Declaring from the beginning the end and from ancient times the things not yet done, (I will be) saying, "My counsel shall stand and all my purpose I will accomplish (11). I will call from the east a bird of prey from a country far away (and it will in union with) the man of my counsel that I have called. I have spoken and I will bring it to pass. I have purposed (determined) this and I will do it."

The phrase, "I will bring it to pass" is conveyed in the Hebrew as: "a-bi'en'nah" which means "to come into (and fill it up)." That is, Plato's idea of the eternal demiurge, i.e., the eternal-divine-immovable God will come "into" his declaration using "time" or "chronos" to do so.

How can eternity and chronos work at the same time (chronos)?

Let's continue with the overriding genius of the scripture to find out: Isaiah 46:12 "...I bring near my Righteousness [Hebrew: *tsid'qatiy*, *tsadoch* – root etymon of *tsid'qatiy*]. It is not far off and my Salvation [*wa-te-su-a-tiy* (root of *yeshua* – *yasha* – "deliverance, salvation, save, saving, security, victory")] will not tarry. I will put in Zion My Salvation [-*su-a-*] for Israel and my Glory."

How does this fit with the platonic universal idea of "coming to be," "universal/particular?" Through God's *logos* (word/category/pagan),

---

5. Chronos would be what we would relate in distance/time = speed. So, simple enough, to find the "speed" by which you accomplished, one would take the distance and divide by time (chronos). Distance equals speed x time. Time equals distance divided by speed. In all 3 cases we are still in the cave.

wyrd (setting forth of fate), *dabar* (word/order/thing/judgment/setting forth the "order," etc.) we can see the "coming to be" in the fullness of times that the fleshly Jesus "coming into being" as God incarnate. He, as logos, —as the pagan calls, *spermatikos logos*, inseminates the entire world with his judgment, word, *dabar*, and grace.

Galatians 4:4 answers to Isaiah 46 and Plato's conundrum of eternity vs. time and the eternal demiurge. Galatians 4:4: "When the fullness of time had come, God having sent forth His Son, to have been born of a woman, born under the law, that those under the law might HE redeem in order that the Divine adoption as sons (and daughters) we should receive."

So we can see that the logos (Greek: word) *dabar* (Hebrew: word) of the immovable – truthful – eternal God is able to enter chronos and fill chronos with eternity. Eternity is truth, therefore, eternity is unchangeable as is "truth."

Let's look one more time at Plato's integrity for holding to word meanings and their history concerning: God, Chronos, eternity, immovability, etc.

In Plato's *Dialogues of Cratylus* 437/B I have paraphrased the *daemon* ("higher mind/god mind") of Socrates into modern English. Socrates wrote with such compression of words and thickness of ideas that only a Greek mind could unravel, I found it necessary to use English by expanding the dialogue. Some things taken out for I didn't think I needed to make a bigger point. All said, you can refer here to Socrates in this footnote.

Socrates: "Let us take up the words for eternity starting with *epistaymay*. It means "upon the standing firm" or "immovable." But in regular speech, we call *epistaymay* "knowledge" for it does not move and can be counted on as an eternal form. Epistaymay, in our Greek language, seems to indicate that it makes our souls "stand still" at things that are transient/movable/trending —not foundational. Hence, *epistaymay* shares eternal quality with the immovable with the moveable. In each case for the beautiful Greek language, we have an opposite meaning for every word by simply adding an "a" in front of the word. Moreover, we can add an "e" or "i" to alter that same word again. The genius of our language is that it is unalterable and can be counted upon to show the "picture negative" of its meaning by the prefix "a'—by which we call, "the alpha privative." So, we can know what something is by what it is not in the Greek case. This is not so for all languages. The genius lies within the simplicity and most important, the "immovability" or "eternal form." Greek allows one to have "dialectics" because Greek is "true, straight, without the shadow of turning." We can "confirm" our forensics "through" (*dia*) the LOGOS of Greek. Take another example: *armateia*. We know this to mean "sin" or "missing the mark." It is an actor's term and used to show the "fallacies" of the actor (*hupokrites* – later: "play actor as hypocrite in society") by which tension and dynamism was given in the play. So, if sin or *armateia* is "missing the mark;" sinful; careless; not accountable; off, etc… then what is its opposite? Take the "alpha privative" off of *amarteia* and we get *marteia*. Well, what does *marteia* mean? It has a complex meaning. Therefore, the "word -complex" *martia* was negated with the alpha privative. *Martia* means to "be accounted for." It means "to remember." It means in the verbal sense, "to account." It is a word for "martyr" for a true martyr will speak eternal words in the here and now, whilst the words bring eternal judgment down (*kata*) upon the "moveable" falsities that go to and fro on this earth. It means merit, meritorious, memorize, think upon and act with thought. It means "carefulness – full of concern." Its first meaning was mero as in a part of the whole body, a comprising-integral thing of the whole. We continue with words like "amathia" – "without math; without knowledge." While *mathia* is the word for disciple – *mathetikon*, other words such as *a'kolasi'a* which means "unrestrained; movement in company with any and all things it comes into contact with." So, the opposite is *kolassi's* or *kolassin* which means a "judgment system unto rectification" or righteousness. This term *kolassin* can be referred to a prison system of rectification of the prisoner who was once *a-kollasin* or *a'kolasi'a*.

Can we not see that Plato (using Socrates' *daemon*) seems to be the predecessor for the Pauline writing in Ephesians 4:13- ff.?!

Paul teaches us in Ephesians 4:13 and 14 the following: "Until we may attain all to the unity of the faith and of the knowledge of the Son of God unto a man a completeness in order that no longer might we be infants being tossed to and fro and being carried about by every wind of teaching in the cunning of men in their craftiness with a view to the scheming of deceit."

Below this paragraph I have emphasized some Greek New Testament words that fit within the epistemology of Plato's "immovability" as the "eternal-divine" of the here and now. Ephesians 4:13, 14: "Until we may attain all (*panta*) to the unity of the faith (*pisteos*) and of the knowledge (*epigno'seo's*) of the Son of God unto a man a completeness (*playro'matosin* – "fullness") of order that no longer might we be infants being tossed to and fro (*kludo'vidzo'menoi* – "being tossed by waves") and being carried about (*periphero'menoi* – rotating in circles – on and on) by every wind (*ane'moi*) of teaching in the cunning of men in their craftiness with a view to the scheming of deceit."

If the kingdom of God is here and now in chronos, what therefore does that mean now that we understand our fusion of Hebrew from Isaiah 46, Plato's Cratylus 438/B and Ephesians 4:13–32? It means the "immovable (eternity)" is here and now (*chronos*) in the eternal" by being (*ontos*) in God's eternal WORD (*logos/dabar*). The WORD is the agent by which eternity fills *chronos*. We are immovable (eternal) in the word at the expense of our flesh's ridicule of others. We can "now see" the world spinning out of control and changing with every emotion, doctrine of deceit, pornography, addictions, etc. They are to be remedied to God. Only scripture can and did fulfill Plato's forms to intellection in his Timaeus:

Conclusion

Let's now go back and sum the original heading for Plato's caveave by finding the fulfillment of it in scripture
Initially: pagan's hope

Plato's Cave

Sensory world: the cave

1. Images: representation (Greek: *eikasia*)
2. Physical things: belief (Greek: *pisitis*)

Intelligible world: outside the cave

3. Thinking (*dianoia* = mathematical reasoning)
4. Forms or ideas: intellection (Greek: *noesis* = philosophical thinking/dialectic)

Fulfilled by the Gospels

Sensory world: the cave

1. Images: representation (Greek: eikasia) — now in word and deed
2. Physical things: belief (Greek: pisitis) — having been witnessed in the tangible body of Christ

Intelligible world: outside the cave

3. Thinking (dianoia = mathematical reasoning) – parables of Christ taught to his disciples (Disciples = Greek: "Mathetikon" – "mathematicians (of the word))
4. Forms or ideas: intellection (Greek: noesis = philosophical thinking/dialectic) – eschatology, teleology, epistemology, hermeneutics, exegesis, etc. of the Greek and Hebrew Scriptures unto apocalyptic understanding

In Plato's cave to metaphysics, I believe Plato only missed the "agency" by which this could have happened. It was not Plato's time yet to see this fulfillment. It is Jesus, the divine extension of eternal God that came into the flesh that was Plato's missing link from cave to metaphysics. Plato would have had no idea what fulfillment could have been in his day. Plato couldn't have dreamed that the "meta-physical" could walk, talk, love, create, save, and be with us forever. With the constituents of scripture, platonic reasoning, high art, etc. I would personally lay down my life to say that Jesus is not only our divine saviour but the missing answer for the aporia of Plato's "agency" that filled chronos with the divine. Jesus, as WORD infusing chronos, gave all humankind a reasonable, philosophical, linguistic, musical, artistic and scientific good and wholesome answer for his and our existence. He gave us "the way" by his example unto death. Therefore, my argument (not agaisnt Plato) is that Plato never witnessed the LOGOS come to the flesh in which Jesus fulfilled Plato's "divine demiurge" as LOGOS and agent for the eternal. Moreover, it was Jesus who entered time (*chronos*) baffling politics, legalisms, religions that stifle and are not in accordance with the Greek and Hebrew language, etc. Rather, the divine which fulfilled all pagan proclamations and prophecies of logic "came to be" in the fullness of time.

Seen here is my sketch and water-color called "The Procession of the Magi." A place of bent time and bent physical dimension. For this sketch and color depicts eternal christ's incarnation. This event has baffled our existence by his supervention. Hopefully, you can associate this sketch and watercolor with your leaving "Plato's cave" and begin to answer how eternity can exist in time.

Chapter Forty

Children Walking and Learning in the Kingdom of God.

THE *PAIDEIA*

The children who are learning to walk in the kingdom of God
"*The Little Footers*"
    What is it like to be conformed to Jesus' image? Especially, here on earth? Matthew 18:1-4 speaks of this "coming to be" as turning to be like children ("worldly regress" to make "heavenly progression"). We can call this process "coming to be into the kingdom of heaven." Clearly, this

was stated by Jesus' to his disciples who had not yet "come to be as little children."

In Matthew 18:1–4 Jesus' disciples (*mathetai*—mathematicians, students, exacting etymologists [cf. Plato's *geometers* as etymologists]), were arguing about who would be the "greatest" (Greek: *meizon* from *mega*)" in the kingdom (Greek: *basileia*—basin, abyss, bath, bottom, basis, foot) of heaven. Being "disciples" of Christ you would think they would have known better than to have asked a question like that. Jesus set them "straight" on the answer, but the Holy Spirit to come would guide them to "understand (*hypostasis* from *hypo* = "under" + "standing"—i.e., have footing (*paideia*) to their thoughts and actions) all things."

Let me explain as to why I can't think of a more tender statement than "the kingdom of God" when one understands the pagan Greek language source brought into first-century Christianity, that is, into the New Testament language, *paideia*[1], and early church Greek-speaking fathers. By terms of the "children" or *paidion* I speak of "those" who go step by step, following the precepts of God's word in his kingdom—walking in humility.

I had heard of a beautiful etymology once from one of my old Greek teachers. He said, "When someone says "the kingdom of God" they usually have no idea how powerful a statement that is. *Basilieia tou Theou* literally means "the little feet of God." He went on to say that *basileia* (basis, etc.) means "the foot" or "feet." Words such as "pediatrics" and "podiatrist" come out of this word for "kingdom." However, it is the "little children" who follow the path (*podos*—feet) of God in their obedience, simplicity, meekness, neediness, joy. Such a power-packed phrase.

In the previous chapter I spoke of the archer in Plato's dialogue of *Cratylus* and the etymologies that are used in the will, trajectory, art, or *poiesis* of the *toxotayce* (archer/shooter). The personal participation of the *toxotayce* might be called getting *into the rous (flow, river, stream, current)*. Such a "flow" that is headed directly to the bullseye also allows the shooter to flow with obedience. Therefore, this flow allows the archer to shoot for personal satisfaction within the scope of obedience.

The *paideia* (from the root for "foot," as *padua* in Greek or "little ones," *pedos*— "little one") was the classical aspect of education given to the early first-century Christians to educate (Latin: *e-* prefix— "exit" + *ducare*— "darkness:" meaning "to bring out of darkness") the Christian

---

1. Cf. Jaeger's works on "Paideia": Volumes 1-3 and especially *Early Christianity and Greek Paideia*.

youth by teaching them the richness of etymologies and analogy. They were taught forensics (the art of argumentation) and logic (reason, mainly from Plato and Aristotle's works) and the classics, for sure, such as Homer's *Iliad* and *Odyssey* (cf. Werner Jaeger's *Early Christianity and Greek Paideia*). Such terms of the *toxon*[2] would have "met" the padua as they also would have understood the doctrines of sovereignty as taught by Paul. Paul's Christian worldview fused the genius of Jewish ideas with the Greek orientation, brought to completion by the Holy Spirit, who would and does teach all things to their completion.

---

2. "the one who receives glory" – Greek *doxa* – as in "doxology."

Chapter Forty-One

Paideia to Archer

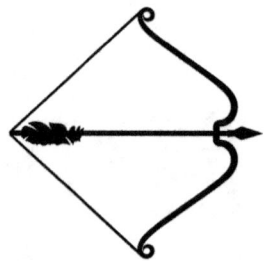

I PLACED THIS ICON at the beginning of my book for it means as much to me as one could comprehend this book and more. As I said at the beginning of the book, this icon conveys to me the "toxotayce"[2] or the lowly "archer" of intent. The true archer holds to the mathematics of the shot. The *mathematician* was called *mathetikon* in Greek. Jesus' disciples

---

1. This is my logo of "the archer" or "toxotayce." You will see it appear throughout my fomcm.com site.

2. Toxotayce (root: toxon – bow/arch/iris/eye/arc) has many sentiments by which I have researched. These fairly archaic words work together in a *conjunction of ideas* that seem to intimate an earlier common root. The first, as I have earlier defined, is "doxa" from which we get "glory," "one who receives glory," "doxology"--i.e., words/hymns of praise (Plato, *Cratylus*, -420 b-c) The other etymological root is "tikto" in Greek meaning "to bring forth." That is, to "bring forth out of its root cause." Jesus is in a sense the tikto of the Father on earth. Jesus receives the praise of the Father as the participant of holiness on this earth and life everlasting. *Tikto* is found in Matthew 1:21, 23, 25, Mat. 2:2; Luke 1:31; Luke 1:57; Luke 2:6, 7,11; John 16:21; Galatians 4:27; Hebrew 6:7: Hebrews 11:11; James 1:15; Rev.12:4, 5, 13. Finally, we find in the *Theaetetus* 194 A, "someone who believes falsely is "like a bad" archer who, in shooting, goes wide of the mark and errs." See Stanford Encyclopedia of Philosophy, "Intentionality in Ancient Philosophy."

were called the *mathetikon*. A Greek, whether Christian or not, who was a *"mathetike"* was one who rightfully divided, assessed, categorized, "allotted the *-ology*" of the shot (i.e., applied the science by which they were involved)." In the case of Jesus' mathetike/mathetikon they were to have applied the WORD unto themselves as Jesus was the WORD. And such an application and *teleos* upon them was much like their leader Jesus, who was "Free" from this world, condemned by this world, and executed by this world.

Not only do we see Christ's disciples/mathetikon as the *padua* of Christ but Jesus as the toxotayce/paduan of God the Father. In pagan antiquity, the stars were referenced in the Bible as the blessed hope for humankind. Sagittarius (also known as "Toxotes" (toxon)—"The Archer"), is the ninth astrological sign and constellation whose "sign ruler" in the heavenlies is Jupiter, the father of the planets ("wanderers"). Sagittarius is the *learned healer whose mental aptitude bridged heaven and earth*. This great "Archer" is represented by the bow and arrow.

The education of the young paideia/paduan/"jedi"

Philosophical understanding plus obedience

The classical Greek *paideia* was originally the classical education for the early Greek youth. The central philosophers such as Plato and Aristotle comprised a large component of this *paideia*. Language, logic, and rhetoric were the primers by which all further study into the sciences could "rationally" be obtained. The language by which these primers functioned was a result of platonic and aristotelian reasoning and cultural bearing.

Therefore, any word used in the *paideia* (language, logic, rhetors) was "refined," delineated, syllogistically filtered, deduced, re-examined, etc. The words found in the *paideia* were therefore known in the sense by which their Greek glossary used its "howness." It is no wonder that the word for "disciple" in the platonic, aristotelian, and, yes biblical New Testament language was *mathetikon* or "mathematician (of the words)."

This "howness" would have been used in its platonic and aristotelian sense. Might I add here that I do not in any way disenfranchise Plato and Aristotle from Greek culture, rather, they simply are the most notable fountainheads of Greek culture.

The New Testament Greek language must be understood from its roots founded in the *paideia* of the ancient pagan (amoral) Greeks. Therefore, the implementation of any word used in the New Testament was based centrally upon the verbal bank of Plato and Aristotle. Yes, there are other "sources" but the well-read philosophers, like Plato and Aristotle, were baptized by their Greek heritage and contemporaries. That is, Plato and Aristotle were the "result" of Greek heritage and, therefore, the consequential "parents" of classical Greek scholasticism.

As a linguist, it is of most import to know the etymologies, morphological rules, socio-linguistic phenomena, etc. of any given language to fully comprehend its worth. It shouldn't be a hard jump to understand that Alexander the Greek, the Hellenizer of Palestine, brought with him the Greek culture into which Palestine was baptized. Moreover, Alexander's teacher was the renowned Aristotle himself. Straight from the horse's mouth to the monarch who would order a new language be spoken across his empire.

Alexander, for sure, was the leopard in Daniel's prophecy and his rule was necessary for the spread of Christianity, via Greek language and reason, to a Hellenized, pagan Europe.

With all that I have said, I conclude with this: there is consensus and concentrated agreement with how the Greek language was implemented in the days of the early Greek New Testament writers. For sure, the Gospel writers were Hellenized. Paul was highly educated both in the Hebrew and Greek systems of thinking and his fluency of both Hebrew and Greek was known and expressed in his writings. Therefore, it would be blasphemous on a secular and theological level to "Anglicize" the *paideia* of the pagan Greeks, the *paideia* of many of the Christian youth of the early church (taught by the Christian mothers!), or the New Testament text.

Deep analysis of the horrid perversion of Anglicizing the rest of the world will begin with the New Testament verses concerning "eternal damnation" in our third piece to this series.

The application of historical-morphological filtering of word meanings down to an "age" of "collective reasoning" is necessarily implemented in order to find biblical "vocabulary agreement." With this said, the Greek New Testament's social context could certainly be viewed as heavily influenced by two forces: (1) socially naturalized verbal usage from logographic/pictographic Proto-Armenian (Syunik) to Hittite, Proto-Georgian Kartvelian and Sumerian pictographic society, and (2) the ingenious handling of Aristotle's deductive syllogism and Plato's agreement of particulars in motion to the fuller receptacle of itself. Such a view synthesized pagan predeterminism with theistic determinism. It has hyper-focused the question of "direction" and "duration" by which the associative words "move forward" in a given society which would therefore be superimposed by a deity. Simply put, Plato's etymological treatments concerning natural elements, their associative words, and the evolution of their abstractions became a grammatical and etymological "theology."

Logic and reason usurped "the collective conscience" of *word and idea* as generated from an *EL* or *YAH* → the prime mover. Thales began to look to his *hupostasis* or "under-root" to all things that water was everything. Things could change but the primary "phusis" was the object of Thales's philosophy that allowed for other philosophies to counter, test, apply, deduce and conclude. To the philosophic and mathematical mind, a "God" was not necessarily needed to be assumed within the objective Thalian view or any scientific view.

The distinctions of "specific-structured" deduction (a.k.a. "probabilities"/"proving")— "proving via observation" vs. "acting within the genius (or "joining") of a community without the weariness of analysis are seen clearly in the disparity of our vast cultural paradigms.

Such examples might be found contrasted in tribal communities. Such as a New Guinean tribe living within their own biosphere perfectly adapted to the genius of the trees, streams, water, food gathering, family life, etc. Such a lifestyle is what we might call, "natural," or "nature." Language is, on the other hand, "abstracted" (literally, "taken from" "taken off" + "structure'—"nature at its origins") from its "root form" of natural elements such as "sky, tree, stream, dirt, earth, fire, wind, etc." To this, there is a "meeting ground" for me that solidifies a verbal-social semiosis within the telegraphed (i.e., to that era studied) socio-verbal bank. One needs the other to exist, past needs present and vice versa. If you will, out-of-time "semiosis."

One might delve into Aristotle's *Rhetoric, generatione et corruptione* (coming to be and going away) and Plato's *Cratylus* for a wonderful side study on word morphologies and the limitations of their interpretations, aka, "semiotics." So beautifully found for me were the "natural" elements that were linguistically "abstracted" into a combined *story*. They had to go somewhere[3]. The morphology of the folktale is all about the natural becoming unnatural and the morphology of the folktale also brought about the *fulfillment* of all things (pleon) in the fullness of time to a mythopoeic and then prophetically instanced culmination of pagan and biblical agreements. In this "eye" I see no contradiction between the movement of pagan tales, scientific-Thalian-Socratic-Platonic-Aristotelian and Semitic logic. I see no distance between biblical archetypes—whether found in the Bible itself or in, let's say, the Norse Volsung Saga, Greek myths, and Rig Veda, etc.—*only movements/motions* aligning to agreement by force of logos.

The *paideia* of the early Greek words found their fulfillments in a Hellenized Christ figure. The origins of Greek society were in their pagan poets such as Virgil, Aeschylus, Sappho, Homer, and others, so, how could these bards and poets be just random mistakes if the God of the Bible created all things?

Such Semitic archetypes, shadows, types, and prophecies did Christ Jesus fulfill! Such European and Hellenized archetypes (spoken of by the bards and poets) did Christ fulfill as the Messiah versus the limited "hero." Jesus was and is the physical fountainhead or "tip of the arrow" to which all myths and folklores point.

FROM HEAVEN TO EARTH AND BACK AGAIN

In Psalms 45:3–5 (ca. 1000 BC) we have the conjoined Pagan and Biblical astrological link to our Christ: "Gird Thy sword upon Thy thigh, O most mighty, with Thy glory and Thy majesty, And in Thy majesty ride prosperously, Because of truth and meekness and righteousness; and Thy right hand shall teach Thee terrible things. Thine arrows are sharp in the heart of the King's enemies Whereby the people fall under Thee."

Revelation 6:2 "I saw a white horse, and He that sat on him had a bow, … and He went forth conquering and to conquer:

The Hebrew and Syriac name of the sign "Sagittarius" is *Kesith*, which means "the Archer." The Arabic name is *Al Kans*, "The Arrow," and the Coptic name is *Pimaere*: "the graciousness/beauty of the coming forth."

---

3. as though I could see the pagan's words as little demiurges who answered to an omnipotent God.

I look at each constellation as another book which has chapters in it telling the narrative of the Christ. When I look at the constellations, namely that of Sagittarius, I am amazed that no matter how far-removed cultures have been from one another over eons of time, the story remains the same.

There are roughly 70 main stars in Sagittarius. Out of the main magnitude stars that comprise Sagittarius we have retained in Hebrew, *Naim*, which means "gracious one." In this same Archer constellation, we have amongst the highest magnitude stars retained in the Akkadian, *Nun-Ki* meaning "Prince of the Earth."

The brightest star in Sagittarius is known as *Vega*, which means, "He shall be exalted." Further back in antiquity, we have the ancient Egyptian Dendorah Zodiac which is contemporary with Sumeria. The Dendorah Zodiac retains *Fent-kar*, meaning "the eagle (or hawk) ruled over the serpent." We see this same ancient high magnitude star retained as well in the Arabic *Al Nesr* and Hebrew *Nesher*. The "ascension as an eagle" is the primary meaning behind these later word and idea relations but all do retain "ascension," "victory," "rule."

Such a history goes far beyond what I present for the "praise-narrative" of Christ in the heavenlies. What I do want to convey through this section is that "word and idea" throughout history have had tremendous effect. Concepts such as "Bringing Forth" "Serpent Ruled Over," "The Eagle," "The Archer," "The Bow," "Sag" (as in Sagittarius), are all inter-related. As I have presented lectures on "picto-graphic societies" I attempted to convey "word and idea" as something far more complex than the linguistic "disparity" of our culture today.

To make one further step back to make this point I will bring in the ancient Armenian word *Sag* which means "tip of the beginning or end of the tip." The verbalization of *Sag* meant "To bring forth," "to gush out," "to emanate." Ancient Armenian language has been identified to be closely related to Sumerian. It is in the Sumerian myth that *Hawarasag* is the mountain where the mother Goddess, *Nin. Hur. Sag.* (Lady of the Emanating Mountain).

So, ancient myth and legend carry the "conglomerate" and inseparable word sandwiching by which these images are fired into the minds of our ancestors. The ancients were "true" to their words in that Ideas could not be so easily separated.

Being in hell must partially mean disenfranchised from the trueness of the words of old and the WORD which binds us all together.

Chapter Forty-Two

A Prelude to Satan/a *shatan*

A "HITTING OF THE MISS"

Dr. Tur Sinai in his book *The Book of Job* makes it clear that "Satan" did not have the suffix "-an" originally–as in "Shat-an" or "Sat-an." Rather, this added suffixial "-an" came later to make it personal, i.e., "THE doer of disparaging- destroying, etc." Such was NOT the case in its original

A PRELUDE TO SATAN/A *SHATAN*

and oldest Semetic case[1]. *Shat* meant "to disparage." Here, we must contrast *Shat/SHT* from "Shatan, Satan, Shaytan." For social convention to the Babylonians and Persians, the Jews in Babylonian and Persian captivity did indeed adopt the ideas of "verbs of motion." These approaches, for sure, gave power to the quality of action as "the mover, intender, actor upon [2](etc.)." This was not so in the earlier conventions of language concerning a Satan – i.e., *SHT* or *Shat*. *Shat* was not a personalized doer, rather, *SHT* was the agency by which destruction occurred in the context of the story.

I find it interesting that the ancient usage of *SHAT* or *SHT*, i.e., "to disparage," is the verb which means "to belittle to nothing; to make someone feel like nothing." It is the VERY equivalent of the Greek "*E-MISEO*" which is used in Romans 9 to mean "hated" in the sense of "reduced to non-importance, dismiss" (hence the Greek: *Miseo*, not count (at least, for now). It is in the little things like this (from Sumerian to Older Hebrew/Semitic to New Testament Greek semiotic/endonymic agreement) that give me solace in the consistent theology of a timeless God and his agents throughout every culture and language.

Another highly interesting point that I have found in scripture is that "the satan/Satan" is used as the actor *of* God and later "dismissed" into non-existence for the story's sake.

Zechariah 3:1 makes it clear that Satan was an "adversary" at the right hand of God. Stumping your toe in a sense is "adversarial" but not a moral issue. So, do we attribute stumping your toe to Satan? Stumping your toe could be defined as a *Ra'ah* which is the Hebrew word used for "evil," "destruction," "breaking down," "injury," "hurt," "pestilence," "disease," etc. So, it is clear in scripture that God did ordain that: Psalm 115:3 "But our God is in the heavens; He does whatever He pleases"; Daniel 4:35: "He does according to His Will in the army of heaven and among the inhabitants of the earth"; Isaiah 43:13: "Indeed, from eternity I am He; there is no one who can deliver out of My hand; I act, and who can reverse it?"

---

1. cf. Sinai, *Book of Job*, 42 and 43.

2. It wasn't until later that the Arabic borrowed the later meaning, Shaytan or Satan, and again, loaned it into the Hebrew language which became a word of assimilation into the Hebrew Culture, which in my opinion causes a perversion of the original meaning. Yes, the Hebrew translators could have used "SHT" for a more contextually fitting "SHT" verses and "rogue actor of evil." This is, for sure, a result of the Babylonian influence on the Pharisees in Babylon which "borrowed" this word as well.

And, yes, Satan was rebuked because Joshua (archetypical Jesus found here in Zecharia's prophecy) would be tempted and overcome. Was the act of Joshua/Jesus THE rebuke, THE dismissal of Satan in this timeless-a-tempo prophetic scenario? I say, YES.

This development of word and idea is shackled in a web of traditions that I plan on solving by going back to the very origin of word and idea in this treatment (vide infra footnote 94).

More offices of the Satan

In Job, we have the Satan figure *coming with* (Hebrew: *bo*) the *bene ha Elohim*. These were the "sons of God" at their "celestial court *presentation* [Hebrew: *la hit yas tseb*] before YHVH." YHVH asked the satan who "came with them" "*where* do you come from?." Satan answered his name! That is, the satan said, "I am going "to and fro [*mi–SHUT*]." We see this attribute of the satan's name in YHVH: 2 Chronicles 16:9 says that "God's eyes roam to and fro throughout the earth . . ."

1. In Zechariah 4:10 we have an apocalyptic composite of God "as the lampstand" and the "seven lamps are His eyes which scan to and fro [Hebrew: *mi-sho-wt*] through the whole earth." The root for God's eyes which "scan to and fro" is indeed the same as "the satan" in Job.

2. Herodotus, a famous Greek historian, tells us of a Persian king, being a contemporary of Ezra and Nehemiah, that had his "eyes and ears which did rove to and fro" seeking out those who might conspire against the king and his family. These "rovers" were called the *shut* or *sht*. They were the "secret service" of the king[3].

3. There was a "satan" of both Jewish and non-Jewish legend who was considered the "horned one" who was "hoofed" and depicted as having a bull's tail. To me, it is the obvious picture of Gilgamesh and his grandfather, Enmerker or Nimrod. Such symbolic animal aspects of the "horned one" or "the Satan" seen here were of a shamanistic idea that one took on the power of what they had conquered. Nimrod, the Bullman, is just that depiction.

---

3. Zech 4:10; Sinai, *Book of Job*, 42–43 —'the eyes for the king/secret service for the king = shut/sht." Arberry, "Legacy of Persia" 9; "The Watcher" (Hebrew: "ir") was applied to certain members of the heavenly court – Daniel 4:13. Satan as a prosecutor: Zechariah 3:1, Psalm 109:6

4. In some biblical references to Satan, as a "being" or anthropomorphized, we see "him" as a seducer, accuser, and trouble maker.

5. The Greeks translated *Sh-t-n* from the Septuagint (LXX) as *diabolos*. Such a Greek sentiment of *diabolos* meant "informer." This nears that of the *SHT*/satan of the Persians in terms of the "Secret Service" to the Persian King (cf. Tur Sinai: pgs. 38–45)/also among the ancient orient). To make the "informant" part of a bigger "sketch" by the "sandwiching/stacking" of a very real, ancient, and universal sense we find that in the very name, *diabolos – dia* = "across," "traverse," "through" + *bolos* = "to volley," "cast," "toss," "throw." It was duly noted in Dr. Tur Sinai's work on *The Book of Job*[4] that this "kind" of *Sht*/satan/*ha shatan* was a "rover, roamer, scanner, sifter, master of language–in terms of interrogation." Dr. Sinai says on page 43: "And if such a roving agent finds no fault with a person or a people, so that he has nothing to report to his master whereby he might prove his zeal and usefulness, he sometimes adopts the role of an "agent provocateur," who incites men to commit offences, in order to deliver them afterwards in the hands of justice (for example: cf. I Chronicles 21:1)."

6. In Job 1:7 – We satan responding to God's question: "where do you come?" – Satan responded: "roaming about the earth going to and fro." Here we have a match in the Akkadian *alakum*[5] which shares in Assyrian, Hebrew, and Arabic the common root, *hallek* –"to walk." But, the Akkadian, I believe, is where the sentiment of "evil" is borrowed into the Hebrew/Jewish idea of the Hebrew participle "*mithhallek*." For "*alakum*" means "to rove about as an armed man being "full of eyes" -i.e., a *watcher*.

---

4. Sinai, *Book of Job*, 43.
5. Huehnergard, *Grammar of Akkadian*, 561.

Chapter Forty-Three

Satan is an Element of Predeterminism: Not a Theological Component Which Substantiates Dualism

DOES DUALISM EXIST OR IS SATAN A PREDETERMINED TOOL USED BY GOD?

It can seem very confusing when reading passages of Satan "acting" in the scripture such as Job and 1 Peter 5:8–9 (para) - *the Devil (aka Satan) walks about like a roaring lion, seeking whom he may devour.* Such freedom to roam as a roaring lion gives us the illusion that he, the Devil, has an independent volition but the "nature" is bound to do what it does[1].

Let's start here in Ephesians 2: "Once (*pote*— "a time when") you walked according to the age (*aeon*—era) of the world . . . of this accordance to the ruler (*archon*) of the air and the *spirit* currently working in the sons of disobedience."

---

1. Remembering a challenge I posed to a former college professor who was teaching that "free will" was an "independent" ability *from* God. I asked him during the class: "Does a dog bark because it chooses to or is it simply in its "nature" to do so?" —that is, is its "nature" a demarcation of what it will do and how could "choice" be distinguished from nature? This might have been an incomplete challenge then but the study of the word "nature" has brought me to understand that predetermined patterns within physics are real and do apply to "nature." Though an atheist, Dr. Sam Harris explains in his book, "Free Will," about the impossibilities of having "free moral agency," "free will," "independent volition" based on being independent of the physics and biochemical reactions that precede your very "actions." My argument stands firm that though Sam is right, we have "God's moral agency" working through us, willing us unto redemption from the hopeless inability to repent of our flesh's nature.

Paul here refers to the "god" of the age (*aeon*/era/*hora*/hour/horizon) previously mentioned in 2 Corinthians 4:4: "The god of the age (*aionos*—era) has blinded (*typhlos*) the eyes of the unbelieving (*apeitheia* = *ap* (not) + *peitho* (persuaded)). So, at one time you, believers, were "hardened, immovable, insensitive, not persuaded so as not to beam forth (*augasai*) illumination of the gospel."

We've got terms such as: "ruler," "authority," "air," "spirit," "now working," in the sons of disobedience. So, we have a "present-day god" who currently (Greek: *nunti*, now) works (*energountos*) in the "sons of *apeitheias*." So, I continue: *who* is this "god"? Well, he walks, talks, rules, blinds, and acts within this age, this time, this duration, this era, this aeon. This is most important for our understanding of what he is by name. Demon. *D'-mn* is the P.I.E. root for "divider of time + god" (in Dr. Joseph Shipley's work on Proto Indo-European root word "Chronos") as in "time" + "god"[2]. Chronos most certainly fits the bill for "the Satan" identified as "tempo" and/or "tempter." Chronos "consumes" us all in his "divisions" of time. He is the parser of time, the parser of us. His consort/bride is Ananke. Ananke was given a tremendous treatment in Plato's *Cratylus*. She/it is the field of thorns and thicket by which one traverses for one's erotic fulfillment at the end of such a telegraph. The outcome is never what it seems to be in one's hopes and initial desires.

It is in the here and now that "the divider" acts. That is, both in space and tempo. Should it be a wonder, therefore, that the Latin Vulgate gives us the Latin *tempus* for "temptation." It means "to be strung across time, to be stretched, pulled, torn, divided, rent—i.e. "*temo*-ed" . . . or, *over-timed*. It is this duration of testing that Job was made even more pure. It was the "testing" that proved that Jesus was the Son of God and did not falter. The trying of the saints—those who were martyred (Greek: *maturos* – "maturing; to make mature; martyr) led to their "sainthood."

Now, as to *who* causes this? —Isaiah 45:7-25 makes it clear that it is God. God is not relegated to our sense perception of "good" vs. "evil." He does ALL things to the betterment of himself and us. But, the tools for "acting" in this world are ordained of God for God is outside of tempo. Therefore, it is not God *directly doing* anything in our tempo/time[3]. God's

---

2. Time as tempter: Demon—Timon (proto-Indo-European: di- "divider, god, demon, etc.")

3. (Let) no one being tempted (*tempo*, Latin; *peirazomenos*, Greek: put through trials, dragged, pulled through (in this age/time/duration)) say, "By God I am being tempted—for God cannot be tempted and he tempts no one. A man is tempted

Will is outside of time's actions of good or evil. In I Corinthians 15:28 the *all in all* is subsumed in eternity past, present, and future. All shall submit to Christ and all shall be returned to the Father in a holy state in order to exist in his presence. If the writer of Ecclesiastes is correct in that all things have been done: past, present, and future then, "IT IS DONE" —even as I type this. All of creation *beginning to end* was in the mind of God. Panentheism (not to be mistaken with *pantheism*) would be a befitting term here. Panentheism (Greek: pan – all + en – in + theos – God) means that "all things are in God. All things work together in synergy in his Will. In 1 Corinthians 15:28 we see that this "all in all" will be just the case. All things will go into Christ and ALL of these "things (creation from the beginning of time)" will be given to the holy Father sealed, daubed, wrapped, secured and restored (apokatastasis) in the Son.

THE LIMITATIONS OF THE FLESH

Sin is the binding of the natural man. It (sin – *harmateia* – "missing the bullseye by the archer") is all that he can do with the fullest of his "natural will, or "natural intent." So, I'm immediately brought to the first chapter of Job in the dialogue of God and "the Satan" (the accuser). Satan was given the boundary lines by which he could "do his work, (the boundary of his authority, authorship, energy, work, etc.), hende, Satan's limitations.

Though known throughout eons of religious/cultural permutations, we have *narratively* picked out "Satan" (mostly influenced within the Perso-Medes influence) as the "bad" Ahriman (vs. *AhuraMazda*) propping a "humanlike" dualistic" nature.

The Hebrew scriptures connote Satan as a "sifter" who does the "sifting (The Strong's Concordance gives further color to "Satan" as "*sifting without mental cognizance*")." Even when "the Satan ("Ha Shatan")" in the book of Job answered YHVH as to what he (Satan) was doing, his reply was, "going to a fro" (i.e., meandering, roving[4]. This was his *nature* (not his choice). In Zechariah 4:10 God's eyes were considered to be "the

---

(*peirazetai*—drawn out, pulled through, dragged, put through) by his own desire (*epithymias*—passions that drive one)—being drawn away and being enticed (*deleazo*— "baited," "lured") . . . *then*, *desire* or your *passions*, having conceived, gives birth to sin (*harmateia*—that which misses the mark). Once sin has become fully grown it brings forth death – James 1:13, 14.

4. cf. my lecture on my site: fomcm.com for a treatment of "The Raven, The Rover, Corvai," —"eye of the witch," "eye of Odin" in the "Articles" section.

Satans" because *they rove in judgment*[5]. His (Satan) was governed by an overriding force. In our terms, this means bound to or limited to that which he could "work" or "sift." In Isaiah 45:7ff. it is God who says, "I, the LORD, create both good and evil." The Hebrew translated here as "evil" is *ra'ah*, which means "falling down, destruction." So, it is God's essence which sets the ordained plan from the *tselem* (Hebrew: "mind/imagination") but the *work* of "evil" is done by God's tool of "evil." Otherwise, "evil" ("breaking down") would exist in God and creation would have evil in its essence via its creator. If this is the case, the creation would fall apart, given the meaning of *ra'ah* (Hebrew: "collapse;" "break down"). Even in the book of Job we see that God was the one who brought evil upon Job, not Satan: Job 42:11 ". . . . and they (Job's brothers, and all his sisters, acquaintances) bemoaned him (Job), and comforted him in house over all the EVIL that the LORD had brought upon him (Job) . . ." So how do we figure this verse from the first few chapters in Job where it seems like Satan was the "actor" in doing evil? Satan's nature was used to do the will of the LORD, which is ra'ah (destruction in Job's case for that moment —only to build Job up). We only think in "time." "Good" and/or "bad" is a fixture to our thinking due to our fall and our myopic view that renders us blind to U.P.A.T. If we could only see that it is God that is doing good and evil for everyone's benefit then we would "get it." But for now, it's all about "look at this, it's evil," "look at this, it's good." The apocalypse of our minds will be opened soon enough–that is: the "cover will be removed" and our eyes shall no longer be fixed on the small picture. We will see God's total plan set before the creation.

Evil entered (*eis*) holy creation but it was ordained by the LORD. Sin is in our natures when faced with the holy. It becomes under judgment "naturally." Nature is not sinful until the holy requires holiness. Going against most current Roman Catholic and Protestant beliefs, I say that sin has nothing to do with the idea of "free agency (neither does "nature")." For the idea of what we think "free will" means is usually the freedom to act. But our only "freedom to act" by our *nature* is to sin in the face of the holy one which is not free agency but universal condemnation upon the works of ALL of us. We naturally sin and sin naturally.

---

5. Zechariah 4:10 "e.ne YHVH *hem.mah miSHT.Tiym* (Hebrew root: *Sht–'to* scan; rove to and fro) *be.kal ha erotz* – "The eyes of YHVH scan to and fro throughout all the earth"

HOLINESS WITHIN CREATION

If Jesus was the lamb slain from the foundation of the world, then *Jesus* was the fashioner of the holy act of creation—including making the evil that man would do to put him on the ordained cross (Revelation 13:8 "... The lamb (Jesus) slain from the foundation of the world...."). Therefore, Jesus created the men who acted within evil[6] and who crucified him. All of this, however, was still under the Will of the Father. These men were never "free" to choose not to do this act against the holy one. In other words, all that was in the mind of God the Father to create through the Son, i.e., the beginning through to the end, i.e., *all* of the sequences of events in between beginning and end were set before they happened in God's creation, and this *was good* (Hebrew: *tov*, "beneficial," "builds upon itself," "anabolic," "supports itself and the next step"). *Tov* or "good," as the Hebrew mind conceives it, is not necessarily "happy" but "beneficial" in the plan of God, even if not in sinful man's plans.

If we can agree to see how scripture is coherent here, then we can conclude that the scripture conveys not only an *ordaining*[7] God but a God of predeterminism, for his abode was and will be in his eternal chamber. Looking at scripture from this view, God did not sin but ordained the "archons" or "rulers" in *his* grand narrative to put Jesus to death at the act of creation (Revelation 13:8) in order that we may go past this world into the next (past the boundary of time and space [a.k.a. "pre – horizon/"pre-time]]). This was not an act of man's "free will" but an act of ordination by God, as explained in Acts 2:23: "Him [Jesus], being delivered by the determinate counsel (*boule* = "the will") and [also] the foreknowledge of God (not just "foreknowledge" like many would argue), ye have taken, and by wicked hands have crucified and slain."[8] This verse goes on to

---

6. Ephesians 2:1–22. explains that we, too, were those kind of people – i.e., people of disobedience, destruction, etc. who followed the spirit of antiChrist and were "damnable" by our very natures. Yet, we received grace anyway.

7. i.e. sequences *in time meeting their termination points* [the antithesis of eternity].

8. take a moment to see that God determined Jesus' crucifixion by wicked hands. It is the "natural man" in his sinful-natural state/existence that God used (just as God used Satan in his "natural state" of fallenness. God cannot be "natural" or "of this world" in all of its dichotomies and bifurcations for he is above that. Yet, the narrative must unfurl for MEANING'S sake that Jesus is the holy one. How are we to understand this holiness if we are holy? We must be fleshly to see the contrast of that which is holy. Holy is not "left or right," "bad or good," etc… "Holy" is above time in all of its divisions and divisiveness.

speak of the "narrative" by which the "actors" do put Jesus to death —you have taken Jesus "and by wicked hands have crucified and slain *him*."

Again, Revelation 13:8 makes it clear that Jesus is the lamb that was slain from the foundation of the world. In other words, at the "creation point" our Father had willed (*boule*) Jesus, his Son, to be put to death. Moreover, Revelation 13:1–8 reveals, literally "un-caps" (*apo* = "off" + *kalypto* = "cap" or "seal[9]" that covers"), the kingdoms of the earth for whom power was given *by God* to mock God in his own holy temple service (by Babylon-Persia (lion), Greece (leopard), and Rome (bear)). As Revelation 13 continues we read that there is yet another beast that had/has not/will have a power likened to that of the first. I believe this first beast was Babylon led by the "god-king" with various names for the various cultures which called him by their view of him: Nimrod/Nebrod/Marduk/Enmerker/Narmer. In any case, it is "new Babylon" with its "final system of worship," much like that of the old kingdom where all bowed to Nimrod. This time though, the "system" would be a full-on contagion that marks the world with his power. Anyone not worshiping his system (a.k.a. "receiving the mark of his likeness") should be put to death. I remember studying the Sumerian/Babylonian word for such "a mark" or "demarcation" of power. The Sumerian word was called: ME. Not as in "me" in the English (yet ironically, exactly what it is). The Sumerian word *ME*, as defined by Dr. John Halloran, meant: "essence, function, office, responsibility, ideal norm; the phenomenal area of a deity's power; divine power; divine decree; cult (the culture beset by the norm of operations); silence as to anything against such a system."

Such a system was *ordained,* yet, the "authority" by which it stands was already mentioned here in reference to Ephesians 2:2: "The ruler of authority of the air, [aka] the spirit now working in the sons of disobedience." Also, read on in 2 Corinthians 4:4, for it speaks of "the god of this aeon." Satan as a "roaring lion"—i.e., his "nature." In all such cases, this Satan character is appointed (hupotasis - "placed upon") as the head of the *cosmokriton* (world) and *aeon* (age) but not the kingdom of men, as we see in Daniel 4:17. All men, whether in the faith or not[10], experience the "roaring lion," Satan, in the world. In 1 Peter 5:8 we read, "Be sober,

---

9. seal: *Kel* – "hell"; "hole," (German: "Hollen" – "Hell") "That which conceals." As we see even in the word, "apocalypse" we have *apo* – "to take off" + "hell" or "that which has been the covering, concealment, hole/unseen place.

10. 1 Timothy 4:10 (Jesus/God) → *Who is the Saviour of all, and especially of those who believe.*

be vigilant; because your adversary the devil, as a roaring lion, walketh about [just as the Satan in Job], seeking whom he *may* [i.e., may be allowed to, living according to his nature] devour: Whom [Satan] resist steadfast *in the faith*, knowing that *the same afflictions are accomplished in your brethren that are in the world.*" Have you been "devoured" today, yesterday, or maybe tomorrow with pride, ego, lust, anger, jealousy, rage, self-pity, etc.? Well, if you have, you were figuratively "eaten" or "*devoured*" by the lion-Satan at that "time" or "division of time." We all are "divided" at times (no pun).

From the oldest book in the Bible, that is, the book of Job[11], we have the narrative agreement as to how YHVH uses Satan to do YHVH's desire. This devouring is done on all men to "accomplish" his perfected will through time in us.

Another example of divine sovereignty is seen in prophecy. Unless everything goes *perfectly* (that is, required, willed—including events both *ra'ah* ("evil") and *tov* ("good")), then prophecy could have never come about. Consider Daniel 8 and 9. Here we find prophecies of an exact number of years for the Messiah to come back concerning the seventy-sevens/*shavua* (490 years) from the decree to Jesus and the final seven years (*shavua*) of the 490 being Revelation's final seven years. Unless Nehemiah was given a decree by Xerxes, the Persian king (most scholars believe this was Esther's "Xerxes"), to go back into Jerusalem and rebuild the temple then we wouldn't have the final prophetical event of Daniel (Jesus, the Messiah riding into Jerusalem as king of kings). If we can understand that prophecy requires the spoken word of the future event with the acts that are continuing as the prophet would speak in the present, then we can reason that one act requires the next —i.e., the seemingly mundane to the great event(s) were prophesied. "Seventy *shavua* (490 years) are determined upon thy people . . . from the going forth of the commandment to rebuild Jerusalem" (Daniel 9:24–25). Historically, we know that this command was issued ca. 445 BC. So, from then until the Messiah will be sixty-nine *shavua* (483 years). This puts Jesus roughly at AD 34–38 (depending on the calendrical formulas proposed by

11. The book of the "man of struggles–IYYOB" was a Mesopotamian text that many believe to be the Job that accounts for the biblical Jobab. If this is the case, we have a fix on the oldest text. Otherwise, Job is still a contemporary text of the culture of Uz capturing many of the endonymic usages found in UZ. For a much fuller treatment read Sinai, *Book of Job*. Cf. Jobab, son of Zerah: Genesis 36:33; 1 Chronicles 1:44, 45. Jobab (Job) would be a contemporary of Abraham putting Job ca 1800 BC at latest and ca 2000 at earliest.

SATAN IS AN ELEMENT OF PREDETERMINISM

numerous "calendricists"). After this, the sons of disobedience (sons of the prince/antiChrist) will destroy the temple (at Jerusalem, ca. AD 70). Then—at a futuristic date— the antiChrist "will confirm a "covenant" for seven years." That is, the last *shavua*.

None of these chain-events could be "random" or left to *chance*[12] if the scriptures concerning prophecy about what will happen are true. There are no dates that the heathen, atheist, agnostic, or anyone has placed on the prophecy of Daniel that would nullify the coming of Christ on a donkey and being praised as the king of kings[13].

---

12. I always address the word "chance" in its Latin form: *cadentia* – [cf. *cado* – Latin, Lewis and Short, *Latin Dictionary*, 258–59, "that which falls out" and its much older root from the Proto-Indo-European: **kad* – "to fall." This word "chance" is never implying a connotative "luck," which, hilariously, means, "to fall to the lot" —i.e., an "ordered sequence." To fall down, to decline, to fall to.

13. May 14, 1948 – Israel became a nation, one stick of Ephraim and one of Judah as "ONE" nation to fulfill Ezekiel's prophecy Ezekiel 37:7–10.

Chapter Forty-Four

A Hyper Focus using Paideia: (Twisting Texts on "Hell")

I AM A FIRM believer that exegesis in the scripture leads to freedom from ignorance both in "theological conundrums" and life's quagmires brought about through seeking one's self satisfactions.

When I say, "educate" I do not mean that we have to all be scholars or academics. Rather, I believe that we must be educated. What do I mean by that? I return to the root of the word "education": Latin: *educare* (*e* = "out of" + *ducare* = "darkness" = "to educate"). Therefore, we have agreement with the Greek *apokalypse* ("to be taken out of hell," "to have concealment removed")" and the Latin "out of darkness"/"from hell into the light."

The culture of the early Jews put the children (paidia) up front of the group where they were nearest to the rabbi. All were taught. The earliest Jews learned together[1].

AS LITTLE CHILDREN

Paideia was the classical Greek education, which would also have been the education of many of the children in the early church. It means, "to walk"—literally "the little footers"[2] One could use the *Star Wars* term "padawan" (same term as *paideia*) for the *young ones* learning the *Force*.

The educational path of the paideia was called the *trivium*. The *trivium* for Christian children in the early church consisted of (1) Greek and Latin language (and the classics such as the Iliad, Odyssey, Antigone, Medea, Metamorphosis, Plato's Dialogues, the Histories of Herodotus), etc. (2) logic (Aristotle's "deductive syllogistic reasoning") (3) rhetoric/rhetors – Aristotle. All such classical education came *directly* out of the early classicists with special emphasis on Aristotle and Plato's philosophies and the classical myths of Homer and beyond.[3] There would have been no conflict perceived between the New Testament texts written by Paul and the *paideia*. Contrary to a conflict between the Gospels, Epistles, and the Classical education of the Greeks, the epistles of Paul would have only complemented each other. Paul said much more on his journeys than just the written epistles. In my mind there's no way that Paul would have not looked for "common ground" to minister to the Greek, Roman, Galatoi (Celts) who migrated to Asia Minor (modern day Turkey).

There are academic arguments that Paul was a Hellenistic Jew and that he was classically trained. To Paul's education, he would have also been able to have fused Jewish beliefs with Christian and even show the

---

1. cf. Ralph Gower's *Manners and Customs of the Jews* concerning education of the youth. Also, Werner Jaeger's *Early Christianity and Greek Paideia*.

2. As I have stated earlier, we see this term in "pediatrics" for medical care for the youth. See Dr. Werner Yeager's treatment on "Christian Paideia" and "Classical Greek Paideia."

3. Cf. treatments on Astrological, Biblical and Homeric ties in Rolleston, *Mazzaroth*; Bullinger, *Witness of the Stars*; Florence and Kenneth Wood's *Homer's Secret Iliad* and *Homer's Secret Odyssey*; and MacDonald, *Homeric Epics and the Gospel of Mark*.

Jew that there is an entire world outside Christianity and Judaism that proclaims Christ —whether unbeknownst or known to them.

I hold that Paul cryptically, if not openly, referred to the classics. Such is the case for Plato's works and more than likely, John's "logos" in John 1:1–51 answers to the Stoics' "spermatikos logos" as "the cosmic order" by which we consist, live and breathe.

In a sense, I lightly call Paul a *Christian culture hero*. Paul was able to use the deep-rooted Mediterranean, European, and Judaistic cultures to promote the grace of Jesus Christ. Paul taught that Jesus was a deeply embedded theme, though hidden at times, within the underskirt of universal (all cultures) wisdom. Paul referenced the great philosophers within his letters.[4] Please read footnote #203 for just a few of them.

With that said, Paul, by inspiration of God, addressed the Greek's religious beliefs of the demiurge and other superstitious ideas at Mars Hill. Paul builds upon their ideas into the fullness of a resurrected God in Acts 17:22-31[5]. The genius of Paul's ministry, in my opinion, was his

---

4. 1 Cor. 15:33 – Paul uses a quote from Menander, a third C. BC writer; Titus 1:12 "The Cretans are always liars, evil beasts, slow bellies" –here, Paul quotes Epimenides – "who is a "prophet" of their own;" Acts 17:24 "God dwells not in temples made with hands" — Seneca: "The whole world is the temple of the immortal gods," and "Temples are not to be built to God of stones piled on high. He must be consecrated in the heart of every man....... Acts 17:26-28: "God made one every nation of men to dwell on all the face of the earth" —Seneca – "We are members of a vast body. Nature made us kin, when she produced us from the same things and to the same ends"; Galatians 5:23: "Against there is no law (i.e., the law of Grace)" —Aristotle "Against such there is no law, the they themselves are a law"; 1 Cor. 9:24 (paraphrased) "all run the race —all win in one" — Aristotle — (same); Romans 7:22,23 – same as Plato's "There is a victory and defeat—the first and best of victories, the lowest and worst of defeats – which each man gains or sustains at the hands not of another, but of himself; this shows that there is a war against ourselves – going on in every individual of us"; Phillip. 3:19 – Plato: "the gluttonous and intemperate souls whose belly was their God (Republic)"; etc... the list goes on.

5. Acts 17 verses 22–31: 22 Then Paul stood in the midst of Mars hill, and said, "Ye men of Athens, I perceive that in all things ye are too superstitious. 23 For as I passed by, and beheld your devotions, I found an altar with this inscription, TO THE UNKNOWN GOD. Whom therefore ye ignorantly worship, him declare I unto you. 24 God that made the world and all things therein, seeing that he is Lord of heaven and earth, dwelleth not in temples made with hands; 25 Neither is worshipped with men's hands, as though he needed anything, seeing he giveth to all life, and breath, and all things; 26 And hath made of one blood all nations of men for to dwell on all the face of the earth, and hath determined the times before appointed, and the bounds of their habitation; 27 That they should seek the Lord, if haply they might feel after him, and find him, though he be not far from every one of us: 28 For in him we live, and move, and have our being; as certain also of your own poets have said, For we are also his offspring. 29 Forasmuch then as we are the offspring of God, we ought not to think

boldness to connect with others' beliefs with an openness to his. Moreover, Paul offered a greater way, a way that freed one up from idolatry and human effort.

Paul's Christ was understood by the Hellenized world. For sure, Christ's association to the heathens of Gadara was possibly one of the ambiguous Gadarene healing Shepherds known in the Greek tongue as "Eubouleus." Such a title as Eubouleus, the "Swine-Herder" or "well caster" or "good-caster" (Kerenyi 1967). One must think what the people of Gadara thought in Luke 8 and Matthew 5 when the possessed man from whom legion spoke out of and was excised from running into the swine and into the abyss. I hold that Jesus was the heathen's idea of their "christ-figure"[6].

---

that the Godhead is like unto gold, or silver, or stone, graven by art and man's device. 30 And the times of this ignorance God winked at; but now commandeth all men everywhere to repent: 31 Because he hath appointed a day, in the which he will judge the world in righteousness by that man whom he hath ordained; whereof he hath given assurance unto all men, in that he hath raised him from the dead".

6. There is quite a bit of romance here for me concerning this Greek myth that held the swine as the chthonic taxi into hell/abyss. I can easily see the Persephone myth brewing alongside this as well. Though this is just my thinking, the common myth of this swine herding Messiah would have been fulfilled in the flesh by Jesus at this juncture in real time.

Chapter Forty-Five

What Is Judgment Again? — (A Recap)

APOKATASTASIS (ACTS 3:21) VS. THE ENGLISH'S "ETERNAL JUDGMENT"

BEFORE WE CONSIDER THE "hell verses" that many use from the English Bibles to support a "forever damnation" due to the works of one's flesh, I have a word to say about what "judgment" means under a gracious Jesus Christ.

It is true that Jesus made it harder to keep his law in Matthew 5:20–48 than the mosaic law by turning the law into a spiritual impossibility. Jesus made getting into heaven impossible by human will. Jesus set a "conundrum." Then, he tells his disciples that though it is impossible with the human will to acquire salvation all things are possible with God (Jesus). So then, there can be no amount of "good willing" to get into heaven.

JUDGEMENT

For Aristotle, the word *kolasis* (judgment) is a kind of punishment inflicted upon the "damned" or "condemned" for the sake of the "condemned" being punished unto reformation. In other words, judgment for remission of the sin—a rectification!

Christians often think of the apocalyptic/eschatological judgment as an "eternal scourging'—mindless pain without end. Such a punishment *could not* have any benefit for the ones being punished. This theology of everlasting punishing comes into our theology in part from a mistranslation of the Greek word *kolasis* and partly from a mistranslation in the Latin Vulgate of the New Testament Greek word *aionios* (meaning "age-long or "pertaining to an age") into the Latin word *aeternus* (meaning "eternity without end"). The Latin Vulgate was the Bible of the Western church for many centuries and was massively influential in shaping its theology. In the minds of many Christians the Bible straightforwardly taught never-ending punishment. And that was indeed true of their Latin Bible.

In contrast to the Vulgate's erroneous translation-usage of *aeternus*, which hugely impacted the High Church medieval mind and then subsequent English translations which corrupted western Christendom, the earliest transmissions of the Greek New Testament spoke of a *kolasin aionion*. What did that phrase convey to its audience? The biblical *aeon* (age, a certain duration of time) and *kolasis* (affliction for the benefit of the afflicted *unto remission of guilt*) were used together to express the "baptism of fire" (Matthew 3:11: John the Baptist said: "I indeed baptize you with water unto repentance: but *he* that cometh after me [Jesus] is mightier than I, whose shoes I am not worthy to bear: *he* shall baptize you with the Holy Ghost and with fire. (12) He is ready to separate the chaff from the wheat with his winnowing fork. Then He will clean up the threshing floor, gathering the wheat into His barn but burning the chaff with never-ending fire." In conjunction with this seeming "hell verse" we read: 1 Peter 4:12 says "Don't think it a strange thing that a fiery trial would take place upon you." That is: the "fiery trials which are here to try (reform/purify) us." These "fiery trials" or "baptisms of fire" do test us and do refine us. The fiery trials sent by God burn out the "evil" aspect of us "unto the remission of sins." These fiery baptisms are experienced in order for one's figurative eye or hand to burn and not oneself. This is, in effect, what Matthew 18:8 is saying: if your hand, foot, or eye causes you to stumble, cast it into "eternal" fire lest the *whole* body be thrown into "eternal" fire!

We can now rest assured that these trials are from God and not sent randomly. In Philippians 2:13 it states: "For it is God who works in you to will and to act in order to fulfill his good purpose." So, any repentance *unto remission of sins* is a good act of the will, choice, doing, becoming, etc. of God, not you. Let's now ask the question: Who is *casting the limbs, eyes, tongue, etc. into the fire* lest the whole body is cast into hell? . . . Looks to me that scripture makes it obvious. The chaff was sent by God to be separated from the wheat and burned by the winnower – i.e., God.

So, what's the difference between parts of us that need purging by fire and those that don't? We are coming to be in the likeness of Christ. Was He not afflicted? How much more should we deserve affliction than Him? If we are "speaking" as "we see" our flesh to be justified then we are very well deluded. If we believe that it is God who is casting out our sin then what more worry must we have? If we read, learn, obey, study, dig deep, etc. into the biblical Greek and Hebrew text we will find that it is God who creates, does, wills all things for the "good" of him and those who have been made to believe in God (Isaiah 45:7ff; 48; Romans 8:28ff, etc.). Is this atonement limited to a few or to all?

It would be psychotic to shed rageful anger and eternal damnation forever upon someone who is governed by *your* will to begin with, as we are governed by God's Will. This would be a *reaction* of anger. Should I say, an "anthropomorphic" attribute. Such a *response* is not consistent with full restoration-predeterminism. But what if I said God – Father is holy and cannot have sin before him? This would explain the necessity of the sacrifice that Jesus did in order to wrap us up in his covering (as the scroll/tsaror of the Hebrews), daub us with his signet and wax seal and hand us "covered," "sealed," "secured," etc. by Jesus back to the Father (1 Corinthians 15:28) where all things will be restored.

Then, what is left is the freedom of being within the infinite web of God's existence. To be his "children" roaming freely in his *mansion* (domicile/dominion/"doom"/judgment (all these are from the same word, etymologically speaking)[1]).

We are eternally bound to his infinite possibilities of joy, love, experience, etc. Not even the Calvinists seem to take "predeterminism" this far. The kind of predeterminism I am advocating for is what leads us to universal reconciliation, yet sadly Calvinists insist on having their eternal judgements! It's a careless approach to scripture to hold to Calvinism's insistence on a predeterminism of "love" for the elect and rageful "hate" for the majority of the world which is considered by Calvinists as the non-elect. Still, if the argument was only made that "God is holy *therefore* he can damn whom he will" (as the late R.C. Sproul taught) then the apocalyptic view that I am offering says this view is incomplete.

Prior to the mistranslations of "judgment" in many English Bibles, such ideas connoted for "judgment" had been astutely addressed by Aristotle (as he defined all things) using his classically influenced Greek

---

1. Cf. my Wyrd Hoard podcast on "doom and fates."

WHAT IS JUDGMENT AGAIN?

language. Such a refined understanding was called for when understanding the milieu of Greek vocabulary. Consider the Greek word that Aristotle contrasted with *kolasin* (punishment) such as *"ekdike,"* or, "revenge." Punishment is *not* revenge—and neither is "doomed unto reformation" – apokatastasis.

Ekdike (literally meaning "out of righteousness") was Aristotle's Greek word for "revenge/vengeful judgment" in his work called *Rhetoric*. Aristotle said that *ekdike* was based on a perverted "hunger-anger-appetite for revenge" (i.e., it was "out of" or "away from" + "that which is right/good/productive/straight").

Another recap: Aristotle said that *ekdike* meant "revenge:" the action of inflicting harm or hurt on someone for an injury or wrong suffered at their hands. It is a "habit based on appetite and is rooted in human emotions" (Aristotle, *Rhetoric*, Book 1, ch. 10, v. 13). The concept of *ekdikes* is connotatively akin to the idiomatic use of "judgment" in most English Bibles. The problem with this usage of "revenge" is that this presents either: (1) God with emotional problems acting out with a humanistic-childish approach to resolving problems with children (hence, the misdirected ideas of "how to handle your children") (2) an all-judgmental God that all shall be punished if we do wrong (3) a reactionary God that did not know what was about to happen. So, do we "justify" such a seemingly anthropomorphic view of a God who simply throws rage out as a tool for "control"? Absolutely not. Doesn't the Bible present this God? Absolutely not when one comprehends the Bible's fullness of meaning. This is what I refer to as the apocalyptic view – i.e., "where the concealment of meaning has been removed."

To the skeptic of the Bible, the anthropomorphic ideas of God can be assumed if the skeptic plans to go no further. To the contrast of the skeptic, the New Testament gives us a consistent theology vs. an idea of contraction within the biblical text. The Old Testament exhibits the Father in his holiness – having no sin before him. We see that ONLY in Christ can we be in the presence of the Father (as in 1 Corinthians 15:28 – where Jesus Christ takes all of our sins unto himself and subsumes us and gives us back to the Father in Jesus' *onoma* or *shem*.

We are sealed[2] in Christ and shielded against judgment now. When looking at the two offices of God here, we have perfect coherence and a

---

2. remembering the study of the Hebrew "Tsaror" in Job's (Abraham's day/pre-mosaic law). It was the seal that was daubed in wax, i.e., a scroll that accounted for all the sins in our lives written down and "looked over" by God. Cf. my lecture article "sin

collective theology. It is damaging to interpolate this kind of judgment into the connotation of *God's* final judgment. And this misunderstanding of divine judgment has nothing to do with the original Greek text of the New Testament or its semiotic committed language.

Remember, the New Testament word for the final judgment in Matthew 25 is not *ekdikes*, revenge, it is *kolasin*, meaning chastisement, judgment for the good of the one judged, and it is aimed at bringing about the full acknowledgement of infraction and the "coming to be" in eventual restitution!

Let's continue. We have seen that in Matthew 25:41 Jesus uses the term "judgment" or *kolasis*— "a penal system which restores us to righteousness". This judgment reaches its climax in this scene: "Then He will also say to those [the goats] on the left hand (sinister gyrate/hand of no blessing), Depart from Me, you cursed, into the everlasting fire prepared for the devil and his angels."

This is yet another verse that needs proper care in the handling of translation then interpretation. This does not mean that those on the right hand (the sheep) won't be "singed" and "remitted" for sins through "the fire that burns." That is, there is a heat or *orge*[3] that we will experience when we break the law. We experience it as Christians, as Paul explains in Romans 13 as when we break the civil laws of the land and pay earthly prices by being arrested, tickets, etc. Yet, this has nothing to do with our salvation. These are entirely two different things: for I was hungry and you gave me no food: I was thirsty and you gave me no drink.

Let's look at the Greek to see what Jesus has said:

Matthew 25:41:

> *Tote* (then) *erei* (will He say) *kai* (also) *tois* (to those) *exs* (on) *euonumon* (the left), *Poreuesthe* (depart) *ap'* (from) *emou* (me) *oi* (those) *katayramenoi* (being cursed), *eis* (into) *to* (the) *pur*

---

and hell unto repentance" on my website: fomcm.com

3. The term for "wrath" is retained in the Greek word *orge* which conveys "orgasm" "rage." We etymologically find the word "rage" in the word "orgasm" and their Greek parent, *orge*. The etymologies, endonyms, idioms, colloquialisms and root meanings do express the feeling of two feelings for the group and at the same time, the individual for "being out of one's senses." Such a word has found itself in "jazz" which means "to ejaculate with excitement," "to burst out," "to flow out." Such slang or vulgar words such as jizz or jizzum still hold to this meaning, therefore keeping its history within the profane. A much older root comes from the Proto-Indo-European "uerg" which simply meant "a *work* ([r – rotex + k – gutteral = g] that brings about)." In *orge's* ancient sense, "a work unto product" is what is conveyed. So, even if God's "wrath" is upon us it would be unto a work by his good intent, not our flesh's desire or will (*thelos*).

(fire) *to* (to) *aionion* (*aeon* – an age/season), *to* (the) *heytoimasmenon* (having been prepared) *toi* (for) *diaboloi* (the devil) *kai* (and) *tois* (the) *angelois* (angels) *autou* (of him).[/EPI]

This is one of the more challenging passages that I have been approached with. It seems to show here that Jesus is indeed sending some to hell and some to heaven. A closer look at the fire which burns everlasting, we see that agency of fire has been a transformative aspect by which the believer is changed. It is indeed an everlasting fire in the English, though, the word "aionios" is used from its derivative, *aion* – meaning, "an age" or "duration." Isaiah 1:25 says, "And I will turn my hand upon thee (Israel/Judah (us)), and purely purge away thy dross, and take away all thy tin – (26) AND I will restore thy judges as at the first, and thy counselors as at the beginning: afterward thou shalt be called, The city of righteousness, the faithful city. Isaiah 1:27 says, "Zion shall be redeemed with judgment." Isaiah continues in verse 30 to say, "For ye (Israel (God's very children/us)) shall be as an oak whose leaf fadeth, and as a garden that hath no water. (31) And the strong shall be as tow, and the maker of it, as a spark, and they shall both burn together, and none shall quench them." Through his chapter God is telling Israel that they will be refined by a judgment that burns and they shall not be quenched. Sounds a lot like Jesus as he spoke of judgment.

It is here that I need to employ the meaning of fire, judgment, and "baptism" (which has been founded upon many archetypes from heathen to early first century Christianity.) In Isaiah 4:4 we read: "When the Lord shall have *washed away* the filth of the daughters of Zion, and *shall have purged* the blood of Jerusalem from the midst thereof *by the spirit of judgment and by the spirit of burning*" — (conclusion: a "restoration" will occur).

I am convinced that the "baptism of fire" (Dale [orig.1874]1995) mentioned by John (mentioned by Jesus in the "hell verse" of Matthew 25:41) is of a *durative* purge/fire that burns your sinful identity out for an unquantifiable[4] time *unto* restoration/regeneration [a.k.a., to be born again (anothen)]. This "kind" of baptism of fire is not an "endless burning (Ramelli 2007/2013)," rather a "fire" from God's eternal abode, hence, an "eternal fire" with purpose *unto* salvation.

Does not John say the same when he says, "This is He (Jesus) who shall baptize you by the Holy Spirit and fire" (cf. Matthew 3:11 water

---

4. that is, not measured with a "chronometer" (as opposed to "without end").

– spirit – fire)? There seems to be 3 meanings relayed here: (1) purification from defilement by the agency which is of an eternal burning and (2) regeneration due to such a purge[5] and (3) trial by the fire of judgement *unto* God's kingdom[6] and his presence. These "fires" are not of our choosing but of God's mercy, no matter how painful the process.

As I have defined in past lectures about "the least and greatest in the kingdom of God," there is no "level of lesser than or greater than" in God's presence but of the kingdom of God mentioned in Romans 14:17 – we see that our level of conditioning is obviously expressed amongst fellow believers in this life, time, space. We must be purged to become more trusted, more resolved, more resolute, etc. There is also a greater sense to a duration of conditioning than a mere mindless burning. This mindless burning forsakes the meaning of "unto repentance" and requires an incoherent theology.

Here's something that needs to be understood before the next paragraph: Jesus is aligning himself with King David, the Messiah to come, the Son, the Father. His words are in unity and conjunction with the line of the Lion (*lebayu*) of Judah. Saul was named the same, Lebayu[7]—the Lion. But his actions of jealousy and murder assigned him a new name or *shem:* Saul[8] was "the LORD's anointed." How can a saved man be in sheol? These are the concepts we must understand to correctly read the Bible. Consider: "in darkness" meant *sheol*—or, in the Germanic, *holen* (in the "hole," "in the place of darkness'— "hell"). The idea of "hell" as

---

5. Greek: a cleansing *pur* – fire – i.e., used within the *aeon*/eon (durative/durational (aeon)) which employs the baptism unto repentance. This "baptism of fire" is here to purge the child of God unto repentance over an "era" or "time" or *aeon*<—which has been taken by many scholars to mean purging "without end." My argument is that the fiery baptism is unto repentance-meaning, an intentional finishing point which required an era or *aeon* to get there.

6. Roman 14:17 "For the kingdom of God is not meant and drink; but righteousness, and peace, and joy in the Holy Ghost."

7. In the letters to Pharaoh Akhenaton, Biridiya of Meggido complains that Labayu was attacking his lands in the Jazreel valley that Saul fought.

8. Saul "name" has meaning found in "sheol" – "hell": "to petition in a dark place," *request* in the dark place; entreat in place of dead; in hell; in concealment; covered; without vision – But his name initially, as Saul, meant "requested," "asked for," "begged for," "fulfill a wish." "To petition" as in an oratorium. A formal plea. All such roots to Saul's name do indeed match that of the "plea in formalities made in a dark place/prison." Just think of this "condition" by which Saul was in. . . . a man in his tortured mind, a constantly bitter and angry warrior, constantly living by the sword. A man angry at the ones who loved him. Yet, the Bible says that Saul was God's anointed: 1 Samuel 10:1–16.

"separation, a dark pace, ignorance," etc., is derived from the Latin *ducare*, which means "darkness." "Coming out of hell" or to "exit hell" is our word "education." Hence, the Latin for "education" is composed as *e + ducare* = "*education*" = "*out of ("e") + darkness ("ducare")*."

Saul's very name suggests that he was in hell or in darkness, ignorance, a lost place, etc. Yet, Saul was God's though he had to fall into darkness as an anointed of God! Has that ever happened to you? Do you ever "fall into darkness, feel like you're in hell—so distant from God due to your "actions" that here and now you are judged unto repentance by the Holy Spirit? I know of no other way. I have no other reference to my life with God but by not being in relation with God. Do I call out to God to help me when I am in "hell"? Yes! Even now. Do I ask God to save me and do I profess the he is alone my only savior while I'm in "hell"?! Yes! I am still in "hell" (German *holen*—darkness; Hebrew *sheol*—darkness; Greek *phylake*—prison [known as the dark caverns guarded by the prison watch])! My sin "calibrates" me to realize I have no other "choice" but to go to *dikaiosyne*— "righteousness." I must "right-afy" (rectify) my sights. I must shoot with the ballistics that "make the shot to the *boulesthai*'— i.e., the "bull's eye."

Here are Christ's words in Matthew 25 echoed in Psalm 6:9: "Depart from me, all ye workers of iniquity; for the LORD has heard the voice of my weeping." David continues this prayer in Psalm 6:10, "Let all my enemies be ashamed and sorely vexed; *let them return and be ashamed.*" Is this *return* not the same as repentance? Is this not a return to the "acknowledgement" of their wrong? Is this not the meaning of repentance (Greek *metanoia*—a changed mind, a repented mind)? Yes, yes it is! Again, is this not the very usage of *kolasis* (judgment) in the Greek New Testament of Christ's words? It is.

GOING BACK TO THE TEXT OF CHRIST'S "JUDGMENT"

Jesus continues to say of those who did *not* show charity: ". . . as you did not do unto the least of them you did not do it unto *me*." These beings who act non-charitably are not the full "being," not the ontological "coming to be" of the whole person who is *finally rectified*. If Jesus had used the word "revenge" or "retribution," it would have referred to an act that benefitted the avenger, but not the avenged. This "revenge" would be in reaction to an act by the infractor of the law. Are works of the law destroyed by Christ? No. They are made manifest in our flesh to be impossible to overcome by human effort. The flesh is the very thing that holds to account damnation upon the infractor of the law[9]!

Again, look at the words in Matthew 25:40: "The King [c.f. Psalms 5–6] will say, "Truly I tell you, whatever you did for one of the least of these brothers and sisters of mine, you did for me. Then he [King David—speaking in the past in foreshadowed language] will say to those on his left, "Depart from me Psalms 6:8 [David's plea to God to relieve him of his enemies], you who are cursed, into the eternal fire prepared for the devil and his angels [Psalms 6:10 – "Let all mine enemies be ashamed and sore vexed: let them return and be ashamed suddenly – K.J.V. —is this not repentance shown in David's heart?!]" . . . ."

Are not even the angels subdued under Christ's feet at the end where death, hell, and all powers and principalities subdued and restored in Christ and given back to the Father in this fully restored and sealed condition (I Corinthians 15:21-28)? Continuing in the misleading English: ". . . will go away into everlasting (*aionion* – an age) punishment

---

9. Romans 7:7,8, and 9 ". . . . *Is the law sin? God forbid. Nay, I had not known sin but by the law: for I had not known lust, except the law had said, Thou shalt not covet. (8) But sin, taking occasion by the commandment, wrought in me all manner of concupiscence. For without the law sin was dead. (9 For I was alive without the law once: but when the commandment came, sin revived, and I died."*

Concerning "the law," It is interesting to me that in the study of the Pre-formative Jews, there existed a *pre-Mosaic law* amongst these pre-formative Jews (Iberu/Hebrews) that could indeed be accounted for and yet wiped away via the *Tsaror* (The Christ Archetype). The Hebrews in Job's day- contemporary with Abraham- used the salvific Tsaror which I have given treatment to in this book. The Tsaror was believed to blot out all of the Hebrew's sin's prior to them becoming "Jews under the law." The Tsaror was an archetype of Jesus. My theological mind thinks of the "pre-law" status – while recognizing "sin" existing – while the future vision of the mighty angel holding up the "one seal" holding "judgment" was a "catcher's mitt" to such an ancient acknowledgment. It seems to me that the early Hebrews were shown grace via the Tsaror, the myopia of thinking one had the free will to keep the law, to the prophetic hope to be saved from this state of fallenness, to salvation in the New Testament Epistles. For, I believe, the book of Revelation must be understood as a collage" of all of these factors—i.e., the apocalyptic view – or, "fully revealed view."

Paul continues this same expression of our own plight in him. We all share this plight. This is part of the "Romans Road" you might have heard of in your church. It leads to salvation within scripture. In many orthodoxies, however, we are offered "a salvation" via your free will to choose or reject Christ. The argument from my thesis (based on Paul's "Romans Road") is that a "dead person cannot make a living decision" so "free will" or "human agency" is corrupt and cannot "choose" a holy God.

(*kolasin* – punishment unto reformation), but the righteous into eternal (*aionion*) life (*zo-'ayn*)." What is "everlasting punishment"?

In Greek it is *kolasin aionion*—a durative penitentiary rectification unto restoration. The affliction is for the benefit of the sinner and it endures for an "age" (or it pertains and takes place in an age—the age to come). The *diakesyne*—the righteous—are already in the kingdom of heaven as little *paideion*. We must employ a little soft algebra here to place who is who. The saved unto eternal life already "are." The penalized are still "coming to be" —emerging "out of darkness" they will eventually come "into the light" and "will be made to confess that Jesus is Lord." These are two different allotments and two kinds of "beings."

The *eternal (for an unquantifiable time – i.e., "era'-aionion*) scourging (and we can set aside here our English idea of "eternity," derived from the Latin mistranslation *aeternus*) is a tool put upon the "evil doer" in order for their eye or hand to burn *and not them!* This is chastisement and not "an eye for an eye" retribution—a mentality for dealing with misdeeds that easily lends itself to war.

Once more: *kolasin aionion* is "a duration or time of beneficial affliction to bring one back to restoration." *This* is the meaning in the classical Greek used by the New Testament. Therefore, terms such as judgment, salvation, faith, God, logos, etc. have been all too familiar for the Greek-speaking New Testament church who knew exactly what they meant when they were edified and taught their children in the paideia. Romans 14:17 says that the "kingdom of God exists."

Is "hell" a real place? Hell might be referred to as an existence set upon those of purgation. Can I see this purgation working now therefore, I see "hell" right here, right now. Therefore, we can understand "hell" as the "eternal fire which purges" us ALL for a "time." Is there a hell which just burns one endlessly *unto nothingness* without direction, end-game, plan unto restoration, etc.? I, so far as I see a consistent theology within the narrative of the Bible, it says no. All of my beliefs are summed up in God having predestined into creation all things for HIMSELF in love and for us all *unto* the fullness of meaning tells me no, there is no mindless burning of a soul "unto" nonce meaning. So, is there an eternal hell? Yes. Of whatever durational "time" or duration (era, eon, age, epoch, interval, season, interlude, etc.) that it exists I don't know but by the 5 core premises that I am establishing the biblical "hell" must be a thing which was created for reformation and restoration.

Chapter Forty-Six

Sin and Hell Unto Repentance

A STUDENT OF MINE told me about a confusion they had concerning sin and hell. They simply did not know what it meant from a modern sense of connotation/denotation. What I reckoned that they were being led to ask was: "how could these two topics make sense if we are saved by grace?" I said that we must know the mannerisms and language used in early first century Palestine. From this approach, we can see how cleanly the words of the New Testament were ordered into the earliest manuscripts substantiating the codex Sinaticus.

TERMS TO KNOW:

Profess – *homologeo* = "to agree in word and deed" —i.e., you don't just "say" "I love Jesus" you must do the deed by acting as He did.

Predestination – *pro – horidzon'* —pre – boundary"or "pre – encircled" "sheep gate with legal food (*nomos bromata*) for grazing"/— pre "Stage and Setting" in our "coming to be" - (Greek: *engeneto* — generated/-ing)

Apokatakollosin = "full restoration" "restored back to original state (Colossians 1:14-17)"

Grace – "unearned/unmerited favor"

Hell – the hidden place – con + CEAL/seal – "cellar"/*Kalupsis* – cover/hid = i.e., APO (off) + KALUPTO (cover) = Apocalypse

Remember: "educate" = "e" = "out"/"exit" + "ducare" darkness

Greek: *Phulake* – darkness of a prison cave or confine

Sin – Greek: *harmateia* —an archer's term meaning: "To miss the mark" or "bullseye," senile – *senex* (Latin), to "sine" – curve away, etc.

Question one:

What is sin? Sin is a path, that if continued by its own nature, ends off the grid, off the range of meaning, into darkness – covered or sealed in darkness – especially, as in a dark hole or place (cf. Old Germanic: *hollen* – hall; hell; cellar), into finality, into non-meaning, death. It is the archery term: *harmateia* which means: "to miss the mark."

Here's the list of those who have sin:

Revelation 21:8 – "But as for the cowardly, the faithless, the detestable, as for murderers, the sexually immoral, sorcery (*pharmakois* – drug users), idolaters, and all liars, their portion will be in the lake that burns with fire and sulfur, which is the second death (see Romans 3:10 – no one is righteous).

Many scholars believe (as I do myself) that Jesus' Gospels are referring to the works of the Pharisees for whom they believed that their works would be acceptable unto God. Many scholars and myself believe that Jesus' Gospels addressed salvation as having come before the Pharisees and contrasted the "two systems." It was the Pharisees that said they were the kingdom of heaven because they brought God's words with them. Jesus didn't have to address the words when he said, "unless your righteousness exceeds that of the Pharisees you shall in no way enter the kingdom of heaven. Here's the play on "the kingdom of heaven": *basileau tou Ouranos* —or, "the kingdom of God": basileau tou Theon. In both Greek cases the *basileau* means, "the basis." Furthered, it means "the feet," "the base," "basin," "pit," "under structure'<— the "abyss" of the thing. All to say, the "root core" of the kingdom of God would be with *word and deed*…not just words and show as the Pharisees did.

Jesus' reference to the Pharisees's "*words*" vs. the actions required by Jesus (the deeds). When Jesus says in Matthew 5:21 – ff. "Ye have heard that it was said by them of old time…" Jesus is referring to the Pharisees. Please start with Matthew 5:17 below:

Matthew 5:17 —

(17) Think not that I am come to destroy the law, or the prophets: I am not come to destroy, but to fulfill (1 Cor. 15:28 – all in all). (18) For verily I say unto you, Till heaven and earth pass, one jot or one tittle shall in no wise pass from the law, till all be fulfilled. (19) Whosoever therefore shall break one of these least commandments, and shall teach men so, he shall be called the least in the kingdom of heaven: but whosoever shall do and teach *them*, the same shall be called great in the kingdom of heaven.

(20) For I say unto you, That except your righteousness shall exceed *the righteousness of* the scribes and Pharisees, ye shall in no case enter into the kingdom of heaven.

Anger and Reconciliation

(Luke 12:57-59; Psalms 90 – God will walk over our sins and will see us no more as tainted)

(21) Ye have heard that it was said by them of old time, Thou shalt not kill; and whosoever shall kill shall be in danger of the judgment: (22) But I say unto you, That whosoever is angry with his brother without a cause shall be in danger of the judgment: and whosoever shall say to his brother, Raca, shall be in danger of the council: but whosoever shall say, Thou fool, shall be in danger of hell fire. (23) Therefore if thou bring thy gift to the altar, and there rememberest that thy brother hath ought against thee; (24) Leave there thy gift before the altar, and go thy way; first be reconciled to thy brother, and then come and offer thy gift. (25) Agree with thine adversary quickly, whiles thou art in the way with him; lest at any time the adversary deliver thee to the judge, and the judge deliver thee to the officer, and thou be cast into prison. (26) Verily I say unto thee, Thou shalt by no means come out thence, till thou hast paid the uttermost farthing.

SIN AND HELL UNTO REPENTANCE

Adultery

(Leviticus 18:1–30)

> (27) Ye have heard that it was said by them of old time, Thou shalt not commit adultery: (28) But I say unto you, That whosoever looketh on a woman to lust after her hath committed adultery with her already in his heart. (29) And if thy right eye offends thee, pluck it out, and cast *it* from thee: for it is profitable for thee that one of thy members should perish, and not *that* thy whole body should be cast into hell. (30) And if thy right hand offends thee, cut it off, and cast *it* from thee: for it is profitable for thee that one of thy members should perish, and not *that* thy whole body should be cast into hell.

Divorce

(Deuteronomy 24:1–5; Luke 16:18–18)

> (31) It hath been said, Whosoever shall put away his wife, let him give her a writing of divorcement: (32) But I say unto you, That whosoever shall put away his wife, saving for the cause of fornication, causeth her to commit adultery: and whosoever shall marry her that is divorced committeth adultery.

Vows

(Numbers 30:1–16)

> (33) Again, ye have heard that it hath been said by them of old time, Thou shalt not forswear thyself, but shalt perform unto the Lord thine oaths: (34) But I say unto you, Swear not at all; neither by heaven; for it is God's throne: (35) Nor by the earth; for it is his footstool: neither by Jerusalem; for it is the city of the great King. (36) Neither shalt thou swear by thy head, because thou canst not make one hair white or black. (37) But let your communication be, Yea, yea; Nay, nay: for whatsoever is more than these cometh of evil.

Love Your Enemies

(Leviticus 24:17-23; Luke 6:27-36)

> (38) Ye have heard that it hath been said, An eye for an eye, and a tooth for a tooth: 39 But I say unto you, That ye resist not evil: but whosoever shall smite thee on thy right cheek, turn to him the other also. (40) And if any man will sue thee at the law, and take away thy coat, let him have *thy* cloak also. (41) And whosoever shall compel thee to go a mile, go with him twain. (42) Give to him that asketh thee, and from him that would borrow of thee turn not thou away.
>
> (43) Ye have heard that it hath been said, Thou shalt love thy neighbor, and hate thine enemy. (44) But I say unto you, Love your enemies, bless them that curse you, do good to them that hate you, and pray for them which despitefully use you, and persecute you; (45) That ye may be the children of your Father which is in heaven: for he maketh his sun to rise on the evil and on the good, and sendeth rain on the just and on the unjust. (46) For if ye love them which love you, what reward have ye? do not even the publicans the same? (47) And if ye salute your brethren only, what do ye more *than others*? do not even the publicans do so? (48) Be ye therefore perfect (teleioi – unto completion), even as your Father which is in heaven is perfect."

(here ends Jesus' rhetors: statement to cause attention/effect.)

But how can we be "perfect"? If *teleioi* means "telegraphed to the end with the fullness of meaning" then, the English has no bearing on this context. Such an example of teleos might be as follows: Aristotle said that the "teleos" of an acorn was the oak tree. We are commanded under his authority with his WORD OVERRIDING US (ADVERSE OF Macbeth's witches' fate) to "become complete unto "the fullness of meaning." I believe we can have homologeo or true profession implemented here as a "spiel/spell/God-spiel" by which Christ casts upon us. As Macbeth's witches cast a spell over Macbeth so did Christ over us — a spell unto repentance which leads to being perfect.

The conundrum:

We sin. Paul says in Romans 3:10 – "For there is no one righteous, no, not one. No one understands, no one seeks for God. All have turned aside; together they have become worthless; no one does good, not one.

Romans 3:10 is simply establishing our natures. While Jesus geniusly commands us "to be perfect." Jesus "presses" us to obtain the answer. Jesus thrusts us into the press which purifies us.

1 Corinthians 15:27 "For God has put all things in subjection under His feet."

If we are "to be perfect" and "all things are subjected under his feet" must we look at a "conjunction" of two events? First, all things are subject under God and we are "to be perfect." Must this "obedience" be the "profession"/'homologeo" that we learned earlier that links word and deed and the sign of Christ working in us? This must be taken as being in context with the Will of God acting on us— or it will simply not make sense in Greek or English!

You're not doing "works unto salvation." Philippians 2:13 "For it is God who works (*energon*) in you, both to Will (*thelein*) and to WORK (*energon*) for His good pleasure." So, the command by Jesus "to be perfect" is without our sinful nature acting. In contrast, it is with our renewed Christ-like nature that is in *homologeo* — agreement with the Will of GOD. This new and "coming to be" will in us does indeed obey, do and speak God's commands. Our homologeo-will is the herald to the world that you are God's beacon and that he is willing and working in you to act as Christ did on earth. I might add that our "wills" are not free from God, rather, infinitely bound to him. In this sense, we are more "free" than ever to act, breathe and think as his children. Therefore, we are "free from" our limited flesh which continues its course unto death and hiddenness.

Refer to the appendix for the fully expanded form of this chapter concerning the "tsaror," or "scroll that will seal all of our sins unto death."

Chapter Forty-Seven

A Kind of Condemnation

OUR EARTHLY PLIGHT STILL remains though we are saved from our fleshly wills until the end (eschatos) of this age when Christ returns. The *law* still remains until the end (eschatos) of this age. Matthew 5:17: "(17) Think not that I am come to destroy the law, or the prophets: I am not come to destroy, but to fulfill. (18) For verily I say unto you, Till heaven and earth pass, one jot or one tittle shall in no wise pass from the law, till all be fulfilled."

Jesus makes it clear that he has not come to destroy the law here on earth but to fulfill it —in order that this law would *condemn all works of the flesh* and will remain until "all be fulfilled." Furthermore, this "kind" of condemnation is ordained to its own condemnation.

WHAT DOES "*ALL*" MEAN HERE?

In James 1:2 we have the beginning of this answer: "My brethren, count it all joy when you fall into *many* temptations. (3) Knowing this, that the trying (*dokimion* – testing unto righteousness) of your faith works patience (*hupomene'* – above the remaining echelon/higher than just to maintain – hyper + maintain). (4) But let patience have her perfect work, that you may be perfect (teleioi – "to come to the end with the fulness of meaning") and entire (*holoklayroi* – sound, whole, perfect, complete, lacking nothing (*holo* – "holy"), wanting nothing."

The works of the flesh are the works of judgment against the flesh. Therefore, the superimposed trials that are put on us by God are the trials by which we must endure. These trials calibrate us unto the better

A KIND OF CONDEMNATION

way/his way/his holy Will unto his Son's "likeness." This is not just pain for pain's sake but a fully intended act upon us with a trajectory unto the fullness of meaning ordained by a sovereign God. Any other "god" or "ideology" is a lesser "god" or "ideology."

We see this in Romans 8:29–31 where we have been predestined to become unto the "likeness" of Jesus. Little by little, we are "calibrated" out of our flesh and into the necessity of righteousness. Still, this necessary flesh must exist. Our very being is still under the law. We are flesh (sarx), phusikos (natural-physical mind and body), spiritos (spirit), phreino (brain), soma (body-organs). These components that make us who we are — are STILL under the law and by the law we are still condemned *until time no more ("at the last trump")*.

In Revelation 6:11–17 we have the sixth judgment vial/sixth judgment/sixth angel in John's vision saying that time will continue a little longer until the final number of the saint's brothers be martyred unto completion (*plerothusin* – fullness/filled to full/nothing else left to fill in/the fullness). Revelation 6:12–16 is nearly identical to the prophecy that Jesus made concerning the final days leading up to his return. In Revelation 19:12 we see the resurrected and returning king Jesus as the word of truth, the logos, the Christ and kings of kings with a name that no one knows but himself, with eyes as a flame of fire and many diadems seen on his head (please read Revelation 19:12 – ff. for a "beautifully – horrific" vision of our Lord who will come back in his new body).

Jesus' words in Matthew 24:31 make it clear that "Immediately after the Days of Tribulation (the 7 judgments found in Revelation) we shall see Him appear (*phanaysete* – physically see) in Heaven." Vs. 29 and 31 match that of the mourning of the earth in their sins for there is still the final release of our identities in the flesh – more or less this is the final rending from our natural man/woman. This final sadness is the *teleos* by which the fullness of the physical world has come to an end of itself.

We have come to the end (*teleos*) of the law which bound us to condemnation. We were and are believers but with a different condition. We now have a new heaven and new earth seen in Revelation 21:1 – "Then I saw a new heaven and a new earth, for the first heaven and the first earth had passed away, and there was no longer any sea. (2) I saw the Holy City, the New Jerusalem, coming down out of heaven from God, prepared as a bride, beautifully dressed for her husband. (3) And I heard a loud voice from the throne saying, 'Look! God's dwelling place is now among the people, and He will dwell with them. They will be His people, and God

Himself will be with them and be their God. (4) He will wipe every tear from their eyes. There will be no more death or mourning or crying or pain, for the old order of things has passed away."

Our old bodies must go away with world's condemnation while the spirit goes with God where we will receive new bodies becoming an eternal soul (body and spirit). Philippians 3:21 tells us that Jesus Christ will transform our lowly body to be like his glorious body, by the power that enables him even to subject all things to himself:

> 2 Corinthians 5:1 "For we know that when this earthly tent we live in is taken down (that is, when we die and leave this earthly body), we will have a house in heaven, an eternal body made for us by God Himself and not by human hands. (2) We grow weary in our present bodies and we long to put on our heavenly bodies like new clothing. (3) For we will put on heavenly bodies; we will not be spirits without bodies. (4) While we live in these earthly bodies, we groan and sigh, but it's not that we want to die and get rid of these bodies that clothe us. Rather, we want to put on our new bodies so that these dying bodies will be swallowed up by life."

BUT WHEN AND HOW WILL THIS WORLD END?

Time table: The last of the 7 trumpets; the last or seventh angel; The last of 7 judgments

1 Corinthians 15:52–58: "In a moment, in the twinkling of an eye, at the last trumpet, For the trumpet will sound, and the dead will be raised imperishable, and we shall be changed. For this perishable body must put on the imperishable, and this mortal body must put on immortality —Death is swallowed up in victory. O death, where is your victory? O death, where is your sting? The sting of death is sin and the power of sin is the law. But thanks be to God, who gives us the victory through our Lord Jesus Christ."

In 1 Thessalonians 4:16 – ff "For the Lord Himself will descend from Heaven with a cry of command, with the voice of an archangel, and with the sound of the trumpet of God. And the dead in Christ will rise first. Then *we* who are alive, who are left, will be caught up together with *them* in the clouds to meet the Lord in the air and so we will always be with the Lord."

A KIND OF CONDEMNATION

Matthew 24: 29 (Jesus' own words) "Immediately after the tribulation of those days the sun will be darkened and the moon will not give light and the stars will fall from the sky and the powers of the heavens will be shaken."

Let's address the final judgment (*Krima*/"crime'–judicial process upon) upon the sinful earth:

Characteristics of our sinful natures (*phusikos*) lead to death. Death (*thanatos*) is our nature's wage (earnings). Revelation 21:8 "But (*di*) as for the cowardly (*tois deilois*) and (*kai*) the faithless (*apistois*) and the detestable (*ebdelugme'nois*)....and... as for murderers (*phoneusin*) and the sexually immoral (*pornois*) and sorcerers (*pharmakois*) and idolaters (*eidololatrais*) and all (*kai pasin*) the liars (*tois pseudesin*) their portion (*to' meros*) is in the lake (*limnos*) that burns (*kaiomene'*) with fire (*puri*) and sulfur (*theio*), which is the second (*deuteros*) death (*thanatos*)." As Macbeth has a "fatal" or "fatalist" reward of fatality ... the reality of the "reward" is death. Might I state here that the "reward" or "portion" is indeed this in the works of the flesh. But there is another very old Jewish understanding of this "kind" of "portion" unto death that is sealed away with all of our sins in it—a "book" of sins of the camp of Israel. Revelation makes use of Jewish customs from their inception into the early church age. This "book" was called the *tsaror* which meant a "bundle" by which a wax seal bound it. This was done by the priests that no one should open. Job says that his sins were sealed in the *tsaror* (Hebrew: bundle, scroll, bag) and daubed with wax to seal over my iniquity (allusion to God as the priest who did the sealing and waxing of Job's spiritual *tsaror*).

Another fantastic support for the "books" of judgments versus the "book" of life could actually be several "kinds" of judgment which are doled out to us in the dispensing of our coming to be. Let's take a look at another scholarly writing: Dr. J. Massyngberde Ford's *Commentary on Revelation; Anchor Bible Series*.

Dr. Ford deals with the Semitic and Greek cultural usage of the phraseologies used in Revelation. With his vantage point we can hack away at a nagging orthodox contention which fixes on Revelation 20: 11-15 the "text for damnation."

Let's start with the point of contention verse: Revelation 20:11: "Then I saw a great white throne and Him Who sat upon it from Whose presence the earth and sky fled away, and no place was found for them. (12) And I saw the dead, great and small, standing before the throne, and books were opened and also another book was opened, which is the book of life; and the dead were judged by that was written in the books according to their deeds. (13) And the sea gave up the dead in it, and Death and Hades gave up the dead in them, and all were judged according to their deeds. (14) And Death and Hades were thrown into the lake of fire. This is the second death, the lake of fire. (15) And if anyone's name was not found written in the book of life, he was thrown into the lake of fire."

The view of damnation from another perspective in Revelation 20 vs.12, the "books" seem to be distinguished from the "other ONE book" in that the books appear to record WORKS and the single book of life to have the names inscribed.

1. Canonized books such as Malachi, Isaiah, and Daniel seem to refer to "books" of "good and evil" deeds that Israel did.

2. According to Exodus 32:32, Psalms 69:28; Isaiah 4:3 Jubilees 30:20, 22, 1 Enoch 103:4 we are given the "memorial of the righteous." The Book of Life (or the Living) culturally referred to the register of Israelite citizens (*and it is here that I believe John drew his poetic-apocalyptic metaphor from*) in the Old Testament. This would touch-base with the idea of "anathema (vehement hatred)" to those who are not Jewish Israelites in the Day when the identity of their Nation was so great to establish a future representation for Spiritual Israel. "Hatred," linguistically retained in the Greek word "Miseo" means to "dismiss" and "disregard" another's words, worth, efforts, existence, etc. Another sense of "hate" — "miseo" meant to "not regard as being on stage to promote meaning for the play's intention." A bystander without meaning to the event of meaning.

3. Specific mention of those who died at sea occurs in vs. 13 of Revelation 20 probably because there was a tradition that only those who died on dry land would rise from the dead. Again, a cultural idea/belief—ultimately used to build upon "traditions" that "participate" in the "figurations" of an isolated society. Though it may be wrong scientifically, it wasn't wrong culturally to "act in accord" with the tribe's order or protocol of beliefs.

4. In reference to Hades giving up the dead: Greek mythology tells us that Hades was the place where the wicked souls had their abode. The connotation to the usage of "Hades" as "unseen" plus its mythology was most certainly carried into the first century Christian mind as a "reference" metaphor. In Greek myth, the evil souls never

resurrected from Hades whereas some Greek traditions held that only the righteous would be resurrected.

5. With all of that, death (the wage of sin) and Hades (the unseen) will be cast into the lake of fire which signals the new heaven and earth seen in Revelation 21.

What I would like to say is that the origins of Judaism can be many. A hotchpotch of inspired truths revealed by God, commanded by God. The Books of Enoch, Jasher, and Jubilees for sure carried many societal references of, let's say, David's time. Many societal views of hell from Enoch, Jasher, and Jubilees were used in Revelation as a tethering to counter the terms unto a salvific rhetoric. Rev. 20:15 "And if anyone's name was not found written in the book of life, he was thrown into the lake of fire." Let me try to answer this from a heart perspective first that I call my "how abouts"?

MY "HOW ABOUTS"

My questions are fearful and simple questions: Could it simply be that no one will be left out of the Book of Life? It never said that there *most certainly would be* "*those thrown into the lake of fire.*" It only said by condition that "*IF*" (Greek: *ei* – "if" as in a condition [cf. Strong's concordance #1487]) anyone's name was not in the Book of Life.

As the Bible states its own theology that the portion (*meros* – allotment) of sin is death. Conversely, the portion of grace is eternal life. So, conditionally, if it were possible to not be in the Book of Life THEN you would receive the wages of sin.

Could Revelation's writer be referring to the Old Testament law that brings death to all and the New Testament Messiah that brings life to all[1]? How about our sins being forgiven as the thief on the cross next to Jesus? How about the ravenous Romans, Pharisees, and Jews who mocked and revealed at the event of Jesus' crucifixion? Did not Jesus tell his Father, "Forgive them for they know what they do"? Could there be hope

---

1. Matthew 10:32 "Whoever *acknowledges* me before others, I will also acknowledge before my Father in Heaven" + Romans 14:11 "Every Knee will bow before me; every tongue will *acknowledge* me" + Romans 10:9 "If you declare with your mouth, "Jesus is Lord," and believe in your heart that God raised Him from the dead, you will be saved." So, putting all of these verses together makes it clear that salvation is without an option since every knee shall bow and confess Jesus as lord.

for all of the nations, tribes, tongues, kings, etc. that come to the throne of God and worship him? Forgive me if I'm wrong but "all" nations, tribes, tongues, kings, etc. probably includes non-Jews, non-Christians, non-believers, sinners of the worst kind, etc. So, isn't there a hope that grace would extend to all of us?

Wouldn't this understanding of the book of judgment within the tsaror mean that our damned sins are our salvation?! As the book of judgment is opened it is opened without our judgment, only our sins which are already judged.

In 1 Corinthians 15:26,27: "Death will be overcome by Christ. Death is the "last enemy" to be destroyed. For God has put all things in subjection under His feet."

Who's not to bear any of these traits, even to the present time? I'm referring to Christians for the moment. You'd be a liar if you denied that you didn't have at least one of these traits. And, being a liar defaults you back to this category of "those whose portion will burn with fire and sulfur. I won't argue the agents of chastisement in the lake but I will approach the "portion" that will be cast out later. I also look at the agents of fire and sulfur as being that which is used by God to overcome and destroy not only the sinful nature of all of us but the reward of sin which is death itself.

Romans 6:23: "For the wages of sin is Death *but the free (xaris – unearned favor) gift* of God is eternal life in Jesus Christ our Lord." Here's the contrast and here and now conflict. We have both. We will have only one later.

So, what did we get out of this Greek columnar text? (1) the wages of sin are death. Therefore, we all die in our sins. (2) but we have the free gift of salvation through God's grace (our unearned favor). Is this clear enough? It took me a lifetime to "get it" after having been "fearful (delio)" of my salvation. All such delio/fear was taught to me day in and day out in the "church." Yet, the word of God teaches us something diametrically opposite. Big business churches don't want you to not fear. Some call this "contractual christianity" —you "do the dos" and "don't do the don'ts" in your church etiquette and somehow you might have salvation.

Chapter Forty-Eight

Are We a Third Party?

Let's go back again to see a consistent flaw in free will as a "fear tactic." If sin continues its will and God continues his salvific Will — who are *we* to "choose"? — if *we* are bound not only to one (sin) state of being but both states of being: sin unto salvation and sin and salvation, then, is there another pre-emptive act that *we* could do prior to sinning or "choosing" salvation? Are "we" known as something else? Are we known as those who have "acted before" we sinned or "chose" salvation? If we are, then we claim to be before the foundation of creation mentioned in Ephesians 1:4, 9 concerning "who chose who?" Did we have preemption before the (a) act to sin or (b) to "be" as a child of God? Our answer lies within "ontology (the study of "being" — "as 'we' are known")" and "profession."

We must add to this cauldron of theological "isness" *with* and *in* God and our former addressment to what "profession" means in order to surmise "being in the state of agreement using your words and your actions in accord with Jesus."

We have all "professed" cowardice. Recapping the word coward we find in scripture a command, not a law, to "not be fearful (*deilia*)." In 2 Timothy 1:7 it says, "God has not given us the spirit of *deilia* (fearfulness)." Yet, in John 14:27, there is instruction given to us to "not let your heart be troubled, neither let it be afraid." Well, if there's instruction given then there is a directive path to come from some state of being to another.

The early church was being addressed concerning their *deilia* that they should not be of this profession. Does this *damn*[1] them to hell due

---

1. Various usages of *damn* were used in Roman society to mean many things of "judgment," "observation" ("critique"), a "choice" – in the sense of the "given discretion

to their prior status if they are "coming to be" or "coming out of" *deilia*? No. How are they "coming to be" as Christians in the likeness of Christ? By their power? No. By God's sovereign predeterminate and foreknowing council before the world began? Yes. Romans 8:29 "For those whom He Foreknew He also predestined (*pro/horisen* = "set before the light came upon it") to be conformed (*sunmorphous* – summed, tied together, joined and shaped into the same) to the image (icon) of His Son, in order that He might be the firstborn among many brothers" . . . . that is, Jesus will be our bigger brother. How sweet is that?! Let's continue this passage: 30, "And those whom He predestined He also called (*ekelasen* —*ek* + *accou* [echo] — sounded out), and those whom He called He also justified (*edikaiosen*), and those whom He justified (*e'dikaiosen* – *dike*" = "make right/make straight" (versus *sine*/"curved") and those whom He justified He also glorified (*edoxsasen* = "the shooter/the bowman/the archer who "participates in the shot that is already done; in the *boule* or ballistics co-rightly to make the shot to the bullseye")." The scripture continues: "What shall we say to these things then?! If God is for us who can be against us? He who did not spare his own son but gave him up for us all (*emon panton*) how will he not also with him graciously give us all things?! Who shall bring any charge against God's Elect? It is God who justifies. Who is to condemn? Christ Jesus is the ne who died and was condemned. More than that, Jesus was raised and sat at the right hand of the Father, who indeed intercedes for us." Romans 9:25 "As He saith also in Hosea, I will call them my people which were not my people; and her beloved which was not beloved. (26) And it shall come to pass that in the place where it was said unto them, "Ye are not my people; there shall they be called the children of the living God."

    Faithless = Greek: *apistos*. John 20:27 – Jesus says, "Be not faithless, but believing . . ." . . . . Why would Jesus instruct this, command this IF there was not a deficiency of faith? The Bible makes it clear that in marriage the *apistia* spouse will be indeed saved by the believing Spouse (1 Corinthians 6: 13, 14). Are there "levels" of being cut off and sent into fiery-sulfuric hell forever? – Well, if there are, then the "cut off" is worse

---

that one has at the time." Such meanings follow from the Roman etymon "Damn-": decision, view the harm of an injury – to make a judgment of an injury, obligation to pay–especially by an heir, injure, to damage/to occasion loss to, judicial doom, full of injury, hurt/harm. Such words are *damnabilis, damnas, damnaticius, damnatio, damnator, damnatorius, damnatus, damnaustra, damnifico, damnificus, damnagerulus, damno, damnoque, damnosus*, and *damnum*. Cf. Lewis and Short's *Latin Dictionary* and Seneca, "On Anger," I. i. 1, 22. ----f.

for the man in 1 Timothy 5:8 – "for if anyone does not provide for his relatives (*idion* – genitive; plural; masculine), and especially for members of his household (*oikeion*), he has denied the *Pistis* or Faith and is worse than an unbeliever (*apistou*). Just to play with this, "my relatives" would only mean in the literal Greek: "of my genes, plural, only the males"—just saying! Now, up till their deaths, I took care of my mom and dad at our own home, cleaning them, bathing them, wiping them, administering their medications, feeding, clothing, putting them to bed…day after day until there's nothing left of me. I thought I would die before them. I didn't.

Here's a "throwback" part of this writing concerning my deceased mother-in-law who was alive at the time: "

> Presently, I'm in the same situation with my mother-in-law who weighs around 275 lbs., has borderline personality disorder, and is bi-polar. My wife and her brother have been tortured by her since their youth. They still can't be around her for too long from such trauma that she imposed on them. Her in-laws and friends (minus one) never come over. No one will have her in their home or can. She is vicious and cruel to me. I am the one who takes care of her from 6:30 am until ca 5 pm when my wife gets back. I'm still sharing the load in helping. I have an eighty-hour week's worth of work from home as an online teacher, recording artist, book writer, graphic artist, podcast and website minister… I have so little time to breathe. I have 3 children under one roof, the aforementioned mother-in-law and wife. Am I an infidel (*apistia*) at 54 if I have done all of these things and something happened to me? Let's say, God forbid, I was rendered physically incapable of not "providing" this kind of care for my *ideon* = relatives, plus my *oikeion* = my own home/house. Would I be an infidel?—There's a gist in scripture that is not tackled by the *literal* Greek nor English. What is it? It's not what the literal says it is. Where do we go from here? The answer begs for a different one than "looking to condemn someone or some situation."

We are now led to see what is condemnable/detestable in God's sight and what is not. Titus 1:16 "They profess to know God, but they deny (*arnoumai/arnountai*) him by their works. They are detestable (*bdeluktoi*) and disobedient (*apeitheis*) and unfit (*adokimoi*) for any good (*agathon* – beneficial/productive/constructive/wholesome/whole) work (*ergon*).

How many of you have gone to a Christian Bible school? How many of you have gone to a Christian university? How many of you, if you are in one of these camps, have professed *(homologeo* – speak as "one in agreement")" Jesus as Lord but was disobedient in youth, at that time, before life's lessons, reality, heaviness of loss, destruction beset you?

Then, destruction came. That very thing that many churches teach us that God does not bring. Yet, Isaiah 45:7- ff says in the King James English: "I form the light, and create darkness; I bring prosperity and create *evil* [Hebrew: *Ra'ah* – destruction/disease/death/war/etc.]: I the Lord do all these things."

How can we claim to "have done" evil against God's Sovereign will, path, plan, direction? Wouldn't this *kind* of faith actually be considered heinous in the twenty-first century generally accepted view (orthodox or secular)?

We have created "two wills" in the church view that is for a lack of a better term, schizophrenic. Good vs. Bad — God vs. the Devil. We have created a fantasy of two "wills" battling it out to see what god/God will win.

What rectifies ("right-a-fies"/makes right) this error is looking at scripture from the purview of predestination with God's full intent. If the term "demonic" could actually mean "against" God's Will then we have this "rectifying" passage: Ephesians 2:1–4 "ALL *(pantes/pan)* of us ("christian/non-christian") were sons/daughters of wrath *(orge* - rage) and disobedient *(apatheia)*." Ephesians continues to conclude God's sovereign predetermination in his grace in Ephesians 2:5 "Even when we were dead in our trespasses, made us alive together with Christ — (therefore) by Grace you have been saved." Continuing this thought in Ephesians 2:8 "For by Grace *(xaris* – "unearned favor") you have been saved through faith. And this is not your own doing; it is the gift of God, not a result of works, so that no one may boast. (10) For we are His workmanship, created in Christ Jesus for good works, which God prepared beforehand, that we should walk in them."

Chapter Forty-Nine

Therefore, What Is Hell?

TITUS 1:16 SAYS IN the passage I just quoted for "those who will receive the burning of the lake of fire and sulphur." Well, isn't that us? Let's continue with the context of Ephesians 2 to eliminate any perverted sense that we had the free will to repent of this detestable nature that will be thrown into fire and sulphur. Ephesians 2:4: "*But* God being rich in mercy, *because* of the great love with which He loved us, (vs. 5) *even when we were dead* (nekros) *in our trespasses, made us alive*, together with Christ – by grace (charity) you have been saved."

Doesn't sound like you did anything to "cause (*ergon*)" your salvation in this passage. It also doesn't sound like any merit is involved on our part. We all naturally have been accruing ("*dedouleumenohn*") hell. We can't even "earn" hell, if God is the one who ordained our salvation! We were dead and, therefore, not conscious to make a living decision to choose our own destruction or salvation. Then who's the author of our lives?

Murderers: Matthew 5:21"You have heard that it was said to the people long ago, "You shall not murder (Greek: murder – *phoneusin*) and anyone who murders will be subject to judgment. (22) But I tell you that anyone who is angry with a brother or sister will be subject to judgment."

See the following passage of 1 Chronicles 22:8: "You [David] have shed much blood and have fought many wars. You are NOT to build a house for MY NAME [*Shem* – authority = Greek: *Nomos* = Name, Authority], because you have shed much blood on earth in my sight." At what point did David sin the sin of "murder" when he "killed" more than Saul? Yet, David was instructed to kill Philistines in the name of God, by God, for God – 1 Samuel 23:1-25, "David asked the Lord, 'should I go and fight these Philistines'?" The LORD answered David, "Yes, go attack the Philistines. Save Keilah." Funny enough, the very next sentence in this verse mentions Israel's Army's own "fear"—the very "character" that gets you thrown into hell in Revelation 21:8! Did Israel's army under David go to hell? I mean, let's stick with the face of the text . . . let's be literal or not! It did say that. I've answered to their "apportionment" that will and the Christ in them that won't. Let's continue. We don't have to have an accountant, only God's reason for categorizing David's heart for having a "portion" of it as being "murderous."

In the story of the young warrior David and Saul, there was a jealousy that came over Saul because David was a greater killer of enemies than Saul and David was getting recognized by everyone for this skill over King Saul. Within this gift that David had to kill Israel's enemies, somewhere, David's heart received a murderous portion. As the Bible tells us, David could not complete building the temple to God and gave the command to his son, Solomon, to finish it. The reason why David could not complete the temple's construction was due to David's "blood lust"—his apportioned murderous heart. God established David as a great warrior, nonetheless, "blood-lustful" or "blood on his hands." At the same time, David had a portion (*merimna*) that was saved, i.e., his heart for God. Do we remember his "sexual immorality" (*porneo*) with Bathsheba that caused a rift throughout his home? Isn't this the same "sexual immorality"–aka "adultery" that gets you into the eternal fiery lake of sulfur? Could this "portion" of David have been purged by the *eternal* (*aiohnios* [from eternity/from God]) lake of fire?

Could this apportionment of *necessary narrative sin* be burning in, from, by the eternal (*aeones* —not *adunae*) lake now until "all be subdued under God's hand" (1 Corinthians 15:25—"The Son Himself (Christ Jesus) Will reign until He has put ALL things under His feet)? Will not death and hell be destroyed by Him?" Revelation 20:14, "Then death and Hades were thrown into the lake of fire. The lake of fire is the second death." There are two births, as Jesus tells us in John 3: "The first is the flesh, the second, the spirit. The "book of life" does account for us, "those that are judged by their deeds are being purged by the lake of eternal fire" . . . just as one is "baptized" by an ever-flowing river when one walks into its depths (and out again—lest they drown)." John 3:14 continues with Jesus saying that "everyone who believes in Him may have eternal life" . . . → John 12:32 Jesus: "And I, when I am lifted up from the earth, will draw

(Greek: *elkouso* = Strongs 1670 – "drag, induce, haul:) *everyone* (Greek: *pantas* = all) to Myself."

So, if *those* who are generated to confess Christ and believe do not receive death in hell (as "modern orthodoxy" presents), then, we should look to the "those" who are the "those" that will profess Jesus as Lord? Romans 14:11- ". . . . every knee Will bow (*kampsei*) and every tongue Will confess (*exs/homo/logesetai* —one word) to God." Following this, Romans 14:13 says, "therefore (*oun* – now, therefore, going forward), no longer should we judge (a sinful act)" because this (thinking) eliminates stumbling blocks and snares for our brothers (and sisters). Backing up to Romans 10:9, "If you openly declare that Jesus is Lord and believe in your heart that God raised Him from the dead, you will be saved." Now, did not the latter verse in Romans 14:11 declare that you would do this very thing!?! Yes, it did. It did by the force of God. How's that for your freedom to die and burn a miserable eternal death in eternal fire and sulphur. You, as you are his, will not die in hell. The portion, the "offending eye," "the offending hand" —the "portions" of the total you will be "cast into the purge" . . . but this is a transcendent or meta way to explain the complexity of the verb, the God, causing the entire narrative to move forward, be, have been written, and conclude. How do we continue to talk "meta" all day long in our physical tempo? I answer, "because it makes sense for a change." I'm still speaking as an incomplete – *coming to be* – human.

> 1 John 3:4 "Everyone who makes a practice (*poein*) of sinning (*harmateia*) also practices lawlessness (*anomos*); sin is lawlessness; sin is lawlessness. You know that he appeared (*ephanerothe*) to take away (*aray*) sins, and in Him there is no sin. No one who abides (*menon* – "remains") in Him keeps on sinning; no one who keeps on sinning has either seen (*eorake*) Him or known (*egnoken/gnoia*) Him."

Who are we to be "known" by? That is, by what "Name (Greek: authority, lineage, heritage, law, boundary, hedge, gate, "sheep gate")" are we retained by? By what name are we becoming more and more like. We see in Romans 8:28–31 that we are predestined to become (becoming) like Christ. The word *sunmorphe* used in the Greek for this predestined "coming to be" literally means, "summing into the shape or form of Christ."

THE FULFILLMENT OF THE LAW

Matthew 5:17 "Do not think that I have come to abolish the Law or the Prophets; I have not come to abolish them but to fulfill them. (18) For truly I tell you, until heaven and earth disappear, not the smallest letter, not the least stroke of a pen, will by any means disappear from the Law until everything is accomplished. (19) Therefore anyone who sets aside one of the least of these commands and teaches others accordingly will be called least in the kingdom of heaven, but whoever practices and teaches these commands will be called great in the kingdom of heaven. (20) For I tell you that unless your righteousness surpasses that of the Pharisees and the teachers of the law, you will certainly not enter the kingdom of heaven.

MURDER

(21) "You have heard that it was said to the people long ago, "You shall not murder, and anyone who murders will be subject to judgment." (22) But I tell you that anyone who is angry with a brother or sister will be subject to judgment. Again, anyone who says to a brother or sister, "Raca," is answerable to the court. And anyone who says, "You fool (*anoaytos* – "not knowing")!" will be in danger of the fire of hell. (23) "Therefore, if you are offering your gift at the altar and there remember that your brother or sister has something against you, (24) leave your gift there in front of the altar. First go and be reconciled to them; then come and offer your gift.

(25) "Settle matters quickly with your adversary who is taking you to court. Do it while you are still together on the way, or your adversary may hand you over to the judge, and the judge may hand you over to the officer, and you may be thrown into prison. (26) Truly I tell you, you will not get out until you have paid the last penny."

ADULTERY

(27) "You have heard that it was said, "You shall not commit adultery (28) but I tell you that anyone who looks at a woman lustfully has already committed adultery with her in his heart.

(29) If your right eye causes you to stumble, gouge it out and throw it away. It is better for you to lose one part of your body than for your whole body to be thrown into hell (30) and if your right hand causes you to stumble, cut it off and throw it away. It is better for you to lose one part of your body than for your whole body to go into hell (so, does this mean the *merimna-* or "portion" of damnable existence goes into everlasting fire? —I think so/the "ontology of the sinful man"/Christ is, for sure, not referring to physical mutilation)."

DIVORCE

(31)"It has been said, "Anyone who divorces his wife must give her a certificate of divorce" (32) but I tell you that anyone who divorces his wife, except for sexual immorality, makes her the victim of adultery, and anyone who marries a divorced woman commits adultery (so there is no forgiveness in Grace here? –I say this is not what Jesus is talking about)."

OATHS

(33)"Again, you have heard that it was said to the people long ago, "Do not break your oath, but fulfill to the Lord the vows you have made" (34) but I tell you, do not swear an oath at all: either by heaven, for it is God's throne; (35) or by the earth, for it is his footstool; or by Jerusalem, for it is the city of the Great King (36) and do not swear by your head, for you cannot make even one hair white or black. (37) All you need to say is simply "Yes" or "No;" anything beyond this comes from the evil one (then why is there advocacy in dialogue amongst the Attorney and Judge? Why is there testimony/oath by the defendant which abides by Romans 13:1 –which is established by God Himself?)."

EYE FOR EYE

(38) "You have heard that it was said, "Eye for eye, and tooth for tooth." (39) But I tell you, do not resist an evil person. If anyone slaps you on the right cheek, turn the other cheek to them as well. (40) And if anyone wants to sue you and take your shirt, hand over your coat as well. (41) If anyone forces you to go one

mile, go with them two miles. (42) Give to the one who asks you, and do not turn away from the one who wants to borrow from you.

LOVE FOR ENEMIES

(43) "You have heard that it was said, "Love your neighbor and hate your enemy." 44 But I tell you, love your enemies and pray for those who persecute you, 45 that you may be children of your Father in heaven. He causes his sun to rise on the evil and the good, and sends rain on the righteous and the unrighteous. 46 If you love those who love you, what reward will you get? Aren't even the tax collectors doing that? 47 And if you greet only your own people, what are you doing more than others? Do not even pagans do that? 48 Be perfect, therefore, as your heavenly Father is perfect.

THE RICH AND THE KINGDOM OF GOD

Matthew 19:16 "Just then a man came up to Jesus and asked, "Teacher, what good thing must I do to get eternal life?"

(17) "Why do you ask me about what is good?" Jesus replied. "There is only One who is good (Romans 3:1–31/ (logically, then, how can anyone do good to get into Heaven and judgement (a kind of judgment does exist – obviously for all who do bad/evil—i.e., all of us). If you want to enter life, keep the commandments."

(18) "Which ones?" he inquired.

Jesus replied, "You shall not murder, you shall not commit adultery, you shall not steal, you shall not give false testimony, 19 honor your father and mother, and love your neighbor as yourself."

(20) "All these I have kept," the young man said. "What do I still lack?"

(21) Jesus answered, "If you want to be perfect, go, sell your possessions and give to the poor, and you will have treasure in heaven. Then come, follow me."

(22) When the young man heard this, he went away sad, because he had great wealth.

(23) Then Jesus said to his disciples, "Truly I tell you, it is hard for someone who is rich to enter the kingdom of heaven. (24) Again I tell you, it is easier for a camel to go through the eye of a needle than for someone who is rich to enter the kingdom of God."

(25) When the disciples heard this, they were greatly astonished and asked, "Who then can be saved?"

(26) Jesus looked at them and said, "With man this is impossible, but with God all things are possible."

This brings me to the point of grace. I feel that many universal reconcilationists do somewhat the same error that all "orthodoxies" (I use this term with tongue and cheek) do. They follow the lead of the commentator, minister, theologian, teacher versus following the truth of what God is really telling us in biblical common sense terms through his Bible. We are afraid (deilois—that damnable term) to think for ourselves lest we burn in hell . . . no joke!!!!

Origin proposed a "free will" that he deemed necessary to fulfill the relationship between us and God that would commence us into *apokatastasis* or universal reconciliation. Without this "free will," said Origen, we wouldn't have the glory, nor would God, of being reconciled together in a marriage at the very end.

To me, Origen's kind of "free will" bears no weight on this holy marriage. Many humanistic terms employed to obtain God's meta actions fall short of explaining God's infinite strings.

But here is the higher point to law and its condemnatory element under grace: The law only showed our inability to "get saved" .... Nothing we could have done would have granted our damnation or salvation "just" by our works. This means that God "caused"/"created" the sin. Let's talk sin. Sin means to "miss the mark" (Greek: Harmateia). It is also conveyed in Latin as *senex* or "one who is *senile* and wanders off the straight and narrow." Then there's the trigonometric function, sine, from the Latin root, *sinus*, or, "fold in a garment, bend, or curve. We have the Arabic geometrical equivalent of sine, *jiba*, which means, "chord of an arc." Furthermore, Sanskrit gives us the same in *jya* for "bowstring" (for a further definition of "the fool"/"the sinner" in the A.N.E. see *Kesil*, the "far darter" – the one who shoots his arrows "amiss").

We are free from our sin (sine: "curving away") by being tightly pulled into the Will (Greek – *boule*: "the arrow's shot to the bullseye") of God by his grace.

His grace gives us a *new* and *eternal* condition, namely, "free *from* the will of the flesh" which does "will" to error without one iota of human ability to stop that. Grace means no judgement (all penalties are dropped past, present and future) because there is no more condemnation from the law that no one could fulfill anyway. If we can collectively look at creation from beginning to end with all of its evolutions, the Bible's story of absolute meaning, message of salvation, sum of energies sutured together in one mass narrative, how can we claim "autonomy"? Can the characters written by the author jump off the page and tell the author, "I refuse chapter 5!"? How much more is creation a narration written by the great author, God himself? Even if creation were only addressed in thermodynamic principles, all energies would have been done already. And from that perspective/reality, I would only need to go back to Solomon for his supporting wisdom.

Let's revisit some of our earlier concepts: *apokatastasis*, *apokatakalleo*, and *telos*: the process aimed at bringing about repentance and salvation, a process aimed by God, through God, and for God.

God declares, "I have sworn by myself, the word is gone out of my mouth in righteousness and shall not return, that *unto me every knee shall bow, every tongue shall swear allegiance*" (Isaiah 45:23). That is the *telos* and God guarantees—even swearing an oath on himself—that he will bring it to pass. This *telos* is brought about in Christ (Romans 14:11, Philippians 2:10, 11 and Hebrews 6:13).

If this is the case, and we are in allegiance to God, who can be against us? If we were driven to God to swear allegiance, then Jeremiah's words in Jeremiah 31:18–19 are applicable to all. It is in Jeremiah's own words here that we see God enabling Jeremiah to repent in order for Jeremiah to come to God. It wasn't pretty either. Jeremiah gives us the process of repentance: "I have surely heard Ephraim bemoaning himself saying thus: "You, God, have chastised me, and I was therefore chastised, as a bull unaccustomed to the yoke: therefore *turn me and then I shall be turned*; for you are the LORD my God" Surely after that I was turned, I, then, repented; and after that I was instructed, I smote upon my thigh because I was then ashamed, yes, I was even confounded, because I did bear the reproach of my youth (and all of my previous sins)" (Jeremiah 31:18–19).

Chapter Fifty

Objective Forms to Abstractions: (Eternal, Eternity, Permanence, Forever, *Aeternum, Aeon*)

ONE COULD SAFELY SAY that until the past century, especially at the point of understanding Einstein's equation $E=mc^2$, "time" was "relatively" not understood. Moreover, the Universe was not understood as to how it worked. *Spatiality*, to the ancient Middle Eastern minds, beheld objects "*relatable*" to the *objective form* and not the abstract. Such cases for infinity, heaven or hell might be a physical "place" "to the top of the mountain from here," "where the land meets the ocean," "the darkness created by the depth of an abyss," "the unseen in the darkness of the waters," etc. Therefore, a "relatable" physical object seen with ocular observance, such as the horizon (i.e. sky touching earth), would have been used to express *where* heaven meets the earth. Hence, the objectively viewed world could be used to see the abstract world.

Such a concrete to abstract example can be found in Genesis 1:1. "In the beginning God *created* (*Bara* – "to make fat;" or "to offer the best of your offerance" at the *Beherith* table).

So, in Genesis 1:1 we see the objective Ancient Near Eastern term for "best of your offerance." If God, in the beginning (*be-roshiyth* [at the head/top/arch/"we begin here"]), gives us the best of what He has to offer —then, Creation, meaning, ending, beginning again, —*new life, eternity* is God's "Bara." What, therefore, do we/can we offer God at the Beherith table? Nothing but our belief in his Son, which even our belief is a gift of God.

Another example: "the sun was the roving eye (*mi-shut-ayin*) of God searching the hearts of humankind and scanning the actions of humankind as it appeared in the sky or heavens where God abided. It is interesting that *mi-shut* is the root for "Satan" – "the rover, the sifter, going to and fro, wandering amongst the earth." This same *shut* can be found doing his deed in Zechariah 4 as God's eyes (scanning to and fro). Of course, in Job when Satan was *going to and fro*.

Chapter Fifty-One

Configurations Unto a Mytho-Theology

The earth might have been seen as "round" and disk-like, but probably not as a globe. Therefore, to the "primitive" genius, the "watercourse" of the seas "circled" the flat-circular earth. It is within these waterways that our primitive-genius ancestors find the lore, of sorts, that "Leviathan" swims his course 'round the earth. What a great story to tell your children when not wanting them to get too close to the water!

These were primitive understandings, sure, but they were not stupid. "Primitive" is the strongest and purest foundation by which all other mental structures are established. So, when I used the expression "primitive-genius," I meant it. "Genius" literally means "to be joined," "to be connected" to everything and "act" or "participate" within this "connectivity" or "genius." For each level of evolution of participation of the figurations of word signaling, we have deeper fulfillment to the higher complexity of the original generative word. The "genius" is pregnant with higher fulfillments yet to come, both semiotically and spiritually. Therefore, I witness that each biblical epoch/era/*aeon*, etc. was needed to fulfill a greater archetype (as do we need the grace to "evolve"). We will see that the terms "permanence" and "eternity" will use the terms "eon'[1], "epoch," "era," and "aeon" to substantiate the vagaries of contextual meaning later on in the biblical text and pagan authors by which the Bible borrowed.

In Joseph Campbell's, "Masks of Eternity," we are presented an array of pagan ideas concerning how "forever" was to be understood. The "event" of "forever" was "participated" through hierarchical festivities, agricultural observances, and various religious observances in order to

---

1. eon: p.i.e. – *aiu* = "vital force;" "life force" (possible link to "vie" or "bio").

"partake" of the masks of eternity. "*Representation*" of eternity now becomes the practical form of communicating eternity.

"Forever," looked at within a time frame, is a very interesting philosophical topic.

As I have stated, eternal time was mythically signified through participation involving dancing, usage of the "masks of eternity," celebrations of the deity's eternal order — such as was found in the Jewish "Hag." The Hag was a "procession" around the "Stone of Order (Hebrew: Dabar (Hebrew: "Thing of Order"; "Stone of Order"; prophecy, judge, bee (animal of the ordered dances)). Likened dances are the *Debka* of the Arabs and Ancient European agricultural/cosmological dances called this "dance of eternity" as they danced the *horo* or "circle."

God might say "forever" concerning his statutes . . . yet, there was no example of specific relatable "time mapping," only conceptualizing of "referred continuance" by the tools given to the *primitive sense* — not *lesser "sense"*: "Forever;" Hebrew: *olam*; Genesis 9:12; Ecclesiastes 12:5; Isaiah 26:4; Psalm 145:13; etc.—all such usages *allude to a "duration" of non-accounting/the unquantifiable time/aeon/olam/era*, etc.

As we delve into the distinct concepts of "permanence" vs. "eternal" we will see "relational differences such as "being with God in a *relationship* that never ends versus a *permanent* ordinance that "never ends" but is superseded by its fulfilments and becomes the stronger "archetype" for its exponential "primacy." That is, we participate in the figuration of eternity through obedience to the eternal WORD. IN THIS, OUR EARTHLY "permanence" is eternally rooted. We come to our telos/intentful fruition as eternal beings that wore "obedience" as the mask of the eternal God.

Therefore, the importance of the biblical patriarchs/matriarchs was that they were the recipients of God's word, though having a limited technological skill set, they fulfilled eternity in their obedience. Obedience is the key word. Obedience is necessary to have completion of God's telegraphed ending to his grand narrative, namely our marriage to him. Here, we see 2 Noble Truths: "The Teleological" view working with "The Prophetic" view.

Chapter Fifty-Two

Messiah vs. Hero

Not that we're at the end of this work yet, but I feel that I'm at a point of conclusion.

If all that I have presented has had no bearing by which a Messiah has been called out "through the rocks" of time, then, what is left? The Hero?

To my way of thinking, "what is left" is decremental if our "option" is to oppose that idealistic humble and most gracious Messiah which has been exalted beyond our abilities to understand and obey by the Father. Must we return to the flesh, the objective might of man, for the hopes of an "answer"? What reasonable thing is there to treat others as Jesus treated the hopeless in this fallen world? What story is there taking over ca 2,000 years to complete at his arrival into Jerusalem that we should follow to make more sense to our lives than this? What Messiah is there other than Jesus the Messiah? Does this scream "sense" to the mighty world of will/flesh worship? I don't think so. Where's the Hero that can save us from plight? Know yourselves before you answer that "it is in me to pull myself up."

We've come to this point of humanity that we see what "religions," "theocracies," secular – humanistic/selfish based enterprises, atheistic corporate bodies can do. They do everything that the Jesus of the New Testament did not do.

We still "naturally" do not account for the meekness of Christ, his words, his deeds, his love, his grace, his peacefulness, his mercy upon our souls. For fleshly might cannot achieve these qualities. We continue to look elsewhere because it seems to be "logical" to do so. Yet, we are still killing each other in the names of corporations and mighty ideas.

I ask: why would we oppose our present selves from what was incomplete in the past? In the secular world, to oppose an "evolutionary idea" of a deity, such as the idea of Jesus the Messiah, is to do as Fredrich Nietzsche said, "now that we've killed the god who shall light the lamps"? This might be one of the strongest rhetorical statements I've read concerning the natural rejection of Jesus.

We've attempted to "be as gods." Is this a new idea? Are our physical and mental capabilities going to give us the "grace" needed to repent when humility is what we need? Logically speaking, when one is above others one cannot commiserate or have empathy with others who are suffering in this world. Yet, to "rise above" others gives a false sense of "freedom" to have to commiserate. Therefore, the mighty hero might think: "*After all, "I pulled myself up by my own bootstraps'---so, what's the problem with the weak who can't? No need to induce suffering upon myself—for that would be ludicrous. Fly high and above others.*"

For the external act upon us to make us humble is a sovereign act. It is an "out of our control act." It must be looked at as such. Otherwise, even the Christian will begin to have resentment against God if they are still infected with this ancient heroic/luciferian "might is right" ideology.

You can see the importance of believing in God's sovereignty lest you, the Christian or non-Christian, try to make sense [1] of anything in this life. "Might is right" is a band-aid motto for those in the middle of their ego-centered limited blindness. For there can be only one (cf. the movie, "Highlander" for a comical reference). If the one is the

---

1. "sense" – Greek: *semion* – a "signal;" "sign;" "indicator of direction (to and from). If "YOU" – the Hero "are it" —that "RIGHTNESS" is where you stand, i.e., the HERO's throne, then, there are no "signals." That is, you technically stand in a place of "NON-SENSE." Where else can you go? There are no more "directions" to go to other than you.

mightiest in this secular world, then, He must be "right." Isn't this the same Nimrodian/Gilgamesh – Hero – idea of antiquity mentioned in the Epic of Gilgamesh and Genesis 11? This motto begs for either (1) a long regressive journey back with the aid of psychiatrist and taking mental/emotional "inventory," (2) staying stative in the same motto which is a bullying Nimrodian idea, (3) or progression to meet those mightier than you. Where will you go then if, in your older age, the mighty men, greater than you, come for you? This question begs for *limited options*[2].

Yet we naturally/unbridledly return to our flesh, dismissing the humble Christ figure, whether in written word, idea, and/or reality. In all of our "above-human" ideologies and technological advancements an archo-neo philosophical movement has arisen called "transhumanism." Basically, attempts (some successful) of enhancement of the human body via new technology — i.e., downloading intelligence through a modem into our neural network, enhancements of bone structures by titanium replacements, etc. All of this to create an "above" or "superior" human. Again, I make the argument that science has nothing to do with the "faith based" system of a scientific-theology/ideology to "replace" the meek Jesus.

It was, and still is, the picture-negative of Jesus that the pagan's "societal "photograph" of the "hero." Beautiful are the efforts of the pagan that "missed the mark" for their acts were consistent in painting the "missing of the bullseye'! That is, the "nature" of all humanity – collectively as "one" – *paints by obedience to God's higher laws what it cannot be.*

The heathen's path showed us clearly what they did not have yet longed for. Naturally, the heathen aimed for joy, selflessness, consistency, and specific direction without necessary cognizance of the Christ. As C.S. Lewis called it, "The Tao." In his *Mere Christianity* C.S. Lewis makes the point that we are always circumnavigating towards or around the central figure – the Christ. Christ truly fills in "the miss *(i.e., what is lacking in the pagan/heathen)."*

Truly, if there was a historical/physical Odin who walked around the backstreets of Norway or Iceland and no witnessing historian wrote down this spectacle we would know the innate man calls out for this All-Father, All-Saviour through his God-given desire. It is therefore, expressed in the myths of the ancient heathen, the desire for Christ.

---

2. such as a hiding place, mercy, re-establishing your world view, an ideology that doesn't praise the will of the flesh over others, etc. Sounds a lot like true Christianity as is taught in the Gospels and Epistles.

Through the poets, bards, story tellers, etc. do we world myths likened to that of Christ without the "witness" to the mythological god's physical and historical effect. Did Krishna sit down to dinner with a local Indian community in historical reality? I think not. All of these beautiful pagan stories allude with cultural color a Christ who was to come and to the solidification of the language, the logos, by which the Greek words in the New Testament submitted and took to their stations[3]. It is within this "imaginative field" of the fantastic that I digress, for I know the literary genius of Tolkien in this world. Yet even Tolkien was a Christian who believed that the "collective consciousness" of all myths had a bearing of logos to which other fantastic worlds could be generated. But Tolkien's focus was just that and by that he accepted the physical trueness of the logos and the power of its deployment upon all the eons of our existence. Maybe this is why I stay within such biblical realities, which are not "sub-created" within a vacuum of humankind's opinion, or technical "idiocy" ("viewed as one perceives").

The efforts of the pagan that "miss the mark" for joy, selflessness, consistency, and specific direction are "naturally" painted without cognizance of the Christ. In my heart and mind, Christ truly fills in the "miss" (i.e., in the lacking of the pagan). Truly, if there is a historical Odin that walked around the backstreets of Norway or Iceland no witnessing historian wrote it down as did the history of Jesus in the Gospels. Jesus "fit the bill" through his words and deeds by acting in accord with the Jewish first century sketch. He interacted in accord with these Jewish social manners, customs and idiomatic paradigms.

Counter to the historical Jesus, only the poets and bards created the pagan's mythos. Did Krishna sit down to dinner with a local Indian community in historical reality? I think not. All of these beautiful pagan stories allude with cultural color to a Christ to come, and to the solidification of the language, the logos, by which the Greek words in the New Testament submitted and took to their stations. It is within this "imaginative field" of the fantastic that I digress, for I know the literary genius of Tolkien in this world. Yet, even Tolkien was a Christian who believed that the "collective consciousness" of all myths had a bearing of logos to which other worlds could be generated. But Tolkien's focus was just that and by that he accepted the trueness of the logos and the power of its deployment upon all of the aeons of our existence. This is why I

---

3. For a further treatment on Osiris/Dionysus as the mythological allusions to the physical Christ, see Jones, "Jesus Is Physically Dionysus."

stay within such realities writing this chapter, realities that are not "sub-created" within a vacuum of humankind's opinion, or technical "idiocy" ("viewed as one perceives").

Lastly, the Greek New Testament should be read within the context by which the Christ was in agreement with the Greek myths/Hellenized *paideia*, Christian *paideia*, The Greek Old Testament (LXX/Septuagint), the great philosophers (Plato and Aristotle), and our parent, the Hebrew Bible, by which YHVH revealed his *rhema, dabar, shem,* and *shekinah,* that we may operate within the confines of his *words*.

Chapter Fifty-Three

Eternity, Everlasting, Era, Limited Duration, Unending

"time" in various understandings within pagan and Christian usages

(especially, in culturally backed usages concerning our salvation)

AIONIOS, THE GREEK WORD for "time segment," is contrasted with *adios*, meaning "infinity." These two terms were used throughout Homeric times and then on into the early centuries of the church. As we better understand the term *adion* (infinity) we will better grasp what *aeon* is *not* (i.e., it does not mean "unending" or "eternal" or "infinite").

I will be clear, the word *aeon* which means "a segment of time," "an era," "an eon," "an age," and "a limited/finite period of time of unspecified duration"—was employed by the biblical writer John in his Revelation (or apocalypse) in order to speak of hell within its "aeon of purpose."[1] Moreover, the ontology or "coming to be" of "an age" of "being a sinful human" requires an aeon/era of hell to refine sinful humans to enable them to be with God. This intimates "direction," therefore the intent of God to create a passageway by which we will be refined, ready, and reserved for the final destination, i.e., union with God.

Since we have seen by its usage that *aeon* is not an "unending" term, we therefore look to *adios*. If we go to the archaic authors of the Greek and Hellenized world, we see that *adios* was socially normalized in its

---

1. For what event or duration could exist outside of God's intent (*thelos*)? Therefore, "*aeon*" implies a "duration" of intent, whether measurable or unquantifiable.

usage. Again, words are used in their participation in the figuration of a culture. I reiterate from my past 3 lectures that the beginning New Testament community (ca AD 30) had its rich linguistic heritage spanning at least 800 years, if not more, from the Classical Greek authors.

ADIOS AND *CHRONOS* WORKING TOGETHER.

Time (1)

One of the earliest cultural usages and accounts of *adios* is found in Homer's "Hymn to Hestia" (ca. 800 BC). Here, the "goddess resides on a throne" with mortals. This, by context alone, should give us ample information to see that there is a kind of "time" that can "participate" in this "throne realm" but is separate from . . . , for if mortality exists there, then "mortality" requires sequential time or *chronos*, which is separate and distinguished from *aidion* as we shall see. *Chronos* is neither subsumed or supervened by *adios* at this aforementioned juncture, rather, they (*chronos* and *adios*) share their "attributes" at certain juncture points for a fuller gestalt of meaning. That is, time and eternity (*chronos* and *aidios*) are "conjunctive" as "time" meets the eternal, or, relating to mortals, the *epiphanal*.

We see Hestia, the goddess of the hearth/throne sitting at her "permanent seat'—*edren aidion elaxes*. Such as "seat/throne" is the hearth at the fireplace. It is where the family convened to talk, eat, share, cook, stay warm, and associate with home. Hestiab was considered love, the beloved, and, in this maiden housekeeper sense, she was divinely eternal, without end. Hestia was called, "She of the Public Hearth." So, there is a sharing of the "time" of mortality and this *aidon* throne. This is no more contradictory than when the eternal God of the Bible talks with the patriarchs, matriarchs, and prophets. How about the answerable Platonic idea of "coming to be" to the fullness of the universal found in the very nature of Jesus Christ "coming to his fullness" (i.e., when the universal meets the particulars)? The "participation" by which the gods act involves such a confluence of different "times."

Time (2)

We find *aidios* inscribed in Hesiod's "Shield of Hercules" saying, *aidion eixon ponon*. This means that no one side can win in this athletic competition. It states the "stasis" by which movability cannot be achieved (therefore, "without end") in the duration of the game. But here's the catch: it is in the "picture" of stasis without resolution. This depiction fires on the mind a never-ending battle for glory without resolve, a state of being, a longsuffering of worldly effort, the battle of the *epos* ("epic ones") or *eroes* ("heroes").

Time (3)

Anaximander's (A.NAX.'uh.MAN.der) Greek says, *tayn aidion kinaysin*, i.e., "the *aidion* is perpetual movement." Therefore, *aidion* shows no retirement of motion, hence, no aging.

Time (4)

Anaximenes (A.NAXIMENEEZ) says, *kinaysin de kai hootos aidion poiei*, agreeing with Anaximander.

Time (5)

Anaximander went on to say, "There is a certain *nature* of the infinite (*physin tina tou apeirou*), and that this nature is *eternal* and *unageing* (*aidion ein kai agayro* ["a" = "not" + gayro" = aging; i.e., 'geriatric']."

Time (6)

Xenophanes (XSE.NAH.'fa.neez) attests that *adios* means that which is "not to be deconstructed, immortal, and ungenerated (i.e., uncreated)." Xenophanes uses *adios* in contrast to anything that is "coming to be" or "generated." For Xenophanes, anything that segways into a subsequent event is not *adios*.

ETERNITY, EVERLASTING, ERA, LIMITED DURATION, UNENDING

Time (7)

Diogenes (DIE-AH.jeh.neez) Laertius (Lay.er.ti.uhs) simply agreed with Xenophanes here.

Time (8)

Anaxagoras agreed with Aristotle that *adios* is "without end'

Time (9)

Heraclitus says, "*Adios* is perpetual motion of things without end." These "things" therefore do not share in the attributes of *aeones*.

Time (10)

Empedocles says, "There is a "*thing of necessity*," an ancient decree of gods eternal" (*Anankayce krayma theon psaypheesma palaion aidion*). Conclusively brilliant, Empedocles continues to his conclusion that *aidion* is "spherical, eternal, and immobile" (*sphairo-eides kai aidion kai akin-ay-ton to hen*).

Time (11)

Parmenides used the term *aidion* to mean "all" in the sense of "all that will always be, all that is ungenerated and imperishable.'

Time (12)

Simplicius says, "nothing that has a beginning and end is *aidion*."

Time (13)

For me, maybe the most important statement is from Metrodorus of Chios who stated, "the all (*to" pan*) is eternal (*aidion*), because, if it came into being at a certain moment, it would come to be from non-being; and it is unlimited (*apeiron*) inasmuch as it is eternal: for it does not have a principle (*archay*) from which it began, nor a limit (*peras*) or an end (*teleutay*)."

"Indefinite time" does not have to mean "infinity," though it could. The way in which *aeon* and *aidion* were used of "indefinite times" were poetically and philosophically expressed as a complimentary union of ideas.

Vocabulary from New Testament Greek

Aion (102 occurrences in the New Testament) – "age," "time period," "unquantifiable time." It can represent the present age, the age to come, or the "universe." *Aion*, as an adjective, follows (in Greek) what it modifies – such as "past *aion*," "present *aion*," "future *aion*." All such adjectival usages of *aion* here indicate a limited modifier. *Aion* is used in contrast to the eternal kingdom of God. We see the Greek cognate, *aemi* – to breathe; the Sanskrit *evas* (*aivas*) – life/breath; Gothic *aivs* – life/breath; P.I.E. **aiw* – "vital force, life, long life,

aidios – "eternal" in the strict sense of infinitude. Aidios coincides with God's attributes as well as God himself.

aionios – Everlasting. This kind of "time" may bear "quantitative" and "qualitative" connotations. The quantitative is in the sense of everlasting and qualitative as belonging to eternity or the age to come. If we remember my treatment in this book on "Plato's Cave" we found that the LOGOS made flesh and dwelling amongst us was the contradiction of the natural mind. The LOGOS made flesh (*sarx*) was eternity in this *kosmokriton, kronon*, aeon, age, era .... Such an event halted our senses to time and space. As salvation (Jesus) came from eternity so did/does his fire (*pur*) which is put upon us all. This is his eternal fire put upon us in this age, kronon, age, era, etc. that exists in time but eternal—that is, from him, as his words are eternal. We see this "baptism" as an overwhelming *agent* of a future of *unspecified duration, completion or repetition* (which represents an "*aionon*"[2] or "aeon" —i.e. an unquantifiable duration) acting

---

2. Hebrews 13: 20, 21 -King James: "Now the God of peace, that brought again from the dead our Lord Jesus, that great Shepherd of the sheep, *through* (Greek: "en" – "in") the blood of the *everlasting covenant*, (21) make you perfect in every good work to do HIS Will –(which is) working in you that which is well pleasing in His sight, through Jesus Christ; to Whom be glory *forever (aionas)* and ever (aionon). Amen." Here's an

upon us *unto* a profitable outcome for us and God. An outcome with both God's and our interests in mind. As for *aionios* life and *aionios* punishment —neither concept carries any implication of "unending temporal duration" ←— for this is an oxymoron in Greek or English. Unending is to be distinguished from eternal here for two reasons: 1) unending is not durative nor temporal/nor the combination of the two 2) everlasting or eternal is without time or temporal modifying. Aionios sustains itself to mean "everlasting" without any modifier to imply "forever" – "eternal" – "without end."

To lightly sum: *Adion* is almost always used in the eternal sense, *Aionion/aiones* is used to show eternal "attributes" of God on earth in his eternal nature, *aion* is an "age" on the earth of *kronon* or "time passages."

Kronon – Time as passages or measured segments such as in the word chronology

Kronos aioniois – not eternal time but eternities of time/aeons of times

Kratos eis tous aionas – power of the ages

Eis tous aionas ton aionon – from generation to generation/from ages to the ages

Kairos – "time at hand"

Kairos idiois – proper time; particular time

Without understanding these different forms of time, we will never understand the eternal nature of God's salvation, nor the eternal nature of judgment from God in the heaven leaves onto mankind by which we are purged in his eternal fire which is here (from God in heaven [i.e., eternal fire]) to try us: 1 Peter 1:7: "That the testing (*dokimion* – testing for genuineness; proving of your faith, which is far more precious than gold that perishes though it is tested by fire, may result in praise and glory and honor when Jesus Christ is revealed." 1 Peter 4:12: "Beloved, do not be surprised at the fiery *(purosei – pur –* "fire"*)* trial *(peirasmon* – "probation," "tempting," affliction, calamity[3] when it comes upon you

---

example of the *aionas* ton "of the" [genitive article] *aionon* having eternal-durative attributes while working in our time upon us *unto* salvation. As stated above, the eternal fire of God, which is here to test us *unto* the second coming of Christ, is more precious than gold which perishes. Eternity meets us in limited time with our interests in God's mind.

3. *Strong's Concordance* #3986.

to test you, as though something strange were happening to you." I Corinthians 3:13: "Each of our works *ergon*: "doings" will become manifest (*phaneron*: shown) as the day (*emera*) reveals it in fire [*ekastou to ergon phaneron genesetai; hay gar emera* (day) *delosei* (will disclose), *hoti en puri* ("fire") *apokaluptetai* ("because in fire it is revealed"); *kai ekaston to ergon, opoion estin, to pur auto dokimasei*] (fire will prove; "make fit," "approve," "put to the test for approval" —i.e. a reason to "burn" something through)."

It is obvious that Satan is not "en-rogue" to "challenge us unto fitness of the spirit." As I have tried to, and will again in my next chapter, show that God's tool is Satan. That is, God uses a satan, or Satan as to be identified as the apocalyptic hinderer, for God's purposes, therefore, our purpose with God. Eternal fire is not to be seen in the Greek sense, *timoria*, which means "to punish for pleasure's sake," rather, chastisement is seen in the biblical text as *kolosin* or "a time of proving unto rectification/right-i-fication" (my newly made-up word). To add to this, Peter makes it clear that this heavenly fire which is here to try us is more precious than gold which melts away (unlike the spirit that is being tried). We see in 1 Peter 1:7 that the fiery trials are already upon us before Christ's second coming. That is to say, the *aionion* fires from God in heaven (i.e., the "eternal fires") are "here and now" in time to "try" us unto the return of our Lord and Saviour. Eternity extends itself unto holiness by heaven's agent – "fire."

The failure of the church at large is that we are postmodernists that think the original language of God's words means little to nothing. That is, we can "have our truths and you can have yours" by being "relative" to one's own accord — so, opine away! This is the natural decline of humankind.

To paraphrase Edward Gibbon, the author of *The Decline and Fallof the Roman Empire*:

Empires fall when the study, usage, retention, and guarding of their language is no longer preserved. Double entendres, business-speak, cultural popular slang, etc. are the beginnings of this sorrow.

Chapter Fifty-Four

Do We Fear the Powerless?

Who is Satan?
What is Satan?

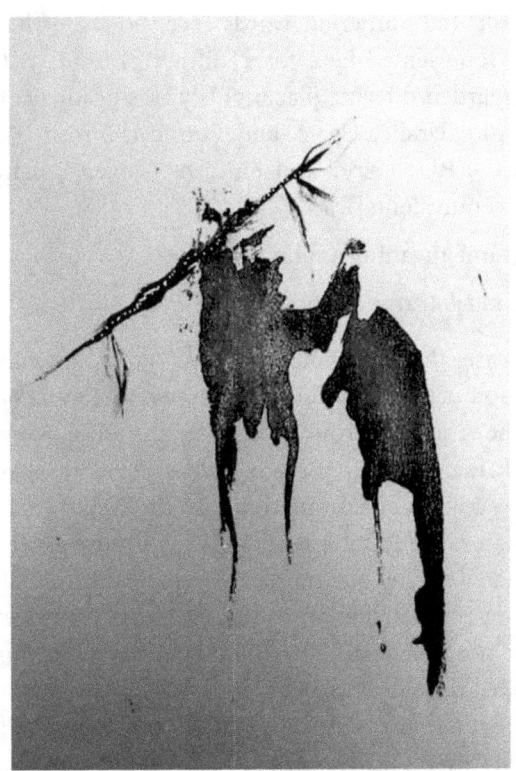

Our ancestors called him the Lord of *Sht*, god of *Ekron*, Lord of the Flies, Beel-zebub. In the earliest cases for "beginnings" of gods, demons, etc., this particular demon god comes to mind simply because of his primacy, simplicity, and relatability to many "next generation" shamanistic and quasi-religious practices that sprung from the primal "dung heap" with him. His names are many but one of his earliest names is "Beelzebub," the chief of demons—though, in the earliest name for *Satan* was the root word SHT, which literally means, "shit," which fits "the stuff" he was made out of. He attracted flies from the camp, and was praised for that. The richness and thickness of the primary belief in this dung god is that he is a myth housed in the simple and "ordinary" by which a "primitive" would have easily believed.

Let's recount from a few chapters back "satan's" original name:

Proto Uralic: *Saksa*, filthy, unclean/*SIT*, to bind/*SITTA*, (slang) shit/*SIJTE*, grove, offering place (garden)/*SIB* (as in the Philistine "fly'—Lord of the Flies) "to cast a spell."

Sumerian: *shesh*" (all Sumerian words received from the Proto-Uralic and *arer* represented here for 1) filthy; 2) bind; 3) (slang) "shit;" 4) grove/garden/offering place; 5) "fly" (as pestilence) are cognates to the Proto Uralic, Ugric, and Finnic (Finnish) (i.e., Sumerian matches the P.U., Ugric, and Finnish — even nearing in spelling [Grimm's equivalents]).

Ugric: *shosh* (same meaning as above)

Finnish: *tade, tadeh* (same as above)

In each case, the morphology of *saksa* and *sit* do fit the original meaning for "shit" as "unclean." In the Hebrew we have "corban," "dung," "filthy," etc. The Arabic borrowed this later meaning, *Shaytan* or Satan, and once again, loaned it into the later medieval Hebrew language, which reinforced it as a word of assimilation into the Hebrew culture. Yes, the Hebrew translators could have used SHT for a more contextually fitting SHT (i.e., "satan") versus our modern "rogue actor of evil." This is, for sure, a result of the Babylonian influence on the Hebrew Pharisees in Babylon, who "borrowed" this word, and I believe it has caused our modern church to be "dualistic" and corrupt.

It is my contention that the Aramaic from the *Peshito* (Aramaic Gospel Text) in Christ's words must be brought in concerning Be'elzebub. In Matthew 12 in the *Peshito* Jesus employs the word *bab'el-zebub* for *Ba'alzebub* or *Ba'alzebul*. But this is in the simplest "translation" of the "active-ness" of the "fly-sounds" which modify the icon of "Baal." Most related "Be'elzebub" as "Ba'al's Dwelling."

In the pagan Roman world during Christ's days on earth, many pagan idol worshipers "housed" their gods. Interestingly, as a tabla player, I have played many Indian performances including those called Bhajeons, which loosely means "a music flow jam session for the god or gods of that particular house." Further, I know of some very wealthy Indians who buy homes for their deity or deities. This is not too far off from Greek and Roman idol worship in their housings or temples nor is it too far off from Catholic images or icons such as Mary or any of the apostles taking "sainted" status. I tread on dangerous ground in that I am not Catholic or Hindu. Yet I find some "kind" of merit in these icons by what they do for those who use them to "shoot past" the icon to an alive idea. This kind of worship seems to attract the tactile senses by which we primitively seek. Oddly, I find myself seeking this kind of primacy through words hoping to find a "tactileness" to the weightiness of their meanings and unions with a grander theology.

WHAT IS "PRIMITIVE"

When I speak above of "what a primitive might have believed," I use "primitive" in a jocund way. My view is that the term "primitive" should be approached in a pure manner. Therefore, in my use of "primitive" I mean "in the sense of the genius (collective consciences holding their tribe together) of the minds of *that time* long forgotten." I do not use it as a derogatory term nor to mean "backwards." To me, a "primitive" had less tools and more genius to make things happen.

Furthermore, such "primitives" would have, with simple clarity, associated such abstract notions as unitive or singular. Their collective and multidimensional (as we see the world now) world was without the fatigue of one important fallacy: the "knowledge" of good and evil for there was no such thing taught, only "known" as a collective culture and as an attached individual to the culture.

As in the story of Adam and Eve, after they partook of the "forbidden fruit" they had their "eyes opened" or "wits" about them and they could see good *and* evil as "binary" moralities. The "genius," "joined," or, "union" of the Garden culture was in its *genesis* of the Fall. They became instantly "incriminated" – "krima" – "krino" —under judgment. Their new-fallen nature did judge. They became "as gods" as the satan said they would. This *double vision* wasn't always so and neither was the view of the "dung god," which was naturally born in the mind of earlier man. If something would take flies away from your village you would reckon it to a force that worked in that way. You would regard it with value and over time venerate it.

THE DUNG GOD'S EARLY REPRESENTATIONS

The "dung god" or "fly god," Beelzebub, seems to be first built upon its sound and then the word-representation of such a sound via onomatopoeia. In the Kartvelian 3, Georgian, and Sumerian 4 (all dating to at least 4000 BC) we have the onomatopoeic *bzz, blzz, v'v*, etc. which was used in such ancient kingdoms to represent a pestilent bug, especially that of the fly.

Words beginning with natural representations such as bird, river, tree, rock, bug, etc., also carried "associative name sounds" or abstract meanings by which they move, act, "are as," etc. Such words can become, over a process of time, assumed social memes. Furthermore, these social memes can be culturally integrated into the fantastic. I use the word "fantastic" in the Tolkien sense here to explain such examples of fables and superstitious associations. Both Tolkien's view of "temporary suspension of disbelief of the ordinary mundane world fused with Owen Barfield's "collective representation" we can find an early world by which pestilence is related to the sound and name is of the "name-sound-thing" called Baal-zebub. Such acts were not viewed as efforts but rather as assimilation into a self-referencing tribal colony.

Therefore, "name-sound-thing," in many early cultures, is one and the same. These societal associations can be hard to detach. Such associations become what we call endonyms, or insular socially based names. These can represent particulars which are a part of insular social structures. From there, linguists can study cultures of focus for their semiotic usages such as signs and symbols by which they once upon a time were interpreted within their mythology/ideology/theology/sociology, etc. These phenomena do take "body" or "social anima" wherewith a particular culture can participate in its daily activities.

ALLUSIONS OF CHRIST IN BEELZEBUB/SATAN;

The Chthonic Taxi "to take away troubles"

Such representations are found in 2 Kings 1:2 where the king of Israel, Ahaziah, fell through a roof injuring himself. Ahaziah, the king of Israel, although knowing YHVH, calls on the god of the flies instead of YHVH. This god of Ekron called Be'el-zebub (god of flies) was an interesting social god that allows for us to view ancient Near Eastern primitive beliefs that many others believed in at that time, both Israelites and Philistines. It is interesting that the "type" of injury was somehow addressed by Ahaziah as an injury that Beelzebub could fix. We see that Ahaziah's belief was in Beelzebub's ability to "take away" an injury.

The boar is considered a Chthonic Taxi into hell. Dr. Marija Gimbutas and Ted Hughes do quite an extensive treatment on the boar as the taxi which "takes away" and "puts into hell." This belief can be seen in William Golding's *Lord of the Flies*. Such a demon and god are interchangeable with Beelzebub, Lord of the Flies, the dung god, and reaching back to biblical stories—the god of Ekron.

Ahaziah, the king of Israel, believed that Beelzebub could "take away" his injury. We can see this same belief predating the Bible in ancient Canaan and concurrent in Jesus's day. This "belief" was so strong that the Pharisees attributed Jesus's exorcisms to Beelzebub. Their misunderstanding of "sending away" or "loosing" was horribly out of context with what Jesus and the Father were doing to promote as the Messiah. Jesus was the only one that could "release" the "binding" that the Father set. Beelzebub had nothing to do with either scenario concerning powers of binding and loosing.

Again, we see a rich verbal imagery in the Lord of the Flies represented as the Boar's head who could take the flies "away" from the camp and give "power" to the leader of the group who was maddened with a sense of brandishing Beelzebub's power." William Golding's "The Lord of the Flies" brilliantly brought this out within his story for it reveals that we have no recourse but chaos when our eyes are blinded to order. In the end, socialism becomes cannibalism – literally and/or figuratively.

So, in the antimony of "God as Satan" we come to a crux that is remedied in the book of Job. The story begins with "representations" of "evil" as a rogue or roving satan nearly ending Job's existence to the end of the book of Job where it was God-YHVH all along who did this destruction to

Job all for the betterment of Job and his rectification with God. The book of Job also remedies any idea of "dualism."

I find this so interesting when reading the Bible in Isaiah 45:7, Romans 13:1–14, and Colossians 1:16–17 that *all things,* "good and evil," are from, by, made for, made of, fulfilled in, determined by the Lord. So then, where is the dichotomy of scripture? Where is there room for dualism in scripture? Who can oppose the prime mover, the only mover, the verb of all things? A pile of dung is a dead thing, nothing more. To "take away" into hell, as a chthonic taxi (per se) must be just another Pagan's allegory to the Christ to come. 1 John 3:5 "And you know that He appeared so that *He might take away* (Greek: aire" [airo'] – "carry away") sin and in Him is no sin." Bear in mind, the anthropomorphizing of a singular autonomous being identified as "Satan" was a Persian idea loaned into Jewish mysticism and early Christian ideas. Nevertheless, the authenticity of the Old and New Testament's language does not bear this heretical mark for the Satan figure as autonomous. Hence, dualism, once again, is not a reality.

Chapter Fifty-Five

Jesus and Beelzebub: Jesus as a "type" of Beelzebub

IN JACOB GRIMM'S *TEUTONIC Mythology*, we see the "shape" of the devil as a fly.[1] Grimm quotes the Greek translation of 2 Kings 1-2 as Baalzeebub to be called in the Greek *Baial muia*, i.e. the fly god. In the ancient religion of Zoroastrianism (possibly dating from as far back as 2000 BC) we see the defiant spirit against Ahura Mazda known as a "devil" named Ahriman. Ahriman is seen in the shape of a fly. In Lithuania, there is a myth of *mussu birbiks*, fly god. Such a god is usually found buzzing and blowing. Fairytales from Germany hold that diabolic spirits can be held in glass or "phials" (vials) like "flies." Likewise, Loki turned into a fly or *fluga* when defrauding Freyja. Loki as a fly can get through keyholes (Norske folktales). There is a Lombard myth, found in Paul Diac. 6:6, about the *malignus spiritus* who settles on the window as a fly and gets a leg chopped off. "*Belsebuc*," in the fragments of Madelghis, is referenced as "a fly such as a spirit shut up in a glass."[2] Hence, the myth "there's a devil in the glass."

About 750 years prior Jesus' stay on this earth he was spoken of prophetically in Isaiah 53. As we read from that oracle in paraphrase: "we did not hold Him up in high regard among ourselves yet, we knew He was punished for our sins and we knew that He was our Messiah." Isaiah tells us that we loved to cast our evils on him—likening him to Ahaziah's view of Beelzebub. How so? In Potts's *Bible Proper Names*, he says that Baalzebub was a "God of wandering" (*vagationis, vel muscarum*), as flies

---

1. Grimm, *Teutonic Mythology*, 3:998-99.
2. Grimm, *Teutonic Mythology*, 4:1604-5.

"wander." Going "to and fro," "roving" like the raven's eye that scans back and forth. Josephus (*Antiquities* 9.2.1) says that King Ahaziah sent his "sickness (as a thing)" to *the fly*—that is, to the god of Ekron, who was the "caster," "carrier," "exorcist," and "receiver." So, the god Baalzebub was viewed by Ahaziah as the god of healing. So, Beelzebub represented a "healing aspect" to Ahaziah while reigning as king under the God of Israel.

COMPLEXITY ABOVE REASON TO THE PHARISEES

Likening Jesus' beliefs to Ahaziah's beliefs, the Pharisees shared somewhat a muddled view of Jesus and blamed him as the Lord of the Flies, for Jesus could "take" the disease from and (I assume) take the disease upon himself, making him both a healer and an unclean thing (according to the Pharisees' accusations).

The complexity lies in the fulfillment of the one who would "loose" or "release" the "binding" by which mankind has been "bound" in prison to sin. The exorcisms Jesus did were an "outward manifestation" of the power that he held and could consistently use. The intriguing tie-in between the word "cast out" in Greek (*ekballo* = *ek* (out) + *ballo* (cast)) and "exorcise" gets close to the primitive view of Beelzebub. The Pharisees were relegating Jesus' works to Beelzebub because many fallen men of Israel, such as Israel's king, Ahaziah, actually believed that Beelzebub could "exorcise" or "cast out" or "take away" an evil spirit.

Already we are dealing with the Pharisees' theological interpretive misunderstanding that "evil (*ra'ah* = "destruction")" is not ordained by God and that in their misunderstanding of the sovereignty of God, they fell into dualism (good vs evil, a Persian idea). Simply put: the Pharisees viewedthe world as a good and evil place by which judgments can be established by the "knowers of the law."

The reason that Jesus offers in Matthew 12:24 is brilliant. Jesus takes sovereign reason to the Pharisees. He shows the difference between "casting" and "loosing." Again, "casting" was believed to be an attribute of Beelzebub and to many shamans throughout the ages. Whether they be smoke and ladders or "real," Jesus showed his own "casting" to be consistent as the power of God, which most Jewish exorcists thought was the proper procedure.

Jesus focused on God's power in order that he not stick out of the crowd as being anything more than a Jewish exorcist. But it was the fulfillment of loosing/releasing that only Jesus had to release what his Father in heaven had bound. In this, Jesus would show not only his title as exorcist but also as healer and fulfiller of Joel's prophecy as the forerunner to the Holy Ghost, who would continue the work of God until the kingdom of God be complete on this earth.

Jesus addresses the Pharisees' blindness to the kingdom of heaven that the Pharisees claimed to belong to. It takes a complete understanding of the distinction between "casting" and "exorcising" to understand the ignorant judgments made by the Pharisees concerning Jesus "casting out" as using Beelzebub's spirit to exorcise when in truth Jesus was "loosing" spiritually and prophetically, though "casting out" physically.

I attempted to bring a modern style dialogue to my understanding of what Jesus said to the Pharisees using the Bible. Here is my paraphrased attempt at Jesus' famous words to the Pharisees based on Matthew 12:24 and following:

> Oh, you wretched Pharisees! How can an unclean thing cast out an unclean thing? How can Satan cast out Satan lest his house collapse? If I am Satan why am I casting out Satan lest I fall? What do you think I am doing then? Can you not see the incoherency in your idle words? If I cast out devils being a devil then by whose authority (*shem*) do your children (disciples) cast out devils? Am I not a Jew? Therefore, what "standard" is held to the Jews to be an exorcist? Am I not exorcising before you? Do you not optically see the healing of this demoniac? Is there more to me than just me being a Jewish exorcist? What draws you to me, a Jewish exorcist who is actually doing his job correctly and by the book? Am I not doing legitimate exorcisms? Do you not see the miracles I do in the physical world before you? Do your eyes betray you? In contrast, are other Jews displaying this power? Are there other Jews in the name of the law and not the prophets that are doing the same things as I? In contrast, are there successful exorcists, who are completing these same miracles, using my name? Yes, there are! Would you argue that they are not? Are they working or not?
>
> I say that there is not only the physical miracle that your eyes see before you here and now but also the fulfillment of the kingdom of God which was prophesied to come. I am that fulfillment of prophecy. Now is the time of which the prophets spoke. I justify not only my acts of exorcism, but the fulfillment

of binding and loosing by which you claim to understand. I am releasing—loosing that which was put into binding by my Father in order to show prophecy's fulfillment concerning myself. It is me and my kingdom, my children of my authority, that are fulfilling not only all righteousness but the grasping for hope in a failing pagan's idea of just who Beelzebub was supposed to be for them. Just and true is judgment and fulfillment of prophecy here and now. I am the judgment. I am the answer for the prophets of the Jews and the archetype fulfilled by which the fallen pagans of this world sought.

Until your time and your children's time has come, your children shall be without knowledge, feigning your judgment. They shall be your exorcists feigning you to be exorcised or exorcising someone that is not needing such an exorcism. You feign loosing and binding yet have no understanding of this time at hand to fulfill such prophecies that Joel spoke of. It is me who is in agreement with what my Father and the Holy Spirit do.

Yet, for now, you define whatever "evil" and "good" means to you and you teach it to your followers. But as to your followers, students, and future Pharisees, who watch and hear me teach the gospel and then listen and watch you incessantly contradict yourselves, they will remember my words to see if your words and your actions hold up. They will see which is evil and good (i.e., that which builds up and that which breaks down upon itself). To those who are twofold, the children of blindness that you teach, they will either judge you by my words, wittingly or unwittingly, or they will judge you by what you call devilish and judge you by the confusion which you have taught them. Loosing and binding is Joel's prophecy concerning this moment. I am the fulfillment of God's Will, that by the Holy Ghost I shall cast out that which is bound by God. You condemn the very Spirit by which I cast out. If I cast out by the Spirit of God then the kingdom of God has come upon you and you are already judged. Again, you call yourselves the kingdom of God, yet ironically enough, you are already in judgement since I am the judgement. All is exorcised now and judgment is already done for I am the judgement. Therefore, if I come "casting out devils" then I am here to cast you out. Yet, this is not what I am doing. I am releasing the bindings that my Father established in order that I might show the power of the kingdom of God is here and now with me. You are either with me or not. You either gather or scatter. But don't you dare mock the Holy Spirit, which releases those who are captive in this world with many sins too grievous to bear. I am here for my little ones who will follow in my *shem*—my authority! You can mock me as a man, but you will not be forgiven in this life if you mock the Holy Spirit that works in me. Nonetheless, you are vipers. Nothing good comes out of your muddled hearts, minds, mouths. You lie in wait to strike, injure, maim, kill. For whatever your heart is, your words will reflect your heart. For your words will either justify you or condemn you.

Chapter Fifty-Six

Jesus as Exorcist

ACTS 2:23 "HIM (JESUS), being delivered by the determined purpose and foreknowledge of God, you have by lawless hands, have crucified, and put to death; Whom God raised up, having loosed the pains of death, because it was not possible that He should be held by it."

There's a theme in the Gospels where Jesus heals, yet, the natural stage by which man plays his role is under God's orchestration. Both the healing and the condition of fallenness are established in the Trinity. The *loosing* and/or *binding* was not something that a human could wield. Both *loosing* and *binding* were created to do one thing: establish the Godhood of Jesus Christ on earth before all humankind as only Jesus and his disciples could heal. The Jewish exorcists and Pharisees (who considered themselves "the kingdom of God" with an overriding sense of dualism [good vs. evil]) could not understand this kind of sovereignty by which one God would ordain both *loosing* and *binding* all for his glory and his children. Not only dualism did the Pharisees believe, but as I have mentioned prior, they professed to have a "communication" between the heavenly Sanhedrin (the powers in heaven) and the earthly kingdom of God which reigns on earth through the Sanhedrin. This gave a faux idea to the common Jew that there was a "tethering" between the high and mighty Pharisees (Sanhedrin) on earth and the council of the Pharisees (Sanhedrin) in heaven–attempting to strike awe in the common Jewish citizen by giving the sense of a "connection" of heaven and earth via the Sanhedrin.

So, it was not hard to understand the reaction by the Sanhedrin to Jesus as Jesus exorcised (*ek-ballo*) spirits of maladies of all sorts. The Pharisee only had dualism as their reference when insulting Jesus for "casting out" demons. For if Jesus was not a Pharisee in agreement with the Sanhedrin, then he was a heretic. And, if a heretic is "casting out" demons he must be casting out his own kind. This gives way to their thinking: i.e., only "they," the Pharisees, thought of themselves as holy and only they could *wield* an exorcism. The very act of Jesus' exorcisms rendered the Pharisees without rebuttal for they had no power to exorcise demons.

Then, Jesus told the Pharisees that they make laws and break them—all which make life unbearable to the sons and daughters of, not only the Pharisees, but those who are common Jews in fear of the Sanhedrin.

Jesus makes it clear in John 8:44 that the Pharisees are the sons (carriers of the *shem* (language, lip, boundary line)) of their father, the devil. It is necessary to understand father-to-son relations in the Jewish community. Jesus was calling the Pharisees "devils," as their "authority–Satan–had fathered them. Did not Jesus call Peter "Satan" when Peter said to Jesus that Jesus should not suffer unto death[1]? In the like manner, the Pharisee could not hold to the doctrine of predestination of the Father without muddling it with that of dualism and the illusory idea that they had self will.

If Satan isn't an independent agent, then are the Pharisees acting on their own *evil* accord? I say no. If Satan is bound to limitation, then it is possible he could be loosed? The scriptures are clear that this is the case in Revelation 20:3. In the same way Satan is bound and loosed as scriptures explicitly show in the earliest book of the Bible in Job and the last book of the Bible in Revelation, the Hebraised use is shown, that Satan and the Pharisees were "antagonists, opposers, scandalizers, anti-Christs." As a portrait of a corporate body of Satan, the Sanhedrin wished to sit in the throne of God. The Sanhedrin were composed of mortal men-Pharisees who, as Edersheim says, "were wont (wished/wanted) to say the Sanhedrin above confirmed what the Sanhedrin beneath had done." It is here where Jesus counters this idea by saying in Matthew 18:18-20, "Truly I tell you, whatever you bind on earth will be bound in heaven..." There is no middle man nor are there two parties or two tingdoms.

We can see that the opposing Pharisees were indeed "satans." For sure, they were "anti-Christs." Their natures opposed the light of the

---

1. Mark 8:33 and Matthew 16:23: Jesus telling Peter: "Get thee hence, Satan" – "*Upage opiso mou, Satana!*" Why did Jesus call Peter, Satan? – For one reason only: Peter's will of the flesh (at the time) wasn't ready to believe the Father's Will was going to be done. That is, Jesus' crucifixion was ordained as Revelation 13 tells us that Jesus was the lamb slain before the foundation of the world.

world. Their *shadowed reasoning* was brought to light by unmitigated truths spoken by our Lord and Saviour. This is why they acted as satans. Who would want to be exposed as liars, especially when your reputation and income counted on conning the society? Jesus spoke, revealed, exposed, prophesied, Yet, Jesus never "reacted." Jesus only spoke the truth and went forward.

Scripture tells us that when Jesus was on the cross, he addressed his Father concerning the Jews, Pharisees, Greeks, Romans, etc. saying, "Father, *forgive them*; for they do not know what they're doing" (Luke 23:34). What more can I say than they are not acting with intent, freedom, knowledge of why, how, or what they are doing? Jesus pleads to the Father to forgive them. The King of Grace has spoken. Where is their "free agency" or "free will" if they "acted" with seemingly full consciousness throughout the entire Gospels and we are finalizing with their absolute innocuous natures. They did not know what they were doing so forgive them, Father.

Christianity had not begun as what we now call Christianity. Jesus was a Jew preaching the *euhados* or the "well way." He was the law-fulfiller. Jesus was the true healer. He was the sacrifice. He was and is the Messiah. He was and is the fulfillment of Isaiah 53—the entire chapter. The Father deemed it necessary to have powerless Pharisees who claimed so many things, which only Jesus could do and did, witness these acts which were "the judgment." These acts were the sign to proclaim Christ our Lord is among us.

The genius by which Jesus' fulfilling of the Old Testament's prophecies as the healer forced the Pharisees (by their only irresoluble-resolve) to "mete out" their judgments on others (especially themselves) with the same scrupulosity as that which they gave Jesus. That is, if the other Jewish exorcists were failing to cast out demons, how much more judgment should the Pharisees meet out on those failing exorcists than the true exorcist, Jesus? If they didn't judge their own failures and lies then the inequity of their judgment would proclaim their hypocrisy and proclaim Jesus' Godhood. Not only did Jesus' exorcism have true power but his meek "style" in which he "exorcised" shamed the snakes-and-ladders approach by the pretentious Jewish exorcist shams with the possibility of being without verbal reproach from Jesus. Exorcisms and healings were sometimes more powerful than words.

To the onlooking exorcists, disciples of Christ of a different clan than the twelve, some of the Romans and Greeks, and even some of the

Pharisees, one would have found a gentle and meek Jesus who healed as he fulfilled his title. His existence was the judgment for anyone who could deny such a sweet spirit. Why couldn't it be that the Messiah was Jesus, that is, that one who was even gentle with those who were backwards in their superstitions and even claiming to be exorcists? Why couldn't it be that Jesus was the promised Lord? He upheld the ordinances, the law, the honoring of the prophets, observing and fulfilling the feast days and the meaning. Jesus was the only one who did not "break the traditions of men" by doing something different according to the formulas for exorcisms? Rather, as Dr. Graham Twelftree points out, Jesus both condescended and abased himself to all men, even those who had no real power to exorcise, enacting the rites of "exorcism" without the reliance of the enactments of the rite. Maybe a lesson could be learned here of going to any church in order to be in touch with Christ and community, regardless of the error of the doctrines? I don't know. I presently wrestle with this.

For further study on this chapter please read Alfred Edersheim's *Life and Times of Jesus the Messiah*. Dr. Edersheim goes at length in discussing "loosing and binding²" all to convey God's non-dualistic sovereignty without the possibility of a rogue agent, namely Satan, which was proposed to oppose God by those who believed in dualism.

I say that Jesus gently respected and implemented the idea of "formulae" for exorcisms as understood by first-century Chrestoi and Jews. Jesus followed the formulae, revealing his sufferance to the incompleteness of such mysticisms within exorcisms. This earmarks the title of Son of Man where he took on all of the fallacies of man while his title "Son of God" is his authority over heaven and earth. Yet, by his true healing hand did he fulfill and reveal his role and the role of the Holy Spirit in the prophecy of Joel 2:25–32. This passage is somewhat shrouded in apocalyptic verbiage but is fulfilled soon after Jesus' resurrection in Acts 1:11. The Holy Spirit is doing his work now on earth to confirm the power of healing, exorcisms, preaching the gospel through the martyrs of the first-century church with signs and wonders. The Holy Spirit's power at that time (ca. AD 35 to 100) was expressed in Palestine and in foreign lands. They continued Jesus' work by casting out or "loosing" those who were "bound" to a litany of sins. They experienced hearing the gospel in foreign languages that were intelligible and understood.

2. "*loosing* (Hebrew: Asar [prohibit, restrain])" and "*binding* (Chittir [to permit")" Life and Times of Jesus the Messiah, ii; 84, 85 and also ii 645.

SATAN'S END/JESUS FULFILLMENTS

Satan's teleology

Therefore, the binding of the "demon possessed" in the first century would be "loosed" by Jesus and his disciples, i.e., the first church martyrs. It was, therefore, in Jesus' "name" or *shem* that his exorcising power would continue with his disciples through the Holy Spirit, which is the seal of God upon these precious martyrs. If there was any "evil," as we symbolically call "evil (falsely understood as evil in and of itself)," the first-century onlookers would have witnessed the "loosing," or "setting loose," of that which God had bestowed. Many of these onlookers became believers due to the ordained demoniacs for which Jesus remedied by *casting out* the known demons by which the possessed housed them (cf. Mark 1: 21-28). Such is the case for Jesus as both the looser or releaser of the possessed and binder of the unclean spirit[3].

I find it necessary to categorize this chapter under 3 Noble Truths: (1) Prophetic View, (2) Predestination, and (3) The Apocalyptic View

1. I say "The Prophetic View" to illuminate the fulfillment of the only one who can release the captive spirits who are in prison (1 Peter 3:19: "After being made alive, He went and made (Himself) a proclamation to the imprisoned spirits." That is, Jesus resurrected to prove his Godship and with that power *and then* he visited the spirits in bondage.

2. I say "Predestination" because God the Father predestined the salvation of the preordained spirits in prison (i.e., the spirits were still "in" bondage and not yet eternally with God's "pre-horizon" or eternal form. Therefore, in the Father's *predestined* plan, his *preordained* children, prior to their births, that *"in the fullness of time,"* would be on stage and setting to reveal Jesus, the Son of God, the Christ who was the only one who could "release/loose" their infirmities. By their sins he was preached. By the exorcisms of Jesus, the power of heaven was found "lacking" amongst the Sanhedrin.

3. I say "The Apocalyptic View" because it is Jesus who *reveals* to us/ *takes off the cover of blindness* that he is the one who fulfills his Father's works and fulfills the prophecies by which he is known to be

---

3. cf. Twelftree, "In the Name of Jesus," 40, 48, 113, 114; 112-28.

the Messiah. We no longer need to be in darkness as to who God is. He is known as Emmanuel – God who is among us – i.e., Jesus.

Note on the terms of the heathen:

The heathen tongue and their veracity with scripture

(the pagan's view is the mother of our natural understanding)

pagan (n.)

Origin of term "pagan" ca. AD 1200– from Late Latin *paganus*— "pagan." In classical Latin: a "villager, rustic; civilian, non-combatant."

Noun use of adjective meaning "of the country, of a village," from *pagus* "country people; province, rural district," originally "district limited by markers," thus related to *pangere* "to fix, fasten" (from PIE root *pag-* "to fasten," a peg set to "stake" or "border where the villagers live).

Pagan is seen as an adjective from early 15c. and the religious sense often was said in 19c. to derive from conservative rural adherence to the old gods after the Christianization of Roman towns and cities; but the Latin word in this sense predates that period in Church history, and it is more likely derived from the use of *paganus* in Roman military jargon for "civilian, incompetent soldier," which Christians (Tertullian, ca. AD 202; Augustine ca. AD 350) picked up with the military imagery of the early Church (such as *milites* "soldier of Christ," etc).

Chapter Fifty-Seven

The Importance of Understanding Platonic Vocabulary as *praeparatio evangelii*

HERE WE TAKE A look at the Greek's view of souls that are "free" to flow in a "kind" of quality vs. the souls that are limited and "bound" in another kind of immovability or lack of motion. I find it interesting that we return to a type of "loosing and binding" that only Jesus could do as an exorcist-Messiah.

I would like to explain the Greek idea that led to Christian language borrowings for the "sons of *apeitheias*" found in 2 Corinthians 4:4, that is, the sons of "immovability, sluggishness, tardiness, unrepentance, incapable of flowing with the *boule* of righteous living, etc."

For a heavier reading on "the hinderer" as the dragon, serpent, devil, etc., one should read Calvert Watkins's, *How to kill a Dragon*, where Dr. Watkins explains "hindrance" (from the societal ideas of "stoppage") such as the stoppage of waterways (or the human soul) which plenish their respective cultures—and the reason why certain cultures pray to their serpent or dragon deity.

In conjunction with Dr. Watkin's work, I used the great dialogues of Plato from the Greek Text found in the Loeb Classics.[1]

SET ONE OF "MOTIONS"

dei'on: "obligation" (root: "to go through")

de'o (root of *dei'on*): "to bind" as a prisoner or animal (Matt 18:18) (cf. "*deismos*" as cognate)

blaberon (cognate)

---

1. Plato; *Cratylus*; 121; vs. 418.

IMPORTANCE OF UNDERSTANDING PLATONIC VOCABULARY

SET TWO OF "MOTIONS"

Plato says that these particular names signify the principle of arrangement and motion

owe-fee'-lee-mohn: "useful'

lusitelon: "profitable'

kerdalay'on: "gainful'

agathon: "good'

ksoom-fe'ron: "advantageous'

euphoron: "prosperous'

SET THREE OF MOTIONS

zaymeeoh'dayce: "that which binds motion'—in a good way (halting from trouble)
(Other spelling: *daymioh'dayce* = good)

SET FOUR OF MOTIONS

hay.doe.nay: "pleasure" (cf. "hedonism")
lupay: "pain'

epithumea: "desire'

SET FIVE OF MOTIONS

haydonay: "the action that tends towards advantage" (root of *haydonay*: *eonay* – PN – to breathe)
lupay: "dissolution of the body which takes place through the process of pain'

ania: "sorrow'—that which hinders motion (root to *ania*: *algaynos*, "distress," "having a hard time'

SET SIX OF MOTIONS

odu'nay: "grief; putting on the pain"
aksthaydon: "vexation," as in weight

aksthos: "burden," as vexation of weight put upon motion[2]

SET SEVEN OF MOTIONS

doxa: "opinion."[3] I.e., "shooting for the goal or intention to meaning without knowledge or certainty as of yet"). In Plato's dialogue, *doxa* comes from the pursuit (*dioxis*) that the soul carries on as it pursues the knowledge of the nature of things, or, most likely, from the "shooting of the bow" (*toxon*);[4] i.e., though we can't say for sure that we have hit the mark, we are aiming with good intention.
oi.'ay.sis: "belief'—the sense of the motion of the soul *towards* the essential nature of every individual thing (i.e., trajectory; intention; goal towards some*thing*; from the universal to the particulars [from the heavenly to the earthly, I might add])

Just as *oi.ay.sis* acts in its motion, so does *boulay*.

boulay: "intention'—denotes "shooting" (*bolay*)

boulesthai: "wish'

bouleu'esthai: "plan" = denoting "aiming at something'

SET EIGHT OF MOTIONS

kara: "joy'
diakoosis: "of the flow of the soul'

terpsis: "delight'

---

2. Plato, *Cratylus*, 125; 420, B, 5.

3. P.I.E. *op* – "to choose;" cf. "option;" Latin: "to desire, to pray for, choose;" Proto-Italic: *opeje*- "to choose, to grab," from P.I.E. *hopeie*- "to choose, grab," etc., Hittite: *epp/app* – "to take, grab;" *avestan*: "has reached, reached for."

4. Cf. Ascham, *Toxophilus – The School of Shooting* and *Toxophilus*.

IMPORTANCE OF UNDERSTANDING PLATONIC VOCABULARY

terpnon: "creeping of the soul," "delightful" (page: 123; vs. 419) (root of *terpnon, -pnoay [pne-]* = "breath")

eufrosy'ne: "mirth" = ("harmony with all things universe) (*eu* – well; good + *synay* – all things "summed"/"joined" (together)

epithymee.ah: "desire;" *thymos* = *thysis* = "boiling over; boiling of;" "*ee. oo.sa* = "goes into *thymos*" – cf. below with above

SET NINE OF MOTIONS

hay.'me.roos: "longing;" "the day" (root: *hay.'mee + rous*)
hay.mee.ros = *emera* + *roos* = longing for the flow; the flow that goes away; takes away; the "rush away as a stream from the soul;" "yearning" (cf. *hay.meh.nos*)

pothos: "yearning'

allothi pou: "that which is elsewhere'

hay.me.roos: "present (object)," "the day that has come upon.'

pothos: "absent'

eros: "flows in from out." (root: *esrei* = *eis* ["into'] + *roos* ["river'] = "flows into as a river [from an outside source]).

SET TEN OF MOTIONS

aboulia: "evil;" "without intention," "ill-advised." The "a" is an alpha privative, a Greek prefix for making negative, negating the meaning. So, *boulay* + alpha privative = *aboulay* – "evil;" "ill advised;" "without intention, plan, goal, desire, wish, trajectory;" therefore, a failure to hit the mark = cf. "sin" = Greek: *harmateia* = sin, senex, sine, *missing the mark (even if one planned to hit the mark)*

anankay: anagkay = *ana'g* ("g" takes the nasal/liquid- "n") *kay*) – "compulsion.'

hekou'sion: "voluntary." *Hekou'sion* comes "in line" with (and not in opposition to) the "events" of motion to the yielding (Greek: *eikon* = English: "icon").

anankay is the converse of *hekou'sion* and is "compulsory" and "resistant," which is contrary to the will and is associated with error and ignorance. *Anankay* is likened to walking through ravines (*ankay* (cf. "angst")), because they are hard to traverse, being rough and rugged, and ritard motion.

SET ELEVEN OF MOTIONS

Converse of noblest and their hindrance terms of motion
aletheia ("to *wander* with" + "god (goddess)" = "to wander with the God/ess"); "divine motion;" the divine motion of the universe.

pseudos: "the opposite of motion;" "held back and kept silent" – hence, associated with "slumberers'—*heu'dousi* (the addition of "*ps*" (or "*psi*"), says Plato through Socrates" daemon (i.e., deity mind), simply conceals the "slumber" word *heu'dousi*.

onoma: signifying "this is *a being about which* our search is.'

These eleven sets of motions lead us to the summation and setting forth of the gospel of Christ via the pagan's language: so, *aletheia*, truth, means "motion forward;" *pseudos* is known by being the opposite of "truth" (*aletheia*)—the slumber from divine motion, and Aletheia, the goddess of truth, wanders where she "will" – signifying what the divine wandering is about. She is open, evident, unconcealed, etc. Aletheia was a daughter of Zeus.

This summation gives us hints to the meanings of our New Testament theology within the Greek words used: nomos and onoma. Galatians 3:24 – "the nomos was our schoolmaster to bring us to Christ." *Nomos* is the law, where *onoma* is "name." Matthew 1:21 "You shall call His name (*onoma*) Jesus." The *Strong's Concordance* gives us the basic definition of "name"- "onoma" to mean "a name, authority, genealogy, character, cause'--etc. James Strong continues to say "According to Hebrew notions, a "name" is inseparable from the person to whom it belongs, i.e. it is something of his/her essence. Therefore, in the case of (the) God, it is specially sacred."

Jesus is the "name" of God represented on earth. His "motion" was *the* sign or *onoma* of God the Father's Will (*boulay*). The disciples followed or wandered with the name of God, the *onoma* of God-the-Father, aka, Jesus. Their "motion" driven by the God on earth followed in line with the narration of the universal divine motion of doing and fulfillment. *Pseudos*, to my view, sheds light on the "hated" mentioned in Romans 9. "Before they were born, God loved Jacob and *hated* Esau." The "slumber" is the meaning of Esau. As the Greek gives us *miseo* for "hate" in this passage of Romans 9, it does *not* say, "I, the Lord, despise you," rather, it means "dismiss," or "not included for the narrative."

THE GRAND HINDERER – THE ULTIMATE DEFINITION OF THE EUROPEAN/NEW TESTAMENT SATAN

So, I continue by asking, *who* is this "god"? Well, he walks, talks, rules, blinds, and acts, acts within this age, this time, this duration, this era, this aeon.

This is most important to understanding what he is by name. Demon. *D'-mn* is the Proto Indo-European (P.I.E.) root for "divider of time" + "god" in Dr. Joseph Shipey's work on P.I.E. roots to the English Language.

Chronos, as in "time" and "god" most certainly fits the bill for "the Satan" as "tempo" or "tempter." Chronos "consumes" us all in his "divisions" of time. His consort/bride is Ananke. Ananke was given a tremendous treatment in Plato's *Cratylus*. She/it is the field of thorns and thicket by which one traverses for one's erotic fulfillment at the end of such a telegraph. The outcome is never what it seems to be in one's hopes and initial desires. One is "hindered" from the *boule* of God and brought into a field of quagmire and stoppage.

It is in the here and the now that "the divider" acts. That is, both in space and in tempo. Should it be a wonder therefore, that the Latin Vulgate gives us the Latin *tempus* for "temptation." It means "to be strung across time, to be stretched, pulled, torn, divided, rent, —i.e. *tempo*-ed" ... or, "across-timed" (i.e., you have been tested in *duration* your faith).

James 1:13,14 – "[let] no one being tempted (Greek: *peirazomenos*; Latin: *tempo*—put through trials, dragged, pulled through (in this age/time/duration)) say, "By God I am being tempted—for God cannot be tempted and He tempts no one. A man is tempted (*peirazetai*—drawn out, pulled through, dragged, put through) by his own desire (*epithymias*—passions that drive one), being drawn away and being enticed (*deleazo*— "baited," "lured") . . . *then*, desire [or your passions], having conceived, gives birth to sin (*harmateia*—that which misses the mark). Once sin has become fully grown it brings death." So, I'm immediately brought to the first chapter of Job in the dialogue of God and "the satan." The satan was given the boundary lines by which he could do his work, delimiting his authority, authorship, energy, work, etc. Satan was always known in the Farsi, old Hebrew, and old Slavic as a word that denotes "sifting without mental cognizance." Even when "the satan" in the book of Job answered YHVH as to what he was doing his reply was, "Going to and fro" (i.e., "meandering, roving"). In Zechariah 4:10 God's eyes were considered "the satans" because they rove in judgment.

The satan was governed by an overriding force and, in our terms, bound or limited in regard to that which he could "work" or "sift." In Isaiah 45:7ff. it is God who says, "I, the LORD, create both good and evil." The Hebrew translated here as "evil" is *ra'ah*, which means "falling down, destruction." So, it is God's essence that sets the ordained plan from the *tselem* (Hebrew: "image") but the "work of evil" is done by God's "*tool of evil*." Otherwise, "evil" would exist in God and creation would have evil in its essence via its creator, which has an essence of evil. If this is the case, the creation would fall apart, by the very meaning of *ra'ah* (Hebrew: "collapse;" "break down").

Chapter Fifty-Eight

Satan Is God's "Cookie Cutter"

EVIL ENTERED HOLY CREATION through sin. But this has nothing to do with an idea of what we think "free will" means. If Jesus was the lamb slain from the foundation of the world (Revelation 13:8) then Jesus was a part of the holy act of creation—*including* the evil that man would do in order to put him on the ordained cross. In other words, all that was in the mind of God to create, from the beginning to the end, and *all* of the sequences of events in the middle were set in place *before* they happened, and this is *good* ("good" from Hebrew *tov*, meaning "beneficial," "builds upon itself," "anabolic," "supports itself and the next step"). *Tov* or "good," as the Hebrew mind conveys, is not necessarily happy, and may not fit into the plans of sinful humanity, but it is *beneficial* in the overarching plan of God.

If we can agree to see how scripture is coherent here then we can conclude that the scripture conveys a predeterminer, i.e., God. Looking at scripture from this view, God did not sin but ordained the "archons" or "rulers" in his grand narrative to put Jesus to death. Such an act of "wicked men's hands" was ordained from the predeterminate will prior to creation. This was not an act of man's "free will" but an act of ordination by God. If men could have chosen not to execute Christ, we would never have salvation. Therefore, the wickedness of man was necessary. "Him [Jesus], being delivered by the determinate counsel (*te boule* = "the will") and [also] the foreknowledge of God . . ." (Acts 2:23). This verse goes on to speak of the "narrative" by which the "actors" do indeed put Jesus to death— "ye have taken [Jesus], and by wicked hands have crucified and slain." But the wicked *acted* as ordained by God, for the salvation of creation. Again, Revelation 13:8 makes it clear that Jesus is the lamb that was slain from the foundation of the world (i.e., at the "creation point" our God-Father *Willed* [*boule*] Jesus be put to death). Moreover, Revelation 13:1–8 "un-caps" (*apo* = "off" + *kalypto* = "cap that covers") the kingdoms of the earth for whom power was given (by God) to mock God in his holy temple service: Babylon-Persia (lion), Greece (leopard), and Rome (bear) only to reveal that they were not in charge, that the world was His stage for meaning. Not just the heathen nations mentioned in the Bible but us, as to how we should play out. As Revelation 13 continues we read that there is yet another beast that had, now has not, but will again have a power likened to that of the first. I believe this first beast was Babylon led by the "god-king" with various names for the various cultures which called him by their view of him: Nimrod/Nebrod/Marduk/Enmerker/Narmer. In any case, it is "new Babylon" with its final system of worship, much like that of the old kingdom where *all* bowed to Nimrod. This time, though, the "system" would be a full-on contagion that marks the world with his power. Anyone not worshiping his system (i.e., not "receiving the mark of his likeness") should be put to death. I remember studying the Sumerian/Babylonian word for such a mark or "demarcation" of power. The Sumerian word was called: "ME." It is not to be confused with "me" in English (yet ironically, exactly what it is). The Sumerian word "ME," as defined by Dr. John Halloran, meant: "essence, function, office, responsibility, ideal norm; the phenomenal area of a deity's power; divine power; divine decree; cult [the culture beset by the norm of operations]; silence as to anything against such a system."

Such a *system* was *ordained* yet the "authority" by which it stands was already mentioned here in reference to Ephesians 2:2— "The ruler of authority of the air *is* the spirit now working in the sons of disobedience." Also read on in 2 Corinthians 4:4 in which the Bible speaks of "the god of this *aeon*" is the spirit of antiChrist. This same *archonta* ("*arch*" or "*head*" or "*Leader*") of the "authority (exousia – existence)" of the air (aeros– air (that which we "breathe")) is Satan as a "roaring lion." All to say, we "breathe" the "anima" of the existence of antiChrist as disobedient children. In all such cases, this Satan character is the head of the *cosmokriton* (world) and *aeon* (age) but not the kingdom of men as we see in Daniel 4:17. All men, *whether in the faith or not*[1], experience the roaring lion, Satan, in the world. In 1 Peter 5:8 says, "Be sober, be vigilant; because your adversary the devil, as a roaring lion, walketh about [just as the Satan in

---

1. i.e., the "witness" to all.

Job], seeking whom he may ["be allowed," acting according to his nature, to] devour: Whom [Satan] resist steadfast in the faith, knowing that *the same afflictions are accomplished in your brethren that are in the world*" (cf. Philippians 2:13; Psalms 138:8).

Is this not universalism? Is this not sovereignty? From the oldest book in the Bible to the New Testament, that is, the book of Job to Revelation, we have agreement as to how Yahweh uses Satan to do YHVH's desire.

This "satanic-Chronos" devouring is done on all humankind TO "accomplish" us. We have read this all wrong in English, especially the American language which has less regard for its European etymologies.

Can we not see how our language, encased in pagan antiquity, has yelled out our very plight? We read the narrative of the Bible in us and in pagan antiquity. The Bible simply tells us what has already happened to us and why. It tells us what will happen. Why do we resist such a beautiful thing? It is because our deeds are evil and we will not be exposed or reminded of our actions which would hinder us all day long.

Another example is *prophecy*. Unless everything goes perfectly (that is: *willed ra'ah* ["evil'] and *tov* ["good']), then prophecy could never come about. Consider Daniel (in chapters 8 and 9), who prophesies an exact number of years before the Messiah comes back, concerning the seventy-sevens/*shavua* (490 years) from decree to Jesus and the final seven years (*shavua*) of the 490 being Revelation's final 7 years. Unless Nehemiah was given a decree by Artaxerxes, the Persian King, to go back into Jerusalem and rebuild the temple then we wouldn't have the final prophetical event of Daniel, i.e., of Christ, to the day, riding into Jerusalem as King of kings. One act requires the next and so on. "Seventy Shavua [490 years] are determined upon thy people ... from the going forth of the commandment to rebuild Jerusalem [historically, we know that this was ca. 445 BC] *until the Messiah* will be sixty-nine *shavua* [483 years] (Daniel 9:24)." This puts Jesus arguably at AD 34–38, depending on the calendrical formulas proposed by numerous "calendricists." After this, the sons of disobedience (sons of the prince/antichrist) will destroy the temple (at Jerusalem—ca. AD 70). Then, at a future date, antiChrist will confirm a "covenant" for seven years —that is, the last *shavua*.

So, these events are "mathematically" set at the beginning of Daniel's prophecy to us. Daniel lived as a Persian captive who knew Persian astrology and probably taught this prophecy to the Persian Magi. Even the horrors of Herod slaughtering all of the children under two years of age (prophesied by Jeremiah [31:15] and fulfilled in Matthew 2:16–18) was a necessary evil to drive Mary, Joseph, and an unborn Jesus to Egypt. Daniel very well could have told the Magi where Jesus would be residing as a paideon (little toddler/little "footer")—otherwise, the Magi were told directly by God. As to the incarnation of Christ's birth, please refer to my 10-part audio lecture series on my site under "Christ of the Zodiac/Vanderbilt Lectures" (as well as my audio interview with Dr. David Lawrence called: "The Finnish Mazzaroth").[2]

Either way, all of these chain events could not be at "random" if the scriptures concerning prophecy are about what *will* happen unto the fullness of meaning. There are no dates that the heathen, atheist, agnostic, or anyone has placed on the prophecy of Daniel that would nullify the coming of Christ on a donkey and being praised as the king of kings.

---

2. Jones, "Christ of the Zodiac"; Jones, "Finnish Mazzaroth."

Chapter Fifty-Nine

The Scapegoat and the Sacrifice: (*A Universal Theme of Christ*)

IN CERTAIN PRIMITIVE RITUALS, our ancestors enacted the dying god as scapegoat, that is, the god worshiped (as enacted as the village's god) impersonated the guileless, naive-innocent. That is, the roles are reversed and it is the god identified as the "nascent-minded," "idiot" or "fool." This seemingly *simple-minded one* or *village idiot* was selected usually for their meek nature which stood out—that is, a stick in the mud of the "not-so-innocent." The "idiot" in the enactment and reality was usually the smartest one in the group and was able to escape the ego-contagion of the villagers until it was his time to be sacrificed due to the fervor of the "satanic contagion." "He's just an idiot, leave him alone." Such a social "idiot" was displayed in William Golding's *Lord of the Flies* in the character Piggy where this innocent becomes the sacrifice. Another example of the village innocent or village *idiot* (one's own-to see things singularly) can be found in the script to movie, "The Wicker Man." This story depicts a reverent Christian police officer looking for a lost child only to find out that he was lured to an island to be sacrificed to the fertility god(s) by a pagan village.

In James Frazier's classic work, *The Golden Bough*, the "idiot" is seen to bring attention to himself or herself by way of their purity. They are the village clowns, the pure of mind, the ones who are like children. Dismissal for such an idiot is natural. Hatred and/or jealousy has its part too. Such a release of tension from the tribal fury is put on the awkward one or "idiot."

We should know from our youthful school days when the focus of the group collective or "clique" was set upon "that different one" or the one who "stands out." The group projects its own "iniquities" onto the "other–the idiot." The more a group amplifies the contagion of hate projected onto the idiot, the less focus is placed on its own inadequacies. Therefore, "naturally" and brutally does the community mock, despise, put their judgment to, discard, dismiss, etc., the village or community "fool" or "idiot.[1]

Anthropologist Rene Girard coins the terms "satanic contagion" or "mimetic contagion" for the acts of collective hate. Furthermore, these collective feelings must have an object of desire—that is, *idolatry* (Greek: "eido-latreia "what the *eyes (eido) serve (latreia)*"). I call this process "social cannibalism." It is here that lust becomes rage/wrath (orge [from where we have "orgasm']) meeting that of sexuality. Collectively speaking, it is an *orgy of hate* upon the object of desire—i.e., the collective rage put upon the innocent, the virgin, the child, the untouched, the undefiled, etc.

Naturally, social cannibalism attempts the enactment of resurrection. We see this in the story of Persephone and Hades' agreement of resurrecting in cycles (the cosmogonic cycle) or that of the Sumerian Dumuzi after being in the underworld for an arguable period of days. We kill and want resurrection. We desire the ability to resurrect but we cannot resurrect on our own. As James Frazier's complete works on sacrifice of the innocent, Rene Girard's books on the Scapegoat and the sacrifice of the innocence, William Golding's "Lord of the Flies," Joseph Conrad's "Heart of Darkness," all point out our primitive natures to filter out the weak through a tribal business mentality eliminating the weakest. Ultimately, as Girard points out: the *satanic contagion*[2] drives humanity to its demise.

The Satanic Contagion, as dubbed by Girard, calls for something "beyond" the natural call for dominance. There is a power greater than the tribal elder whose "power" was regarded as a "warrior who could

---

1. Fyodor Dostoevsky wrote a novel called *The Idiot* based on his fictional character Lev Nikoayevich Myshkin, whose Christ-like persona led to people judging him for being an idiot. Dostoevsky wanted to provide a litmus test within his novel of pure good amongst a chaotic world. Dostoevsky describes the Christ-like Myshkin as "the positively good and beautiful man." "Idiot" in the Greek means, "eido + tace" or "what I see is what I place." In many ways, "idiot" can convey "holy."

2. the sickness of sin that has infected all of the world creating a group collective mindset evocating self-preservation as the prime need.

subdue." In Rome, a "legion" was a large number of Roman soldiers estimated ca. 5 to 6 thousand fighting men. So, when "legion" is mentioned as a "demonic force" in Luke 8, the early Church had associations of this kind of power. Yet, we see a pathetic legion fleeing from the presence of Christ into a herd of pigs/swine which were known in Christ's day as a *chthonic*[3] taxi. That is to say, the herd of swine were seen not only in Christ's day but in our most primitive representations as the carrier of souls to hell (or the underworld); Luke 8.[4]

We need a god/God who will resurrect and overcome an overwhelming and inherited multiplicity of desires which drive our wills to enact the mimetic contagion of social cannibalism.

Read the Old Testament, Sir James Frazier's works, Rene Girard, Kerenya, Joseph Campbell, etc., and find out what only the Gospels answer. In the Gospels you will find the genius of the true God, the undying God, that resolves our double vision. We enact the prophecy of Christ by doing everything else but what Jesus did.

The True Scapegoat and Sacrifice are found in Isaiah 53.

> (1) Who has believed our report? And to whom has the arm of the LORD been revealed?
>
> (2) For He grew up before him like a young plant, and like a root out of dry ground; He had no form or majesty that we should look at Him, and no beauty that we should desire Him.
>
> (3) He was despised and rejected by men, a man of sorrows and acquainted with grief; and as one from whom men hide their faces He was despised, and we esteemed Him not.
>
> (4) Surely He has borne our griefs and carried our sorrows; yet we esteemed Him stricken, smitten by God, and afflicted.
>
> (5) But He was pierced for our transgressions; He was crushed for our iniquities; upon Him was the chastisement that brought us peace, and with His wounds we are healed.
>
> (6) All we like sheep have gone astray; we have turned—every one—to his own way; and the LORD has laid on Him the iniquity of us all.

---

3. underworld.
4. For further study on this, see C.K. Kerenya's work on Eleusis.

(7) He was oppressed, and He was afflicted, yet He opened not his mouth; like a lamb that is led to the slaughter, and like a sheep that before its shearers is silent, so He opened not his mouth.

(8) By oppression and judgment He was taken away; and as for His generation, who considered that He was cut off from the land of the living, stricken for the transgression of my people?

(9) And they made His grave with the wicked and with a rich man in his death, although He had done no violence, and there was no deceit in His mouth.

(10) Yet it was the will of the LORD to crush Him; He has put him to grief; when His soul makes an offering for guilt, He shall see his offspring; He shall prolong His days; the will of the LORD shall prosper in His hand.

(11) Out of the anguish of His soul He shall see and be satisfied; by His knowledge shall the righteous one, my servant, make many to be accounted righteous, and he shall bear their iniquities.

(12) Therefore I will divide Him a portion with the many, and He shall divide the spoil with the strong, because He poured out His soul to death and was numbered with the transgressors; yet He bore the sin of many, and makes intercession for the transgressors.

Conclusion: hope in Christ is the hope in the God who was ordained to be slain from the foundation of the world: "And all that dwell upon the earth shall worship *him*, whose names are not written in the Book of Life of the *Lamb slain from the foundation of the world*" (Revelation 13:8).

As I have addressed already, Romans 10:9–11 makes it clear that those who confess and believe that Jesus is Lord shall be saved. Shall not all that dwell on the earth worship him? I conclude here that the Book of Life must mean something of a figuration to the temple census of the tribes of Israel and Judah or a *toledoth* which is a list of genealogies by which the houses of Israel and Judah were accounted for. In Hebrew, *toledoth* means "generations" or "genealogy." *Toledoth* is the second word in the sixth weekly Torah portion of reading in which the Parasha tells of the conflict of Jacob and Esau as well as Isaac's passing off his wife Rebekah as his sister, and Isaac's blessing of his sons. My focal point of the Parasha is to mention that in Romans 9:13 God says "Jacob have I loved (*eygapeysa* from *agape*) and Esau have I hated (*emisaysa* from *miseo*, "to dismiss")."

I should for a moment address again the root word *miseo*. Esau was "dismissed" from the stage and setting of God in the Old Testament. The point is that Esau (i.e. the Arabic tribes of the ancient Near East up to present day) are the generations (*toledoth*) of Ismael and they were not promised to bring the promised seed of salvation. In this sense they were dismissed from the narrative of the prophecy of the Messiah. The scriptures teach us that Christ would be "brought forth" through a Jewish line (Jacob's line). It is here that we look to the *prophetical view* as one of the noble truths: Isaiah 7:14 makes this Jewish line clear all the way into the Gospels: "Therefore the Lord Himself shall give you a sign; Behold, a virgin shall conceive, and bear a son, and shall call His name Immanuel (Hebrew: "God is among us"). This scriptural rectification of "*hate before they were born*" can be clearly seen in God's sovereign plan. Think of the worst "hate" you've experienced. It probably wasn't someone yelling at you. It was probably from someone or some group who "dismissed" (*miseo*) you from their company. You were "put away" from their company. Maybe you were "dismissed" from a class due to your conduct or bad grades. This is an overwhelming feeling, but it does not take hope away. Or, a girlfriend or boyfriend who broke up with you with or without good reason—this can definitely be an example of "hate" or *miseo*.

There's always hope with Jesus. Might I add that those painful events that we feel over time are all aimed to complete the fullness of God's meaning. To understand this is to understand the *telos, pro'horidzo, prophetayce, apocatastasis*, and universal salvation of God.

Recap:

Recapping my "values" system and summarizing our journey. to: I end with hope. I am obviously inclined to show how Jesus is at the center of everything, as Colossians 1:14–17 states. He is the one through whom creation comes and the one for whom it is made. He is the *telos*, or the fullness of meaning. Jesus is the "all in all" ([*apocalyptic* and *apokatastasis*] Colossians 3:11). Jesus is not bound to culture, religion, creed, race, tongue, time, space etc. Rather, Jesus fulfills *all* meaning *in himself*. *All things* lead from, by, to, for, and of *him*. Therefore, our *telos* (fullness of meaning) is to be[5] conformed to his image (the fullness of meaning) and united to him (*apokatastasis*). That ties in with *predeterminism* and *telos* with Christ. Jesus will take all things back unto himself (*universal salvation*), from whence all things were created, wrap them in his gracious arms and by his protective holy covering, *he* shall give us back to origin of intent, that is, the Father (*apokatastasis*) in that all things may be returned in their original state ([apokatastasis]cf. 1 Corinthians 15:28).

Divine providence is demonstrated through Jesus on the cross—in which natural animosity/human rebellion against God *reaches its height in its "natural decision"*[6] to rebel and murder the innocent one. Yet, this "natural decision" was a predetermined plan of God (Acts 2:23: "Him [Jesus], being delivered by the determinate counsel *and* foreknowledge of God (Father), you have taken, and *by your wicked hands* [your hands = the *tools* by which the cutting must be done], have crucified and slain [him] (*predestination/prophetic/teleos*)." As we see, this "wickedness" was "determined"/predetermined and "foreknown" by God/Father. We see that this "delivered over" to these "wicked hands" was ordained and foreknown by God. The importance of these unimaginable horrors to the natural man forces the unbeliever to question "why." That is, what is the *teleos*, teleology" or aetiology[7] of the thing? Only if these heinous "acts" were unfurled into time would we have the meaning of resurrection as an *apocalyptic* event. Such heinous acts revealed the hidden *telos* of humanity and creation from the foundation of the world. All such "acts" were predetermined with the intent of the Father.

---

5. Even "those" who are "not written in the book of life" will worship him. What is this saying? "All that confess that Jesus is Lord shall be saved and believe in your heart that God raised him from the dead shall be saved" (Romans 10:9). The argument now falls upon the apocalyptic usage of the Hebrew "Tsaror" or "Book of Life" because the *mode of salvation* has been completed upon those "who confessed that Jesus is Lord."

6. Rene Girard's "Satanic Contagion/Satanic Mimesis"; cf. my lecture on "Social Cannibalism" on my site: fomcm.com

7. etiology or aetiology = "science of causes or causation." Greek: *aitia*: "cause"; Proto-Indo-European: *ai-t-ya = ai – "to give, allot" + -*logia = "a speaking; "origin."

Chapter Sixty

The Five Noble Truths Summed

THE FIVE NOBLE TRUTHS posited in this book's preface (predestination, universal salvation, apocalyptic view, prophecy, and teleology) are to be read as a "sandwich" or a "stacking"[1] when circumnavigating the scripture.

Biblical Greek, borrowed secular ancient and contemporary koine Greek, the Tanakh (Hebrew Old Testament), Latin, and Aramaic (esp. in the Peshitta) support these Five Noble Truths. The languages and cultures created a matrix or hologram by which Jesus could speak through. He fulfilled the Christian paradigm in doing so.

Our biblical parents represented in the *Jewish* localization could only speak contemporaneously to the customs, languages, religion, socio-economic, and superstitions of the day. They understood more of what Jesus was referring to in his day than we could occidentally comprehend. Not just intellectually, but on a familiar level that would have touched the childlike nature in all of us. Even today, his words command without commanding a call to innocence.

The consistent limitation of cultural barriers and hardships echoed through scripture as a constant resounding theme, with real stories and the names to fit them. Such characters, names, meaning of names, geographical and emotional landscapes, diverse legal boundaries, etc., all poured into a cauldron by which a narrative of "true-ness" could be sensed on a visceral level. It is his Narrative[2] that holds a *reality with inner*

---

1. I do like the idea of "sandwiching" or "stacking" because the term offers separate ways to read the scripture. Sandwiching implies a "stacking" upon each other bringing forth a new paradigm of biblical sight.

2. I capitalized Narrative to express the "Gospel" within the Gospels. There is

consistency. Such an "inner consistency," which rings true to history and the biblical narrative, matches that of outlining history that we continue to construct. Whether *neighboring* (to the Jewish and Christians) secular, heathen, pagan, mystae, or gnostic sources of language, the "trueness" of these archaic word usages are wrapped into their own histories. Whatever means by which they were accessed, the New Testament authors deemed these borrowed languages as good enough to be Christianized. Such a rich endeavor to study biblical history through the medium of its borrowed words!

Such a pocket of time which is true to itself, and surrounding outer realities of history, does indeed confirm other historical secular realities. The Bible is an account of good history that saves you. Such pregnant biblical words are these! Heavy laden are they with meaning as they were used in the days of Christ for him alone to speak through. Such a linguistic womb waited for language's birth to occur through, by, and into one physical man, Jesus.

For sure, these pregnant words have unfurled eternity's force upon us all taking the Gospel into the modern world. This I call the eternal logos. Such "archaisms" have humbled us all for our lack of breadth, width, scope, and dimensionality without his narrative to clarify meaning itself. Yet, Jesus poetically bound such seeming entropies into order through the drama of his stage in his Gospel years to us. He, Jesus Christ, is the ultimate joy found in our words of *strong limitations*, squelching the "noise" out of our fallen flesh meanwhile expressing his eternal being[3].

OSTENSIBLE MADNESS AND RE-CONFIGURING REALITIES

In our current society we are barraged by the challenges of seeming biblical contradictions or scriptural antinomies[4]. These perceived biblical

---

"another" Gospel, not in any way different or in opposition (only supportive) to the Gospels that can be found in the reconstructive process of exegesis, eisegesis, normative claims, using tangential historical facts, linguistic affiliations, etymons, contemporary mythological verisimilitudes, the anthropological end to the answer for the ultimate sacrifice and/or scapegoat, etc. that tell the tale of Jesus Christ.

3. I.e., we are "reduced" to *only* seeing God's majesty. It is interesting that "holy"— "holos" in Greek means *"without mixture'*—this is the very meaning of the *linguistic noise reduction* unto the full limitation of meaning.

4. antinomy: a contradiction between two principles, statements, or conclusions that appeared to be reasonable.

contradictions usually occur at the failure to apply a scholarly approach but the lack of using the sandwiching of these Five Noble Truths which I have proposed throughout this work. I do believe that all theological contentions could be resolved with my offered approach. I also believe that holding a position with theological error would also have to go. That is to say I am claiming here that there is an ultimate non-contradictory truth called the WORD or LOGOS. We just have to whittle away the superimposed theologies that do not remain consistent to the WORD governing the manifested circumference of the original Hebrew and Greek Bible.

Imagine the ageless "versus" arguments such as: "free will" versus "predestination" versus "universal salvation," versus "damnation (and all of its hellologies)," etc. finally working together in a theological resolve and synergy.

When we finally understand that God predestined our very thoughts, feelings, salvation, responses, reactions, evil, and good *unto* a *salvific end*, i.e., our *"teleon"* and *"apokatastasis,"* we can then have the blessed assurance (the hope) that our relationship is secured in our saviour. I am more careful than ever to state that "sin" is a determined "act" within nature. Nature sins "naturally" against God when required to act within the boundary lines of the "kingdom"—*basileou*— "walk/foot/basis/podos" of God. Our natures are determined/ordained to sin against God. Our natures are made to show us that we cannot "choose" God by our nature. Our nature is ordained to be burned off. Though this has been repeated in my work several times it is of utmost import that we understand that predestination is a marital term and pre-existing condition of our "once holy" state. Predestination is a condition that governs our return to that *once holy marriage*, i.e., our restoration or apokatastasis existence with God. We will one day (again) be completely *free from* the flesh and be able to "will" only God's Will. We are headed to this "freedom" in his Will and will be "free from" our deathly/fatal natures that can only choose death. Therefore, yes, sin is ordained of God, it is pre-ordained by him but only for our "coming to be" which uses our natures to calibrate us into his Son's image. Nothing exists without or outside of God, nothing, including sin which so many want to "rectify out" in terms of a western ill-defined ideology of "free-will" which we have covered somewhat extensively in this work.

Though still in our sin-natures we have "new found freedoms" to will from. These new-found freedoms are the infinite conditions by which we experience God's motions upon us. We find ourselves each day a less and less "limited" carnal state. We also find ourselves (here comes a mind bender →) more and more limited to the infinite possibilities of God.

This is a revelation (*apo* – "off" + *kalupto* – "cover;" "seal;" concealment; "hell") by the understanding of "marital-predeterminism" and not Calvinistic predestination for the few "select -elect." We (everyone will kneel and confess Jesus is Lord and be saved) are free from this aeon, or duration of hell on earth in his salvation but through his eternal fire which are sent for our limited duration on earth to be *purged unto* eternal life. This is the Gospel of grace without a ceiling. Be joyous and draw close to the one who loves you the most in all of creation. Yes, while we sin, we are still eternally his.

Chapter Sixty-One

Final words: Synthesizing vs. Sandwiching

Since we have covered the Five Noble Truths (5NT) I would like to juxtapose two terms that might or might not have been a relevant thought concerning exegeting the scripture. Let us now look at the differences between the *synthesizing* and *sandwiching* approaches.

It is not enough to look at scripture from a compressed sense of "synthesis" which narrows my vision down to "simply believing" what has been handed to me. In the synthesized "sense," our English version Bibles are much like what I complain "synthesis" to be. For example, a church official might approach you or someone concerning "their faith." They might say to you or someone you care about: "It's right there in the Bible" (as he hands you/your friend an N.I.V. or ESV Bible).

English "versions" are *synthesized* products. That is, they "place together" the Greek and English into a "composite" by which we are to accept the impossibility of a *one-to-one ratio* "translation" of the New Testament Greek to English "versions." Such English versions are configured with the Latin Vulgate, King James, Geneva, or Tyndale versions and are promoted as "the Bible." I do find this alone to be problematic to say the least.

Again, such English versions/"bibles" are the expressed synthesis as to what I am addressing here. Shockingly enough, you might find me to say that such versions of synthesis are not necessarily a bad thing when understood either in innocence, safehoused, or used as a launching pad for a deeper dive into the depths by which the English percolated out of. From my positivist point of view, the synthesized bible versions do offer a doorway to a greater responsible reading of scripture if one is inspired to purchase commentaries, lexicons, topical dictionaries, etc. The most important thing to take away from this chapter might be that only the original scripture can be denoted from. Connotations "at" the original or connotations "at" English *versions* can potentially start theological wars when looked at as "holy writ." This is how divisions were and are made within Christendom. Nonetheless, these divisions, are they not prophesied and ordained to come? I think so.

SEGWAY INTO THE "STACKING" OF THE APOCALYPTIC VIEW OF JESUS

Such eternal themes spoken from Christ in Revelation clue us into the *apocalyptic view*. We read the mode in which Christ spoke within two *meeting points*[1]. Both eternal and chronistic, Christ is able to convey His essence through his truth. Let's see what I mean.

Such an honest expression of this dynamic tension between us and our eternal Christ can be found in Revelation 2:1–29. Jesus both praises and condemns (*krima*/incriminates) the fallenness of his own significant earliest Church bodies. It seems that in the eyes of the Lord found here that many of the New Testament churches became heretical and "fell away" for a duration.

Whatever the state of "salvation" is, I find it most revealing when Jesus addressed the angel (evangelist/minister/church father) in Pergamum by saying: "These are the words of him who has the sharp, double-edged sword. (13) I know where you live—where Satan has his throne. Yet you remain true to my name. You did not renounce your faith in me, not even in the days of Antipas, my faithful witness, who was put to death in your city—where Satan lives. (14) Nevertheless, I have a few things against you: There are some among you who hold to the teaching of Balaam, who taught Balak to entice the Israelites to sin so that they ate food sacrificed to idols and committed sexual immorality." –Jesus Christ–

Jesus continues with his juridical charges from his holy eternal court. All fleshly acts are "incriminated" in his holy district. We read Jesus' words in Revelation 3:1–7 as he attributes the Church of Ephesus as being that Church which has not fatigued in its perseverance, intolerant of wicked people, tested those who are not apostles, yet, in all of this laudation, Ephesus has fallen. Jesus tells them in vs. 5 to repent and turn

---

1. Greek: *saymeio sunantaysayce* – "meeting point" [i.e., some kind of conveyed apocalyptic *hendiadys*].

to your first ways or "*I will come to you and remove your lampstand from its place. (6) But you have this in your favor: you hate the practices of the Nicolaitans, which I also hate.*"

So, it would *seem* that our *futuristic* Jesus "condemns" either from impersonal will, whim, or worse yet, a *conditional reaction* to those who sin. This, however, is not what is happening. Jesus was not speaking from the "future," He was speaking "*out of time.*" Jesus was speaking "apocalyptically." He was/is/will always be in the Hebrew "olam"; Jesus Christ is the alpha and omega as He speaks.

The Hebrews looked at olam as "beyond the horizon of measurement. The Greek Chronos was a parcel of time. It is a measurable, perceived sense of duration. Olam is beyond time or chronos.

The eternal Christ is where/when you were born and when you will die. He "is" "when" you sinned in the past "now." He is when/where you repented in the future. He is honest to his judgments and his judgments are true. Jesus is bound to the Father to condemn (indict/incriminate) and at the same existence, through his holiness, he has assumed the throne in grace not willing that any should perish but that all should inherit eternal life. Jesus is speaking that which is true. Was he supposed to be partial with sin at all even with the "best" of us? No. This is the point. The "acts" of righteousness which are the expressed nature of God through us are found in Philippians 2:13 "for it is God Who works in you to will and to act in order to fulfill His good purpose." We are "incriminated" in Jesus' court either way, we are "decided" upon as good actors and evil actors—sometimes/many times at the same time—especially as we see Jesus Christ speaking in the "apocalyptic form" or "apocalyptic poesis." Time is no more in Christ's time. All of us are both incriminated as sinners and "have been repented" by him, not ourselves. Nonetheless, we are all looked at from God's perspective, as both sinner and saint. In this apocalyptic vantage point, Jesus is not contradicting his nature but being true to his nature that he cannot lie when his eyes are upon the acts of humanity in time, over time, past, present, and future. His "trueness" can now be witnessed in the *seemingly* contradictory nature of the Jesus of Revelation.

One might look at it like this: You drive by a homeless person literally every day. Some days you have the time, patience, and generosity to stop at the inconvenience of yourself and those behind you who are just trying to get home to their families in order that you might give the homeless some money. Some days, however, you speed past, fail to engage eye contact, and hide behind other cars in the opposite lane from where the poor vagrant is asking for help just to "get through" this awkward situation. You have been judged good and evil in the timeless court of God. Thank Jesus that we are not to be proud of our "good works" and damned by our bad works.

Our confusion in reading the "face value" of the English or Greek Jesus is (1) in the exhibit of an *if- then* condition—which is the particularization by which we live in the here and now. (2) Jesus speaks eternally where eternal themes could not flow in contradiction by their very eternal "natures." (3) Revelation is the opposite of a "condition of "dualities" or "contradictions." Rather, Revelation is the meeting ground by which heaven and earth are paradoxically joined. Such a "place" needs "a language" by which eternity can transmit to the "time and space"—conditioned listener/reader. I see this "language" as being "spoken" prophetically, apocalyptically, pre-determinately, analogously and poetically (all "seen" in the apocalyptic view). In this third point we can try on the idea that the *apocalyptic approach* or *view* of reading scripture is a binding of heaven and earth using "honesty" to express "both sides," not in contradiction but in agreement of eternity and time.

We, through our temporal senses, have all too often defined a fictional "Jesus" into being. He is someone who is vengeful, wrathful, hubristic, lustful, proud, i.e., "*a Jesus*" who is more like them. What would remedy this opinion of the "judgmental Jesus" is within the apocalyptic approach of John's Revelation, for all things are past, though accounted, all things as Colossians 1:16–21 tell us that "all things were created in Him, all things in the heavens, upon the earth, whether thrones, powers, dominions rulers or authorities, all things through and unto Him have been created." Paul continues with the necessary contract that creation has with Jesus. Finally, in vs. 20 Paul says that "all created things will be reconciled (*apokatallazai*) to Him. . . ." This is the language that we must carry. This is creation's hope. It is the Gospel. This is also an apocalyptic truth if we know the end and the why of all things, that is, our existence is made to be saved. But saved from what? This question begs to ask and answer with "freedom" from the flesh, the world (*kosmokriton* – the world of judgments, hate, lies, etc.), the fated end of sin.

But here lies the truth of the matter: He exists out of time in John's apocalypse. He speaks "to the things as they are seen in all of their totality and in all of their particularizations. What a statement for the trueness of Jesus Christ's new position as his speech patterns are "caught" in John's Revelation.

So, we go forward in our time with human entropy that still resides in the "nature" of the believers in Christ such as the "angels" at Pergamum, Ephesus, Thyatira, Sardis, etc. of the first century. These are those who were contemporary "witnesses" either having seen Jesus in the flesh or a close second generation to which they had associations with several of the Gospel and/or Epistle writers! Yet, their natures fell. They were condemned, not unto eternal hell without hope but a pruning of their natural selves.

As we do so do they. All of the churches "fell short." All of them were "condemned" by the court of Christ. All shall stand trial. All shall be "sentenced." All shall be "rectified" unto righteousness, not by the will of our natures but by the Will of God.

Ephesians 2:8-9 "For by grace are ye saved through faith; and that not of yourselves: it is the gift of God. (9) Not of works, lest any man should boast."

Therefore, Christ is not reactionary, should I say "shocked," for he knows us as our creator. He knows our "dilemma" concerning the nature of the flesh and the longing for the soul to return home to its maker. So, our works are not capable of *saving or damning* us but to confirm our need for him. It is Christ eternal that speaks to us in the fullest sense. He saves us in the fullest sense. He is honest. He is true. He spans across eternity not bound to the god of the age. Christ's words settle all things anew both in earth and heaven.

THE DULL BLADES OF PLATO AND ARISTOTLE

Much like knowing[2] Plato's universal view of "coming to be into the ultimate reality," we can find through a healthy theological approach using the Five Noble Truths that Plato's work compliments Aristotle's anatomizing teleological view of the *thing* which acts, does, is, etc. etc. in this world of measurability.

The faulty view: likened to Aristotle, if we take scripture to only "anatomize" its message without "stacking" or "sandwiching" the Five Noble Truths we would subtract the *universal idea* or "the fullness of

---

2. i.e., *gn* or "joined"; Sanskrit: *jaina* – "to know"; "to be joined"; "sexually procreate," "genius," [*yoni*].

meaning" from that which the Bible is supernaturally expressing. Hence, we would be taking *faith* out of the picture knowing that faith *is the substance* of things hoped for. Furthermore, and etymologically speaking, "faith" finds its root meaning to be a kind of nest of substance by which we can rest in and launch out of. . . . cf. P.I.E. *bheidh.

Using Aristotle's reasoning, we would discount all biblical prophecy which is tethered to all things *provable* in scripture. Therefore, the immeasurable/unquantifiable God of scripture cannot factor into Aristotle's observation in the immediacy of "actions." This alone proves Aristotle's limitation. It takes faith to implement the 5NTs which allows us to circumnavigate scripture with a proper methodology.

Plato, on the other hand, can be without relation to the "motion of the thing" in the immediacy of time, yet capture/apprehend the full "apocalyptic view" because the "apocalyptic view" is Plato's universal view. Plato's problem with Aristotle was in Aristotle's immediacy of "observing[3]."

Plato's downfall with me concerning the Five Noble Truths is that Plato believed the "real world" was a flawed imitation of a perfect world of forms, accessible through reason. We have read in this work that even the "fallenness" of this creation is in perfect order unto his master plan. Therefore, God's reason and intent —which are pre-creation forms – are predestined to actuate or instantiate (which Plato did not believe in "real instantiations," only illusory representations of a single unitary existence). This means that all *things (tangible, intangible)* are not at all flawed but specifically meaningful or "full of meaning" as they are coming to be in their universal sense—or, "wholeness of being." But here I digress from Plato for he fought against meaning as we "see things."

On the other limited-hand, the Aristotelian view, i.e., the *anatomizing* or *particularizing* view, which most present-day secular universities are bound to, is an unsafe approach, theologically and apocalyptically speaking—that is: that which could only be seen, touched, tasted, smelled, felt, —a.k.a. sensory perceptions are limited to time and space.

If we only use the "the eternal sense of forms," i.e., the Platonic view that there are no real instances, only metaphysical forms reduced to "shadows" then we disregard the Aristotelian particulars" approach by which the Universal mass movement uses time/space to hold together a bending quantum "fabric"—therefore disregarding elements necessary

---

3. *eido*: "wit, witness, see, see at."

to defend scripture from a *particularized linguistic perspective* (such as knowing declensions, inflections, intonation, accent rules, syllabification, etc.).

I also look at the "fabric" by which God called out creation from: (Hebrew:the *tohu va bohu*) "formless and void" "waters" (*mayim* – Hebrew – "bacterial soup; urine; piss; semen") –cf. Strong's Concordance of Genesis's "waters" that the Holy Spirit hovered over in creation). Therefore, I also look at biblical *sandwiching* from the Aristotelian and Platonic view. This combination of both views of Aristotle and Plato can be somewhat of a correlative supporter, if taken from their "trueness" and strengths, of reason for the Five Noble Truths. Nonetheless, both views are not to be affiliated with my belief system, especially for Plato's belief in one of his major influencers, Parmenides, who believed that "all was one" as did Plato. Thus begins all of the entrapments of eastern philosophies as they found their way into western "philosophies" and religions.

Therefore, I could not make a Platonic/Aristotelian *synthesized* case for the Bible (from both sides) for in all of their extensive human reasoning, they still do not give us a wholesome answer for biblical reason nor metonymic usage by which we could "deduce" as analogue or "imaginative" of the universal Christ. Having grown up with Aristotle and Plato (Plato's works especially), it pains me to say that to use such blunt philosophical tools as these great philosophers for biblical exegesis is to *i*mpede the sense of *rous* or "flow" of sensory meaning. Ironically, I am echoing Plato's wonderful etymological treatments against him as I keep his denial of particularism as a denial of application of tangible realities–for tangible realities are, in a sense, particulars. And again, the very foundation by which abstractions came to full blossom of expression in the New Testament, I use Aristotle's deductive syllogisms against him for they would require the "sensory" world to never evolve *naturally* into higher meaning over time-immeasurable (a.k.a. – *aeon/aeonnes*) for "eternity" would require that which is against nature. We would then be left short changed by the greatest of human minds of the philosophical age to "deduce" or "universalize" a good theology. *Natural* is a case condition in theology which cannot logically prove itself to *win out* from the eternal sense.

LATEST PHYSICS

Latest physics leaves us with the measured world and that alone. I say, recent findings in physics and astrophysics are screaming "universal restoration," "total restoration" ←- as in total "conservation of energy" being restored as to who will "be again (Greek: "anothen", "born again" [John 3:3-Jesus])." Such "storage facilities" are black holes. Within the quantum entanglement hypothesis, they contain intelligence and every feeling we've ever had. So, in a sense, our future looks as though it will return to "a beginning." A reverse "predeterminism (at least "determinism")" might need to be thought out philosophically as well as theologically. So much information presses us to respond.

Some of the greatest of unbelieving physicists tell us to *only think*: "we have enough, we know enough, isn't this enough?" What kind of "reason" is this when they don't apply these same philosophical or deductive reasons to "go on" and do no more to find meaning within the confines of science? Meanwhile, they scream "conservation of energy retained in black holes" stored as "bits." These "bits" are waiting to be "released" into and through a new big bang, i.e., a new creation. Biblically speaking: couldn't this be the restoration of Colossians 1:20? Could this not be the one and only same story of a new creation? The Bible tells us this will happen but not in the jargon of quantum physics. Quantum physics tells the biblical story without claiming "religion, theology, God, the divine, etc." Quantum physics' *apokatastasis* is without the jargon of biblical restoration as being in a loving marriage. Rather, it is just a measured restoration.

There are simply too many "reductions" and "limitations" to a synthesized view of the Bible. I somewhat liken this to Edwin Abbott's 2-dimensional square in which the story *Flatland* is conveyed[4]. In *Flatland* a 3-dimensional sphere went to great lengths to explain what 3 dimensions are to the 2-dimensional square. This short book conveys marvelous analogies to both theological and mathematical reasoning. It should be of no surprise that Dr. Abbott was both a mathematician and theologian.

Again, remember that Aristotle watched "the thing" as it "did its course" calling the thing by its action of observance with a limited teleon, hence "probation" or "proving" under observation –which means

---

4. somewhat like the 3-dimensional sphere was to the 2-dimensional square in *Flatland*.

that the "proving" of the thing is only relegated to the observer's abilities, however complex and far-reaching they are.

With all of that said, Aristotle's *observation of actions* of a particular thing was either in opposition to Plato's *universal coming to be* or complimentary. I say complimentary, as was humanly possible for their time. I am reminded of the term "university" as it should be known: university – "the whole, aggregate, corporation, entire, etc." if one is "willing" to apply both Aristotelian and Platonic ideas (and many more), i.e., the observable and the universal. For many other ideas that came from Aristotle and Plato might not be as applicable to what I am trying to convey, but their deductions, syllogisms, analysis, etymological treatments, syntheses, etc. have carried on to this day . . . and never to be deemed as unworthy for these two major intellectual giants live on today as groundwork for future scientific and theosophical thinking.

Conclusion Recap:

I cannot make a Platonic/Aristotelian *synthesized* or *sandwiched* case for the Bible. With absolute respect for the fathers of philosophy in all of their extensive human reasoning, they still do not give us a wholesome answer to our existence as does biblical reason. Also, Christ cannot be "deduced" as analogue nor "imaginative" through either or both philosopher's systems of thought. The universal christ supervenes that which is anatomized or humanistically/philosophically "quantified."

Chapter Sixty-Two

Teliko Sumperasma

THE EMPHASIS OF THIS work is likened to that of Edwin Abbott's "Flatland[1]" in finding the "sandwiched" Five Noble Truths (The 5 Dimensions) which are already built into scripture as healthily denoted. Now that you have been prepared to approach the scripture from a fresh-multi-dimensional perspective, one just needs to look for these Noble Truths as they signal you past the turbulent English versions' connotations.

One could look at the Five Noble Truths as going to an optometrist. While you're there at the optometrist's office you will need to be tested with *multiple "correcting lenses"* for *calibrating* what you specifically need for wearing corrective glasses. Many of us have different vision issues that need correcting but the "correct" lens is only used to make you see "correctly" and not made for you to see something *"other than"* — (or to "alter" of your view[2]). Likewise, I believe these "Five Noble Truths" are the corrective lenses which allow us to see the *genius*[3] of scripture.

I encourage you that you can have a coherent view of scripture if you apply this book's 5NTs approach to your theological studies. Through this sandwiching or stacking of these Five Noble Truths you will "see" clearly that you now have a key to unlock scripture, maybe for the first time in your life. May God bless you and your journey with Christ. We all

---

1. cf. Abbott, *Flatland*.

2. to this point I make an argument against hallucinogenic drugs which alter the corrective lenses already given to us in scripture by way of truth and sufferings unto completion (i.e. to holiness).

3. Genius: root: *gn* – to "kindle" –i.e., "off-spring;" "generation;" to "join;" to "connect."

have different roads to travel. It is my deepest belief that we are all being "corrected *unto*" him, i.e., the bullseye.

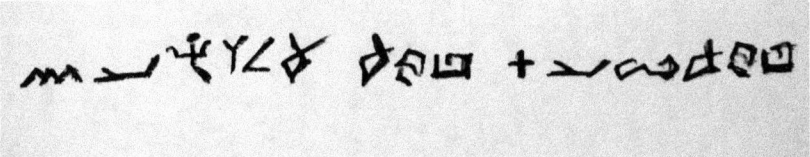

"In the beginning God created" – written by me in Proto-Sinaitic Pictograms: *Barashiyth Bara Alohiym*. This style of writing would have been prevalent in ca. 1800 BC.

POSTSCRIPT

THIS BOOK PRESENTS THE argument that we are all (Greek: *panta* – "every," "all") predestined to go through fiery trials *unto salvation*[1] through the *period of correction* (i.e., the *kolosis aionios*) in Christ Jesus. In this work I presented the case for universal salvation (or *apokatastasis*: full redemption) in Jesus Christ alone vs the English's "eternal punishment" from the "Flatland" or "synthesized" approach. Concerning this particular topic of biblical *apokatastasis* I went to numerous extant sources to support its value and usages amongst the ancient Greeks. Of many Greek sources, one in particular interested me the most: the vocabulary and

---

1. 1 Peter 4:12. "Beloved, think it not strange concerning the fiery trial which is to try you, as though some strange thing happened to you." Also, cf to 1 John 4: 17, 18: "*En toutoi teteleiotai agape meth heymon hina parresian exomen en tei emerai tayce kriseos (sentence; accusation [cf. krino]), hoti kathos ekeinos estin, kai haymeis esmen en toi kosmoi toutoi (18) phobos ouk estin en tei agapie all hey teleia agapay exso ballei ton phobion, hoti ho phobos kolasin exei; ho de phoboumenos, ou teteleiotai en tei agapei*" —> King James: 1 John 4: 17, 18: "Here is our love made perfect (*teleia* – *telos* – complete), that we may have boldness in the day of judgment *kolasin* (purging unto perfection; pruning; whittling away at our sin unto perfection): because as He is, so are we in this world. (18) There is no fear in love; but perfect love casts out fear: because fear has torment. He that fears is not made perfect in Love." *Kolasin* – a penal or juridical term to state "a corrective measure unto righteousness." This was known to have been a horticulturalist's "pruning" term used by the ancient Greeks. William Barclay wrote:

"The word for punishment is *kolasis*. The word was originally a gardening word, and its original meaning was pruning trees. In Greek there are two words for punishment, *timoria* and *kolasis*, and there is a quite definite distinction between them. Aristotle defines the difference; *kolasis* is for the sake of the one who suffers it; *timoria* is for the sake of the one who inflicts it. Plato says that no one punishes (*kolazei*) simply because he has done wrong – that would be to take unreasonable vengeance (*timoreitai*). We punish (*kolazei*) a wrong-doer in order that he may not do wrong again (*Protagoras* 323 E). Clement of Alexandria (*Stromateis* 4.24; 7.16) defines *kolasis* as pure discipline, and *timoria* as the return of evil for evil. Aulus Gellius says that *kolasis* is given that a man may be corrected; *timoria* is given that dignity and authority may be vindicated (*Attic Nights* 7.14). The difference is quite clear in Greek and it is always observed that *Timoria* is a retributive punishment where *Kolasis* is always given to amend and to cure."

usage of ancient juridical Greek terms – especially that of Kolosin – a "damnation *unto* restoration."

I addressed the complexities and contradictions of hell, free will, damnation, punishment, etc. spawned from the dull blade of the Vulgar tongue retained in English from the Latin Vulgate. Though, the Latin Vulgate remains closer to the era of the original Greek manuscripts such as the early third century Oxyrhynchus *leaves* ("papyri"), early to middle second century Bodmer leaves, Chester Beatty leaves (late second to early third c. AD) than our King James or most English and American "translations," and so on, I hold that we need a concerted effort to have a greater academic interpretation of the Greek New Testament in the spirit of J.B. Phillip's scholarly but rounded and comfortable English interpretation. This allows us to "understand" the Greek notions without the impossible synthesized "one to one" ratio "translations." Intimations or hints hidden within the Greek New Testament can be more easily conveyed within the freedom to use more English words of interpretation as we put them to the cauldron of meaning and its coherent flow if we are mindful of the 5 Noble Truths. In this process we could understand scripture better, especially in the "story telling" sense.

I realize the onus is on me to present a bullet proof case that supports such a seemingly "outside" claim as universal salvation and predestination, especially when both terms are "trigger terms" in many orthodox circles. But, I have somewhat garnered slivers of genius found "inside" the early Christian Koine speaking world which have aided me in showing a systematic and consistent methodological approach to the Bible. Biblical predestination (as opposed to "select"/"non-elect" Calvinism) and universal sanctification are two of this work's *five main categories of realities*[2] that, I claim, synergistically work together to make a sound theology. Such a maxim is what I call predeterministic universal salvation (*pronteterministikay katholikay*[3] *sotayria*).

My "arguments" are not to "win" but to guide us all out of anxiousness concerning each other's "salvation status" and rise above the vagaries of "hellologies."

To take my theological views to a marital relationship: a spouse wouldn't threaten you to *be a spouse or else* they will send you to hell, divorce you forever, kill you, etc. Likewise, I have come to many conclusions

---

2. which will be called "Noble Truths" later in this text.
3. "catholic/katholikay" as *universal* and not "Roman Catholic."

in my studies that neither does true salvation equal us "believing in God *because* we are fearing going to hell." Reeling the passage out of Hosea 2:16: "And it shall be at that day, says the LORD, that you shall call me *ISHI* (endearing and loving husband); and shall no more call me *Baali* (owner of chattel/feudal lord/baron/owner)." Our salvation is not "contingency" based. Our "works," "wills," "faith," "trials" are all generated by God and shared in his loving purpose.

Seems biblically-fitting to not judge but spread the Gospel. Being *beside myself*[4] in the joy of universal grace, I testify not only to my "state" or "condition" of salvation but yours too! But it is the sober responsibility that I lay out a clean and reasonable explanation for such a case.

The "facts" rest in the *words* of history (and the history in the words) supporting both the truths of scripture and extant secular works, as you shall see through this work. In biblical research, studies such as archaeology, decipherment of archaic writings, comparative histories, verisimilitudes ("truth-likenesses"), etc., are combined to produce the "*bones*" or "*facts*" of early Jewish and Christian realities, not "fancies." For each field of study in the aforementioned categories has been applied to this brief work.

Over the past 30+ years I have accrued thousands of pages of journal material in which I am still ordering out in my thoughts. I call these stacks of journals my "compendium" – which I have recently put most to print. My compendium is filled with sparkling ideas, unfinished and finished lectures, glossaries, etymologies, a parallel Bible I attempted to make in Latin, Greek, Anglo Saxon, Sumerian, Sanskrit, Proto Indo-European (P.I.E.) roots, etc. The book you are reading is only a fraction of my compendium. I chose to write this book on this topic for two main reasons: (1) to thwart secular "replacement ideologies" which would have biblical beliefs null and void in a post-modern society (2) Dr. Robin Parry's advice to narrow down my knowledge to a main focal point (which seemed impossible at the time) in order to systematize my thoughts.

Most of this filtered (some non-filtered) material worked its way into my lecturing of audiences within classrooms (such as Vanderbilt University, Trevecca, Belmont, etc.), radio (Vandy radio), recording to audio and/or video on YouTube, my website (fomcm.com), and even small group studies. I am indebted to Brandon Heinzelman for creating our website called "The Fullness of Meaning Christian Ministries.com"

---

4. 2 Corinthians 5:13 "If we are "beside ourselves," it is to God" or whether we be sober, it is for your cause."

for which my ever-surmounting lectures would have been lost. Instead, thanks to Brandon, they found their way into my website as a "thought-repository" for the public, myself included.

I profess that I am wholly incapable of convincing others, especially in mass, into *"getting saved"* nor manipulating a liquid form of baptism upon those who just "got saved" into what I believe is now the "continuance" case of holy fire from God's eternal abode to purge us from our sins. Ephesians 4:5 makes it clear that there is now one Lord, one faith, and one baptism (*Baptisma* [noun-neuter singular]). There were 6 accounts for "baptisms" used and mentioned in the Bible. This last "baptism" was in the nominative/noun case. If we return to John's Baptism, we return to a prior portent of Christ. If we return to Jewish ordinance and/or laws we make Christ's life null and void. If we obey ordinance and outward profession, this is respectful to the people and legislators for whom we should show respect to (Romans 13:1–14). But, the "continuance" of fiery trials is indeed a noun as found in the word *baptisma* that doesn't stop until we are through "being repented" into heaven. This will be a segue for answering the conundrums created by our English translations of eternal "damnation" with fire that has been so horribly translated from the Vulgate. Universal salvation can indeed find a place to rest within the study of continued baptism. I will refer to this reasoning over and over in this work to show us that "eternal fire" from the eternal court of God is sent upon us "unto repentance." It is, therefore, God who does the "convincing" in his time through these two separate and very distinct "acts" upon us.

The "acts" of saving and baptizing, I believe as a biblical linguist, are incongruous with scripture and reality as we understand more concerning biblical exegesis. For it is simply impossible to superimpose a "continuance of stativeness" of salvation or the "continuance of the action of fiery trials" without quantifiable duration by human hands. I say this on the basis that "being saved (Greek: *sodzo* – as in sodium/salt)" is a "state" of being preserved from point A to B and not a specific point in time. Our salvation is by God who "generates" us to do his will for his good pleasure. This is a personal and individualized experience between you and God from eternity, into time, a lengthy period of time, and unto your *teleos* (meaningful trajected end). Phil. 2:13 "For it is God who works [*energon*] in you to will [*Thelon*] and to act [*energein* – superlative "working" to *energein* – the recipient] in order to fulfill His good purpose." This is not only a "sharing of wills" but a receiving of his Will to do his Will.

The "participation" of wills, as I covered in this work, calibrates us into the image of Christ (Romans 8:29 – "For whom God did foreknow, He also did predestinate to be conformed [*sum-morphous* – "come together in shape" – similar to – Hebrew: *damah*- "resemble;" Hebrew – *Tselem* – "image" or "likeness"] to the image of his Son ....)." Over time, and not a point, do we find ourselves "being saved" in the journey with God, our Lord—not "got saved." As to when our beginnings of "getting saved" began is unanswerable due to God knowing, loving, choosing, ordaining, predetermining, our salvation before the foundation of the world (Ephesians 1:4; 1:9; Romans 8:28–31, etc.). There was no "got saved" because this indicates a mortal-time based salvation rather than a "reckoning" by which we are more than ever aware that we are wholly dependent upon God for our salvation before the foundation of creation which "carries us" through this time and tempo and back out again into eternity.

Other facets of my views in this work:

The biblical-historical Jews of scripture are not only supported in scripture but by the testimonies of their surrounding neighbors and captors such as the Egyptians, Assyrians, Babylonians, etc. Such historically/biblically marshalled witnesses have been included in the scripture as concomitant testimonies to both secular and biblical histories. There would be no reason, biblically and secularly speaking, to discount what both sides of the fence propose of each other's existence.

Time suspended as the prophets speak from the heavenlies

One should also consider the Jews who were socially adjoined to the prophets of the Bible (*navi'i' hitna'tech*). For these *ne'evim*/prophets foretold events which augured the secular and heralded biblical timelines (for which I have come to see as one and the same). The power of God's word, *dabar*, and *rhema* was shown through these *ne'evim*.

Such a ne'evi who spoke of the restoration of Israel was Ezekiel. God spoke through Ezekiel and said in Ezekiel 37:19: "Thus saith the Lord God; Behold, I will take the stick of Joseph, which is in the hand of Ephraim, and the tribes of Israel his fellows, and will put them with him, even with the stick of Judah, and make them one stick, and they shall be one in mine hand. (20) And the sticks whereon thou writest shall be in thine hand before their eyes. (21) And say unto them, "Thus saith the Lord God; Behold, I will take the children of Israel from among the heathen, whither they are gone, and will gather them on every side, and bring them into their own land (22) And I will make them one nation in the land upon the mountains of Israel; and one king shall be king to them all: and they shall be no more two nations, neither shall they be divided into two kingdoms any more at all."

Such a fulfillment of "the one stick/one nation-Israel" was to signal the *last generation* mentioned by Jesus in Matthew 24:32 where Jesus referred to Israel as "the fig tree." In Matthew 24:29, 30, and 31, Jesus had just made a segway to His Second Coming. Jesus' apocalyptic poetic diction (Barfield 1973) clearly conveys that "immediately after the tribulation of those days shall the stars fall from heaven, and the powers of heaven shall be shaken and then shall you see the Son of Man." "Those days" of Matthew 24: 29 are the "summer" of Matthew 24:32's "fig tree." That is, when Israel is one nation again, "this generation (70–80 years)" shall not pass until all things are fulfilled (Matthew 24: 34). Interestingly, king David said in Psalms 90:10: "The days of our years ("generation") are threescore (3 x 20) plus ten years, and 80 with much effort and sorrow, to be cut off and we fly away." So, a "generation" was ca. 70–80 years to the Jewish mind in the days of David and probably useful to a prophetic-poetic way of speaking in the New Testament, especially in the apocalyptic nuances.

The prophet Daniel (Daniel 9:25) had specifically told us that Jesus would be heralded in as the Messiah on the back of a donkey (Zech 9:9 -> fulfillment: Luke 19:28-40). This divine entrance of Jesus as Hosanna was prophesied to occur *after* the 69 *Shavua* (or 483 years) once the commandment to rebuild Jerusalem was enacted (Nehemiah 2:1-8). The entire chapter of Isaiah 53 gives us the portrait of Jesus' sufferings unto death, His reason for doing so, and his resurrection. Ezekiel 38 tells us of the alliance between Russia (Gog) and Iran's (Persian) "last days" attack on Israel. Ezekiel calls Israel by name, "Israel," which had been long gone in Ezekiel's day for Israel's last days were in 722 BC via the Assyrian "taking away." God told Ezekiel to perform a pantomime in Ezekiel 37:16-22 by joining two sticks together: one Ephraim (N. Israel) and Judah as "one stick." God said that this "one stick" is the future Israel reunited never to be two nations again. The next chapter is "the next generation" which concludes to the "end of days."

POSTSCRIPT

Ezekiel was a true prophet. God's word bore fruition through Ezekiel on a secular and applied theological level. The seed of prophecy through the prophet Ezekiel was planted in the hearts, minds, bodies of the Jewish people. Such people heard the voice of God through Ezekiel. God's words through his prophet came into being as a historical reality — i.e., an undivided Israel, a literal reborn nation, re-established on May 14, 1948.

Had this secular/historical and prophetic occurrence not happened as prophetically promised through the mouth of Ezekiel we would not be looking at the "last day events." Ezekiel made it clear that "Israel" would be attacked by Gog (Russia) and Persia (Iran) at *Megiddo* (*Har-Megiddo/* i.e., "Armageddon")[5]. If one reads secular-historical timelines of the Jews one will be able to collaborate the prophets with the secular-historical accounts of the Jews. It was Jesus who mentions Daniel as an authoritative prophet concerning these matters in Matthew 24:15-35; Mark 13: 24 - ff; Luke 21:25-33. The stress of the prophet's messages rest on Jesus' timeline of his entrance as Hosanna and Israel's rebirth (1948 May, 14) —which is the "generation" from the time of Israel's rebirth until the last 7-year period - or —> "shavua" Within this last shavua will be Revelation's narrative of 7 years, 7 vials, 7 judgments, 7 churches, 7 golden c andlesticks/eyes of the Lord.

For further study on the historical mentionings of biblical patriarchs and their associated *Ne'evim*/prophets please refer to Chaim Potok's work, *The Wanderings of the Jews*; David Rohl's, *A Test of Time, Legends of Avaris, Legend*; Schurer's *A History of the Jewish People in the Time of Jesus Christ*, and Dr. Alfred Edersheim's *The Life And Times Of Jesus The Messiah*, Strong's and McClintock's *Cyclopedia Of Biblical, Theological, And Ecclesiastical Literature* (full volume set).

With a heartfelt tug I conclude this work with the Archer's icon. The meaning of this icon should be obvious to most of you by now as to why I placed it at the beginning, roughly at the middle, and here at the end.

---

5. Ezekiel 38:2 *Gog* and *Magog* [Arabic *Ya'juj wa Ma'juj* = ascribed to individuals, tribes, or lands in the Quran. The Biblical Narrative of Ezekiel 38:5: says that the armies of "Persia (Iran), Ethiopia, and Libya" will join with Gog and Magog to attack Israel at the "last Days. We see in Ezekiel 38 that "Meshech and Tubal draw genetic lines with Tiblisi and Meskhe (Meskhe 2023/2024). Revelation 20:8 Gog and Magog are to go out to the far compassing regions of the earth and fool the nations, gathering them to war against Israel.

DOES GRACE HAVE A CEILING?

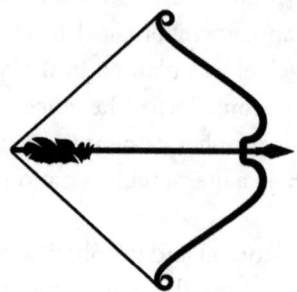

Appendix

The tsaror: *(Universal salvation proclaimed in Job's Pre-Mosaic form of yhvh worship: the scroll that took away the sins of humankind in the days of Job)*

This is the expanded look at Job 14's Proto-Sinaitic "tsaror." I believe this study will shed some light on the scrolls of final judgment found in Revelation 5:1,3,4,7,9; 6:14; 10:9

Papyrus from Elephantine, folded and tied, with seals on the strings. From Emil C. Kraeling, The Brooklyn Aramaic Papyri (New Haven 1953).

Job 14:1, 14–22.
Job 14:1: "Man born of woman, Short-lived and sated with strife[1]"

---

1. please refer to my video lecture: "Job and Macbeth – a comparative analysis" on my website: fomcom.com (in the video lecture section) "Man of Woman Born is a theme Shakespeare understood to mean "the fate of the flesh."

APPENDIX

14 "If a man die, shall he live again²? all the days of my appointed time will I wait, till my change come³.

15 Thou shalt call, and I will answer thee⁴: thou wilt have a desire to the work of thine hands⁵.

16 For now thou numberest my steps: dost thou not watch over my sin⁶?

(17) My transgression is sealed up in a *tsaror*/bag⁷, and thou daub/sewest⁸ up mine iniquity⁹.

(18) And surely the mountain falling cometh to nought, and the rock is removed out of his place.

2. i.e., "will a man live after he dies?"

3. i.e., after his death, he "waits." He "waits" in Sheol, as understood by the Jews and A.N.E. (ancient near east) thought among certain circles, later, the Jews. "Until my redemption comes." To be changed from the "state" of being in the "abode of the dead/shadows" is redemption to the A.N.E. God "believer" and, later, the Jew. Cf. to Dr. Irving Finkel's "Mesopotamian Ghosts"; Tur Sinai's "The Book of Job"; Marvin Pope's "Job" (The Anchor Bible Commentary series. In verse 19, there is a grim maxim for the "state of man." Job says in 14:19 "The waters wear the stones: thou washes away the things which grow *out* of the dust of the earth; and thou destroyest the hope of man." But, this is the "state" and "plight" of mortal man. Many commentators do not account for the shade or soul of man not being of the "adama" or "soil, earth"). I believe this is a spectacular passage to the contrast of many commentators. A hope in an eternal soul to continue.

4. the hope that God calls to us, that he acts upon us.

5. a continued thought to the first part of this verse: Thou Acts upon me and Does the works of His Hands. Again, God is acting and doing upon us, ←-i.e., "us" = those who are already in "the Shadows" of sin, death, remorse, iniquity, hell.

6. As Dr. Tur Sinai says in his "Book of Job" pg. 240/241, "this is not "affectionate watching" but persistent watching as "a lion lieth in wait for His prey (Hebrew: *ych-sph*)." Satan, as the "eyes of the Lord" was the "watcher" as we see his attributes in the Hebrew words mentioned in scripture: *m-SHT* – the "rover/satan/purger/challenger/rogue/etc." In Zechariah 4:10 we have the "eyes of the Lord" as "m-SHT," or, the "satan" of the Lord, the roving watcher. Cf. to 2 Chronicles 16:9; Jeremiah 16:17; and Hebrews 4:13 as well. Job's sin is not overlooked but as we shall see, Job is in the next verse alluding to not just Job's gift of grace from God but mankind's gift.

7. Tsaror – "sealed up/tied up document." This mentioning, by Tur Sinai's words, meant a document of the living (cf. 1 Sam. 25:29: "but the soul of my lord shall be tied up in the *tsaror* of the living." That is, in this book, the *Tsaror* of Job, the *Tsaror* was tied up and contained the names of all living persons who were inscribed. Cf. Ps. 139:16: "his days are tied up (in the *Tsaror*) and none can be added."

8. "thou sewest" = "daub; daubest; seal" over my iniquities.

9. Here we see the contrast of judgment unto the "cutting off" or *sheol* to the Salvation imbued us all through the Tsaror. "My transgression/(and iniquity) (*pishiy*) is "sealed up (chatum)" in a "bag (tsaror)"/You cover (*wat-tit-pol*) my iniquity (*a'woniy*). This is, I believe, stated to contrast the fate of "mortal man" with that of universally sanctified man as an eternal being, and not mortal.

APPENDIX

(19) The waters wear the stones: thou washes away the things which grow out of the dust of the earth; and thou destroyest the hope of man[10].

(20) Thou prevail for ever against him, and he passes: thou changest his countenance, and sends him away [cf. ft. note# 254-part b].

---

10. as I stated: the plight of mortal man, "fatalism," "fate, fatality, the "end result of mortality." Nature is determined to be destroyed as we know it.

Bibliography

Abbott, Edwin A. *Flatland: A Romance of Many Dimensions*. Toronto,: Dover Thrift Editions, 1992.
Albright, William Foxwell. *Archaeology and the Religion of Israel*. Baltimore, MA: Johns Hopkins Press, 1946.
Arberry, A.J. *The Legacy of Persia*. Oxford: Clarendon, 1963.
Aristotle. *The Basic Works of Aristotle*. New York: Random House, 2001.
Ascham, Roger. *Toxophilus*. London: King's College printing: 1545.
Auerbach, Erich. *Mimesis: The Representation of Reality in Western Literature*. Princeton, NJ: Princeton University Press, 1953.
Bachvarova, Mary R. *From Hittite to Homer: The Anatolian background of ancient Greek epic*. Cambridge, UK: Cambridge University Press, 2016.
Barfield, Owen. *Poetic Diction: A Study in Meaning*. Middletown, CT: Wesleyan University Press, 1973.
———. *The Rediscovery of Meaning: and other essays*. San Rafael, CA: Barfield, 1977.
———. *Saving the Appearances: A Study in Idolatry*. Middletown, CT: Wesleyan University Press, 1998.
Barney, Stephen A. *Word-Hoard: An Introduction to Old English Vocabulary*. New Haven, CT: Yale University Press, 1977.
———. *Allegories of History, Allegories of Love*. Hamden, Connecticut: Archon Book Publishers, 1979.
Bergson, Henri. *Laughter: An Essay on the Meaning of the Comic*. Eastford, CT: Martino, 2014.
Black, Jeremy and Anthony Green. *Gods, Demons and Symbols of Ancient Mesopotamia (an illustrated dictionary)*. Austin: University of Texas Press, 2000.
Boman, Thorlief. *Hebrew Thought Compared with Greek*. Bristol: Western Printing Services, 1960.
Bosworth, Joseph. *An Anglo-Saxon Dictionary*. Oxford: Oxford University Press, 1972.
Botterweck, Johannes G., and Helmer Ringgren. *Theological Dictionary of the Old Testament* (full volume set). Grand Rapids: Eerdmans, 1964-1921.
Brown, Francis, Driver, S.R. and Charles A. *Briggs-Driver-Briggs Hebrew and English Lexicon*. Peabody, MA: Hendrickson, 1906.
Brown, Raymond E. *The Birth of the Messiah*. Garden State, NY: Doubleday, 1977.
Bullinger, E.W. *Figure of Speech used in the Bible: Explained and Illustrated*. Grand Rapids, MI: Baker Books, 1968.
———. *The Witness of the Stars*. Grand Rapids, MI: Kregel, 1893.

Campbell, Joseph. *On James Joyce: Wings of Art* (6 audio cassette tapes). Carbondale, IL: Southern Illinois University, 1995

Campbell, Joseph and Henry Morton Robinson. *A Skeleton Key to Finnegans Wake.* New York: Viking, 1967.

Chambers, E.K. *The Mediaeval Stage.* London: Oxford University Press, 1903.

Clement (of Alexandria), *Stromateis ('patchwork')*: Washington, DC: The Catholic University of America Press, 1991.

Cohen, Mark E. *An Annotated Sumerian Dictionary.* University Park,: Pennsylvania State University Press, 2023.

Comfort, Philip Wesley. *The Text of the Earliest New Testament Greek Manuscripts (2 vol.).* Grand Rapids: Tyndale House, 2019.

Dale, James W. *Christic Baptism: An Inquiry into the meaning of the Word as determined by the usage of The Holy Scriptures and Patristic Writings.* Phillipsburg, NJ: P&R, 1995.

———. *Classic Baptism: An Inquiry into the meaning of the Word as determined by the usage of The Holy Scriptures and Patristic Writings.* Boston: P&R, 1989.

———. *Johannic Baptism: An Inquiry into the meaning of the Word as determined by the usage of The Holy Scriptures and Patristic Writings.* Phillipsburg, NJ: P&R, 1993.

———. *Judaic Baptism: An Inquiry into the meaning of the Word as determined by the usage of The Holy Scriptures and Patristic Writings.* Wauconda, IL: P&R, 1991.

Dodds, E.R. *The Greeks and the Irrational.* Berkeley: University of California Press, 1951.

Dostoevsky, Fyodor. *The Idiot*: Harmondsworth: Signet Classics, 1969.

Eco, Umberto. *The Aesthetics of Chaosmos: The Middle Ages of James Joyce.* Cambridge, MA: Harvard University Press, 1982.

Edersheim, Alfred. *Life and Times of Jesus the Messiah.* Oxford: Hendrickson, 1910.

———. *Sketches of a Jewish Social Life in the days of Christ.* Grand Rapids: Eerdmans, 1992.

———. *The Temple.* Grand Rapids: Eerdmans, 1992.

Flieger, Verlyn. *Splintered Light: Logos and Language and Tolkien's World.* Kent, OH: The Kent State University Press, 2002

———. *There Would Always Be a Fairy Tale.* Kent, OH: The Kent State University Press, 2017.

———. *Green Suns and Faerie: Essays on Tolkien.* Kent, OH: The Kent State University Press, 2017.

Ford, Massyngberde J. *Revelation: Introduction, Translation and Commentary.* The Anchor Bible. Garden City, NY: Doubleday, 1975.

Frazier, James. *The Golden Bough: A Study in Magic and Religion.* 12 vols. New York: St. Martin's Press, 1990.

Frye, Northrop. *Fearful Symmetry: A study of William Blake.* Princeton, NJ: Princeton University Press, 1947.

———. *The Great Code: The Bible and Literature.* New York: Harcourt Brace Jovanovich, 1982

———. *Words with Power: Being a Second Study of the Bible and Literature.* Orlando: Harcourt Brace Jovanovich, 1990.

Gellius, Cornelius A. *Noctes Atticae (Attic Nights).* Oxford: Oxford University Press, 1990

George, A.R. *The Babylonian Gilgamesh Epic*. 2 vols. Oxford: Oxford University Press, 2003.
———. *House Most High: The Temples of Ancient Mesopotamia*. Winona Lake, IN: Eisenbrauns, 1993.
Gesenius, Heinrich Friedrich. *Gesenius' Hebrew Grammar*. Oxford: Oxford University Press, 1985.
Gibson, George Sinclair. *Wake Rites: The Ancient Irish Rituals of Finnegans Wake*. Boca Raton: University Press of Florida, 2005.
Gilles, Quispel. *Man and Time*. Papers from the Eranos series/ Bollinger series 30, volume 3). Princeton, NJ: Princeton Press, 1933.
Gimbutas, Marija. *The Language of the Goddess*. New York: Harper & Row, 1989.
Girard, René. *The Scapegoat*. University of Michigan: Johns Hopkins Press, 1986.
———. *Things Hidden since the Foundation of the World*. Stanford, CA: Stanford University Press, 1978.
Golding, William. *Lord of the Flies: Bloom's Modern Critical Interpretations*. New York: Infobase Publishing, 2008.
———. *Lord of the Flies: Casebook Edition Text, Notes & Criticism*. Toronto: Penguin, 1988.
Gonzalez, Justo L. *The Story of Christianity: The Reformation to the Present Day (vol. 2)*. New York: HarperCollins, 1985.
Gottschalk, H.B. *Heraclides of Pontus*. Oxford: Oxford University Press, 1980.
Gower, Ralph. *The New Manners & Customs of Bible Times*. Chicago: Moody Bible Institute, 1987.
Graves, Robert. *The White Goddess: A Historical Grammar of Poetic Myth*. New York: Farrar, Straus and Giroux, 1948.
Grimm, Jacob. *Teutonic Mythology* (4 vol.). Darmstadt, Germany: Dover, 2004.
Halloran, John Alan. *Sumerian Lexicon: A Dictionary Guide to the Ancient Sumerian Language*. Los Angeles: Logogram, 2006.
Harbus, Antonina and Russell Poole. *Verbal Encounters: Anglo-Saxon and Old Norse Studies for Roberta Frank*. Toronto: University of Toronto Press, 2005.
Hardy, Robin and Anthony Shaffer. *The Wicker Man*. New York: Three Rivers, 1978.
Harris, Murray J. *Prepositions and Theology: In the Greek New Testament*. Grand Rapids: Zondervan, 2012.
Harris, Sam. *Free Will*. New York: Simon & Schuster, 2012.
Heidegger, Martin. *Being and TIme*. San Francisco: HarperCollins, 1962.
Hirsch, Edward. *A Poet's Glossary*. New York: Houghton Mifflin Harcourt, 2014.
Hislop, Alexander. *The Two Babylons*. Neptune, NJ: Loizeaux Brothers, 1916.
Hoehner, Harold W. *Chronological Aspects of the life of Christ*. Grand Rapids: Zondervan, 1977.
Huehnergard, John. *Grammar of Akkadian*. Harvard Semitic Studies 45. 3rd ed. Winona Lake, IN: Eisenbrauns, 2011
Hughes, David. *The Star of Bethlehem: An Astronomer's Confirmation*. New York: Walker and Company, 1979.
Hughes, Ted. *Shakespeare and the Goddess of Complete Being*. New York: Barnes & Noble, 2009.
Hughson, Thomas. *Neanderthal Religion?: Theology in Dialogue with Archaeology*. Eugene, OR: Pickwick, 2024.

BIBLIOGRAPHY

Jaeger, Werner. *Early Christianity and Greek Paideia.* Vols. 1-3. Cambridge, MA: Belknap, 1961.

Janik, Vicki K. *Fools and Jesters in Literature, Art, and History: A Bio-Biographical Sourcebook.* Westport, CT: Greenwood, 1998.

Jeremias, Joachim: *Jerusalem in the Time of Jesus.* Gottingen, Germany: Vandenhoeck & Ruprecht, 1967.

Jones, Kyle. "Anatomy of Will." Fullness of Meaning Christian Ministries, Feb. 9, 2016. https://fomcm.com/anatomy-of-will/.

———. "Christ of the Zodiac." Fullness of Meaning Christian Ministries, Nov. 10, 2015. https://fomcm.com/christ-of-the-zodiac/.

———. "The Finnish Mazzaroth." Fullness of Meaning Christian Ministries, June 12, 2017. https://fomcm.com/finnish-mazzaroth/.

———. "God's Two Creations." Fullness of Meaning Christian Ministries, May 5, 2022. https://fomcm.com/gods-two-creations/.

———. "Holy Cheese: Part 1." Fullness of Meaning Christian Ministries, Feb. 7, 2021. https://fomcm.com/holy-cheese/.

———. "Jesus Is Physically Dionysus, Odysseus, and Osiris: Written in the Stars." Fullness of Meaning Christian Ministries, Aug. 21, 2021. https://fomcm.com/jesus-is-physically-dionysus-odysseus-and-osiris-written-in-the-stars/.

———. "The National Monuments Started in Genesis 11." Fullness of Meaning Christian Ministries, June 9, 2017. https://fomcm.com/the-national-monuments-started-in-genesis-11/.

———. "Prophetic View 1." Fullness of Meaning Christian Ministries, June 22, 2025. https://fomcm.com/prophetic-view/.

———. "Shadows of Job." Fullness of Meaning Christian Ministries, [missing details].

———. "Theodicies of the Goddess." Fullness of Meaning Christian Ministries, Jan. 5, 2016. https://fomcm.com/theodicies-of-the-goddess/.

———. "Trauma, Drama, and Thing." Fullness of Meaning Christian Ministries, Dec. 25, 2015. https://fomcm.com/drama-trauma-and-thing/.

Josephus, Flavius. *The Works of Josephus.* Peabody MA: Hendrickson, 1987

Joyce, James. *Finnegans Wake.* Harmondsworth: Penguin, 1976.

Kashani, Abbas Aryanpur and Manoochehr Aryanpur-Kashani. *The Combined New Persian - English and English - Persian Dictionary.* Lexington, KY: Mazda, 1986.

Keel, Othmar, and Christoph Uehlinger. *Gods, Goddesses, and Images of God: In Ancient Israel.* Minneapolis: Fortress, 1998

Keil, C.F. and F. Delitzsch. *Commentary on the Old Testament.* 10 vols. Peabody, MA: Hendrickson, 1996.

Kelley, Henry Ansgar. *Satan: A Biography.* Cambridge, UK: Cambridge University Press, 2006.

Kerenyi, Karl. *Eleusis: archetypal image of mother and daughter* (mythos/ Bollingen series 65, vol. 4. New York: Princeton University Press, 1967.

Kittel, Gerhard. *Theological Dictionary of the New Testament.* Grand Rapids: Eerdmans, 1928 - 1985.

Klimov, Georgij A. *Trends in Linguistics: Etymological Dictionary of the Kartvelian Languages (documentation 16):* New York: de Gruyter, 1998.

Kloekhorst, Alwin. *Etymological Dictionary of the Hittite Inherited Lexicon.* Leiden Indo-European Etymological Dictionary Series. Boston: Brill, 2008.

BIBLIOGRAPHY

Koester, Craig R. *Revelation: A New Translation with Introduction and Commentary*. Anchor Yale Series. New Haven, CT: Yale University Press, 2014.

Kramer, Samuel Noah, and Diane Wolkenstein. *Inanna Queen of Heaven and Earth: Her Stories and Hymns from Sumer*. Cambridge, MA: Harper & Row, 1983.

Ladd, George Eldon. *The Blessed Hope*. Grand Rapids: Eerdmans, 1956.

Leisegang, Hans. *The Mysteries: Papers from the Eranos yearbooks: The Mystery of the Serpent*. Princeton, NJ: Princeton University Press, 1955

Lewis, C.S. *The Allegory of Love: A Study in Medieval Tradition*. New York: Oxford University Press, 1958.

―――. *Studies in Words*. New York: Cambridge University Press, 1996.

Lewis, C.T. *The Latin Dictionary*. Oxford: Oxford University Press, 1879.

Lonergan, Bernard J. *Verbum: Word and Idea in Aquinas*. Notre Dame, IN: University of Notre Dame Press, 1967.

MacDonell, Arthur Anthony. *A Practical Sanskrit Dictionary: with transliteration, accentuation, and etymological analysis throughout*. Oxford: Oxford University Press, 1991.

Machen, Gresham, J. *The Virgin Birth of Christ*. New York: Harper Brothers, 1930.

Magiera, Janet M. *Aramaic Peshitta: A New Testament (vol.1,2, and Lexicon)*. Light of the Word Ministry: www.lightofword.org, 2005 - 2009.

Maimonides, Moses. *The Guide for the Perplexed*. New York: Dover, 1956.

Martirosyan, Hamlet S. *Lion Character: In the Petroglyphs of Syuniq and the Ancient World*. Yerevan, Armenia: Edit Print, 2013.

Martirosyan, Hrach K. *Etymological Dictionary of the Armenian Inherited Lexicon*. Leiden: Brill, 2010.

Matthew, Victor H., and Don C. Benjamin. *Old Testament Parallels: Laws and Stories from the Ancient Near East*. Mahwah, NJ: Paulist, 1997.

McClain, Alva J. *Daniel's Prophecy of the Seventy Weeks*. Grand Rapids: Zondervan, 1969.

McHugh, Roland. *Annotations to Finnegans Wake*. Baltimore, MA: The Johns Hopkins University Press, 1991.

Meredith, George. *An Essay on Comedy*. Garden City, NY: Doubleday Anchor, 1956.

Meskhi, Anna. *Kartvelian Linguo-Culturology of the Past*. Tbilisi, Georgia: Center for Research of Kartvelian Civilization, 2018.

Meskhi, Ann. *The Unwritten History of the Meskhis*. Tbilisi, Georgia: Center for Research of Kartvelian Civilization, 2023-2024.

Molnar, Michael. *The Star of Bethlehem*. Wheaton, IL: Tyndale, 1999.

Murray, James. *Oxford English Dictionary (complete/ unabridged/ reproduced micrographically)*. Oxford: Oxford University Press, 1971.

Otto, Rudolf. *The Idea of the Holy*. New York: Oxford University Press. 1958.

Parpola, Simo. *Etymological Dictionary of the Sumerian Language*. Vols.1,2, and 3. Winona Lake, IN: Eisenbrauns, 2016.

Parry, Robin A. *Universal Salvation: The Current Debate*. Grand Rapids: Eerdmans, 2003.

Parry, Robin A., and Hanna Parry. *The Biblical Cosmos*. Cambridge, UK: Lutterworth, 2015.

Phillips, J.B. *The New Testament in Modern English*. New York: MacMillan, 1958.

Plato. *Plato, Complete Works*. Indianapolis, Indiana: Hackett Publishing Company, Inc. 1997.

———. *Plato IV Cratylus, Parmenides, Greater Hippias, Lesser Hippias.* Cambridge, MA: Harvard University Press. 1926.
Pope, Marvin. *Job.* The Anchor Bible series. New York: Doubleday Dell, 1973.
———. *Song of Solomon.* Anchor Bible Series. New York: Doubleday, 1977.
Potok, Chaim. *Wanderings: The History of the Jews.* New York: Knopf, 1978.
Qafisheh, Hamdi A. *NTC's Gulf Arabic-English Dictionary.* Chicago, IL: NTC/Contemporary Publishing, 1997
Quaknin, Marc-Alan. *Mysteries of the Alphabet.* New York: Abbeville, 1999.
Raglan, L. *The Hero: A Study in Tradition, Myth, and Drama.* New York: Knopf, 1978.
Ramelli, Ilaria. *Terms for Eternity: Aionios and Aidios in Classical and Christian Texts.* University of Michigan: Gorgias, 2007.
Ramelli, Ilaria and David Konstan. *The Christian Doctrine of Apokatastasis: A Critical Assessment from the New Testament to Eriugena.* Danvers, MA: Brill, 2013.
Ricoeur, Paul. *The Symbolism of Evil.* Boston: Beacon, 1967.
Robertson, Archibald, Thomas. *A Grammar of the Greek New Testament in the Light of Historical Research.* Nashville: Broadman, 1934.
———. *Word Pictures in the New Testament.* 6 vols. Nashville: Broadman,
Rohl, David. *Legend.* London: Random House UK, 1998.
———. *A Test of Time.* London: Random House UK, 1995.
Rolleston, Frances. *Mazzaroth. The Constellations, Parts I-IV, Including Mizraim: Astronomy of Egypt.* York Beach, ME: 2001.
Rucker, Rudolf. *Geometry, Relativity and the Fourth Dimension.* Toronto: General Publishing, 1977.
Schurer, Emil. *A History of the Jewish People in the time of Jesus Christ.* 5 vols. Edinburgh: Hendrickson, 1890.
Shakespeare, William. *MacBeth.* Arden Shakespeare Series. London: Bloomsbury, 2015.
Shipley, Joseph T. *The Origins of English Words.* Baltimore: Johns Hopkins Press, 1984.
Shippey, Tom. *The Shadow Walkers: Jacob Grimm's mythology of the monstrous (vol. 291).* Tempe, AZ: Brepols, 2005.
Sinai, Tur. *The Book of Job.* Jerusalem: Kiryath Sepher, 1957.
Skeat, Walter W. *The Concise Dictionary of English Etymology.* Hertfordshire: Wordsworth, 1993.
Stanford Encyclopedia of Philosophy. "Intentionality in Ancient Philosophy." Oct. 18, 2019.
Strong, James. *Strong's Exhaustive Concordance of the Bible.* Nashville: Abingdon, 1980.
Strong, James and John McClintock. *Cyclopedia of Biblical, Theological, and Ecclesiastical Literature.* 12 vols. Grand Rapids: Baker, 1867 - 1887.
Thavapalan, Shiyanthi. *The Meaning of Color in Ancient Mesopotamia.* Leiden: Brill, 2020.
Tindall, William. *A Reader's Guide to Finnegans Wake.* New York: Farrar, Straus and Giroux, 1969.
Tolkien, J.R.R. *The Monsters and the Critics: and other essays.* London: George Allen & Unwin, 1983.
Tuchman, Barbara W. *A Distant Mirror: The Calamitous 14th Century*: Toronto: Random House, 1978.
———. *England and Palestine from the Bronze Age to Balfour: Bible and Sword.* New York: Random House, 1956.

BIBLIOGRAPHY

Turner, Alice K. *The History of Hell*. Orlando: Harcourt Brace & Co., 1993.

Twelftree, Graham H. *In the Name of Jesus: Exorcism among Early Christians*. Grand Rapids: Baker, 2007.

———. *Jesus The Exorcist: A Contribution to the study of the Historical Jesus*. Peabody, MA: Hendrickson, 1993.

Virgil. *Eclogues, Georgics, and Aeneid*. Translated by H. Rushton Fairclough, revised by G. P. Goold, Loeb Classics 1-6. Harvard, MA: Harvard University Press, 1999.

Walton, Frank Edward. *Development of the Logos-Doctrine in Greek and Hebrew Thought*. London: John Wright and Sons, 1911.

Walvoord, F. John, and Roy B. Zuck. *The Bible Knowledge Commentary*. 2 volumes- Old and New Testament. Wheaton, IL: Victor Books, 1985.

Watkins, Calvert. *The American Heritage Dictionary of Indo - European Roots*. New York: Houghton Mifflin, 2000.

———. *How to Kill a Dragon: Aspects of Indo European Poetics*. Oxford: Oxford University Press, 1995.

Weston, Jessie L. *From Ritual to Romance*. Garden City, NY: Cambridge University Press, 1957.

Wigram, George V., and Ralph D. Winter. *The Word Study Concordance*. Wheaton, IL: Tyndale House, 1978.

Wood, William. *Social Cannibalism: The Educationalist of Anti-Human Development*. Ann Arbor, MI: U.M.I., 1994.

www.ingramcontent.com/pod-product-compliance
Lightning Source LLC
Chambersburg PA
CBHW071142300426
44113CB00009B/1055